THE GENESIS OF THE FRONTIER THESIS

A Study in Historical Creativity

THE GENESIS
of the
FRONTIER THESIS
A Study in Historical Creativity

by

Ray Allen Billington

Senior Research Associate,
The Henry E. Huntington Library and Art Gallery

THE HUNTINGTON LIBRARY
SAN MARINO, CALIFORNIA
1971

COPYRIGHT © 1971 BY THE

HENRY E. HUNTINGTON LIBRARY AND ART GALLERY

Library of Congress Catalog Card Number 74-171108

PRINTED IN THE UNITED STATES OF AMERICA

BY KINGSPORT PRESS, INC.

DESIGNED BY ROBERT SHAW AND MARY STODDARD

PUBLISHED WITH THE ASSISTANCE OF THE

UNION PACIFIC RAILROAD FOUNDATION FUND

To three grandchildren
who have brightened my life
Christine Marie Billington
Michael Scott Billington
and
Kevin Charles Billington,
and to their parents
who have endowed them with such perfection,
this book is gratefully dedicated

CONTENTS

PREFACE   ix

SECTION I The Years of Preparation, 1885–1892   1

CHAPTER I *The Frontier Thesis in Retrospect*   3

CHAPTER II *Fred J. Turner: Background and Training, 1885–1889*   9

CHAPTER III *The Emerging Hypothesis, 1889–1892*   39

SECTION II Formulating the Thesis, 1892–1893   63

CHAPTER IV *The Social Climate*   65

CHAPTER V *The Intellectual Climate*   85

CHAPTER VI *Reading and Speculation, 1892–1893*   119

CHAPTER VII *The 1893 Essay and Its Reception*   147

SECTION III Frederick Jackson Turner Remembers   179

CHAPTER VIII *The William E. Dodd Correspondence, 1919*   181

CHAPTER IX *The Constance Lindsay Skinner Correspondence, 1922*   203

CHAPTER X *The Carl Becker Correspondence, 1925–1927*   221

CHAPTER XI *The Merle Curti Correspondence, 1928–1931*   253

CHAPTER XII *The Luther L. Bernard Correspondence, 1928*   287

BIBLIOGRAPHICAL NOTE   299
INDEX   305

PREFACE

This book is a by-product (perhaps "spin-off" would be a more accurate term) of a biography of Frederick Jackson Turner on which I have labored for far too many years. Its beginnings can be accurately dated, for on January 2, 1960, the Turner Papers at the Henry E. Huntington Library and Art Gallery were opened to use by scholars; I was there, and my love affair with Turner began. My purpose then was to explore only his views on the frontier hypothesis for a volume that appeared six years later as *America's Frontier Heritage*. Such a modest ambition did not take into account the magnetic effect of Turner's personality, even if reflected only through his letters. No reader of his correspondence could escape his charm, or fail to be stirred into a deeper and deeper interest in the man and his ideas. That has happened to others who have dipped into his papers since 1960; it happened to me at that time.

So I returned to the Huntington as often as possible until 1963 when the director, Dr. John E. Pomfret, was gracious enough to offer me a permanent position on its staff as Senior Research Associate. That meant not only a constant immersion in the Turner papers, but an opportunity to explore various aspects of his life and thought that seemed especially significant or intriguing. One problem that transcended all others in my scale of interests was the genesis of his frontier hypothesis. This suggested itself to me as I read the dozens of cryptic notes scattered through his research files, notes that indicated the books he was reading as he prepared his first courses at the University of Wisconsin or the ideas that occurred to him as he read. Why not, I thought, retrace his steps by reading the same books and articles, fitting his fragmentary comments into the pattern as I did so, and seeing how the thesis developed in his mind? This modest program soon expanded; I found that I had to investigate the intellectual and social atmosphere that encouraged his efforts, the expression of his theory as it developed month by month in his mind, the youthful experiences that helped shape his beliefs, and the elements of his education that contributed to his conclusions. I found also that I must learn something about the creative process, a quest that led me to consult friends in the psychological fraternity for advice, and spend more time than I had intended reading in the extensive literature of that field.

All of this began in the belief that I was assembling material for a chapter in the biography that was my final objective (and that will, hopefully, be published in 1972). When I added up my accumulation of information, however, I found that a chapter of some 200 pages would be needed to tell the story properly. To compress that story into the thirty pages that no chapter should exceed meant discarding material that seemed worthy of a better fate. At this point the inspiration came; why not edit the five groups of correspondence in which Turner in his later years speculated on the origin of his thesis, add a hundred-page introduction, and produce a little book that would, in effect, be a case study in the field of creative thinking? This would have a dual value; it would serve on the one hand as a thoroughly documented example of historical creativity, and on the other demonstrate the unreliability of the human memory, for Turner's recollections of his early years were usually as wrong in detail as they were in reconstructing the overall pattern. Unfortunately, the "little" book that I planned grew mightily as it progressed, until the "introduction" to the Turner letters overbalanced them by far. Perhaps my own enthusiasm for the subject, and for Frederick Jackson Turner, has warped my judgment, but I feel that this extended examination of the genesis of his thesis is justified, if not by the importance of the thesis, at least by the light that it sheds on creativity in historical writing.

My search for information on Turner and his ideas has taken me to many libraries where I have been graciously treated by a number of very helpful people. A few stand out in my mind because of the nature of the materials they administer no less than because of their own generosity. Mr. J. E. Boell, Director of Archives at the University of Wisconsin, not only gave me free access to the riches over which he presides, but went beyond the call of duty by installing a desk in the stacks where I could sample and copy to my heart's content. Miss Josephine L. Harper, Curator of Manuscripts at the State Historical Society of Wisconsin, gave me equal freedom with the collections that she administers so efficiently. In addition she has personified kindness in answering repeated questions by mail, often questions arising from my own carelessness in recording information. Dr. Clifford K.

Shipton, former Custodian, and Mr. Kimball C. Elkins, Senior Assistant, at the Harvard University Archives not only made enjoyable a summer of research in the papers of the Harvard Commission on Western History, which are rich in Turner materials, but on subsequent visits called to my attention other items that might have escaped my notice. Several weeks in the Division of Manuscripts at the Library of Congress proved again the courtesy and knowledge of the staff there as they guided me through the intricacies of the papers of J. Franklin Jameson, Woodrow Wilson, and the American Historical Association.

My greatest debt, however, is to my colleagues on the staff of the Henry E. Huntington Library and Art Gallery. Few six-month periods of my life have been as pleasant as that spent in the spring of 1960 as Wilbur R. Jacobs of the University of California at Santa Barbara and I first explored the newly opened Turner papers under the guidance of the charming lady who had catalogued them so expertly, Miss Norma B. Cuthbert. To her, special thanks are due. They are due also to Dr. John E. Pomfret, director of the library at that time, whose help and encouragement were limitless, and to Dr. James Thorpe, his successor as director, who has helped make the Huntington Library even more of an academic heaven for those fortunate enough to live under his benefactions. To all these, and to many more, I owe thanks for such merits as this book possesses; for its faults I am alone responsible.

San Marino   Ray Allen Billington
February, 1971

SECTION I The Years of Preparation
1885-1892

The features of Frederick Jackson
Turner's background, training, and
early teaching that equipped him
to propose the frontier hypothesis.

CHAPTER I

The Frontier Thesis in Retrospect

When in the summer of 1893 a young historian named Frederick Jackson Turner addressed a gathering of his fellow craftsmen on "The Significance of the Frontier in American History" he advanced a theory that shook the academic world to its foundations. The traits and institutions of the American people, he told his listeners, had not been transplanted unchanged from Europe, but were in part products of the American environment. The most unique feature of that environment was an ever-moving frontier of settlement that for three centuries offered men unlimited opportunity for self-advancement. As they moved ever westward to exploit free land and resources, they found that habits and customs suitable to a land where men were many and land scarce were unworkable in a region where land was plentiful and men few. There, in a plastic new society, class distinctions weakened, social and political equality were demanded, cultural ties with the past dissolved, and a new spirit of individualism and nationalism shaped the attitudes of the people. Frontiering, Turner insisted, helped explain why the United States was different from the Europe that gave it birth.

This was heresy. Historians of that generation stood almost solidly behind the "germ" theory to explain the genesis of their nation's institutions. Each had evolved from an English institution, and beyond that from its "germ" in the forests of medieval Germany; this was demonstrably true because comparisons revealed unmistakable similarities with ancient Teutonic practices that were sure proof of common origins. To suggest, as Turner did, that this was untrue, and that American customs were shaped by contact with the wilderness no less than by inheritance from a medieval brotherhood flew in the face of tradition, logic, and common sense. So it was that the frontier hypothesis received short shrift among historians at first, gaining converts only slowly for a decade. By 1910, however, it was generally accepted, and between that time and the Great Depression of the 1930s it dominated the profession so completely that the American Historical Association was branded one great Turner-verein. This overacceptance generated an inevitable reaction between the 1930s and the 1950s; for two decades aspiring young historians made their reputations by leaping on the anti-Turner bandwagon with books and articles proving both his theory and his statement of that theory to be false. Again in the 1950s the tide turned; since that time the "Third Generation" of the frontier hypothesis has been more interested in testing than in glorifying or rejecting Turner's theories.

Whatever the validity of the frontier thesis—and most of today's scholars accept its basic premise as accurate—it did more to vitalize the study of American history than any other interpretation with the possible exception of Charles A. Beard's economic hypothesis. Our purpose in this book is not to argue for or against its correctness, or to rehash the controversy that has raged over Turner's statement of his hypothesis. Instead we will address ourselves to one problem: what was the genesis of this startling new concept? Was it the result of a single inspiration that came to Turner in a flash of revelation? Had its elements shaped in his mind over the course of months until they were ripe for expression? Why should he, rather than one of his contemporaries, stumble upon this unique interpretation? What in this young man's background, training, and mental attainments equipped him to advance the frontier thesis rather than another historian of his day? These are the questions that we will try to answer in this book.

Several times in his mellowing years Turner was prodded into trying to answer them himself; on no less than five occasions he wrote lengthy letters seeking to isolate those aspects of his background and education that made the hypothesis possible. These letters form the last section of this volume. He was inclined, when reminiscing in this fashion, to single out a few events or persons that he deemed especially influential. The fact that he was born in Portage, Wisconsin, in 1861 when "the region was in the later stages of a frontier community" always seemed important to him; there he lived in a forming community where the wilderness was near and "representatives of many nationalities and many American sections" met and mingled to form a new society.[1] He recalled watching a composite nationality emerge there, as cheap lands acted as a catalyst to bring affluence to the poor and higher status to the downtrodden. He remembered visiting Indian villages on the nearby

---

1. Frederick J. Turner to Luther L. Bernard, November 24, 1928. Frederick Jackson Turner Papers, Henry E. Huntington Library, TU Box 40. Hereafter referred to as HEH TU. This letter, and all others cited in this chapter, is reproduced in Section III of this volume.

Baraboo River, watching the lumber rafts as they made their way southward along the Wisconsin River from the "pineries" of northern Wisconsin, seeing lynched men hanging on trees, talking with families on their way westward to still newer frontiers.[2] Experiences such as these, Turner believed, placed an indelible stamp on him, and played a role in interesting him in the frontier as a molding force.

He was also inclined to credit his training at the University of Wisconsin with a major significance in shaping his historical concepts. His guiding star there was Professor William Francis Allen, a teacher of remarkable ability whose specialty was classical and medieval history, but who taught his young disciple to study the people rather than their rulers, and to focus on the social and economic forces that governed political events rather than on the events themselves. "His breadth of interest in social classes, economics, and cultural factors," Turner remembered, "was ahead of his time in this country."[3] Allen grounded his pupil in research techniques and taught him to rely on source documents, without at the same time placing a straitjacket around his ideas, for Allen's only course in American history was a brief, one-term survey. Turner had no choice, as he later recalled, but "to think out my own conceptions of what American history meant."[4] This he did by applying the methodology of medieval studies to the United States, to discover truths that had eluded others with different training. "I saw even then," he wrote many years later, "the possibility of dealing with American history on similar lines in a new way."[5] Turner was also eternally grateful to Allen for allowing him to prepare his thesis for the master of arts degree on an American topic —the Wisconsin fur trade. He recalls that as he mastered this subject he discovered "some of the underlying conceptions that shaped my thesis."[6]

In his retrospective moods, Turner felt that the academic year 1888–1889 spent at the Johns Hopkins University where he earned his doctoral degree a year later offered him fewer challenges than his Wisconsin years, despite the fact that he studied under such masters as Herbert Baxter Adams, Richard T. Ely, Albion W. Small, and Woodrow Wilson. Strangely he assigned little

2. Turner to Carl Becker, December 16, 1925. The original of this letter, and the others of this series written by Turner to Carl Becker, is in the Collection of Regional History and University Archives, Albert R. Mann Library, Cornell University. Photostatic copies are in HEH TU Box 34.
3. Turner to Merle Curti, August 8, 1928. HEH TU Box 39.
4. Turner to Bernard, November 24, 1928. HEH TU Box 40.
5. Turner to William E. Dodd, October 7, 1919 [Rough draft]. HEH TU Box 29.
6. *Ibid.*

credit to Ely and Small as he reminisced about those days, stressing instead the influence of Adams and Wilson, one negative, the other positive. Adams, he admitted, stirred his interest in "institutional history as related to society in general" and encouraged him to forsake narrative history for analytical,[7] but aroused his ire by insisting that all American institutions were transplanted unchanged from Europe. Turner's rebellion against this nonsense, he remembered, came when Adams announced that his seminar, "having dealt with American local institutions, had exhausted the opportunity for new contributions in the field of U.S. history and would turn to European history for its next work."[8] "The frontier," Turner wrote in 1925, "was pretty much a *reaction* from that due to my indignation."[9]

If Herbert Baxter Adams was remembered as a negative influence, Woodrow Wilson stood forth for his positive suggestions among the hierarchy who contributed to Turner's frontier concept. "All my ideas and ambitions," he wrote in 1919, "were broadened and enriched by Woodrow Wilson's conversations, and—though less so—by his lectures, expounding *politics* in a larger sense, discussing the evolution of institutions and constitutions as 'vehicles of life,' as expressions of society and human beings rather than as formal and dead things. It kindled my imagination."[10] Wilson, Turner recalled, introduced him to the works of the English political economist, Walter Bagehot, whose *Physics and Politics*, with its emphasis on "breaking the cake of custom," left a deep impression when he began to think of the part the West had played in American history.[11] He remembered, too, that Wilson's interest in the South as a section neglected by New England historians sharpened his own loyalties to the West and heightened his determination to win recognition for his own region.[12]

These were valuable lessons, but their influence on Turner falls far short of explaining Turner's basic conceptions of history or his fascination with the West. Whence came his interest in the social and economic forces that underlay the surface events of the past? This he could not answer, no matter how often he reminisced. "I can't," he confessed in 1925, "tell you just *how*

7. Turner to Becker, December 16, 1925. HEH TU Box 34.
8. Turner to Dodd, October 7, 1919. HEH TU Box 29.
9. Turner to Becker, December 16, 1925. HEH TU Box 34.
10. Turner to Dodd, October 7, 1919. HEH TU Box 29.
11. *Ibid.*
12. *Ibid.*

the '*how*' instead of the '*what*' came to appeal to me." [13] Nor could he dredge from his memory the circumstances that directed his interests toward the frontier and its significance. "I got absolutely nothing of suggestion on either frontier or fur trade from H. B. Adams," he remembered, "or so far as I can recall, regarding frontier, from anyone." True, someone had called his attention to the census maps that showed successive frontier lines, but Turner was vague on who this was and when it took place. In the end his reconstruction of the evolution of his theory went back to Allen's influence; "I applied historical data and interpretation to those maps," he wrote, "with Mediaeval historical processes as a more or less conscious guide." [14]

To sum up Turner's memories of the genesis of his hypothesis is to recognize that he recalled precious little. He had no recollection of the books he read, the lectures he heard, or the colleagues who contributed to his development. He forgot that the intellectual and social atmosphere of the 1890s was as important as his educational training in encouraging him to think along new lines. He failed to remember the encouragement he received from other young historians whose emergence paralleled his own and whose rebellion against historical traditionalism gave him the incentive to evolve his own interpretations. He did not recall that he built his hypothesis on theories borrowed from biologists, geographers, and statistical cartographers, each providing an essential brick for its foundations. He forgot the hours spent poring over atlases and census data as the image of the westward movement took shape in his mind, or the days of speculation as the accumulated information fell into an orderly pattern. Nor did he remember that he spent months reading about the West in guidebooks, travel accounts, and contemporary journals, or that he found rationalization for his theories in the works of political scientists, social philosophers, economists, and historians.

These mental lapses were understandable; the human memory is fallible, and total recall after a quarter-century almost impossible. This does not mean that the genesis of the frontier theory must remain a mystery. Fortunately Turner's legacy included not only his reminiscences, but a vast bulk of tangible records that allow us to retrace the steps that led him to his hypothesis. A magpie by instinct who threw nothing away, he bequeathed to the Henry E. Huntington Library no less than thirty-four file drawers crammed with

13. Turner to Becker, December 16, 1925. HEH TU Box 34.
14. *Ibid.*

7

notes, lectures, clippings, and assorted jottings, in addition to numerous other drawers and cases containing an amazing variety of historical debris of every sort. From this mass of useful and useless information, two types of notes offer clues to his chain of thought as the frontier thesis evolved. He was in the habit, in those days, or recording bits of information on 3 x 5 notepads that were filed in one of his cases under the heading "Social and Economic History." Most were fragmentary: a few words to record a thought that flashed through his mind, a book that he had read or should read, a random idea and its implications. Just as valuable to the modern-day investigator of his emerging theories were his voluminous reading notes, usually taken in purple ink on typewriter-size paper. These not only allow us to reread the books that he examined as the frontier hypothesis evolved in his mind, but to learn his own reaction to them, for his notes included frequent asides to record an idea that suddenly dawned as he read. By following the trail that Turner blazed, we can not only trace the emergence of the frontier thesis in his mind, but even identify phrases and metaphors that he borrowed from this author or that.

The purpose of this book is to retrace Turner's steps as he developed the concepts that merged into his paper on "The Significance of the Frontier in American History" in 1893. Yet no hypothesis of this importance is the product solely of reading and speculation. Turner, as he correctly recalled, began to prepare himself as a frontier historian during his boyhood amidst quasi-frontier conditions, and continued that preparation at the University of Wisconsin and the Johns Hopkins University. To understand *why* as well as *how* he rather than some other scholar advanced that unique interpretation of the American past we must review those aspects of his background and education that prepared him to make his contribution.

CHAPTER II

Fred J. Turner: Background and Training

The Wisconsin village of Portage, where Frederick Jackson Turner was born on November 14, 1861, was ideally suited to be the home of a future historian of the frontier. Nestled against the Wisconsin River, it took its name from the Fox-Wisconsin portage route used from time immemorial by Indians and French traders on their way from the Great Lakes to the Mississippi River. There Marquette and Jolliet paused during their momentous voyage of discovery. Nearby was Old Fort Winnebago, built by the federal government in 1828 to guard the waterway, and now crumbling into ruins. Young Fred Turner played about its walls as a boy, but such were the inadequacies of schooling in those days that he never heard of Marquette and Jolliet, and knew but little of the French and British traders who followed their trail.[1] His interests then were not in the past, but in the pleasant hamlet where he lived.

This was fortunate, for Portage provided experiences that helped mold his career. Incorporated as a city in 1854, it boasted only 2,879 inhabitants when Turner was born, one-third from abroad, the remainder drawn largely from Ohio, Pennsylvania, New York, and the New England states, with a sprinkling of southerners including nine Negroes.[2] Visitors commented on its neat, cream-colored brick buildings fashioned from a local clay, and were impressed with its hustling infant industries: a four-story flour mill, an iron works, a grain elevator near the railroad station, and two breweries whose generous production challenged the capacity of the small population.[3] Signs of progress were everywhere during Fred's early years: the first fire engine

1. Turner, "Notes for Talk to Harvard History Club," April 24, 1924. HEH TU Box 56.
2. U.S. Census Office, *Population of the United States in 1860; Compiled from the Original Returns of the Eighth Census* (Washington, 1864), 543. The city was incorporated on March 10, 1854, with three wards and a fourth soon to be added. The town's early history is described in James E. Jones, *A History of Columbia County, Wisconsin* (2 vols., Chicago, 1914), I, 184–94.
3. John W. Hunt, *Wisconsin Gazetteer* (Madison, 1853), 177–78; *The History of Columbia County* (Chicago, 1880), 633–37.

purchased by the town fathers in 1863, an imposing courthouse towering three stories tall built a year later, six oil lamps to shed light on the tree-lined main street added in 1868.[4] One of the principal boosters of this modernization program was Fred Turner's father, Andrew Jackson Turner, joint owner and publisher of the *Wisconsin State Register* and one of the city's leading citizens.

These signs of progress were deceptive, for Portage refused to grow as rapidly as its promoters hoped. By 1870, when Turner was nine years old, it still contained less than 4,000 inhabitants, and in 1880 when he left for college only 4,346.[5] These modest gains could not wipe out the relics of a frontier past that was only a few years away. All about were reminders of that earlier day which would impress a small boy. Through the town's streets lumbered prairie schooners loaded with "emigrants" bound for the free government lands of northern Wisconsin. Scarcely an issue of the local newspaper but told of Indian wars in the West, flavored by the editor's damnation of "savages" who massacred honest settlers in the Modoc War or wiped out Custer's command on the Little Big Horn.[6] Occasionally happenings nearer home reminded him that civilization was still in its swaddling clothes: a hunting party formed to track down wolves that were ravaging the countryside, vigilantes organized to aid the sheriff in capturing an overambitious horse thief.[7] The wilderness was not quite subdued, and young Turner felt its influence.

Now and then frontier lawlessness touched even closer to home. Twice in 1869, when he was seven years old, vigilantes turned Portage into a wild-west town. In mid-September that year two hot-headed Irishmen who had feuded since the Civil War—Barney Britt and William H. Spain—met and quarreled on the main street. Spain, losing his temper completely, pulled a revolver, shouted "Take that, you son of a bitch," and shot Britt to death. Law officers were shouldered aside by the mob that formed, captured Spain, and raised the cry of "Hang him, hang him." A rope appeared, the luckless offender was dragged to a nearby tree, and strung up—all within thirty minutes.[8] Less than a week later a notorious trouble maker, one Pat Wildrick,

4. Portage *Wisconsin State Register*, May 2, 1863, October 24, 1868.
5. U.S. Census Office, *Statistics of the Population of the United States at the Tenth Census (June 1, 1880). Vol. I* (Washington 1887), 367, 425, 456.
6. Typical editorial comment of this sort is in the *Wisconsin State Register*, April 26, May 3, 1873, April 20, 1878.
7. *Ibid.*, February 13, October 19, 1872.
8. *Ibid.*, September 18, 1869. A brief account of the lynching is in *A History of Columbia County*, 294–95.

was arrested after bludgeoning and robbing a Norwegian with whom he had been drinking. He was arrested, but the local newspaper, acting in the best tradition of the wild west, declared that he would probably squirm out of a jail sentence as he had before and hinted strongly that only a lynching would provide justice.[9] This invitation was answered when two mobs of men converged on the local lock-up, bound the officers in charge, and hanged Wildrick from the nearest tree. There his nude body was found the next morning.[10] These were events that no seven-year-old boy could ever forget, and Turner remembered them to his dying day.

He remembered, too, the great lumber rafts that passed the city almost daily during the summer months, bound from the "pineries" of northern Wisconsin to the Mississippi River and markets on the prairies of Illinois. The half-dozen men who maneuvered these cumbersome craft over the rapids of the turbulent Wisconsin River were lawless extroverts, glorying in danger and hardship, and ready to "take over" the town on the slightest excuse. Fred Turner rubbed elbows with them often as they came ashore to celebrate passage over the worst of the river's rapids just north of Portage.[11] He was close to the wilderness then, just as he was when he talked with Irish and Scandinavian lumberjacks from the north who dropped by to refresh themselves after coming down the river. The "Old Pinery Road" from Portage to Conant's Rapids on the upper Wisconsin ran by the Turner's front door. Twice the lad was taken by his father to visit the lumber camps, traveling on one of the first trains to reach the Lake Superior country through a narrow aisle cut like a gash through the virgin pine forest.[12] There he saw lumberjacks felling the giant trees, and there he watched pioneers building their cabins on recently cleared fields[13] either homesteaded or purchased from

9. *Wisconsin State Register*, September 18, 1869.
10. *Ibid.*, September 25, 1869. The *Register* was severely criticized by the state and national press for inciting this lynching. It defended itself by saying that the men responsible were from outside the city, and could not have read its inflamatory statements. *Ibid.*, September 25, October 2, 1869.
11. An excellent description of rafting on the Wisconsin River is in A. G. Ellis, "The Upper Wisconsin Country," *Third Annual Report and Collections of the State Historical Society of Wisconsin for the Year 1856* (Madison, 1857), pp. 441–44.
12. Turner to Mrs. William Hooper, February 13, 1921. HEH TU-H Box 5.
13. In 1877 and again in 1878 Andrew Jackson Turner was invited to visit the pineries in connection with his land-holding and railroad interests; each time young Fred Turner went along. On the first visit the train traveled for miles through virgin lands where the countryside was filling with newly arrived settlers and where vast tracts still awaited occupants. A. J. Turner's account of this journey, printed in the local newspaper, showed the deep impression the frontierlike conditions made on him, and must have made on his son. *Wisconsin State Register*, July 28, 1877, July 5, 1879. A delightful picture of life on a pioneer farm near Port-

speculators at five dollars an acre, one-quarter down.[14] Farther west, he was told, even newer lands in the valley of the Red River of the North were being transformed into "bonanza farms"; beyond them on the plains of the Dakotas former residents of Portage were staking out their claims and writing glowingly to the Portage paper of their pioneering experiences.[15]

He was close to the wilderness, too, when he mingled with the Indians who clung to their tribal lands near Portage. The Winnebago, to be sure, ceded their Columbia County hunting grounds in 1837 and the Menomonee in 1849, but many refused to move to the Nebraska reservation assigned them and continued to fish and hunt along the Baraboo and Wisconsin rivers.[16] Fred Turner visited their villages on his frequent fishing trips; he saw the red men under less favorable circumstances when they wandered into Portage to trade or beg, or to drink themselves into trouble with the authorities.[17] He also read in his father's paper frontierlike demands that these "worthless savages" be driven by the government from "a community where they are utterly despised, disgusting everyone with their filthiness and alarming timid women by their frightful appearance as they go begging from door to door." [18] Portage was near enough its pioneer days to believe that the only good Indian was a dead Indian.

Fred Turner shared the town's satisfaction when these demands were met and a detachment of troops arrived early in 1873 to drive the red men to their Nebraska reservation.[19] They refused to go, meeting instead in tribal council to launch legal proceedings and send a delegation to Washington to plead for mercy.[20] These protests were in vain; instead troops herded parties westward all that summer, some almost at bayonet point.[21] The die-hards who hid in the forests to escape the troops were rounded up that December while gathered in tribal council, marched through Portage, and herded on railroad cars that would carry them westward. Turner witnessed these events, and he read in

age, also stressing the frontier atmosphere, is in John Muir, *The Story of My Boyhood and Youth* (Madison, 1967), pp. 199–238.

14. *Wisconsin State Register*, September 1, 1877.
15. *Ibid.*, August 16, 1879.
16. *A History of Columbia County*, 330–33.
17. The *Wisconsin State Register*, February 17, 1866, reported that drunken Indians were so numerous that they menaced life and property in Portage.
18. *Ibid.*, August 9, 1873.
19. *Ibid.*, April 27, 1872, February 15, 1873.
20. *Ibid.*, April 19, June 14, June 21, 1873.
21. *Ibid.*, July 12, July 26, 1873.

the local press that Portage was well rid of the lot of them. "The great mass of them," the editor proclaimed, "are regarded as nothing more than unmitigated nuisances, in every particular, and their departure for other lands is hailed with joy." [22] Scenes and sentiments that so accurately mirrored the frontier could not fail to impress a twelve-year-old boy.

Nor were those scenes to disappear, for despite the vigilance of the troops, many Winnebago stayed on in the brush country along the Baraboo, trapping muskrats, and making annual pilgrimages to nearby blueberry plains and cranberry bogs. Others who found life on the Nebraska reservation intolerable joined them there, until their villages were familiar sights to Fred and his fishing companions. [23] He was often among them, "hearing the squaws in their village on the high bank talk their low treble to the bass of our Indian polesman," as he paddled down the river in a dugout canoe, "feeling that I belonged to it all." [24]

Fred Turner lived close to the hither edge of the wilderness during his boyhood years. He also lived in an emerging society, plastic and rapidly changing, as were the societies near all frontiers. Newcomers arrived daily in Portage and Columbia County, drawn from much of the nation and many countries of Europe. Of the 20,500 native Americans living in the county in 1880, some 15,000 were born in Wisconsin, 800 in the other states of the Old Northwest, 3,000 in New York and Pennsylvania, and more than 700 in New England. The 7,500 foreign-born came from more divergent homelands, 1,500 from England and Wales, 1,500 from Ireland and Scotland, 3,000 from Germany, more than 1,000 from Scandinavia, and a sprinkling from France, Bohemia, and other nations. [25] Roughly one-third of the inhabitants of Portage were born abroad, and the percentage was even higher in the nearby towns Turner visited on his fishing expeditions. Caledonia contained only a handful of American-born, while Scots, Welsh, and Germans were almost equally

22. *Ibid.*, December 27, 1873. These events are also described in Jones, *History of Columbia County*, I, 29–31.
23. *Wisconsin State Register*, July 5, 1874, January 13, 1883.
24. Turner to Carl Becker, December 16, 1925. HEH TU Box 34A. Turner wrote similar accounts of his boyhood experiences to Miss Constance L. Skinner, March 15, 1922 (HEH TU Box 31) and Mrs. William Hooper, February 13, 1921 (HEH TU-H Box 5). His letters to Becker and Miss Skinner are printed below, pp. 234–44 and 205–16. Becker's appraisal of the effect of these experiences on young Turner is in Carl Becker, "Frederick Jackson Turner," in Howard W. Odum, ed., *American Masters of Social Science* (New York, 1927), pp. 301–02.
25. U.S. Census Office, *Statistics of the Population of the United States at the Tenth Census (June 1, 1880)*, *Vol. I*, 446, 534–35.

divided.[26] Lewiston's 234 settlers numbered 95 Germans, 33 Scandinavians, 35 Irishmen, and 53 American-born.[27]

Fred Turner did not need these census figures to tell him that he was part of an ethnic hodgepodge that was slowly blending into the "composite American nationality" that he was later to describe. He knew that the Welsh from all Columbia County assembled at Portage at Christmas time for their traditional Eisedfod where musicians, poets, and literary figures displayed their wares and discussed cultural matters.[28] Sometimes he joined the celebration of Robert Burns' birthday when the county Scots met at the Ellsworth house for music, speeches, and feasting, or took part in the annual ball staged by the Liederkranz Society.[29] Fishing trips carried him into nearby farm communities where no English was spoken; "he couldn't speak a word of English" he reported of one host, "so I had a little taste of continental life, and had to brush up on my Teutonic." [30] He probably learned from his father when he was eleven years old that the Portage city council was made up of one native of Ireland, one of Baden, one of Prince Edward Island, one of Prussia, one of Wurthenberg, one of Holland, one of Wales, one of Massachusetts, and one of New York—a mixture to be found only in an emerging community on the fringes of settlement.[31] Before his eyes Turner saw men from a variety of backgrounds coalescing into a society that blended the culture of each of its contributors, but emerged with a culture of its own. This he never forgot. "It was a town with a real collection of types from all the world," he recalled some years later, "Yankees from Maine and Vermont, New York Yankees, Dutchmen from the Mohawk, braw curlers from the Highlands, Southerners—all kinds. They mixed, too, and respected and fought each other." [32]

These youthful impressions were still fresh in Turner's mind when he began his speculations on the nature of American society; they were part of him, not something he learned from books. They altered his perspective in two important ways. First, he knew himself to be the product of a social order where life and values differed from those of established communities. "I am," he wrote in 1887, "placed in a *new* society that is just beginning to realize

26. *A History of Columbia County*, 706.
27. *Wisconsin State Register*, September 17, 1870.
28. *Ibid.*, October 24, 1868, January 2, 1869, *A History of Columbia Country*, 487–98.
29. *Wisconsin State Register*, September 27, 1862, January 21, 1865.
30. Turner to Caroline Mae Sherwood, July 19, 1886. HEH TU Box A.
31. *Wisconsin State Register*, April 13, 1872.
32. Turner to Carl Becker, December 16, 1925. HEH TU Box 34A. This letter is printed below, pp. 234–44.

that it has made a place for itself by mastering the wilderness and peopling the prairie, and is now ready to take its great course in universal history." Cultural progress might lag as men turned to the material tasks needed to conquer the wilderness, but the fresh social views generated there were worth any sacrifice. "The west looks to the future," he believed, "the east toward the past." [33] Turner sensed the differences that distinguished the pioneering Wests from the stabilized Easts even before he launched the studies that led to his frontier hypothesis.

Secondly, his close contact with nature heightened his sensitivity to his fate, and the fate of the nation, when free lands were exhausted and expansion ended. Turner's boyhood pleasures planted in him an almost Emersonian sensitivity to the wilderness; he acutely resented civilization's assault on the primitivism that he enjoyed as a child. Hence he saw nature as a generative force, transforming frontier social orders into something approaching completely new societies.[34] In this transformation he saw explanations for many of the problems that had long troubled American historians. Had Turner been city born and bred, he would almost certainly not have evolved his frontier thesis.

Before he could do so he must be equipped with the tools and techniques of a trained historian. This meant college, and to a Portage boy college meant the University of Wisconsin in nearby Madison. There Fred J. Turner (as he then signed himself) enrolled in the fall of 1878, and there he compiled a respectable academic average of 90.8% before a near-fatal attack of spinal meningitis forced him to leave school.[35] When he re-enrolled in the spring of 1881 he was still not completely well, but able to attend classes and begin the career in the Adelphia Literary Society that won him fame as an undergraduate orator. Not until he was a junior did his historical training begin, for not until then did he enroll in courses taught by Professor William Francis Allen. From the moment he did so he was a lost soul, so dedicated to history that everything else seemed unimportant. Turner often testified in later life that no other person influenced his future so completely, and this was only a slight exaggeration. This wise and good man shaped him into a first-rate historian, and kindled the enthusiasms that sustained him for the rest of his days.

33. Turner to Caroline Mae Sherwood, September 5, 1887. HEH TU Box B.
34. William Coleman, "Science and Symbol in the Turner Frontier Hypothesis," *American Historical Review*, LXXII (October, 1966), 46–47, makes this point.
35. *Wisconsin State Register*, August 16, August 30, September 6, September 20, October 4, November 22, November 29, 1879, February 14, May 8, 1880.

A classicist by training and a medievalist by choice, Professor Allen brought to the classroom the rigorous "scientific" techniques that he had learned at Harvard and Gottingen, and that were revolutionizing historical studies in the United States.[36] His courses were strictly conventional—in the junior year a three-term sequence in "Dynastic and Territorial History" that surveyed political events from classical times onward, another two-term course in ancient institutions, mythology, and art, and the required one-term introduction to American history; in the senior year a three-term sampling of medieval institutions, the English constitution, and the history of civilizations [37]—but whatever the subject, his students entered a world of instruction far removed from the usual rote learning-recital technique then almost universally employed. In some Allen lectured, but in most he used the "topical" method, sending undergraduates to the sources to investigate assigned topics, prepare fifteen-minute papers, and present their findings to the class with the aid of a syllabus, charts, and maps.[38] Fred Turner learned history by research in the sources, spiced with the thrill of exploration and the excitement of discovery. Had Professor Allen followed the usual practice of textbook quizzes, his prize pupil might have been so repelled as to choose a journalistic career, as he intended at the time. Instead he found that history offered incomparable pleasure, at the same time developing his critical faculties by weighing and

36. A capable biography of Allen is Owen P. Stearns, "William Francis Allen: Wisconsin's First Historian," an unpublished master of arts thesis at the University of Wisconsin, prepared in 1955. Its author has kindly loaned me a copy and allowed me to use some of the mass of materials he has gathered. A brief biographical sketch by his friend Professor David B. Frankenburger is in William F. Allen, *Essays and Monographs by William Francis Allen: Memorial Volume* (Boston, 1890), pp. 3–20. A bibliography of Allen's writings, compiled by Turner, is in this volume, pp. 366–83.
37. Turner recorded his impressions of these courses some years later. He recalled that the course in "Dynastic and Territorial History" dealt only with the "exterior" of the past, and was "unevenly successful, better training for some of us than others!" The institutional courses, he recalled, filled important gaps in the narrative story it told. These were conducted as graduate seminars, even though offered to juniors. Turner judged that on "The History of Civilization" less able than the others, largely because Allen's mind "was not so philosophical as to attract him to the interpretation of large movements. Perhaps it should be said that his scholarship was too exact and thorough to permit him to generalize with facility." This appraisal, in Turner's hand, is in HEH TU Box 56. Allen believed his American history course to be one of the first required in the United States. Allen to Herbert Baxter Adams, August 2, 1886, in W. Stull Holt, ed., *Historical Scholarship in the United States, 1876–1901: as Revealed in the Correspondence of Herbert B. Adams* (Baltimore, 1938), p. 88.
38. Allen explained his teaching techniques in a letter to Herbert B. Adams, August 2, 1886, printed in *ibid.*, p. 88. He also wrote extensively on his methods in an article in the undergraduate newspaper, *University Press*, February 10, 1883, and an essay on "Gradation and Topical Method of Historical Study," in G. Stanley Hall, ed., *Methods of Teaching History* (Boston, 1884), pp. 251–56.

comparing original documents and by shaping his findings into a structured report.

Just as important for Turner's future as the methods Allen employed was the content of his courses. He saw history not as a chronicle of war and politics, but as a search for the hidden social and economic forces that underlay political behavior, a concept that was revolutionary for that day.[39] It vastly influenced Turner; his search for the subterranean currents that explained the American past led him directly to his frontier and sectional hypotheses. Professor Allen also saw history as an exercise in cause and effect; the historian's duty was not to record the event but to determine the causal force behind it. "No historical fact has any value," he wrote, "except so far as it helps us to understand human nature and the working of historical forces." [40] This too was a viewpoint vastly important to Turner, and one that underlay his entire concept of history.

Allen's methodology was also revolutionary for his time. He preached the heretical doctrine that historians should use any available tool in their quest for truth; to him the study of the past was impossible for a person not versed in metaphysics, theology, military science, political economy, and jurisprudence.[41] When Turner, in later years, urged the use of economics, political science, sociology, and anthropology he was only echoing his master. He echoed him again by using maps to illuminate the nation's expansion westward and its division into sections. Allen was a pioneer in this technique both in the classroom and research, and indoctrinated his students in its value. His own studies of the expansion of ancient Rome were based on a series of carefully drawn maps, while the catalog descriptions of his courses regularly noted that "historical charts and maps are constantly used." [42] Turner later testified that his passion for mapping all possible data dated back to his days in Allen's classes.

The most important lesson learned in Allen's courses was an understanding of the historical process as one of constant growth and relationship. Societies, he taught, changed constantly, just as did the biological organ-

39. Allen recorded his views on the nature of history in an article in the *University Press*, February 17, March 2, March 16, April 1, April 16, May 1, 1874, entitled "The Study of History."
40. Quoted in the biographical sketch of Allen by David B. Frankenburger in Allen, *Essays and Monographs*, p. 13.
41. Allen, "The Study of History," *University Press*, February 17, 1874.
42. *Catalogue of the University of Wisconsin for 1881–1882* (Madison, 1882), p. 49.

isms then being popularized by Charles Darwin and his fellow evolutionists. Allen saw the great break-throughs in man's progress—the invention of the bow and arrow, the domestication of animals, the smelting of iron ore, the development of a phonetic alphabet—as steps in "the evolution of society," each forcing a series of changes that altered the social structure.[43] To him the shift from community to private land ownership was the final step in "the evolution of barbarism into civilization." [44] Allen's course on medieval institutions, taken by Turner during his senior year, was largely a study of institutional response to social and economic change.[45] Turner learned two essential lessons from his teacher's emphasis. He saw society as constantly changing, and he realized that the pace of change could be measured by using comparative techniques; the evolution of a medieval village, for example, could be understood better when compared with the growth of a primitive village in New England or the Illinois country.[46] These were essential concepts to Turner, for his belief in society as an evolving organism underlay his entire understanding of the past, and his application of medieval problems to the American West lead him closer to his frontier theory.

Despite later, half-joking remarks that his lack of training in American history fitted him to view the subject from a fresh perspective,[47] Turner absorbed a great deal from Professor Allen's one-term course on that subject. This included an overall interpretation surprisingly modern for that day, and a stress on the importance of expansion that was probably not wasted on the future historian of the frontier. Allen saw the age of colonization as a phase of the expansion of Europe, and an end product of the rise of national states, the ferment of the Reformation, and the intellectual explosion of the Renaissance.[48] He conceived the spread of settlement across the American conti-

43. Several of the notebooks in which Turner recorded Allen's lectures have been preserved. The first, dated September 6, 1882, is labeled "Course I. Ancient Institutions;" the second, dated October 20, 1883, bears the title "History of Medieval Institutions." Both are in the Frederick Jackson Turner Papers, State Historical Society of Wisconsin. Hereafter cited as SHSW: Turner Papers. The quotation is from the notebook on "Ancient Institutions," first lecture. Turner's lecture notes for the course on "Dynastic and Territorial History" were apparently not preserved.
44. Turner, notes for "Course I. Ancient Institutions," second lecture. SHSW: Turner Papers.
45. Allen's notes for his lectures on the "History of Civilization," dated 1883, are in the William Francis Allen Papers, State Historical Society of Wisconsin. Hereafter cited as SHSW: Allen Papers.
46. Turner, notes on "History of Medieval Institutions." SHSW: Turner Papers.
47. Turner to Merle Curti, August 8, 1928. HEH TU Box 40. This letter is reproduced below, pp. 257–65.
48. Allen's notes for his lectures in this course, in a notebook labeled "American History Notebook," are in the SHSW: Allen Papers.

nent as a continuation of Europe's expansion and the Louisiana Purchase as a watershed in the early history of the Republic. Even the slavery conflict was to Allen a by-product of expansion. "It must be noticed," he told his class, "that it was the *extension of slavery* that thus became the leading issue. The *existence* of slavery in the States was wholly a different question, and one which under our political system could never be more than a moral issue." [49] Allen also recognized that expansion increased the power of the central government, especially as the demand grew for federal control of slavery in the territories. When Turner wrote, as he did in 1893, that "loose construction increased as the nation marched westward," he was parroting Allen's wisdom. [50] Perhaps he remembered but few of the specific lessons taught in that course, but they remained in his mind and served as a backdrop when the frontier thesis was emerging in his consciousness.

He may also have recalled the few challenging ideas read in the books Allen assigned his students in American history. Most were dreary chronicles; students of the 1880s endured the boredom of the chronological outline that passed as a textbook—Alexander Johnston's *History of American Politics* (1879)—or absorbed the prejudices of such venerable tomes as John Marshall's life of Washington or the multivolume histories of John Schouler, George Bancroft, Richard Hildreth, and Hermann von Holst. Turner may have found a few items on Allen's reading list more to his liking: the works of Francis Parkman on the French and Indian wars, J. G. Shea's *Discovery and Exploration of the Mississippi Valley* which was judged "indispensible to the student of western history," and Consul W. Butterfield's *Washington-Irving Correspondence*, which was listed as "an important work on the history of the Northwest." [51] These works may have stirred Turner's interest

49. Allen, review of Hermann von Holst volume in the *Constitutional History of the United States* covering the period from the annexation of Texas to 1850 in *The Nation*, XXXII (April 21, 1881), 280.
50. The quotation is from "The Significance of the Frontier in American History" in Frederick J. Turner, *The Frontier in American History* (New York, 1920), p. 25. Wirt A. Cate, "Lamar and the Frontier Hypothesis," *Journal of Southern History*, I (November, 1935), 497–501, holds that Turner borrowed his ideas on nationalism from Lucius Q. C. Lamar, who published on the subject in 1888. Even if Turner had read Lamar's essay, which seems unlikely, he had developed his own concepts earlier than this, and partly due to Allen's influence.
51. Allen expressed his judgment of these books in his *History Topics for the Use of High Schools and Colleges* (Boston, 1883), in a "List of Books for Reference on the History of the United States," *The Badger*, February 15, 1883, p. 3, and in his "Notebook for United States History," SHSW: Allen Papers. Turner laboriously copied the entire list of books in the "Notebook for United States History" into his own notebook. This is in HEH TU Vol. XIII.

in the West, but he gained far more from a less pretentious one-volume *History of the United States* published in 1876 by a young Englishman named John A. Doyle.

Doyle's study was largely traditional, but he defied orthodoxy in one significant way. Illustrating his prosaic text were four colored maps drawn by Francis A. Walker, professor of history and political economy at Yale's Sheffield Scientific School, and later editor of the census volumes from which Turner gained much of his inspiration. One map showed the territorial expansion of the United States; the other three illustrated the westward movement of its population by using four-color gradations to depict the density of settlement from frontier areas with fewer than six persons to the square mile through the fully occupied portions with more than forty-five. Here was a graphic presentation of frontier expansion that must have impressed Turner. Doyle's comments were also enlightening; he argued that American history could be understood not as a study of coastal regions but as "the history of a movement from the coast towards the west." This was made "by new settlers, or those born in America who wanted land, gradually moving westward without losing their connection with the original settlements." [52]

Even more challenging was Doyle's comment on the effects of expansion. The westward movement, he wrote, was responsible for "many of the features which distinguish America from the Old World." Land was held in little value, and tenancy was unknown. This would change when expansion ended, and land increased in value as it had in Europe, driving many wage earners into manufacturing. "Hitherto men in the United States have always had before them the possibility of bettering themselves by a change in abode," Doyle wrote. "Moreover the great demand for labour has given them a free choice of occupation, and thus led to rapid changes. The ease too with which money can be made has led men to concentrate their energies in business, and thus the luxuries and refinement of life has been to a great extent neglected. When the power of extension towards the west is at an end,

52. John A. Doyle, *History of the United States* (New York, 1876), p. 7. The American edition of this work was reviewed by Allen in *The Nation*, XXII (May 4, 1876), 296. The importance of Doyle's book in shaping Turner's views on the frontier is appraised in Fulmer Mood, "The Concept of the Frontier, 1871–1898: Comments on a Select List of Source Documents," *Agricultural History*, XIX (January, 1945), 27–28. Mood's excellent essay on "The Development of Frederick Jackson Turner as a Historical Thinker," *Transactions of the Colonial Society of Massachusetts, 1837–1942.* Vol. XXXIV (Boston, 1943), 283–352, is the best work on the evolution of Turner's ideas now in print. Doyle's influence is appraised on pp. 298–300.

all this will change, and we may reasonably suppose that the United States will become far more like the great nations of Europe." [53] This was a remarkable statement for that time. In it Doyle isolated many of the characteristics that Turner was to identify with free land: the mobility of the people, the greater opportunity for self-advancement, the tendency toward materialism. When Allen recommended Doyle's book as "an excellent English work" he was pointing his best student in the right direction.[54]

Allen also gave his protegé his first opportunity to use the fascinating documents of frontier history. This arose when Allen received a request from Herbert Baxter Adams of the Johns Hopkins University, soon to be Turner's mentor there. Could Allen provide any information on early land holdings in Wisconsin that would illuminate Adams' own study of the origins of New England towns? [55] Allen could. He had six capable students in his course who would be asked to investigate land tenure among the original French villagers. "One of them," he told Adams, "is going to examine the records of Portage where is an old French grant (Grignon)." [56] Thus originated Turner's first research project. He set to work with enthusiasm, plying his father and his father's friends with questions,[57] poring through volumes of the *Annals of Congress* and the *American State Papers*, reading reminiscences of old settlers in the State Historical Society library, and combing documents in the Portage court house.[58] Here was Turner's first chance to apply the lessons learned from Allen, and he found the venture an exciting one.

The result was hardly a historical masterpiece, but it did display its author's skill as an investigator. Turner described the land claim purchased by Augustin Grignon from John Lecuyer, the dispute over ownership that forced Grignon to appeal to a congressional land commission in 1823, the reaction of Lecuyer's heirs, the patent issued by President Andrew Jackson

53. Doyle, *History of the United States*, pp. 386–87.
54. Allen, *History Topics for the Use of High Schools and Colleges*, 105; Allen, "Books of Reference on the History of the United States," *The Badger*, February 15, 1883, 3.
55. Herbert Baxter Adams to William F. Allen, April 6, 1882, quoted in Stearns, "William Francis Allen," pp. 241–42.
56. Allen to Adams, April 16, 1882, in *ibid.*, p. 242.
57. At his son's request, Andrew Jackson Turner wrote to L. J. Porlier, the son-in-law of Augustin Grignon, April 16, 1883, asking for information. This letter is in the State Historical Society of Wisconsin, Green Bay and Prairie de Chien Papers, Vol. XXVII, 56 (Wis. MSS C).
58. An excellent discussion of Turner's research for this essay is in Fulmer Mood and Everett E. Edwards, eds., "Frederick Jackson Turner's History of the Grignon Tract on the Portage of the Fox and Wisconsin Rivers," *Agricultural History*, XVII (April, 1943), 113–14.

on the commission's recommendation, and the history of the tract from that time to the present.[59] Little interpretation was necessary, as the facts spoke for themselves, but the thoroughness of the research, the expertness of the critical judgment, and the logic of the presentation testified to the fact that Turner had learned his lessons well. It showed also that he viewed history as a record of social growth, and could picture the evolution of Portage in two generations from an Indian campsite to a settled community.

Viewed in perspective, Turner's study of the Grignon tract was principally important for setting him to thinking about the differences between land tenure in the United States and Europe—an important step as he moved toward the frontier hypothesis. Why was the quasi-frontier area about Portage a land of small farms, or of "peasant proprietorship" as he phrased it? That he asked himself that question, and sought answers, we know from the jottings that he recorded in the "Commonplace Book" kept at the time— a paper notebook in which he copied quotations that pleased him, notes on books that he read, and speculations on historical topics. "Investigate land-holding peasantry about Madison," he wrote in 1883, "(e.g.) just as one would from the remains of ancient land systems (census—Ag[ricultural] Reports—Talks) etc. How many acres average. What kind of houses live in? Food? Manners—sports etc. Need of village system. Significance of Eng."[60] Again he noted that "if our lands in the west had not been opened to and filled with foreign immigrants it is not unlikely that they would have fallen into the hands of capitalists and have been made into great estates, e.g. Dalrymple farm." This would have reversed the democratic trend in the United States—"the revolution going on which is to raise *man* from his low estate to his proper dignity." Instead "such institutions as the peasant proprietors" served as a force "all the stronger that it works quietly in the great movement."[61] Turner was realizing, even as a junior in college, that Amer-

59. The essay was published in the *Wisconsin State Register*, June 23, 1883. It has been reprinted from this source in Mood and Edwards, eds., "Frederick Jackson Turner's History of the Grignon Tract," *loc. cit.*, 114–20.
60. Turner, "Commonplace Book for 1883," HEH, TU Vol. III (2), 1883.
61. *Ibid.* Turner's interest in the relationship between land and social institutions was probably derived from Allen. In a review in *The Nation*, XIV (February 8, 1872), 89–90, Allen praised a book of Cobden Club essays that dealt with this subject, applying some of its theories to the United States. He speculated as to what would happen after farmers had "skinned the land" of the entire continent as they already had New England, and wondered if farm areas would then revert to control by a few capitalists, thus threatening the democratic system. These were concepts later to be developed by Turner.

ica's unique institutions were due partly to the existence of an area of free land which discouraged aristocratic tendencies, and strengthened the trend toward democracy.

These speculations suggest that when Fred Turner graduated from the University of Wisconsin in 1884 he left with a sound training in historical methodology, an appreciation of the value of comparative studies in American and medieval institutions to the understanding of United States history, and an unquenchable enthusiasm for the study of the past. For a man thus burdened, graduate study was almost inevitable. Turner resisted his impulses for a time as he practiced the journalism that he intended for a career, but this interlude was brief and ended in the spring of 1885 when Professor Allen departed for a sabbatical leave amidst the treasures of classical Europe. Would Turner care to teach his classes for a term? Turner would; newspaper work was proving unsatisfactory after the excitement of historical research and he had been neglecting it to give himself a thorough course in historical reading—"his favorite theme in literature," one of his fellow reporters noted.[62]

There was little time for speculation in the months that followed, or during the next two years when Turner pursued his graduate studies, supporting himself first as an instructor in rhetoric and oratory, then in rhetoric and history. But reading was necessary, and more and more he made his home the library of the State Historical Society of Wisconsin, then housed in a wing of the state capitol. There he gravitated more and more to the history alcoves, and especially to those housing books on the American West. "The more I dip into American history," he wrote in 1887, "the more I can see what a great field there is here for a life of study. One must even specialize here. I think I shall spend my study chiefly upon the Northwest and more generally on the Mississippi Valley. The history of this great country remains to be written. I shall try to add my mite in the way of studying it."[63] A few months later he was even more enthusiastic. "I do not talk anything now but Western history. . . . I have taken a fever of enthusiasm over the possibility of the study of the great west and of the magnificent scope of United States history in general."[64]

62. *Wisconsin State Journal* (Madison), April 11, 1885.
63. Turner to Caroline Mae Sherwood, September 5, 1887. HEH TU Box B. Turner's letters to his fiancée, written between 1886 and 1889 when they were married, provide an excellent picture of his development while in graduate school.
64. Turner to Caroline Mae Sherwood, March 25, 1888. HEH TU Box C.

Whence came this zeal for a subject then little known and largely unrecognized by historians? Turner could never answer that question, nor can we today. Awareness of his western heritage, the realization (brought home to him during his first trip east in 1887) that this differed from that of New England, an eagerness to apply the techniques of medieval history to an unexplored segment of the past, an awakening consciousness of the emerging social order about Portage—probably all had some influence. Whatever the reason, Turner was aware of the boldness of his decision. "I have," he wrote, "started in a line that is not well travelled and I can see a way of treating it that is out of the usual line." [65] Did he even then have a glimmering of the theory that he was to advance six years later?

Again that question is unanswerable, but clues in his commonplace books suggest his line of thought. On one occasion he copied a line from Benjamin Franklin that mirrored his belief in the frontier as a safety valve for the downtrodden: "The boundless woods of America which are sure to afford freedom and subsistence to any man who can bait a hook or pull a trigger." [66] On another he jotted a topic to be investigated: collate the facts showing the date of each permanent settlement in Wisconsin with the causes of migration. [67] On others he pondered the impact of immigration on the changing social structure of the region about Portage. "Need of Study of Foreign Groups," he wrote. "Anthropology, political economy, sociology, politics. Votes by districts. Why are Nor[wegians] Rep[ublicans]. Irish Dem[ocrats]?" [68] In the autumn of 1887 he added: "Our Composite Nationality. Glances through a microscope in the historical laboratory. Biological methods applied to the study of typical groups of immigrants. The Pomeranian settlement at Portage. Evolution." [69] Turner was obviously speculating on an important problem—why did American civilization differ from that of Europe?—and finding a partial answer in immigration. Newcomers were crowding older Yankee settlers from their lands, and by doing so altering both their own behavior and the behavior of those about them. He was groping toward the realization that cheap lands held the key to an understanding of much of the nation's past. "If I fill my letters with speculations about the evolution of American society from the diverse elements of European origin," he wrote his fiancée during the summer of 1887, "—don't think

65. *Ibid.*
66. Turner, "Commonplace Book" [1886]. HEH TU Vol. III (3).
67. *Ibid.*
68. "Commonplace Book II." HEH TU Vol. III (2).
69. "Commonplace Book" [1886]. HEH TU Vol. III (3).

I am insane or that I love you the less; it will be simply an experiment in enthusiasm!" [70]

This excitement sustained him as he buckled to the preparation of his master's thesis. He and Allen agreed on a topic some time in the fall of 1886 when Turner became a formal candidate for the degree. The subject had lingered in the back of his mind since he prepared the paper on the Grignon tract during his junior year; while poking about the collections of the State Historical Society he found bundles of letters from French fur traders that promised glamorous reading, for they were old, water-stained, tied with leather thongs, and written in what he described as execrable French.[71] Why not write a thesis on the early fur trade of Wisconsin? This assured pleasant research, and might add a chapter of interest to the state's history.[72] So the subject was chosen, at the beginning of the 1886–1887 school year, but Turner was a compulsive procrastinator, and not until a year later did he begin serious work. Even then progress was slow, for it involved mastering scarcely legible manuscripts in a language that he learned only with difficulty. Fortunately he did his best work under pressure and by the spring of 1888 was so immersed in his subject that he fell into bad grace with his professors, his friends, and even his fiancée. "The gay chant of the Canadian voyageur rings out . . . in my nightly dreams," he wrote early in May, "and I murmur fantastic French in my sleep." [73] This total immersion, and frequent sessions lighted by midnight oil, allowed his paper to be finished on time to read before the Madison Literary Club later that month, and in expanded form to Professor Allen a few weeks later.[74] Allen was immensely pleased, suggesting that the thesis was worthy of publication in the *Collections of the State Historical Society*, where it eventually appeared.

Turner's first major effort was a no-nonsense history, jam-packed with information seldom relieved by interpretation. Yet it brought him a step nearer his frontier hypothesis, for his was no mere chronicle, but an exercise in *why* the fur trade developed and *how* it influenced later settlement. The

70. Turner to Caroline Mae Sherwood, [August 21], 1887. HEH TU Box B.
71. Turner to Carl Becker, December 16, 1925. HEH TU Box 34. This letter is reproduced below, pp. 234–44. A similar comment is in Turner to Reginald F. Arrogon, July 4, 1916. HEH TU Box 26.
72. Turner to Andrew Jackson Turner, September 23, 1885. HEH TU Box A. Turner at this time was considering writing a history of the fur trade about Green Bay, Wisconsin.
73. Turner to Caroline Mae Sherwood, [May, 1888]. HEH TU Box B.
74. Turner to Caroline Mae Sherwood, May 17, 1888. HEH TU Box B. The meeting was described in the *Wisconsin State Journal*, May 15, 1888, the *Wisconsin State Register*, May 26, 1888, and the manuscript "Journal of the Madison Literary Club, 1877–1903," I, 210–13. This is preserved in the Division of Manuscripts, State Historical Society of Wisconsin.

"why" forced him to master the geography of the state, to show how the traders' advance into successive river systems determined the location and chronology of each extension.[75] The "how" brought home to him the manner in which the trade was the first step in the evolution of Wisconsin's civilization. "The Indian village," he wrote, "became the trading post, the trading post became the city. The trails became our early roads. The portages marked out locations for canals. . . . In a word, the fur trade closed its mission by becoming the pathfinder for agricultural and manufacturing civilization." [76] Turner here voiced a concept basic to his frontier thesis: that society evolved in recognizable steps on each frontier from primitivism to an advanced stage of civilization. When he applied that principle on a broader canvas he had laid another stone for the foundation of his hypothesis.

Before doing so more training was needed, and for this a change of scene was required. With the Master of Arts degree safely tucked away, Turner entered the Johns Hopkins University in the fall of 1888 to resume his studies in what was then the Valhalla of the academic world. There he spent one of the most rewarding years of his life, absorbing learning in vast quantities, mingling with the great and near great of the historical profession, forming enduring friendships, and glorying in the fact that he was in the center of the nation's learning rather than a small backwash. His hope was to complete work for the doctor of philosophy degree in one academic year, using an expanded version of his master's thesis as his dissertation, but these dreams were dashed when he failed to master the French and German needed to satisfy requirements. Instead he returned to Madison in the spring of 1889 without his doctorate, but with enough accomplished to assure the degree a year later when he passed the series of examinations required.

Turner's single year in Baltimore altered his historical perspective and equipped him with the learning needed to construct his frontier hypothesis. Some among his instructors made such a slight impression that they were

75. Six sheets of paper containing notes in Turner's hand on the river systems and passes through the mountains were probably made at this time. They are in HEH TU File Drawer 15, Folder: Physical Geography of U.S.
76. Turner's thesis, in somewhat revised form, was later printed as "The Character and Influence of the Fur Trade in Wisconsin," *State Historical Society of Wisconsin Proceedings*, XXXVI (Madison, 1889), 52–98. The quotation is from pp. 97–98. What was apparently a fragment of the first draft of his thesis was preserved by Turner in the form of four typed half-sheets containing roughly the same material that is on pp. 72–78 of the published work. The writing is less restrained than in the printed version, with a freer use of colorful language. HEH TU File Drawer 8D, Folder: French Fur Trade.

seldom mentioned in his letters or reminiscences, but four stood out as intellectual guides whose influence was second only to that of Professor Allen: Herbert Baxter Adams, Albion W. Small, Woodrow Wilson, and Richard T. Ely. To appreciate the contribution that each made to Turner's mental development is to better understand the genesis of his historical beliefs.

Herbert Baxter Adams' role must remain an enigma. New England born and German educated, Adams was at this time the high priest of the profession; he was secretary of the American Historical Association, supreme potentate of the then popular "scientific school" of historians, and dominating member of the Johns Hopkins history department. Adams recognized Turner's superior ability at once and entrusted him with tasks and responsibilities far beyond the call of necessity; Turner served as his assistant in the extension courses he was conducting, took over his classes during absences from the city, and was selected to lecture on "The Conquest and Organization of the Old Northwest" for a series Adams arranged to enlighten Washington schoolteachers.[77] This trust was reciprocated; Turner respected and admired his teacher, as his letters of the time clearly showed. He acquired from Dr. Adams, Turner remarked shortly after he left Johns Hopkins, "an added enthusiasm for historical research and a definite desire to relate history to the present." Never did he meet another man who could surpass his teacher in inspiring men with enthusiasm for serious historical work and bring out the best in them.[78] These were the sentiments of a sincere admirer, and Turner admired Adams as he did few others among his teachers.

This was surprising, for in his later years he often testified that he was in rebellion against Adams' ideas when he developed his frontier thesis. What irked him especially, he remembered, was his teacher's insistence that the evolution of every American institution from its "germ" in medieval Germany had already been traced, and the subject so exhausted that students were advised to turn to European history instead.[79] If Adams ever gave his

77. Turner delivered a lecture on the same subject to the Madison Contemporary Club in 1887, so that little preparation was necessary. A printed program of the series in which he appeared was enclosed in a letter to Caroline Mae Sherwood, March 29, 1889. HEH TU Box D., in which he anguished over the thought of having to appear before eight hundred school teachers. His lecture was reported in the *Wisconsin State Journal*, February 22, 1889, and *The Aegis*, April 5, 1889. The latter was an undergraduate newspaper at the University of Wisconsin.
78. Turner to Richard T. Ely, January 28, 1902. State Historical Society of Wisconsin, Richard T. Ely Papers. Hereafter referred to as SHSW: Ely Papers.
79. Turner made this remark in a talk to the Harvard History Club in 1924. His notes for this are in HEH TU Box 56. His friend and former student, Joseph Schafer, remembered

seminar such advice (and the seminar records contain no evidence that he did) he was not speaking seriously. To him the graduate seminar was a laboratory in which students from all the nation gathered, each bringing a specialized knowledge of his home community. There they would learn the techniques needed to investigate the institutions of their local villages or counties, tracing those institutions back to their Teutonic origins. In Adams' eyes there were as many topics crying for investigation as there were towns in the United States. Only a few had been studied—the genesis of New England towns, the origins of some southern and Maryland parishes, the background of a few French villages in the Midwest, and certain educational practices. There were enough topics left, he wrote in 1884, to keep students busy for a hundred years. Institutional history was "untouched as were once the forests of America." [80] Turner's memory lapsed when he accused Professor Adams of holding that research topics in American history had been exhausted.

Nor did he give Adams credit for an interest in western topics that paralleled his own. For some time Adams had been encouraging comparative economic studies, and especially those revealing the similarity between western land policies and certain medieval institutions. His students were directed into investigations that would shed light on these matters: in 1885 one studied the history of land legislation in the United States, in 1886 others reported to the seminar on the land question in Nebraska, Indiana, Wisconsin, and California. [81] On one occasion Adams remarked to the seminar that the nation's entire history was shaped by agrarian problems, and speculated that immigration was "greatly influenced by the desire of the emigrants to obtain

that Turner often described Adams' attitude, and always with indignation. Joseph Schafer, "The Author of the Frontier Hypothesis," *Wisconsin Magazine of History*, XV (September, 1931), 91–92. Turner repeated it in a letter to Carl Becker, December 16, 1925. HEH TU Box 34.

80. Herbert B. Adams, "Special Methods of Historical Study as Pursued at the Johns Hopkins University and at Smith College," *Johns Hopkins University Studies in Historical and Political Science*, II (Baltimore, 1884), 15.

81. *Johns Hopkins University Circulars*, No. 4 (April, 1880), 47–48, contains announcements by Adams that show his interest in land studies. In 1884 one of his students, Charles H. Shinn, reported to the seminar on land laws of western mining camps. Shosuke Sato followed a year later with a report on land laws in the United States, and in 1886 students reported on the land question in Nebraska, Indiana, Wisconsin, and California. Minutes of the Johns Hopkins University Seminary, October 31, 1884, December 4, 1885, October 15, 1886. These manuscript minute-books are in the Johns Hopkins University Archives. Photocopies, essential in studying Turner's year at the university, were generously supplied the Henry E. Huntington Library, and are now in that institution's collection of Turner Papers.

large landed estates like those of the gentry in England and France." [82] This might be poor history, but it did recognize free land as an attracting force. Adams also pointed out to his students the relationship between land and the free-silver question, with the "people in the West and South being the debtor classes" wanting cheap money, and "the people in the East being the capitalists" favoring the gold standard.[83] This was the type of history that Turner most liked.

What he remembered as dislike of Adams was more likely resentment against the smug self-satisfaction that was the earmark of eastern historians in that day. All, he found, were disdainfully indifferent to his own Middle West. New Englanders especially found the alpha and omega of life in their one tight little section, and scarcely recognized that the United States extended west of the Hudson or south of the Potomac. This bruised Turner's strong local pride. "Not a man here that I know," he wrote Professor Allen, "is either studying, or is hardly aware of the country beyond the Alleghanies." [84] When he testified, as he did in his later years, that "my essay on the 'Frontier' was a protest against the tendencies of the eastern historians at the time it was written," he was nearer the truth than when he laid it on the doorstep of Adams' supposed insistence that topics in American institutional history had been exhausted.[85]

For his other instructors at Johns Hopkins, Turner had only praise both at the time and later. One from whom he benefited was Albion W. Small, later a famed sociologist, but at this time an advanced graduate student who had been drafted as instructor to replace an absent faculty member. Small's course for a group of selected students on "The Growth of American Nationality" was admirably conducted; its members dug deeply into the source materials of the early Republic to find evidence of the transfer of power from state to nation.[86] This meant an invaluable lesson in the nature of

82. *Ibid.*, December 4, 1885.
83. *Ibid.*, October 15, 1886.
84. Turner to William F. Allen, October 31, 1888. HEH TU Box 1.
85. Turner to Helen Solliday, May 27, 1920. HEH TU Box 44.
86. Eighteen pages of manuscript notes kept by Turner in this course are in HEH TU File Drawer 15A, Folder: Notes of A. W. Small. They show something of Small's teaching methods, and of the content of the course. Small used the course as the basis for a study of "The Beginnings of American Nationality," *Johns Hopkins University Studies in Historical and Political Science*, VIII (Baltimore, 1890), 7–42. He had already published a textbook on *The Growth of American Nationality* (Waterville, Maine, 1888) which the students were required to read. Turner's copy of this book is in the Huntington Library, Accession No. 246586.

nationalism. The emphasis that Turner later placed on the frontier as generator of a nationalistic spirit was due in some measure to his immersion in the subject at this time.[87]

Woodrow Wilson played an even greater role in his training. A Johns Hopkins graduate, currently teaching at Wesleyan College, Wilson was imported during the spring term for a course on "Administration" in which Turner enrolled. This proved immensely valuable, partly because Wilson was in mild rebellion against the dominant "germ" theory of institutional transplant. His revolt had not gone too far; he still saw the New England township as "a spontaneous reproduction of the ancient Germanic Mark," and a "direct lineal descendant from the primitive communal institutions" of the days of Caesar and Tacitus.[88] But he also taught that environment altered these imported institutions so that the colonies "without losing their English character, gained an American form and flavor." This was because each "borrowed what was best suited to its own situation."[89] Wilson conceived institutions not as unchangeable monoliths but as dynamic organisms that responded to pressures upon them. This was a concept fundamental to Turner's historical beliefs, and while it had been planted by Professor Allen it matured under Wilson.

Even more important than formal instruction were the hours of conversation as Wilson and Turner walked together or bantered away their evenings. These began as soon as Wilson arrived in Baltimore, for like all visiting historians he put up at the boarding house of Mary Jane Ashton where Turner was already a roomer. The friendship formed there was immediate and lasting, moreover it was invaluable in shaping Turner's ideas. Wilson was an unreconstructed southerner, Turner a staunch westerner; both resented the condescending disrespect with which their homelands were viewed by easterners. Drawn together by this common bond, they explored the reasons for this alienation and agreed that each must write history that would restore

87. Turner later recalled that the principal task of the students was to investigate the instructions and powers of representatives of the thirteen colonies to the continental congress as a means of determining the degree of sovereignty assigned the emerging national government. Turner to Luther L. Bernard, November 24, 1928. HEH TU Box 40. This letter is reproduced below, pp. 289–96.
88. Six pages of notes taken by Turner on Wilson's lectures are in HEH TU File Drawer 1A, Folder: Mass. Town Lands. Wilson was lecturing at this time from his soon-to-be-published book, *The State: Elements of Historical and Practical Politics* (Boston, 1889). Presumably he used comparable phrases in the lectures that Turner heard. The quotations are from p. 526.
89. *Ibid.*, 450.

his own section to respectability in the eyes of the nation.[90] They also talked much of the nature of nationalism, a subject always dear to Wilson's heart and much on Turner's mind due to Albion W. Small's course. One significant point emerged: they agreed that the role of the West as a nationalizing force had been neglected by historians.[91] If this were the case, had not expansion influenced American development in other ways? Should not the whole history of the section be investigated to discover unsuspected truths that easterners in the profession refused to recognize? These were key ideas in Turner's growing interest in the frontier, and he remembered with gratitude Wilson's part in their generation. "It would be hard to overstate his influence upon my general conception of history and politics," he wrote some years later, and this time he spoke the truth.[92]

No less influential was Richard T. Ely, the eminent political economist who introduced Turner to the study of economic history and supplied him with both beliefs and methodology essential to his development. Ely played this role because of his advanced ideas; he was the bell wether of a group of young economists rebelling against the prevailing Ricardian view that man's behavior was governed by immutable natural laws, and arguing that social improvement was possible. Their duty was to point the way toward human betterment by studying mankind's economic behavior and suggesting reform.[93] These were radical views for that time, but they reinforced Turner's growing belief in the changeability of the social order. Ely saw to that, for he was captivated by his young pupil from their first meeting, drafting him into serving as substitute instructor during his own frequent absences from the classroom, and subjecting him to almost total immersion in economic theory. In all Turner took three courses with Ely during that year at Johns Hopkins: "The History of Political Economy," "Elements of Political Econ-

90. Turner to Constance L. Skinner, March 15, 1922. HEH TU Box 31. This letter is reproduced below, pp. 205–16.
91. Woodrow Wilson to Turner, August 23, 1889. HEH TU Box 1.
92. Turner to William E. Dodd, October 7, 1919. HEH TU Box 29. This letter is reproduced below, pp. 193–98. Brief descriptions of Wilson's Johns Hopkins' experiences and his relations with Turner are in William E. Dodd, *Woodrow Wilson and His Work* (Garden City, New York, 1920), pp. 27–28, and Henry W. Bragdon, *Woodrow Wilson: The Academic Years* (Cambridge, [Mass.] 1967), pp. 188–94.
93. Full accounts of Ely's contributions to economic studies are in Hugh Hawkins, *Pioneer: A History of the Johns Hopkins University, 1874–1889* (Ithaca, 1960), pp. 169–86, Jurgen Herbst, *The German Historical School in American Scholarship* (Ithaca, 1965), pp. 134–36, and especially Benjamin C. Rader, *The Academic Mind and Reform: The Influence of Richard T. Ely in American Life* (Lexington, Kentucky, 1966).

31

omy," and "Special Economic Questions." Ely also helped conduct the seminar that occupied all students from eight to ten each Friday evening.[94]

This was a heavy dose of learning, not lightened by the fact that clarity of expression was never an objective of writers in that discipline.[95] Ely assigned his introductory students representative books in both the classical and modern school—John Stuart Mill's *Principles of Political Economy* and Francis A. Walker's *Land and Its Rent*—then used the classroom to contrast the two views and expound his own. He also had them read all or part of John K. Ingram's *A History of Political Economy*, John B. Clark's *Capital and Its Earning*, and Henry George's *Progress and Poverty*.[96] The students in Ely's advance course, which focused largely on theories of rent, read thoroughly a modern textbook by Simon H. Patten, *Premises of Political Economy*, and listened to Ely's lectures, soon to be published as *An Introduction to Political Economy*.[97] By examining these books, we can gain a

94. Turner to Caroline Mae Sherwood, November 21, 1888. HEH TU Box A. The courses offered at Johns Hopkins that year, with the names of all students enrolled in each, are in *Johns Hopkins University Circulars*, VIII (No. 68, November, 1888), 6. Turner's record at the University is contained in Johns Hopkins University, "Transcript of the Graduate Record of Frederick Jackson Turner." A copy of this document was supplied the Henry E. Huntington Library by Irene M. Davis and Ellen G. Klages of the office of the university registrar.
95. A typical sentence from one of the texts used by Turner, Simon N. Patten, *Premises of Political Economy* (Philadelphia, 1885), p. 158, read: "Every increase of capital and skill reduces the quantity of labor necessary to obtain from land the present produce, and if they displace more labor than the additional labor which can be employed at a diminishing return, the return as a whole will be greater in proportion to the labor expended." Little wonder that Turner's fellow student, Charles M. Andrews, wrote his mother that after three nine-hour days spent on political economy he was ready to throw the books into the river and go on a spree. Charles M. Andrews to "Mama," February 10, 1889. Charles M. Andrews Papers, Historical Manuscripts Division, Yale University Library.
96. Turner pasted a list of the books read in the course in his copy of John Stuart Mill, *Principles of Political Economy* (London, 1886); this copy is in the Huntington Library, Accession No. 211882. The books he read included: Francis A. Walker, *Land and Its Rent* (Boston, 1883), John K. Ingram, *A History of Political Economy* (New York, 1888), John B. Clark, *Capital and Its Earnings* (Baltimore, 1888), and Henry George, *Progress and Poverty* (New York, 1882). Turner's own copies of the books by Ingram and George, dated in his hand in October, 1888, are in the Huntington Library, Accession Nos., 113711 and 152218. He apparently did not own a copy of Walker's volume. That he read Henry George at this time is interesting in view of his later statements that he did not know of *Progress and Poverty* until after presenting his frontier thesis. Turner to Merle Curti, January 5, 1931. HEH TU Box 45. This letter is reproduced below p. 282. We know that Turner not only owned a copy of the book, but read it carefully. His copy is heavily underlined; moreover one of the examination questions that he answered in one of Ely's courses was: "Compare Turgot, John Stuart Mill, and Henry George on Taxation." A copy of this examination is pasted in Turner's copy of Mill, *Principles of Political Economy* in the Huntington Library.
97. Turner to William F. Allen, October 31, 1888. HEH TU Box 1, describes the courses in which Turner was enrolled. His copy of Simon N. Patten, *Premises of Political Economy*, dated November 10, 1888, is in the Huntington Library. Accession No. 204811. It is heavily

fair idea of Turner's indoctrination in economic theory, and particularly into two aspects that were to influence his frontier hypothesis: the stages of social evolution and the theory of land rent.

That all social organisms evolved in well-defined stages was the basic belief of all political economists of that day. The concept was first advanced by the German scholar, Friedrich List, whose *National System of Political Economy* (1856) distinguished between the savage state, pastoral, agricultural, agricultural-manufacturing, and manufacturing-commercial.[98] Ely borrowed List's classifications with slight variations and incorporated them in his lectures and textbook. He saw civilization dawning when men learned to kindle fires, eat meat, and live in political communities. From then on they progressed in five stages: hunting and fishing, pastoral, agricultural, trading and commerce, and industrial. Each of these he explained in detail.[99] This lesson was not lost on Turner. When he described the march of civilization across the American continent in clear-cut stages—hunters and trappers, herdsmen, miners, pioneer farmers, equipped farmers, and urban dwellers— he was merely applying Ely's concept to the expansion of settlement in the United States. We know today that his—and Ely's—explanation was oversimplified; men seldom follow the well-ordered paths that political economists believe they should. But the truth was unimportant; another idea had been planted in Turner's mind to be used as his frontier hypothesis emerged.

He adopted an even more essential concept from his study of the theory of rent. "Rent," as the term was used by political economists, meant simply the return upon land. Land that returned nothing to society, and hence had no immediate value, was "free land." Land was "free" in unsettled or sparsely settled areas; as population thickened and markets emerged, its "rent" increased in the form of higher returns from its use or a mounting market value. What determined these increases, or the amount of "rent" that land yielded? Here political economists differed, with the classical economists offering one explanation and the newer revisionists such as Patten and Ely another.

---

underlined, indicating a careful reading. The Huntington Library copy of Richard T. Ely, *An Introduction to Political Economy* (New York, 1889), was presented to Turner by Ely in June, 1889, as the inscription on the flyleaf indicates.

98. Friedrich List, *National System of Political Economy* (Philadelphia, 1856), p. 72. Ely, in his *Studies in the Evolution of Industrial Society* (New York, 1903), p. 21, states that he borrowed the concept of stages of economic progress from List.

99. Ely, *An Introduction to Political Economy*, pp. 40–41.

John Stuart Mill, a traditionalist, held that the world's supply of land was limited, and that production would slow as its total utilization approached. This would not come abruptly, for inferior lands would be pressed into production as the supply of good lands dwindled. Mill saw the available supply as a "highly elastic and extensible band, which is hardly ever so violently stretched that it could not possibly be stretched any more, yet the pressure of which is felt more severely the nearer that limit is approached."[100] The greater the strain, the more the amount of "rent" the land should earn. Yet limitation in quantity did not solely determine rent. So long as land existed that yielded no return, the rent on land that did yield returns would be determined by the advantages it enjoyed in productivity and nearness to markets. The measure of any land's advantage was the quantity of its rent. This Mill illustrated by pointing to the United States, where farms were poorly cultivated and yielded less than their capacity because land was so plentiful and labor so dear that intensive agriculture was uneconomical.[101] An abundance of land, combined with a scarcity of markets, lowered the profit, or "rent" that could be taken, and hence the value of the land. Mill saw that there was no "free" land in the United States, but much that was relatively "free" because its value in terms of rent was less than in populated areas.

Francis A. Walker, whose *Land and Its Rent* Turner read in Ely's advanced course, refined Mill's theories and in doing so taught his readers a great deal about the nature of "free land" and "rent." Basing his reasoning on the American experience, Walker argued that "rent" was the price that land commanded in the open market, and was measured not only by productivity, but by adjacency to markets, the efficiency of transportation systems, demand, and other variables. If a canal or railroad opened new lands to production at a cost comparable to that in older areas, the older tracts could not compete. No one could cultivate them at a profit "so long as there is a limitless extent of free land on which can be raised with a small expenditure of labor and capital" the same goods produced by old lands.[102] This explained the decline of English and Irish rents as American produce flowed eastward with reduced transportation costs. Walker held that in the United States the availability of land, its distribution without cost by the government, and the excessive mobility of the people ("their almost ishmaelish

100. Mill, *Principles of Political Economy*, p. 109.
101. *Ibid.*, pp. 110, 261.
102. Walker, *Land and Its Rent*, pp. 25–26.

34

proclivity to change of place," he called it) combined to bring actual and theoretical rent close together.[103]

More essential to Turner's training than Walker or Mill was Simon H. Patten, whose *Premises of Political Economy* was an outspoken attack on the classical Ricardian theory of rent. The principal cause of "rent," he held, was social rather than physical; changing popular tastes, wastefulness, and inequities in distribution affected the demand for commodities, and hence the "rent" chargeable on lands producing them. The changing ownership pattern also had its impact. Ignorant and inefficient proprietors inevitably displaced the skilled and intelligent because their living standards were lower and their wants fewer, allowing them to subsist on less and dispose of a larger proportion of their surpluses. This displacement meant less efficient production in the long run, and with it declining food supplies and higher "rents" for lands being utilized.[104] Turner lost little time in applying this principle to his observations of the farm lands about Portage where immigrants from abroad were replacing the original Yankee stock.

These were valuable lessons, but they were made even more valuable by Ely's interpretative lectures. Ely's view of "rent" was not unlike Patten's. "What," he asked, "determines the amount of rent?" He answered by arguing that in a country where lands of varying degrees of fertility and use were cultivated, some were "marginal lands," or "lands on the margin of cultivation." These paid no rent; they provided their owners only a return on capital and labor expended. The United States contained a great deal of land of this sort that "just paid" for its cultivation. It also contained even more land that was better situated or more fertile, and hence did more than "just pay" for its use. The difference between the usable yield of this land and the land on the "margin of cultivation" was the amount of rent.[105] Both Ely and Patten agreed that this varied with the density of population. When a country was new, thinly settled, and distant from markets, land of high fertility would be classed as "poor" and yield no "rent"; those same lands when settled by later generations would be judged "very good," and return

103. *Ibid.*, pp. 45–47.
104. Patten, *Premises of Political Economy*, pp. 11–12. The passage stating this theory was heavily underlined by Turner. He later copied it to send to Professor Allen in a letter written on December 31, 1888. HEH TU Box 1. Patten also attended a meeting of the Johns Hopkins seminar while Turner was at Johns Hopkins, to speak on his book and answer questions. Johns Hopkins University, "Seminar Records, 1888–1889," pp. 406–08.
105. Ely, *An Introduction to Political Economy*, p. 215.

a high "rent." [106] In the first stage, when land paid no or little "rent," it was "free land."

From this formidable dose of economic theory, Turner distilled several concepts essential to his frontier thesis. He learned that returns from farm lands, or "rents," were determined by a variety of social and physical factors, including soil fertility, transportation facilities, adjacency to markets, and relationship to cheaper lands. He knew that "free land" in the traditional sense was nonexistent, but that some produced such a low margin of profit that it could not be advantageously cultivated. He realized that these "free lands" would be no longer free, but would provide a steadily increasing "rent" to their owners as population thickened and markets became available. These concepts were important to Turner's understanding of the settlement process of the United States. They are equally important to those who today would read his essay on the frontier with understanding. When he spoke of "free land" in the West, as he often did, he thought of lands that were not actually "free" but that paid a lesser return than those more favorably situated or endowed. He thought, too, of such "free lands" vanishing when settlers and markets emerged, allowing that land to command ever-increasing "rents." These definitions underlay his later thinking, and stood him in good stead as he developed his hypothesis.

That he applied these theories well was shown by a remarkable letter that he wrote Professor Allen that year. "Wisconsin," he told his old mentor, "is like a palimpsest. The mound builders wrote their record and passed away. The state was occupied . . . by the most various peoples of the Indian race. Then came the French. Then a wave of Northern New York and Vermont fur traders—those who lived near the Lake Champlain route or the Great Lakes caught that fur trading spirit. At nearly this time came the miners from the South. Then the emigration from the *New York parallel* again to the farm lands. Now begins the State's policy of attracting immigration," and the coming of Germans in large numbers. Their lower living standards allowed them to displace the New Yorkers who settled before them. "I do not," he went on, "regard the movement as entirely to be feared. I think peasant proprietorship is not being weakened by these German settlers. The quick settlement of lands in small farms has, I judge, prevented the absorption of such territory into great estates." [107]

106. Patten, *Premises of Political Economy*, pp. 28–29.
107. Turner to William F. Allen, December 31, 1888. HEH TU Box 1.

36

Turner was still leagues away from his frontier thesis when he wrote those words, but he was on his way. He was aware that society in the newer West was an evolving organism as society in the stabilized East was not, responding repeatedly to the intrusion of newcomers. He recognized that the relative ease with which "free land" could be acquired there, and the low "rent" that it exacted, served as democratizing influences, checking the growth of "great estates." Most important of all, he knew that by applying theories learned in the classroom to his native Wisconsin he could test historical concepts just as a biologist tested new substances in a tube. Turner had discovered the laboratory that would serve through his lifetime, and had learned to use it intelligently. His Portage boyhood, his years at the University of Wisconsin and Johns Hopkins, gave him both the tools to produce a major historical premise and the incentive to do so.

Fred J. Turner (as he still signed his letters) left Baltimore that June of 1889 without his doctoral degree, but well endowed with both learning and ambition. His immediate future was secure; an assistant professorship waited him at the University of Wisconsin, where he was slated to relieve Professor Allen of instruction in American history. Now it was up to him to justify his appointment by earning his spurs as teacher and scholar, first by completing work for his doctorate, then by building on the theories absorbed at Johns Hopkins to erect his own historical edifices. Gone was the lethargy that had slowed progress toward the master's degree during his earlier years in Madison. "I discover that my year away has had the effect to stir up the most inordinate amount of ambition in my nature," he wrote that fall.[1] So it had. The next three years were among the most productive of his lifetime.

The first product of his unaccustomed energy was published that summer: an excellent review of the first two volumes of Theodore Roosevelt's *The Winning of the West*. Turner was so eager to display some of the erudition for which Johns Hopkins was famous that he could not resist parroting some of the nonsense learned from Herbert Baxter Adams; he commented on the "forted villages" of the Kentuckians described by Roosevelt in which "reappeared the old Germanic 'tun,' their popular meetings, 'folk-moots,' and their representative assemblies, 'witenagemots'."[2] But he balanced these

1. Turner to Caroline Mae Sherwood, July 4, 1889. HEH TU Box D.
2. Turner, Review of Theodore Roosevelt, *The Winning of the West* in *The Dial*, X (August, 1889), 71–72. Turner's copy of *The Winning of the West* (4 vols., New York, 1889–1896), is in the Huntington Library, Accession No. 139455. All four volumes are heavily underlined and with marginal notations by Turner. One passage in the first volume which may have influenced his thought read: "The vast movement by which this continent was conquered and peopled cannot be understood if considered solely by itself. It was the crowning and greatest achievement in a series of mighty movements, and must be taken in connection with them. Its true significance will be lost unless we grasp, however roughly, the past race-history of the nations who took part therein." Roosevelt, *Winning of the West*,

absurdities with some sound thinking on the influence of the West. Beyond the mountains, he wrote, and not in New England or the East, lay the "center of gravity" of the nation. "To give our history the new proportions which this fact makes necessary, must be the work of the younger generation of students."[3] Their rewards would be great. In the West "a new composite nationality is being produced, a distinct American people, speaking the English language, but not English." They were forming "self-governing communities, peaceful as regards each other, drafting constitutions and growing into states of a federal union." Students of economics would discover there forces altering the economy of the nation and Europe, students of immigration mass migrations comparable to the *Völkerwanderung* of the Middle Ages.[4] The West must be understood if American history was to be understood. Here was Turner's challenge to the Wise Men of the East who viewed the United States from New England. It was also a watershed in his own thinking; he remembered later that preparing that review brought home to him "the need of a history of the continuous progress of civilization across the continent."[5] His long-developing ambition to study the history of the West was taking a solid direction.

For a while he was delayed by practical demands on his time—the teaching of overcrowded courses in general American history, sections in Allen's "Dynastic and Territorial History," and a new offering of his own on the "Constitutional and Political History of the United States" for a select group of advanced students.[6] This was bad enough, but worse followed when Professor Allen sickened with pneumonia and died suddenly on December 9, 1889. Few mourned his passing as deeply as his protegé, and few were so personally affected.[7] There were tears to be shed, and Turner shed them,

I, 7. Gilman M. Ostrander, "Turner and the Germ Theory," *Agricultural History*, XXXII (October, 1958), 258–61 interprets these remarks on Teutonic survivals to mean that Turner believed at this time that any Germanic peoples placed in a forest would develop self-governing institutions as had the Teutons in Germany and the Anglo-Saxons in England. This seems unrealistic in the light of Turner's growing belief in environmental pressures.
3. Turner, Review of Roosevelt, *Winning of the West, loc. cit.,* 71.
4. *Ibid.,* 71.
5. Turner to Constance L. Skinner, March 15, 1922. HEH TU Box 31. This letter is reproduced below, pp. 205–16.
6. University of Wisconsin, Instructional Report, Fall Term, 1889–1890. University of Wisconsin Archives. This was a disappointment to Turner, who had hoped to teach more advanced subjects. Turner to Caroline Mae Sherwood, September 15, 1889. HEH TU Box E.
7. Turner to Herbert B. Adams, December 10, 1889. HEH TU Box 1; printed also in Wilbur R. Jacobs, *The Historical World of Frederick Jackson Turner* (New Haven, 1968), pp. 22–23. This letter reveals the depths of Turner's sorrow. Some of Allen's friends later insisted that

but there was additional work to be done, and it was his task to shoulder the principal burden. Allen's final book, *A History of the Roman People*, completed only four days before his death, must be shepherded through the press and a special introduction added. There were Allen's classes to be taught, even though that meant further burdens on an already overburdened schedule. Turner's teaching load that spring of 1890 was an impossible one: sections in "Dynastic and Territorial History," the French Revolution, Nineteenth-Century Europe, the History of Society, and the Constitutional and Political History of the United States.[8] Moreover, the seminar was now his sole responsibility, and required endless preparation. "I am finding my hands full," he wrote that January with genuine feeling.[9] If this were not enough, Turner was forced to spend hours daily preparing for his Johns Hopkins doctoral examinations in May, for to postpone them now might mean that a more prominent historian would be picked as Allen's successor. Miraculously he completed his courses, survived the three-hour oral examination that won him the degree (although doing so badly that he was thoroughly ashamed of himself),[10] and in June was rewarded with a professorship that increased his salary from $1,500 to $2,000 a year.[11]

With the future secure, and with his Johns Hopkins friend Charles Homer Haskins added to the department to relieve him of instruction in European history, Turner enjoyed the slight degree of freedom needed to develop his

---

Turner borrowed his frontier thesis from an essay that Allen prepared on "The Place of the Northwest in General History." Richard T. Ely, *Ground Under Our Feet: An Autobiography* (New York, 1938), pp. 181–82. Actually the essay was prepared at Turner's invitation for a series of talks that he arranged for the Contemporary Club of Madison, and was later read by him at the meeting of the American Historical Association in Washington in 1889. The secretary of the Association reported that it described "that march across the continent which really constitutes America." *Papers of the American Historical Association*, III (New York, 1889), 251. This was a slight exaggeration. Allen's papers, printed in *ibid.*, 331–48, was a straightforward history of the Old Northwest, with little on the westward movement as a whole and nothing to suggest Turner's hypothesis. A discussion on this point, held by the Madison Literary Club in 1934, is reported in Joseph Schafer, "Turner's America," *Wisconsin Magazine of History*, XVII (June, 1934), 447–65.

8. *Catalogue of the University of Wisconsin, 1889–1890* (Madison, 1890), pp. 98–100; Instructional Report for Term Beginning January 6, 1890, April 8, 1890. University of Wisconsin Archives.

9. Turner to Herbert B. Adams, January 11, 1890. HEH TU Box 1. This is also printed in Stull W. Holt, ed., *Historical Scholarship in the United States, 1876–1901: As Revealed in the Correspondence of Herbert B. Adams* (Baltimore, 1938), pp. 123–24.

10. On several occasions Turner encouraged his students by telling them how badly he performed on his doctoral examination. Turner to Lois K. Mathews, March 21, 1906. HEH TU Box 6; Turner to Thomas P. Abernethy, March 12, 1926. HEH TU Box 35.

11. *Wisconsin State Journal*, June 17, June 18, 1891.

own interests. This must be used in the classroom rather than the study, for the hours of preparation needed to perfect his several courses left little time for research. His seminar, especially, served as a laboratory where his ideas could be tested and his knowledge broadened. This did not mean that he unleashed his students on topics in western history; Turner was interested in *all* the American past and determined to master its every aspect, not just one. His plan was to direct his seminar pupils into the study of era after era, from the colonization of Virginia to the present, with only the Civil War period omitted as too well known to require investigation.[12] No topic within these periods would be neglected, so long as source materials were available, for every report had to be based on thorough documentary studies, and must probe the subsurface economic and social forces that influenced political affairs.[13] Yet circumstances dictated that many of the seminar topics lie in the field of western history, for the resources of the State Historical Society library were unparalleled in that area.

Turner's first seminar, offered in 1890–1891, was on "The Old Northwest," which meant the study of Wisconsin history. Most elected to investigate the coming of Germans to the state, a subject much in the public eye at that time as debate raged over the Bennett Law requiring public instruction in the schools to be in English. The students found Turner a stimulating instructor and their investigations exciting intellectual exercises. "The seminar in Wisconsin history that meets Tuesdays at the historical library," reported the student paper, "provides much interesting work for its members. Each person has a department and they are to master it by the study of original sources." [14] Turner, highly pleased by this reaction, planned to direct his students in 1891–1892 into the study of the 1830s with special emphasis on the reciprocal influence of East and West, but their interests were too divergent to be funneled into any one channel.[15] One studied the westward move-

12. In "Notes for a Lecture to Harvard History Club" given in 1924 Turner wrote: "Seminary. Successive periods from Colonial times." HEH TU Box 56. He also described his plan in a letter to Merle Curti, August 8, 1928. HEH TU Box 39. This letter is printed below, pp. 257–65.
13. *The Aegis*, May 27, 1892, printed a lengthy article describing the work of the history seminar during the 1891–1892 academic year.
14. *Ibid.*, October 10, 1890.
15. Turner to Herbert B. Adams, October 19, 1891. HEH TU Box 1. This is also printed in Holt, ed., *Historical Scholarship in the United States*, pp. 168–69. *The Wisconsin State Journal*, September 26, 1891, and *The Aegis*, October 2, 1891, reported that the seminar would deal with the 1830–1940 period.

ment of population across New York between 1750 and 1810, another the coming of German Lutherans to Wisconsin, another the development of the German colony of St. Nazianz in Manitowoc County, still another the relations between New England town government and that of English parishes in the seventeenth century.[16] A year later the fare was just as varied, with papers on federal relations with Iowa, Germans in Wisconsin, the influence of the Erie Canal on the economy of New England and the West, the relation of the Panic of 1837 to the national land system, and the Ordinance of 1787.[17] Despite their diversity, most of the topics dealt directly or indirectly with expansion or the effect of expansion on the nation. As Turner read along with his students, his knowledge of the West grew steadily.

It grew still more as he nursed his first graduate students toward their degrees. His first, Emory R. Johnson, added only slightly to his master's knowledge with a master's thesis on "River and Harbor Bills,"[18] but his second, Kate A. Everest, plunged into a study more to his liking. Her seminar report on "Early Lutheran Immigration to Wisconsin," based on a careful study of data from pastors of local churches as well as printed documents in German and English, was a capable presentation, showing that religious conditions in Prussia accounted for the large migration of 1839–1845. Turner thought so well of it that he read it before the Wisconsin Academy of Sciences, Arts and Letters, thus speeding it toward publication.[19] This success encouraged Miss Everest to continue her studies, completing a master's thesis in 1892 and a doctoral dissertation in 1893 on "German Immigration into Wisconsin."[20] Both her methods and findings were dear to Turner's heart. Relying on personal interviews, church and government records, and printed archival materials, she addressed herself to a significant question:

16. *The Aegis*, May 27, 1892.
17. *Daily Cardinal*, December 13, 1892.
18. The fine discussion of Turner's early graduate students in Fulmer Mood, "The Development of Frederick Jackson Turner as a Historical Thinker," *Transactions of the Colonial Society of Massachusetts, 1937–1942*, XXXIV (Boston, 1943), 328–31, could scarcely be improved upon. I have drawn upon it heavily for these passages.
19. *The Aegis*, January 8, 1892. Miss Everest's paper on "Early Lutheran Immigration to Wisconsin" was printed in the *Transactions of the Wisconsin Academy of Sciences, Arts and Letters*, VIII (Madison, 1892), 288–98.
20. Miss Everest's master's thesis appeared as "How Wisconsin Came by Its Large German Element" in the *Collections of the State Historical Society of Wisconsin*, XII (Madison, 1892), 299–334. Her thesis was listed in the college catalog as "German Immigration into Wisconsin," the same title used on her doctoral dissertation a year later. *Catalogue of the University of Wisconsin, 1892–1893* (Madison, 1893), p. 151.

why did Wisconsin have a higher percentage of German-born than any other state? There was no single answer, she found; instead the concentration was due to conditions in the homeland, the low price of lands in Wisconsin when the migration began, effective advertising, and the happy coincidence that the state's lands were opened just as economic and social forces in Germany were forcing an exodus. These conclusions were bolstered, in Turnerian fashion, by a map showing the distribution of Germans in 1880 by degrees of color density.[21]

If Turner gained something from his first students, he benefited even more from the speaking activities forced upon him by his fame as an orator. From his undergraduate days when he captured Wisconsin's most prestigious prizes in public speaking, he was always welcome on lecture platforms throughout the state, often to the detriment of his scholarly interests. Now and again, however, he was called on to develop a western theme, giving him an excuse to read widely in his favorite subject. Such an opportunity presented itself in March 1890, when he participated in a series of lectures before the Madison Contemporary Club on "Crossing the Alleghanies."[22] His topic was tailored to his talents—"The Land and the People"—and allowed him to paint a "panorama of brilliant word pictures" (so said the local reporter) that held the overflow audience enraptured.[23] His remarks were hardly earth-shaking; he described the Allegheny mountain wall and its passes, pictured the coming of the French to the Mississippi Valley and their challenge by English traders, and showed how both were pushed aside by Yankee and Scots-Irish farmers who invaded the over-mountain country. Yet his closing words were not without significance: "Indian with his painted face and eagle feathers, voyageur with his turban handkerchief, his beaded moccasins and his birch canoe, trader with his peltry-laden pack horse, all are doomed. For the backwoodsman was in sight; clad in hunting shirt, axe and rifle in hand, attended by wife and children, he bears with him the

21. Her doctoral thesis appeared as "The Geographical Origin of German Immigration into Wisconsin," in *ibid.*, XIV (Madison, 1898), 341–93. A two-page questionnaire, in German, which she apparently circulated widely throughout the state is attached to Kate A. Everest to Sehr Geehrter Herr, November 28, 1892. HEH TU File Drawer 18A, Folder: German.
22. *Wisconsin State Journal*, February 13, 20, March 19, November 11, 1889; *The Aegis*, February 21, October 3, 1889.
23. The lecture was fully reported in the *Wisconsin State Journal*, March 5, 1890. A brief summary and a list of the topics to be treated was printed on the program for the occasion. A copy of this is in HEH TU File Drawer 15C, Folder: Lecture Series. Crossing the Alleghanies. 1890.

promise of the clearing and the farm, the promise of local self-government." [24]
Turner was lifting his sights from the glamorous fur-trader to the prosaic
backwoodsman as the true hero of the westward migration. Realism and a
mounting concern for the socioeconomic basis of society were pushing
frontier romance aside.

He was moved distinctly nearer a still better understanding of the frontier
social order by another speaking engagement that took an undue share of
his energy during his first teaching years. This was on the extension circuit
established by the University of Wisconsin to bring instant culture to the most
remote corner of the state. Turner was naturally in the vanguard when such a
program was planned; his own experiences with Herbert Baxter Adams and
other pioneers of the adult education movement in the East and his own enthusiastic faith in extension as the savior of the nation's democratic institutions
destined him to carry a heavy burden when the university embarked on its
program.[25] So it was that he was drafted to serve as President Thomas C.
Chamberlin's principal advisor during the planning stages, and so it was that
he was elected to provide publicity when an extension series was launched
during the 1890–1891 academic year.

Turner took two steps, one minor, the other significant in his future career.
The first he accomplished by bringing Professor Herbert Baxter Adams to
the campus in January 1891, to preach the gospel with a lecture on "The
Higher Education of the People," an appearance that attracted statewide attention, for not every year did such an eminent scholar visit the Wisconsin
wilds.[26] The second Turner took unto himself when he accepted an invitation
to speak before the Southwestern Wisconsin Teachers' Association at its meeting in Madison in August 1890. Here was a chance to show this influential
group that history was more than dull antiquarianism. If he could infect its
members with the excitement of research and convince them that the past

24. *Wisconsin State Journal*, March 5, 1890.
25. Turner, "The Extension Work of the University of Wisconsin," in George F. James,
ed., *Handbook of University Extension* (2nd edn., Philadelphia, 1893), pp. 313–15; Turner to
Herbert B. Adams, December 8, 1890. HEH TU Box 1. The letter is also printed in Holt,
ed., *Historical Scholarship in the United States*, pp. 144–45.
26. *Wisconsin State Journal*, January 28, January 31, 1891; *The Aegis*, February 6, 1891.
Adams' address was printed in the *Proceedings of the Thirty-Eighth Annual Meeting of the
State Historical Society of Wisconsin* (Madison, 1891), pp. 68–96. In it Adams embarrassed
and delighted his former pupil by describing his doctoral dissertation as "a brilliant contribution to the economic and social history of Wisconsin" and proclaiming its author "a
worthy transmitter of that rare spirit of historical research which Professor Allen represented
for twenty-two years among the students of this state."

was relevant to the present they would become local ambassadors for the extension lectures that would soon be seeking audiences across the state.[27] This was the incentive that led Turner to prepare his remarkable paper on "The Significance of History." Given first before the Teachers' Association, and printed in 1891 in the *Wisconsin Journal of Education*, it probably had little impact on the school teachers to whom it was directed.[28] It did, however, reveal Turner as a forerunner of the Progressive school of history and a scholar of outstanding originality.

"The Significance of History" pushed its author's principal interest into the background for the moment, but it did show an understanding of the past that helps explain how he was able to advance his frontier hypothesis a short time later. His thesis was that "the focal point of modern interest is the fourth estate, the great mass of the people." To probe their past the historian should focus on economic rather than political questions; "the age of machinery, of the factory system, is also the age of socialistic inquiry." All the ages of man must be resurveyed to show how the ordinary people lived and thought and acted. History was no longer past politics alone; "history is past literature, it is past politics, it is past religion, it is past economics." Economic and social life on the one hand, and political on the other, constantly touched, modified, and conditioned one another; they in turn had been modified by religious life. All were elements in "society's endeavor to understand itself by understanding the past." So modern historians must restudy the records from this new viewpoint. "Each age," Turner reminded his audience, "writes the history of the past anew with reference to the conditions uppermost in its own time." Events might not change, but our comprehension of those events constantly altered.

Viewed in this light, history was "ever *becoming*, never completed." Each generation borrowed from its predecessors and bequeathed much to its successors. History could not be conveniently partitioned, for society was an organism, constantly growing, ever changing. Hence American history could be understood only as a continuation of European history under the

27. *Wisconsin State Journal*, August 27, 1890; *Wisconsin State Register*, August 30, 1890; *Portage Daily Register*, August 28, 1890.
28. Turner, "The Significance of History," *Wisconsin Journal of Education*, XXI (October, 1891), 230–34, and (November, 1891), 253–56. The essay has been reprinted in Turner, *The Early Writings of Frederick Jackson Turner* (Madison, 1938), pp. 41–68, and Ray A. Billington, ed., *Frontier and Section: Selected Essays of Frederick Jackson Turner* (Englewood Cliffs, New Jersey, 1961), pp. 11–27.

conditions of the New World. It must be viewed, too, as part of the broader panorama of world history. Tribal history that sufficed for tribal societies had been outmoded by national history for national states; today this was in turn outmoded. Historians of the present realized "how profoundly is our present life interlocked with the events of all the world." Economic ties bound the United States to Europe, Asia, and Africa; political ties would follow. "Our destiny," Turner said, "is interwoven with theirs; how shall we understand American history without understanding European history? The story of the peopling of America has not yet been written." Global migration patterns and the world-wide influence of American trade and ideas must be comprehended. "Local history must be viewed in the light of world history."

This posed problems for the historian. Study of the total life of the people meant an astronomical multiplication of the volume of source materials to be mastered. History would now encompass "all the remains that have come down to us from the past, studied with all the critical and interpretative power than the present can bring to the task." The tools of the historian could no longer be simply books and chronicles; he must master all the papers, customs, languages, monuments, coins, medals, titles, inscriptions, charters, and documents that mankind had produced over the ages. Wherever one found a flint, a fragment of pottery, a picture, a poem, or a coliseum, there was history. All must be comprehended in the light of their relationships to world culture. This was an imposing assignment, but the rewards were worthy of the effort. "The priceless service of history" was to show man the richness of his inheritance, better his life, and reveal the grandeur of the present. These were ends worth achieving.[29] Here was the gospel of history according to Turner.

Had "The Significance of History" been written by an eastern historian of repute, and published in a national journal rather than a local educational quarterly, it might have been hailed at the time as the charter of the "New History" that was to sweep the profession during the next quarter-century. In it Turner advanced most of the concepts that were to be popularized a generation later: "relativism" with its recognition that each age restudied the past in the light of its own experiences, "presentism" with its understanding that the principal importance of yesterday was to explain today, "socialism" (as Turner would have phrased it) with its creed that all facets of

29. Turner, "The Significance of History," in *The Early Writings of Frederick Jackson Turner*, pp. 41–68.

human behavior were worthy of study, and "globalism" with its belief that localism had vanished in the modern world and that all men were so tightly linked that the actions of one affected all. These were doctrines as modern as tomorrow. By voicing them Turner was throwing down the gauntlet to the dominant "scientific" historians of his day who believed that the absolute truth could be revealed by piling fact on fact with a minimum of interpretation. He was also proclaiming his intention to investigate the underlying social and economic forces that explained *why* and *how* the United States related to Europe. This was the quest that led him to his frontier hypothesis.

The extension program that inspired "The Significance of History" was responsible for another lecture that brought him to the brink of his thesis. This was a by-product of his popularity on the adult education circuit. He began his appearances there in the fall of 1890 with courses of six lectures each in two nearby towns,[30] then in 1891–1892 expanded his program so widely that he spent much of that year on the road. Turner was fabulously successful with extension audiences. Five hundred persons crowded into the assembly chamber of the state capital building to hear the opening lecture of his Madison series; hundreds were turned away from Milwaukee's Plymouth Church when he began his course there; and at tiny Poynette two hundred of the town's six hundred inhabitants enrolled.[31] In all Turner gave seven extension courses of six lectures each in as many communities scattered about the state, spending much of his time on trains or in hotels and boarding houses, and enlightening hundreds of knowledge-hungry adults on "The Colonization of North America," "American Politics, 1789–1840," or "American Development, 1789–1829." [32]

This was dismally hard work—Turner soon complained that "I must have some time for *intension*"—but there were rewards in addition to the ten dollar fee for each lecture.[33] For Turner these were significant. His series on

30. Turner, "The Extension Work of the University of Wisconsin," in James, ed., *Handbook of University Extension*, pp. 313–14; *The Aegis*, November 14, 1890; *Portage Daily Register*, January 31, 1891; *Wisconsin State Journal*, January 24, 1891. Turner offered one course at Columbus, Wisconsin, in the fall and another at Stoughton in January and February.
31. *Wisconsin State Journal*, October 22, November 6, November 13, November 30, 1891; *The Aegis*, November 13, 1891.
32. Turner, "Biographical Sketch Sent to William J. Truesdale, March 26, 1902," University of Wisconsin Archives, College of Letters and Science, Department of History, Turner Correspondence, 1901–1905, Box 1, Folder F. Hereafter referred to as U. of Wis. Archives, L&S. Turner Corr., 1901–5.
33. Turner to Herbert B. Adams, January 18, 1892. Printed also in Holt, ed., *Historical Scholarship in the United States*, pp. 174–75.

"The Colonization of North America" focused his attention on the problem of migration, and forced him to embark on a reading program that taught him a great deal about *where* people moved, and *why*. Both the breadth of his subject and the paucity of materials on it decreed this. His lectures spanned several centuries: the pre-Columbian period, Spanish colonization, the Devonshire seamen, the peopling of the southern and middle colonies, the occupation of New England, and the conquest of New France. Simply to force his extensive knowledge of colonization into these neat packages required reorganization and speculation that allowed him to view migration patterns in a fresh way. So did his reading, for texts on exploration or settlement were few in those days and he must garner kernels of information from a variety of peripheral books and articles. As he arranged these tidbits in his mind he distilled many of the theories that he could apply to the frontier process.

The bibliographies prepared for his students suggest the extent of his own preparation: Herman Merivale, *Lectures on Colonization and Colonies* (1861), J. S. Cotton and E. J. Payne, *Colonies and Dependencies* (1883), John A. Doyle, *English Colonies in America* (2 vols., 1882–1887), George C. Lewis, *An Essay on the Government of Dependencies* (1841), a half-dozen volumes by French and German authors, and many more.[34] As he read, Turner occasionally stumbled on passages that gave him a clue to the nature of the migration process, or that sparked his own imagination; when he did so the sentence was copied into his notes or the speculation hurriedly recorded on one of the 3 x 5 slips that were his constant companions. To retrace his steps as he learned about colonization, following the clues that he left along the way, is to witness his burgeoning interest in the westward expansion of the American people.

The causes of migration interested Turner particularly. He learned from his books that overcrowding was one force that drove people to move; Merivale's *Lectures on Colonization* told him that come-outers from Puritan Boston were willing to endure isolation and risk Indian attack farther westward "because the Bay was overstocked." [35] This set Turner to thinking, and he jotted down a series of motives for migration: overcrowding, love of

34. Turner, "Colonization Bibliography." HEH TU File Drawer 15A, Folder: Colonization Bibliography. This is a single sheet, dealing only with "Colonization in General," and apparently only a portion of a larger bibliography that he compiled for his own use.
35. Herman Merivale, *Lectures on Colonization and Colonies* (London, 1861), pp. 267–68.

adventure, fear of military service, the hope of social and economic betterment, a desire for a more congenial religious climate.[36] He read in Cotton
and Payne's *Colonies and Dependencies* that agricultural societies spawned
emigrants more rapidly than industrial, lacking the manufactures to absorb
an excess population.[37] Doyle's *English Colonies in America* demonstrated
that geographic factors helped shape the course of migrations, with mountain
barriers and river highways playing an important role;[38] after reading that
passage Turner noted that population movements followed the path of least
resistance whether along the lower Danube or on the Hudson River.[39]
Merivale's *Lectures* showed him that land systems used in the American
colonies had a major influence on repelling or attracting settlers.[40] These
were fragments of information, none of them particularly noteworthy, but
Turner tucked them away in his notes and mind, to be resurrected when
needed.

More important to his emerging theories were suggestions in his reading
that life in the colonies differed from that of England or Europe. Doyle's
English Colonies in America stressed the English origin of the ideas and
institutions of the New World, but made clear that alterations took place as
they adjusted themselves to a different environment. He saw in this adjustment a microcosm of the whole course of civilization; within a brief span
each colony retraced mankind's history as it advanced from infancy to
maturity. "We can," Doyle wrote, "trace their life and institutions from the
very fountain-head. In their cases we can see those stages of growth going
on under our very ideas which elsewhere can be traced only imperfectly and
obscurely."[41] This basic concept, sharpened later by reading in the works of
the Italian economist, Achille Loria, Turner was to apply to all the pioneer
communities that the westward advance planted across the continent. Similarly, Merivale's *Lectures on Colonization* emphasized the uniqueness of the

36. These notes are in HEH TU File Drawer 15D, Folder: Colonization Bibliography, 1891.
They fill three sheets, and are largely his reading notes on George C. Lewis, *An Essay on
the Government of Dependencies* (London, 1841).
37. J. S. Cotton and E. J. Payne, *Colonies and Dependencies* (London, 1883), p. 117.
38. John A. Doyle, *English Colonies in America. Virginia, Maryland, and the Carolinas* (New
York, 1882), pp. 5–7.
39. This notation in Turner's hand is in HEH TU File Drawer 15D, Folder: Colonization:
Oriental, Roman, Teutonic, 1890.
40. Merivale, *Lectures on Colonization and Colonies*, pp. 394–450, is an extended discussion
of land disposal in the colonies.
41. Doyle, *English Colonies in America*, pp. 1–2.

American experience, pointing out that one reason for this was an abundance of cheap land which encouraged farmers with worn-out soils to move to fresh fields rather than manure or rotate their crops. Here were other nuggets to be stored and used.[42]

That these random bits of information were patterning and repatterning themselves in Turner's subconscious mind was shown by the occasional flashes of inspiration that he experienced during these months when the colonization problem was constantly with him. One evening when marooned in the Atherton Hotel of Oshkosh while waiting for the hour when his lecture would begin, he dashed off a sentence that was to be rewritten into one of his best-known passages: "Beneath the constitutional forms and ideas, beneath political issues, run the great ocean currents of economic and social life, shaping and reshaping political forms to the changes of this great sea, which changes continuously." [43] With the unhappy metaphor discarded and the syntax improved, this was to appear in the essay on "The Significance of the Frontier in American History" as: "Behind institutions, behind constitutional forms and modifications, lie the vital forces that call these organs into life and shape them to meet changing conditions." [44] On another occasion, pondering what he had read on the colonization of Virginia and New England, Turner recorded another perceptive observation: "How the beginnings of Virginia show differences from N. England. The hypothesis of the German tun. Absurd. Real difference lies in mode and ideals of first colonists, and the physiography of the region." [45] The more he studied colonization, the less his respect for the "germ" theory and the greater his realization that environment helped shape American institutions.

These developments in Turner's thinking were demonstrated both when he wrote and spoke about expansion into the New World. Thus the several syllabi that he prepared for the use of his extension classes mirrored his progressing ideas. His first was apparently compiled in 1891, for he wrote Her-

42. Merivale, *Lectures on Colonization and Colonies*, pp. 257–58.
43. Turner prepared six pages of a lecture while sitting in his hotel room, noting at the top the circumstances under which they were composed. They are in HEH TU File Drawer 5D, Folder: Extension Lecture.
44. Turner, "The Significance of the Frontier in American History," in Frederick J. Turner, *The Frontier in American History* (New York, 1920), p. 2.
45. Turner made these notes while preparing a lecture on the colonization of Virginia. They are in HEH TU File Drawer ID, Folder: The Colonization of Virginia.

bert Baxter Adams that fall seeking advice on how to go about the task, and asking for samples from Adams' own collection.[46] This was a mimeographed outline and bibliography for those taking the course for credit; it listed fifteen topics for study, ranging from the geography of North America through Norse, Spanish, French, and English colonization to a final chapter on "The Colonial Governments," all with a wealth of detail and a minimum of interpretation.[47] A second syllabus, probably prepared a year later, and issued in printed form for the large numbers who listened to his lectures without taking examinations, was more enlightening, particularly in Turner's introductory statements. "The History of American Colonization," he wrote, "shows how European life entered America and how America modified that life." Its nature could be realized only by understanding the European conditions that led to migration, and the American conditions that the newcomers encountered. One must also recognize, he went on, that "American colonization is part of a great historic movement—the Aryan migrations. Much of the United States of to-day lay in germ in the old colonies. Europe too has been profoundly affected by the colonization of America." [48] This was a suggestive statement, indicating that Turner was thinking in terms of the effect of the New World environment on the Old World and its institutions. Turner was to repeat it, in somewhat more emphatic form, in a third syllabus printed in 1893.[49]

The lectures that were prepared for the extension courses were largely cut-and-dried narratives, burdened with the glowing rhetoric that genera-

46. Turner to Herbert B. Adams, October 19, 1891. HEH TU Box 1. This letter is printed in Holt, ed., *Historical Scholarship in the United States*, pp. 168–69.
47. Turner, "The Colonization of North America." HEH TU Vol. VI (1). This syllabus is undated, but was probably prepared in 1890 or early 1891. Turner had added to it, in his own hand, a list of books published after 1891, such as John Fiske, *The Discovery of America* (2 vols., Boston, 1892), that were not available when the original listing was prepared.
48. Turner, *Syllabus of a University Extension Course of Six Lectures on the Colonization of North America* (Madison, n.d.), pp. 1–20. A copy of this is in HEH TU Vol. VI (2).
49. Turner, *The Colonization of North America from the Earliest Times to 1763* (Madison, 1893), pp. 1–28. A copy is in HEH TU Vol. VI (2). Fulmer Mood, who made the first serious investigations of Turner's scholarly career, undertook an intensive study of these syllabi in an effort to date each exactly. He came to the conclusion that the first printed syllabus, *Syllabus of a University Extension Course*, was published in 1891. More probably it was printed in 1892, for it lists books and articles published late in 1891. A series of letters between Mood, Merrill H. Crissey, Max Farrand, and Livia Appel on the subject are in HEH TU Box 52. Turner's syllabi were apparently widely circulated and generally used for some time. A librarian who began her career at the Chicago Historical Society in 1901 remembered that they were in her hands from morning until night. "Without them," she wrote Turner some years later, "I would have been lost." Caroline M. McIlvaine to Turner, October 12, 1931. HEH TU Box 46.

tion loved to hear and lacking the generalizations that would make his hearers think. The Norsemen were "dwellers of the North," the "grandeur of the gloomy fjords upon them, the salt gusts of the sea buffeted their dwellings, the rugged cliffs and lofty mountains stamped their impress on the race"; [50] New England was a land "shut in by fogs and snow, and snarling breakers" that "invited to no easy life as did the Spanish southland, and no broad plantations stretching along the slow flowing rivers as did the Virginia region." [51] Tucked away among these extravagances, however, were occasional kernels of interpretation that showed Turner was shaping his views on expansion. One passage demonstrated that he was applying to the American scene the concept of social stages learned from Richard T. Ely. "The Hunter Type," he told his listeners, was unique to the American wilderness; there lived men and women who had seceded from civilization and were happy only where they found elbow-room to move freely about. "They loved to hear the crack of their long rifles, and the blows of the ax in the forest. A little clearing, edged by the woods, and a log house—this was the type of home they loved. All along the uplands from Pennsylvania to Georgia, forming a cordon of defense to the colonists of the lower lands toward the east, lived these pioneers." [52] Turner was thinking of colonization as a concept that applied to the interior as well as the seacoast, and visualizing the reversion to primitivism that took place among the first-comers to the frontier.

He had an opportunity to weld these random thoughts and observations into a logical pattern when he was invited to speak to the Madison Literary Club at its February 1891 meeting, on "American Colonization." This was too broad a topic to be treated in an hour's talk if he clung to the narrative style adopted for his extension courses; it could better be presented by an interpretative analysis of the forces responsible for migrations and a comparative study of the results. This was a challenging assignment, and the skill with which it was met showed Turner as the master historian that time was to prove him.

He began in the best Johns Hopkins tradition with a description of the folk-wanderings of antiquity, moved rapidly to the geography of the eastern United States, and discoursed for some time on the manner in which rivers,

50. A copy of this lecture is in HEH TU File Drawer A, Folder: Norsemen as Colonizers.
51. HEH TU File Drawer 15A, Folder: Colonization of New England.
52. "The Hunter Type," consisting of several sheets of paper in Turner's hand, described the backwoodsmen. This is in HEH TU File Drawer 15B, Folder: Hunter Type. It is reprinted in Wilbur R. Jacobs, *Frederick Jackson Turner's Legacy* (San Marino, California, 1965), pp. 153–55.

mountain chains, and portage routes helped shape the course of expansion.[53] "It was natural," he pointed out, "that colonization should seek the lines of least resistance." Having set the stage, Turner moved in his actors with a hurried story of the Elizabethan sea dogs and early colony planting. This was necessarily a superficial treatment, but he still managed to inject interpretations that were heretical for that day. Thus he saw New England towns not as the offspring of Teutonic "germs," but as the product of local conditions. "The hostile Indians made it desirable for the colonists to settle in communities; nor did the country invite to broad plantations. The region required that men should make their struggle for existence in compact isolated communities." Nor did physiographic forces shape the settlement pattern in New England alone; the whole history of colonization illustrated the manner in which imported institutions adjusted to the demands of a virgin continent. "American history," Turner emphasized, "is the account of how the environment was occupied by a new organization. It is the history of the application of men and ideas to the physical conditions."

Because this was the case, "colonization" must be redefined in the United States to embrace more than the story of population movements from one country to another. In American usage, and in American practice, it meant the migration of any considerable body of people of the same nationality to an unoccupied territory, bearing with them the characteristics of the region they left behind. "Taking this liberal use of the term," Turner told the club members, "we may call much of the European settlement of the West, colonization." This movement deserved investigation, just as the folk-wanderings of the remote past had been investigated. Students should forget Pocahontas and stop arguing about who was the first child born in Brown County; they should study "where and by what means the characteristics and the population of western states like Kansas and California and Wisconsin were produced." They should ask what was contributed to each by New England, by the Middle States, by the South, by Spain. Only when these questions were answered would Americans understand their own country and satisfy history's need to "know the present by the study of its development from the past." Scholars making these investigations should realize, however, that

53. Turner, "American Colonization," is a thirty-three page manuscript, typed, with underlining by Turner. A notation on the first page indicates that it was delivered at the Madison Literary Club on February 9, 1891, and prepared in January, 1891. HEH TU File Drawer 15A, Folder: Lecture, American Colonization.

colonization did not end with the Puritans of Massachusetts or the Cavaliers of Virginia. Latecoming immigrants played just as important a role. "They have brought to us not merely so much bone and sinew, not merely so much money, not merely so much manual skill; they have brought with them deeply inrooted customs and ideas. They are important factors in the political and economic life of the nation. The story of the peopling of America has not yet been written."

Now the "colonizing era" in the nation's history was drawing to a close. "I do not hesitate to say," Turner went on in language that was to be paraphrased in his 1893 essay, "that this fact is the key to American history. As the occupation of the New World transformed Europe, so the occupation of the Great West has determined the flow of American energies, been the underlying explanation of American political history, and has had profound reactive effects upon the social and economic life of the East." This story must be investigated. "What first the Mediterranean sea and later the New World were to the Aryan peoples, breaking the bonds of custom, and creating new activities to meet new conditions, that the undeveloped West has been to the American descendants of those Aryans."

Turner brought his 1893 essay on "The Significance of the Frontier in American History" to a climax with a polished version of that sentence, but he had one more point to make before the Madison Literary Club. Even though the "passive age of colonization" was over, expansion would go on, for the energies developed in peopling the West would now be directed elsewhere. "Our organism has been completed," he told his hearers. "We have a national self-consciousness, a self-sufficient industrial organization. Will not this organization bud as did the trans-Allegheny organism?" Turner thought that it would and saw indications of the direction it would take in the Pan-American Congress that had been held in Washington in late 1889 and early 1890. The United States, he predicted, would soon attach South America's economic life to its own as a substitute for the colonization of its own frontiers.[54]

54. Turner made two notes on the back of this manuscript, apparently during the discussion period following its presentation. Both quote Dr. John W. Stearns, a professor of philosophy and pedagogy at the university, as saying that Anglo-Saxon institutions and ideals were moulding Latin America into a replica of Germany, and that the improved transportation facilities which allowed the flood of immigration then going on was the product of the Germanic spirit in industry. Apparently Turner did not convince all his audience that environmentalism was more important than Teutonism in explaining the American past.

When Turner, in January 1891, prepared that paper for the Madison Literary Club, he had come far along the road to the hypothesis that he was to pronounce two years later. He saw the western settlements as "colonies" of the Atlantic coastal regions, transplanting their civilization to the interior just as Puritans and cavaliers transplanted England's civilization to America in the early seventeenth century. He recognized that those new civilizations differed from their parents, and that the differences were due partly to the impact of different environments. He sensed that the forthcoming occupation of the continent would close one period of the nation's history—the period of "colonization"—and force alterations in the economic, social, and political structure. These were basic concepts to his frontier thesis. Yet still more must be added before it was completed. Turner had yet to use the word "frontier" in his writing, or to visualize the process through which expansion went on. He must investigate the alterations made in the characteristics of the people and their institutions by three centuries of expansion. Yet he had, by January 1891, laid down the basic premise of his frontier hypothesis. Little more was necessary to equip him for the preparation of his 1893 essay.

One intermediate stage in his realization of the frontier's significance was needed, and Turner was inspired to take that step by the undergraduate newspaper at the University of Wisconsin. In the autumn of 1891 *The Aegis* announced that it would publish during the year a series of articles by faculty members on their research, including one by Turner on "New Aspects of the Early History of Wisconsin." [55] Fortunately Turner delayed preparing his essay until the last moment, as was his custom. By this time he was so deeply involved in his study of colonization that his earlier interest in Wisconsin's beginnings had paled. Why not, he probably asked himself, discard his assignment and write instead on some of the newer interpretations that were revising his own understanding of American history? This would popularize his department's offerings by demonstrating to students that history was an exercise in logic rather than a chronicle of names and dates, a vehicle for understanding rather than an exercise in rote memory, and an exciting adventure in creative thinking. His was a happy inspiration, for the result was his "Problems in American History," published in *The Aegis* on November 4, 1892, and destined to take its place among the most

55. *The Aegis*, October 9, 1891.

significant contributions made by Turner to the understanding of the nation's past.[56] In it he detailed the subjects that must be investigated by scholars before American history could be fully comprehended, and indicated the areas of research that were to occupy his own attention.

Former historians, he began, had erred by ignoring "the fundamental, dominating fact in United States history," the expansion of population from sea to sea.[57] "In a sense American history up to our own day has been colonial history, the colonization of the Great West. The ever retreating frontier of free land is the key to American development." To study this expansion would be to reveal the underlying forces shaping the nation's past and to explain the evolution of its own self-consciousness. Such investigations would revise our understanding of every facet of its history. Politics would take on a new dimension, for "behind institutions, behind constitutional forms, lie the vital forces that call these organs into life and shape them to meet changing conditions. The peculiarity of American institutions is the fact that they are compelled to adapt themselves to the changes of a remarkably developing, expanding people." Proper understanding of the role of the frontier in the United States meant also a proper understanding of European history and an appreciation of the extent to which America differed from Europe. "In the settlement of America," Turner pointed out, "we have to observe how European life entered the continent, and how America modified that life and reacted on Europe." What scholar, he asked, would measure the effect on the Old World of free land in the United States? Who would evaluate the impact of American expansion on freedom of speech, the progress of democracy, and the economic alterations that had transformed Europe since the age of discovery? Here were "problems in American history" that deserved the attention of historians.

56. *Ibid.*, November 4, 1892. A copy of this issue was preserved in a manila folder on which he wrote: "Contains first form of my doctrine of frontier. Prior to my paper in AHA 1893 I had not read Ratzel, or Godkin, or other writer who deals with this problem." HEH TU Box 54. Turner's reference was to the German environmentalist, Friedrich Ratzel, and to E. L. Godkin, editor of *The Nation*, whose contributions to frontier theory are discussed below, pp. 96–101. A second copy of the "Problems" essay was given the Huntington Library by Turner, to be kept among the rare books with Accession No. 126772. On this copy Turner wrote: "This with my fur trade thesis constitute the beginning of my writing on the frontier as a symbol of the western movement and its reaction on the East and the Old World." The essay has been reprinted in Turner, *Early Writings of Frederick Jackson Turner*, pp. 71–83, and Billington, ed., *Frontier and Section*, pp. 28–36.
57. Turner, "Problems in American History," in Turner, *Early Writings of Frederick Jackson Turner*, pp. 71–83.

Their complexity meant that those attempting a solution would have to equip themselves with new tools. Historians must add other methodologies to their own, beginning with a thorough knowledge of "the physiographic basis of our history." They should borrow the techniques of geologists, mineralogists, biologists, and geographers. Only by mastering these skills could scholars understand the ebb and flow of westward expansion, and explain why the frontier advanced and receded irregularly, or why some areas were untouched while others were overrun by population. Only by adopting the methods of many scientists could they show why American cities were located at one place rather than another, or the extent to which regional physiographic forces altered the social and economic behavior of the people. Without such investigations the record of the past would remain woefully incomplete.

Turner also pointed out in this provocative essay that the expanding frontier created a succession of "sections" formed when intruding stocks reacted with the natural environment. Each group that journeyed westward —Yankees, Yorkers, Southerners, Europeans—carried with it its own system of local government, culture, and economic practices. As the newcomers met and mingled in frontier communities they merged their traits and institutions to create a distinctive society, differing from any of those contributing to its membership. This was further modified by the physiographic features of the area being occupied. The result was a series of "sections," each differing from the other in economic enterprise, governmental practices, and cultural interests. These were responsible for two conflicting pressures on the national state. One was divisive and more destructive of national unity than state particularism "for whatever force the latter had came in a large degree from its association with sectionalism." The other was cohesive; the blending of peoples from divergent backgrounds served as a bond of unity nationally. "This is what explains the nationalization of the United States as time goes on," Turner wrote. "State sovereignty is lost in the West, where appears a checkerboard division of states which recruit their population from all parts of the Union."

Before these complex relationships could be understood, there were all manner of problems for historians to solve. They must investigate the impact of immigrants on American society, for the new arrivals brought with them traditions, habits, ideas, and customs born of their European existence, all of which reacted with the native culture. "We shall not," Turner declared, "understand the contemporary history of the United States without studying immigration historically." Historians must also study the disposal of the public domain, the building of the nation's internal improvement network, the construction of the railroad system, the whole question of interstate migration. Political practices must be reinvestigated to understand the role played by free land in democratizing governmental institutions. The West was the neglected key to American history, and until it unlocked the secrets of America's emerging years the national story would be imperfectly understood. Turner concluded with an improved version of the sentence that he had used before: "What the Mediterranean Sea was to the Greeks, breaking the bond of custom, offering new experiences, calling out new institutions and activities, that the ever retreating Great West has been to the United States directly, and to the nations of Europe more remotely."

Turner's "Problems in American History" ranks with his essay on "The Significance of History" as a landmark in his historical progress. In it he identified the two fundamental forces—frontier and section—that he believed responsible for much of the distinctiveness of American civilization. Perhaps more important, he isolated material causes stemming from changes in the economic status of individuals as basic in the historical process, rather than the mysterious hereditary factors venerated by that generation. This was a giant step forward. So was his insistence that the tools of social and physical scientists be added to the kits of historians, thus placing him in the front rank of those urging interdisciplinary techniques. These bold suggestions reveal Turner as original in thought, rebellious of convention, and inventive in both the concepts and methods of historical investigation. They also show that he had burst the chrysalis of localism that hampered his intellectual growth until this time, and was ready to focus his attention on the nation's evolution, not on the progress of a single state or region. The time had come for him to step from Portage and Columbia County onto the national stage.[58] Turner was not far wrong when he wrote a quarter-century later that in his "Problems in American History" "I said pretty nearly everything I have said since." [59]

He felt well enough of the essay to send copies of *The Aegis* in which it

58. The importance of this essay in American historiography is stressed in Merle Curti, *Frederick Jackson Turner* (Mexico, D.F., 1940), pp. 20–22; Avery Craven, "Frederick Jackson Turner, Historian," *Wisconsin Magazine of History*, XXV (June, 1942), 408–10; Fulmer Mood, "The Historiographic Setting of Turner's Frontier Essay," *Agricultural History*, XVII (July, 1943), 154–55; and Per S. Anderson, *Westward Is the Course of Empires: A Study in the Shaping of An American Idea: Frederick Jackson Turner's Frontier* (Oslo, Norway, 1956), pp. 49–62.
59. Turner to Max Farrand, October 13, 1916. HEH TU Box 26.

appeared to friends and acquaintances throughout the profession, but with disheartening results. His views were too far ahead of their times to be understood, let alone appreciated. The first paragraphs reminded Professor George E. Howard of Leland Stanford University of some of his own experiences, and he apparently read no farther.[60] Professor Simon N. Patten felt that it offered "a very helpful way of looking at our social problems" (which it certainly did not),[61] while Turner's former student, Professor Emory R. Johnson, was willing to have it noticed in the *Annals of the American Academy* but seemed principally delighted with the improvement of *The Aegis* since his college days.[62] Professor Francis N. Thorpe found Turner's outline for "an extensive district of political activity" worthy of congratulations but pointed out that it would have been improved by a wider use of Thorpe's own writings on constitution making.[63] Turner's Johns Hopkins friend, Professor Charles M. Andrews, was not sure that "we are ready to write the history of our expanding life" when "we are only just getting into form in this country to write our colonial life."[64] A Madison lawyer echoed these sentiments in less laudable form when he suggested that western history should not be studied until the study of eastern history was completed—and particularly the story of the Indian wars on which he was working.[65]

These less-than-enthusiastic appraisals were balanced by two letters from friends that warmed Turner's heart. Albion W. Small was "delighted" with the paper, announced that it would be read to his seminar, and deplored the fact that it appeared in an undergraduate newspaper rather than a national journal.[66] Even more meaningful was the praise lavished by Turner's old mentor, Herbert Baxter Adams. Adams was not only "much interested" in the paper and promised to call his seminar's attention to "your suggestive views" but felt its author worthy of a place on the program of the American Historical Association at its next meeting. Would Turner prepare a paper for the sessions scheduled for Chicago in July 1893?[67] Thus, ironically, the

60. George E. Howard to Turner, December 24, 1892. HEH TU Box 1.
61. Simon N. Patten to Turner, November 14, 1892. *Ibid.*
62. Emory R. Johnson to Turner, November 14, 1892. *Ibid.*
63. Francis N. Thorpe to Turner, December 11, 1892. *Ibid.*
64. Charles M. Andrews to Turner, November 29, 1892. *Ibid.*
65. B. J. Stevens to Turner, December 11, 1892. *Ibid.*
66. Albion W. Small to Turner, November 9, 1892. *Ibid.*
67. Herbert B. Adams to Turner, November 29, 1892. *Ibid.* Because Adams was secretary of the American Historical Association, his invitation virtually assured Turner a place on the

invitation that resulted in "The Significance of the Frontier in American History" came from the man whose views were so archaic (at least in Turner's later memory) that the essay was written as a protest against them!

The months of study on the history of colonization meant that Turner was approaching the point where he could accept Adams' challenge. He had, in essence, advanced his frontier hypothesis in the paper prepared for the Madison Literary Club in January 1891, and had defined that thesis more sharply in the essay written for *The Aegis* in the early autumn of 1892. He had, however, built a speculative structure on scant foundations. Now bricks and mortar were needed in the form of proof; alteration of the framework was necessary as further investigations demanded architectural refinements. This meant that the next months must be spent pouring over maps, studying census statistics, reading widely in the few writings that described the West accurately, and exploring the works of political economists, students of government, publicists, geographers, and biologists to find theoretical justification for his conclusions. Busy times lay ahead, but the pot at the end of Turner's rainbow was richly laden and well worthy of any effort. He earned that reward, however, not because he was capable of heroic exertions, but because he alone among the young historians of that time could find in the background and training he had experienced, the learning that he had absorbed, and the intellectual and social atmosphere of his day, the ingredients needed to postulate a completely new interpretation of American history. In Turner, and not in any of his contemporaries, were balanced the intellectual attainments and social sensitivity necessary to formulate the frontier thesis. Why did he, above all others, possess these attributes? That is the question we must try to answer in the next section of this book.

program. In later years the "Problems" paper received the acclaim that it deserved. Guy Stanton Ford, one of Turner's early students, wrote in 1920 that it was "so illuminating and so concrete that I have never lost the impression it made on me when I read it as a sophomore." Ford to Turner, November 24, 1920. HEH TU Box 30. One of Turner's close friends, Max Farrand, recalled that when he was a graduate student at Princeton in 1892 Woodrow Wilson handed him the article and suggested that he find a dissertation subject among the "problems" remaining unsolved. As a result he prepared his thesis on "Legislation of Congress for the Government of the Organized Territories," Farrand to Carl Becker, April 27, 1927. HEH TU Box 36.

SECTION II Formulating the Thesis
1892–1893

How the social and intellectual atmosphere
prepared the way for the hypothesis,
and the reading and speculation that
made the essay on the significance of the
frontier possible.

CHAPTER IV *The Social Climate*

Frederick Jackson Turner's background and training admirably equipped him to prepare his essays on colonization and the problems of American history as a prelude to the full-blown statement of hypothesis that he was to make in the summer of 1893. His boyhood experiences permanently infected him with an interest in evolving societies and an almost mystical belief in the generative powers of nature; he *knew* that men could be altered by contact with the wilderness because he had witnessed their alteration. His education equipped him with the tools needed to translate his beliefs into scholarly theories, and his early teaching offered him the opportunity to do so. But why should Turner of all the younger historians of his day, develop that hypothesis at the time he did? What in the social and intellectual climate of that day decreed that he should proclaim his thesis in 1893, rather than in 1883 or 1903? [1]

1. Two theories of the genesis of Turner's frontier hypothesis have been advanced that do not lend themselves to the type of analysis undertaken in this book. Edward Channing, his unsympathetic colleague at Harvard University, sometimes entertained his seminar by pulling from a desk drawer a mysterious pamphlet, brandishing it in the air, and saying: "Here, gentlemen, here is where Turner got his ideas from." The identity of the pamphlet was never disclosed, and Channing carried its secret to his grave. This story is authenticated in Fulmer Mood, "Turner's Formative Period," in Frederick J. Turner, *The Early Writings of Frederick Jackson Turner* (Madison, 1938), p. 3. Mood, needless to say, took the story no more seriously than did Channing. On a different level is the contention of Alan C. Beckman, a psychiatrist, who finds an explanation for the frontier hypothesis in the working of Turner's subconscious. Beckman holds that the "hidden theme" of the thesis is its symbolic reenactment of the family triangle, with the West the bountiful mother, the frontiersman the child nurtured at her breast, and the East the father seeking to assert authority over his migrating children. Beckman argues that this concept emerged in Turner's subconscious mind when he was named Allen's successor in December 1889. He had earlier rejected his own father by abandoning a journalistic career, substituting Allen as a surrogate father. Yet he deeply wanted the departmental chairmanship and subconsciously wished Allen's removal. When this occurred Turner was haunted with guilt feelings. These set his subconscious mind to working, and the hypothesis resulted. Beckman holds that this explanation makes two parts of the thesis clear: first Turner's insistence that pioneers inherited nothing from the East (their father) but were shaped by the environment of the West (their mother); Turner held this view because he felt too guilt-ridden to be indebted to his father in any way; second,

In seeking answers to those questions we must realize that Americans for generations past had been aware of the frontier's existence, and had often speculated on the way in which it influenced their lives and institutions. All who toyed with the problem agreed that three centuries of westering had endowed Americans with traits that, while rooted in the European inheritance, differed in some subtle and little-understood way from those of Englishmen. Some among them went so far as to isolate characteristics that they ascribed to the frontier experience—faith in democracy, a tendency to move about, inventiveness, an exaggerated nationalism—just as Turner was to do in his 1893 essay. Yet their message went unheard. The time was not ripe to popularize a theory that stressed differences rather than similarities, or that pictured the Americans as a people apart. Now, in the 1890s, the situation changed. Turner found ready listeners for his theory, and an embarrassingly large number of disciples. If we can understand why the United States in the 1880s was unwilling to glorify its frontier heritage, and in the 1890s was eager to do so, we can better appreciate the social climate that stimulated Turner to advance his hypothesis.

Basic to such an understanding is the realization that his thesis was far from new and that both the manner and effect of westward expansion had been understood for a century or more. As early as the 1830s the able French commentator Alexis de Tocqueville pictured Americans as advancing steadily westward in a massive column, dividing occasionally to sweep by a natural barrier, then uniting again to press relentlessly on—"a deluge of men rising unabatedly, and daily driven onward by the hand of God." [2] As they moved they followed a regular pattern, repeated over and over again, as new communities were founded to merge with the older civilization behind them. Thomas Jefferson believed that a traveler journeying eastward from the Rocky Mountains would encounter in succession men "in the earliest stage of association," then those in the "pastoral state, raising domestic animals to supply the defects of hunting," next those "semibarbarous citizens" who

---

his concept of the East as an authoritarian symbol, stemming from the fact that the three men who most influenced Turner—his father, Allen, and Herbert B. Adams—were easterners. Beckman also contends that Turner's guilt feelings kept him from writing; his inner conscience punished him for being jealous of his surrogate father by forbidding him to finish the books that he desperately wanted to produce, and thus enjoy the satisfaction of accomplishment. Alan C. Beckman, "Hidden Themes in the Frontier Thesis: An Application of Psychoanalysis to Historiography," *Comparative Studies in Society and History*, VIII (April, 1966), 361–82.
2. Alexis de Tocqueville, *Democracy in America* (2 vols., Cambridge [Mass.], 1863), I, 512.

were "the pioneers of the advance of civilization," and finally through "the gradual stages of an improving man" the stabilized society of the eastern seaboard. Jefferson thought of this progression as "equivalent to a survey, in time, of the progress of man from the infancy of creation to the present day."[3] Another European observer, Friedrich List, was impressed with the fact that in the United States a region passed "from the condition of the mere hunter to the rearing of cattle, from that to agriculture and from the latter to manufactures and commerce" in a single generation.[4] Here was the concept of the frontier as a microcosm of the world's civilization that Turner popularized. That he read Jefferson or Tocqueville or List seems unlikely, but their views were common currency to the end of the century.

So was the understanding that cheap lands fostered democracy. Tocqueville believed that American prosperity rested on the progressive exploitation of virgin resources, and in turn sustained the nation's democratic institutions;[5] others viewed the West as a "safety valve" that drained excess workers from the East so effectively that class discontent was unknown. This was accepted unquestioningly on both sides of the Atlantic. When supporters of the English reform bills in 1832 and 1867 argued that democracy operated without disorder in the United States, their opponents answered that free lands drained off "all the peccant political humours of the body politic." "The safety-valve is open," one declared; "the high pressure has not yet commenced on the engine. But wait until the huge receptacle of discontented multitudes is filled up."[6] Such sentiments were never questioned, for they were universally believed. Thomas Babington Macauley spoke for all Europe's enlightened when he wrote in 1857 that so long as unoccupied lands remained, the laboring population would be more at ease than their overseas cousins "and while this is the case the Jefferson politics may continue to exist without causing any fatal calamity."[7]

3. Andrew P. Lipscomb and Albert E. Bergh, eds., *The Writings of Thomas Jefferson* (20 vols., Washington, 1903–1904), XVI, 74–75.
4. This paragraph from List's works was first called to Turner's attention in 1924 by his friend James Westfall Thompson of the University of Chicago.
5. Tocqueville, *Democracy in America*, I, 371–82.
6. William M. Tuttle, Jr., "Forerunners of Frederick Jackson Turner: Nineteenth-Century British Conservatives and the Frontier Thesis," *Agricultural History*, XLI (July, 1967), 219–27, deals with the English background of the safety valve doctrine. The quotations are from *Blackwood's Edinburgh Magazine*, XXXVIII (September, 1835), 399–400.
7. Thomas B. Macaulay to H. S. Randall, May 23, 1857, in G. O. Trevelyan, *The Life and Letters of Lord Macaulay* (New York, 1909), II, 451–54. This concept was also current in Germany. In his *Philosophie der Geschichte*, published in 1837, Wilhelm Friedrich Hegel

Turner was less likely to have read the letters of Macauley or parliamentary debates over reform than the writings of Tocqueville and List, but he certainly did read some of the countless American writers who echoed their views. He could scarcely have escaped that sentiment in the authors of the Golden Age whom he studied avidly. Ralph Waldo Emerson, whose essays were admired and copied more than those of any other writer, constantly preached the importance of the frontier as a preservative of American democratic values. "The nervous, rocky West," Emerson wrote in his "The Young American," "is introducing a new and continental element into the national mind." [8] Turner copied that remark into his "Commonplace Book," just as he did Henry David Thoreau's observation that Americans were "filibustering toward heaven by the great western route." [9] Francis Parkman, another of his favorites, believed that easy access to the interior checked the growth of despotism in New France,[10] and that long residence on the frontier was responsible for "many of the peculiar traits of the American backwoodsman." There geographic conditions, climate, and conditions prevalent in a new country shaped the character of individuals, communities, and states.[11] James Russell Lowell saw the frontier as the mother of equality, optimism, and self-reliance, just as it was of the ingenuity and generosity that were so

---

observed that the United States had not been plagued by economic pressures as had Europe because of westward expansion. "By this means," he wrote, "the chief source of discontent is removed, and the continuation of the existing civil conditions is guaranteed. . . . North America is still in the condition of having land to cultivate. Only when, as in Europe, the direct increase of agriculturists is checked, will the inhabitants, instead of pressing onward to occupy the fields, press inward upon each other,—pursuing town occupations, and trading with their fellow citizens; and so form a compact system of civil society, and require an organized state." Turner had not read Hegel when he wrote his 1893 essay, but the sentiment expressed was well known to him, and to most Americans. W. Stull Holt, "Hegel, the Turner Hypothesis, and the Safety-Valve Theory," *Agricultural History*, XXII (July, 1948), 175–76.

8. Ralph Waldo Emerson, *The Works of Ralph Waldo Emerson* (Boston, 1883), I, 349. This and other references to Emerson are borrowed from two capable articles: Herman C. Nixon, "Precursors of Turner in the Interpretation of the American Frontier," *South Atlantic Quarterly*, XXVIII (January, 1929), 83–89, and Ernest Marchant, "Emerson and the Frontier," *American Literature*, III (May, 1931), 149–74.

9. The notebook into which this was copied is in HEH TU File Drawer 15, Folder: Notebook Kept By Turner c. 1913.

10. Francis Parkman, *The Old Régime in Canada* (Boston, 1898), 462–63. Parkman's social views as shaped by his study of the frontier are the theme of Wilbur R. Jacobs, "Some Social Views of Francis Parkman," *The American Quarterly*, IX (Winter, 1957), 387–97, and Edward N. Saveth, *American Historians and European Immigrants, 1875–1925* (New York, 1948), pp. 103–05 and 110–11.

11. Parkman, *Old Régime in Canada*, p. 461. Parkman's influence on Turner is appraised in Dean Moor, "The Paxton Boys: Parkman's Use of the Frontier Hypothesis," *Mid-America*, XXXVI (October, 1954), 211–19.

marked in western settlements.[12] These were all characteristics that Turner was to identify with frontiering.

If the impact of cheap land on the American character was recognized by these self-centered New Englanders, it was even more apparent to westerners and others living nearer the frontier. All accepted as beyond dispute the belief that pioneering endowed Americans with their most laudable traits, and said so emphatically in the guidebooks, travel accounts, magazines, and newspapers that awaited Turner on the shelves of the State Historical Society library. They agreed that men whose character "had been moulded by constant contact with western scenery and people"[13] were unusually energetic, enterprising, patriotic, democratic, and zealous for cultural self-improvement.[14] Others saw westerners as "generous, though crude, unmindful from habit of the luxuries of life, endowed with great boldness and originality of mind,"[15] or as "quickened in energy and activity."[16] "The price of land," wrote one, "is the thermometer of liberty—men are freest where lands are cheapest."[17] These were views that Turner was to echo in his 1893 essay, and they were accepted as commonplace by all Americans through much of the nineteenth century.

Of those who speculated on the significance of the frontier, none anticipated him more accurately than E. L. Godkin, editor of *The Nation*, whose 1865 essay on "Aristocratic Opinions of Democracy" might have served as a model for its better-known counterpart of thirty years later. "Frontier life," Godkin believed, was responsible for most of the differences that distinguished Americans from Europeans. One by one he ticked these off. The frontier "gave democracy its first great impulse." It fostered individualism by separating settlers from compact social groups until "each gets in the

12. Lowell's views were particularly well expressed in his address, *The Independent in Politics* (New York, 1888). His speculations on the American frontier are considered in Harry H. Clark, "Lowell—Humanitarian, Nationalist, or Humanist," *Studies in Philology*, XXVII (July, 1930), 431–32.
13. *North American Review*, XLIII (July, 1836), 2.
14. J. M. Peck, "Elements of Western Character," *Christian Review*, XVI (1851), 95. Rush Welter, "The Frontier West as Image of American Society, 1776–1860," *Pacific Northwest Quarterly*, LII (January, 1961), 5, remarks that Peck's article "reads like a primitive version of Turner's thesis."
15. James H. Lanman, "The Progress of the Northwest," *Hunt's Merchants' Magazine and Commercial Review*, III (July, 1840), 39.
16. *Fry's Traveler's Guide and Descriptive Journal of the Great North-Western Territories* (Cincinnati, 1865), pp. 261–63.
17. Nixon, "Precursors of Turner," *loc. cit.*, 84–85, and Welter, "The Frontier West as Image of American Society," *loc. cit.*, 5, cite many comments of this sort, all taken from magazines of the period. The quotation is from *DeBow's Review and Industrial Resources*, XII (April, 1858), 272.

habit of looking at himself as an individual, of contemplating himself and his career separate and apart from the social organization." It stimulated "a self-confidence that rises into conceit" among frontiersmen. It bred "a prodigious contempt for experience and for theory," as well as "a devotion to material pursuits." When Godkin added to this list a lack of respect for training, indifference to the future, "the absence of a strong sense of social and national continuity," and a lack "of taste in art and literature and oratory," his catalog of traits traceable to the pioneering experience was an imposing one.[18]

He also projected his analysis into the political realm, as Turner did after him. Americans, he noted, distrusted men with nothing but book learning "mainly because persons who have passed the early part of their lives in learning out of books or from teachers are generally found less fit to grapple with the kind of difficulties which usually present themselves in western life." This prejudice meant that business leaders who were both untrained and self-made enjoyed unwarranted political popularity, whatever their competence in a legislative body. This frontier-bred attitude, Godkin believed, was now universally held, just as was the West's faith in the infallibility of the majority. With typical western optimism he predicted that these views would diminish and eventually disappear when men were no longer attracted to frontiers. Only then would the United States achieve the cultural maturity of older nations.[19]

We know that Turner did not stumble on Godkin's essay until three years after his own was written,[20] but we can be equally certain that he did read similar views in the works of economists, political theorists, and historians who wrote in the latter part of the nineteenth century. William Graham Sumner, Yale University's famed political economist and publican, was a case in point. In fifty or more articles in leading magazines and scholarly journals,

18. Edwin L. Godkin, "Aristocratic Opinions of Democracy," *North American Review,* CCVI (January, 1865), 212.
19. *Ibid.,* 218–25.
20. Andrew C. McLaughlin of the University of Chicago showed the essay to Turner in 1896, shortly after it was published in book form in Godkin, *Problems in American Democracy* (New York, 1896). Turner read it carefully, chuckled, and said: "Godkin has stolen my thunder." McLaughlin recounted this episode to Harold R. Shurtleff of Cambridge, who told it to Fulmer Mood. Mood, "Turner's Formative Period," in Turner, *Early Writings of Frederick Jackson Turner,* 39. In a syllabus prepared about 1909 Turner cited as references to a section on "The Influence of the West on American Democracy" two of his own articles, and that by Godkin. HEH TU Vol. VI (3). Syllabus of Lectures. History of the West.

many of them frequently sampled by Turner, Sumner credited the vacant lands and underpeopled territories of the West with stimulating individualism, capitalism, and democracy. Some of his statements were not unlike those used by Turner: "the democratic tide in America has owed much of its force and violence to the frontier," or pioneering made the people "bold, independent, energetic, and enterprising." [21]

Sumner held no monopoly on these speculations, for other scholars were writing in the same vein. Typical among the historians who followed the pattern was the Californian, Hubert Howe Bancroft, whose little volume called *Essays and Miscellany*, published in 1890, contained three essays that came tantalizingly close to developing a thesis not unlike that of Turner. Bancroft, true, was still a slave to the Teutonic school of interpretation, and saw the westward sweep across the continent as the crowning climax of Anglo-Saxon achievement. In his eyes the Pacific states were the "western world's end" to the great migrations that had been redistributing mankind since the Middle Ages. "What Egyptian and West Asiatic civilization did for Greece," he wrote in language reminiscent of Turner, "what Greece did for Rome, what Rome did for western Europe, all the world has done for these Pacific states." [22] This was because a century of pioneering had developed "the practical adaptibility and self-reliance inherited from the mother race," [23] changing Americans into a new breed of men. They were more prone to move than Europeans, took less pride in their heritage, ignored old customs, and sought to make a mark in the world by whatever means. [24] The frontier gave them "more room for the exercise of native skill and enterprise than in satisfied societies with fixed habits." [25] Bancroft was certain that the West was a transforming force, and that every change was for the better.

Whether Turner was familiar with the writings of Bancroft, Sumner, and Godkin is as unconsequential as whether he had read Tocqueville, Jefferson, and List. He, like them, lived in a land where frontiering was part of life, and the frontier's influence on the whole nation generally acknowledged. Americans had been aware of the significance of that frontier for generations. True,

21. Quoted in Edith H. Parker, "William Graham Sumner and the Frontier," *Southwest Review*, XLI (Autumn, 1956), 360. Miss Parker concludes that Sumner's articles included "the most important ideas set forth by Turner in his essay," a conclusion that hardly seems warranted by the evidence she advances.
22. Hubert H. Bancroft, *Essays and Miscellany* (San Francisco, 1890), pp. 40, 48–49.
23. *Ibid.*, p. 43.
24. *Ibid.*, p. 191.
25. *Ibid.*, p. 189.

no one of them demonstrated that significance as systematically and convincingly as Turner, but all accepted its importance as so obvious that no proof was needed. The wonder is not that he voiced those convictions; someone else would have done so had Frederick Jackson Turner never existed. The wonder is that his message had such an impact on both the public and the historical profession. Clearly the United States was ready in the 1890s to look anew at its frontier heritage as it had not been in the 1860s when Godkin advanced a similar thesis in scarcely less convincing terms. Why this change in public attitudes? What in the intellectual and social climate of Turner's day allowed his essay to stir the popular consciousness and glorify him as the "father" of the frontier hypothesis?

An answer to that question requires us to take a second look at the image of the West common among most informed Americans, but to do so from a different perspective. Through the nineteenth century the frontier was viewed not only as a retreating area of free land, but as the "Garden of the World" where a bountiful nature washed all newcomers of evil and transmuted them into models of republican virtue, all endowed with a lofty morality that matched their physical strength. This agrarian myth was basic in the nation's folklore. Scarcely a literate American but recognized that the republic's most treasured values—democracy, individualism, patriotism, prosperity—flowed from West to East. Scarcely one but knew that the boundless plains of the Mississippi Valley offered a haven for those dispossessed of the seaboard who fled westward to find the strength and wealth that awaited all. So long as the "Garden of the World" existed, the nation and its ideals were secure. So long as yeoman farmers lived and multiplied, republican principles were safe. But once free lands were exhausted, once that garden was threatened, the whole moral fabric would collapse and the land descend into the state of depravity and tyranny that overcrowded Europe already knew. A threat to the garden was a threat to the nation's future.

This myth was almost universally accepted through the nineteenth century, but its roots lay deep in the past.[26] "The small land holders," wrote Thomas Jefferson, "are the most precious part of a state," and the nation agreed

26. The West as an American myth is admirably described in Henry Nash Smith, *Virgin Land: The American West as Symbol and Myth* (Cambridge [Mass.], 1950), Henry Nash Smith, "The West as an Image of the American Past," *University of Kansas City Review*, XVIII (Autumn, 1951), 29–39, and Welter, "The Frontier West as Image of American Society," *loc. cit.*, 1–6.

72

with him.[27] The regenerative powers of the frontier on decadent easterners was a theme played over and over again, decade after decade, by newspaper editors, guidebook writers, essayists, politicians, real-estate promoters—by all, indeed, who could speak or hold a pen, and who had the good of their country at heart. Little matter that many westerners who embroidered the agrarian myth were speculators who wanted to sell land, or politicians truckling for votes. They were believed, for what they said was too logical to be disbelieved. Everyone knew that easterners who went west were transformed as soon as they left the "old fogy settlements"; everyone could see, as did one editor, "his mind expand, his eye light up with the fire of renewed energy, and his whole nature grow to the liberal standard of nature's doing in the West." [28] Stephen A. Douglas testified that he found his mind liberalized and his views enlarged as soon as he stepped on the broad prairies of Illinois "with only the heavens to bound my vision." [29] Those fortunate enough to reach the "Garden of the World" were assured affluence forever, for there a kindly climate promised abundant harvests year after year, and wealth piled on wealth.[30] There ill health was unknown. "Farmers and their children are strong, and innocent and moral almost of necessity," wrote one westerner; [31] their elevated morality could be realized by comparing the easy deportment of the pioneer with the "stiff, reserved, haughty and domineering manners of a southern black leg, or a northern coxcomb." [32] This was the image of the garden engrained in the American mind. Any threat to the yeoman farmer was a threat to the moral and political foundation on which the nation's greatness rested.

This threat arose in the closing decades of the nineteenth century. The twin serpents of industrialism and urbanization were responsible. As factories multiplied and poured out their wealth, as the center of national influence shifted from country to city, as the business leader displaced the farmer as a popular folk hero, as the glamor of Broadway challenged the romance of the prairies, Americans began to doubt whether the Garden of the World was

27. Paul L. Ford, ed., *The Writings of Thomas Jefferson* (10 vols., New York, 1892–1899), VII, 36.
28. *Keokuk (Iowa) Whig*, quoted in Nathan H. Parker, *Iowa as It Is in 1857* (Chicago, 1857), p. 31.
29. Quoted in William J. Peterson, *The Story of Iowa* (New York, 1952), I, 355–56.
30. Rufus Easton of Missouri to Senator William Hunter, quoted in *Niles' Weekly Register*, X (August 24, 1816), 428–29.
31. Timothy Flint in the *Western Monthly Review*, I (July, 1827), 169–70.
32. Isaac Galland, *Iowa Emigrant* (Iowa City, 1950), xi.

quite the Eden that had been pictured by the mythmakers. Every dispatch from the western plains heightened their doubts, for there the agrarian depression of the 1880s and 1890s shattered legends of frontier affluence. The sturdy yeoman farmer, skin tanned and muscles rippling beneath a clean blue shirt as he raked sweet-smelling hay, seemed suddenly to vanish. In his place were agitators and troublemakers: spokesmen for the Farmer's Alliances demanding a larger share of the national wealth, Populists drafting an Omaha Platform that urged social reforms hostile to traditional individualism, orators urging farmers to "raise less corn and more hell" to win their crusade against injustice and poverty. Was this the "Garden of the World"? And if it were not, had that Garden ever existed save in the dreams of promoters and romanticists?

In this moment of doubt, just at a time Turner was formulating his frontier thesis, writers about the West suddenly awakened to a new cause. Why pen romantic pictures of western affluence and moral regeneration when the West was no longer playing that role? Why not describe it as it really was—a grim, depression-ridden land where the East's dispossessed sank still deeper into the mire of poverty? This was the incentive that produced a whole school of starkly realistic writers during the 1880s and 1890s, all bent on aiding social reform by demolishing the myth of the Garden. E. W. Howe was one; his *Story of a Country Town* pictured the West as a world of fading hope and shattered dreams. Hamlin Garland in his *Main-Travelled Roads* (1891) and Jason Edwards with his *An Average Man* (1892) added dimension to the emerging picture. These were bitter novels; they peopled the plains with avaricious land speculators, greedy railroad builders, and money-hungry mortgage holders rather than sun-tanned yeoman farmers; they painted it as a land of poverty and despair. "So this is the reality of the dream," wrote Hamlin Garland as he ended his tragic tale. "This is the 'homestead in the Golden West, embowered with trees, beside a purling brook!' A shanty on a barren plain, hot and lone as a desert. My God!" [33]

These were harsh words, tearing at a myth deeply implanted in the nation's folklore, and they tended as did so much that was written in the 1880s and 1890s to focus attention on the rural past. The dream remained for many, including Turner; his faith in the values of agrarian America—the "real, genuine America" of which Walt Whitman sang—was too deep ever to be completely

33. The literary attacks on the "Garden of the World" symbol are admirably described in Smith, *Virgin Land*, 230-49.

dislodged. This was an emotional reaction, not a rational one. His reason told him that the Garden was gone forever; he listened disapprovingly to the plaints of the Populists and piled data on data to show the ruinous effects of speculative greed on the aspirations of western man. But his heart told him that life in the Garden had been good; this was the rural land that he knew and loved, as did many of his contemporaries. When Turner wrote of the frontier he was recapturing a segment of the past to which he belonged, and glorifying that segment for a later generation who could never know its blessings. He may well have written his 1893 essay had there been no myth of a Garden and no revelation of its falseness, but the task was easier because he believed so fervently in the agrarian values that it glorified. The folklore of the frontier, no less than the reality of the frontier, helped shape his hypothesis and endow it with the sincerity that made his essay so appealing.[34]

If the shattering of the Garden myth jolted Turner and the nation, so did the realization that the frontier was closing and the era of free western lands at an end. This disturbing fact gradually permeated the national consciousness during the last two decades of the century, and as it did so conjured into being a whole Pandora's box of troublesome problems. How could the United States adjust to a closed-space existence? How could its people weather economic storms without the safety valve of western lands? How could its industries prosper without rejuvenating transfusions of virgin natural resources? As politicians and publicists pondered these questions in books, magazine articles, pamphlets, and speeches, the frontier was in the spotlight as never before. Turner would have been insensitive had he not felt concern. And he would have been a poor historian if he had not asked himself an obvious question: if the closing of the frontier threatened to alter the country's social structure, how had its existence during the past three centuries affected the life and institutions of the people?[35] His search for an answer to that question led him nearer his hypothesis.

Public concern was based on the most terrifying of all fears—the fear of

34. The manner in which Turner's views were shaped by the "Garden of the World" myth is discussed in *ibid.*, 123–25, 250–51.
35. Lee A. Benson, "The Historian as Mythmaker: Turner and the Closed Frontier," in David M. Ellis, ed., *The Frontier in American Development: Essays in Honor of Paul Wallace Gates* (Ithaca, 1969), 3–19, holds that the closing of the frontier had no impact on the popular mind until after 1896, and that Turner's essay was responsible for creating much of the interest evidenced thereafter. The best answer to this argument is the article by Benson cited in the next footnote.

the unknown. This was a new world into which the United States was venturing, a closed-space world with no precedents to serve as guidelines. For three centuries frontier resources had provided them abundance and frontier values sustained their democratic institutions. Did they face a future of poverty and despotism? This seemed not unlikely, for already the knowing found signs that the social structure was crumbling. The depression that gripped the nation between 1873 and 1896 bore every mark of permanence; to make matters worse escape to the West was impossible, for there the Populists had proven that the Garden was no more. This was alarming, but even more threatening were the remedies suggested by social critics who rose to dissect America's ills. In past depressions prophets preached optimism, pointing out that renewed expansion westward was inevitable and that this would rejuvenate the country's economy. Now they sang a new tune. Edward Bellamy urged a "New Nationalism" built on the socialization of production and distribution; Henry George wanted a radical alteration of the tax structure; Thorstein Veblen questioned the worth of a society that produced profits for the few rather than benefits for the many. Newspaper headlines told of workers and farmers who demonstrated for radical change in their own way: with crippling railroad strikes, the Haymarket Riot, the shrill demands of the Knights of Labor and the People's Party for a more equitable distribution of the nation's wealth. Critics were questioning basic American values and proposing unheard-of changes. Did this portend the fate of the United States now that free lands were exhausted? Would it be racked for all time to come with class conflicts and faced with revolutionary demands as was overcrowded Europe?

Actually the frontier did not abruptly close at the end of the nineteenth century; more government land was homesteaded after 1900 than before. Nor did the threat of its closing bring on the economic disasters that plagued the country between the 1870s and the 1890s, even though this was the popular impression. Instead the "Commercial Revolution" was to blame. This was a product of the mechanization of means of distribution; within a few decades after the 1850s railroads and ocean-going steamships completely disrupted marketing patterns that had endured for centuries as hitherto isolated regions were brought into competition with traditional areas of production. Overnight, it seemed, the whole world began producing farm goods for markets long monopolized by the United States; overnight traditional patterns in commerce and finance must be readjusted to a global scale. This disrupted trade patterns everywhere, but nowhere more violently than those servicing American agriculture. Farmers in the Mississippi Valley now had to compete not only with each other, but with farmers in Australia, Canada, Russia, Egypt, India, and the Argentine. They were faced with an economy where the price of cotton was set by conditions in the Nile Delta, and the price of wheat by the size of Siberia's crop. Worst of all, they must realize that food supplies had outstripped the world's capacity to consume them as previously unproductive areas entered the market place. Not the closing of the frontier, but forces generated by the Commercial Revolution, drove agricultural prices downward after 1873 and nurtured the discontent that underlay Populism.[36]

Whatever the reason, the effect was once more to focus attention on the West, for there the disruptive effects of the revolution were more immediately apparent than in the East. Could agriculture survive there when faced with competition from nations with lower living standards? And, if it could not, what fate awaited the country's democratic institutions? Could they endure pressures from the giant corporations, the nationalized economic enterprises, the immigrant-crowded cities that were altering the nation's profile? Where amidst this industrial monolith was there a place for the individual? Those who sought to answer these questions usually looked backward rather than forward. Their solution was to reiterate the virtues of rural America and reaffirm their faith in traditional values; publicists and politicians alike insisted that the United States could survive only if individualistic democracy triumphed over the urban-industrial Frankenstein's monster that was threatening the land. Those values were centered in the West, the area that Lord Bryce called "the most American part of America." If they were to endure the West that fostered them must be investigated and understood as never in the past.

The focus on the West of those who pursued this line of reasoning was sharpened by others who sought a cause for the disrupted economy and the plight of the farmer. Few recognized that a global Commercial Revolution was responsible; instead they sought an answer in local conditions. They found one at once: free lands were running out and the era of ex-

36. Lee A. Benson, "The Historical Background of Turner's Frontier Essay," *Agricultural History*, XXV (April, 1951), 59–82, brilliantly explores this theme. It has been reprinted in Lee A. Benson, *Turner and Beard: American Historical Writing Reconsidered* (Glencoe, Illinois, 1960), pp. 42–91. The discussion that follows is borrowed largely from this source.

pansion closing. This was easily demonstrated. Between 1870 and 1890, they pointed out, 407,000,000 acres in the West were occupied and 189,000,000 placed under cultivation—more than in all the previous history of the nation. If this mass migration went on the supply would be exhausted within a few years. As early as the summer of 1880 *The Nation* warned that "the picket-lines of the approaching army of settlers from the East and from the Pacific have met in the middle belt of Colorado and Utah," and predicted that free lands would vanish within a decade.[37] The alarm was sounded again in Josiah Strong's immensely popular *Our Country*, published in 1885. Americans, he wrote, must face a new way of life in the future, for their high wages, general welfare, and contentment had all rested in large measure on the abundance of free land. "When the supply is exhausted, we shall enter upon a new era, and shall rapidly approximate European conditions of life." Strong foresaw the not-too-distant day when skyrocketing land values would drive the mass of the people into cities, dooming the rural values that had sustained America from its birth.[38]

These prophets of doom were few during the 1880s, but as the depression deepened during the grim 1890s they grew into a discordant chorus that all could hear. As Turner was shaping his frontier thesis magazines and public utterances overflowed with references to the West and predictions that free lands would soon disappear. C. Wood Davis of Kansas typified the host of writers who exploited this theme. In a number of articles in popular magazines he laid the depression to overproduction, which in turn had been fostered by "a practically unlimited area of fertile land, free as the air we breathe." As a conservative businessman he had no truck with the reforms suggested by Populists; he believed that agricultural prices would start upward within five years as the exhaustion of the public domain stabilized production.[39] Davis' views were eagerly embraced by many farmers and even by some Populist leaders; others took sharp exception to his figures and insisted that reforms were necessary. The clash between those who held these opposite viewpoints stimulated a lively debate in the public prints; between 1890 and 1892 scarcely an issue of the *Country Gentleman* but

37. "An Agricultural Outlook," *The Nation*, XXXI (August 19, 1880), 127.
38. Josiah Strong, *Our Country* (New York, 1885), 153, 137.
39. Davis' many articles are analysed in Benson, "Historical Background of Turner's Frontier Essay," *loc. cit.*, 66–70, and more briefly in Nixon, "Precursors of Turner in the Interpretation of the American Frontier," *loc. cit.*, 88.

contained articles arguing for or against the views of Davis and his Populist opponents.[40]

Particularly significant to those interested in tracing the origin of Turner's concepts was that many of these debaters used ideas and language not unlike those he himself would employ in his 1893 essay. Davis, writing in the *Country Gentleman* in June 1891, credited the "unexampled prosperity of the United States, and our comparative freedom from the social and economic problems long confronting Europe" to the existence of "an almost unlimited area of fertile land to which the unemployed could freely resort." With this on the point of exhaustion, the United States must face radical readjustments. Davis saw a not-too-distant day when a growing army of unemployed would create "social disturbances of grave significance," when a peonlike caste system would divide the people, and when a giant standing army would be necessary to provide work for those who could no longer escape to the frontier.[41]

Western publicists such as C. Wood Davis found an unlikely ally in spokesmen for eastern bankers and capitalists. The interest of these business men was purely commercial; they recognized that every prediction of the closing of the frontier was an effective sales device for the western lands that they owned or the farm mortgages that they were eager to peddle. What was safer than a mortgage on a Kansas farm, they asked? With free lands soon to disappear, and a premium placed on those already under cultivation, farms were absolutely certain to increase in value.[42] Every eastern banker who advertised the mortgages that he had for sale helped bring the closing of the frontier closer to the people. So did agricultural experts who began to preach in the early 1890s that farmers must "Europeanize" their techniques by abandoning the wasteful, soil-exhausting practices that were feasible so long as free lands were available. "The farming of the past was land-skimming," wrote an agricultural advisor in 1892; "the farming of the future must be land-culture. . . . Our agriculture—still the greatest of our industries—is under the necessity of accomodating itself to new conditions." [43]

40. Benson, "Historical Background of Turner's Frontier Essay," *loc. cit.*, 66–70.
41. C. Wood Davis, "Some Impending Changes," *Country Gentleman*, LVI (June 25, 1891), 513.
42. J. Willis Gleed, "Western Mortgages," *The Forum*, IX (March, 1890), 93–105.
43. A. W. Harris, "What the Government is Doing for the Farmer," *Century Magazine*, XLIV (July, 1892), quoted in Nixon, "Precursors of Turner in the Interpretation of the American Frontier," *loc. cit.*, 89.

Farm experts, eastern bankers, and western alarmists might disagree on the cure for the nation's ills but they united in their diagnosis: its troubles could all be traced to the closing of the frontier. This belief was so much a part of the social climate of the 1890s that it could not fail to make its imprint on Turner, interested as he was in all the West.

Nor could he ignore the less laudable demands of propagandists who used the end of free lands to justify restrictions of immigration from abroad. The real object of their campaign was the "New Immigration" from eastern and southern Europe then flooding the land. Restrictionists made a sharp distinction between the Anglo-Saxons and Germans who had migrated to the United States in the past, and the "swarthy," "indolent," "unruly," "anarchy-prone," Italians, Hungarians, and Jews who constituted the bulk of the arrivals after the 1870s. America's melting-pot image was too deeply rooted to allow an openly racist attack on these newcomers; instead the anti-immigrationists fastened on the closing of the public domain as justification for closing the gates against all immigrants.[44] This devious bit of logic was popularized during the 1880s. The high priest of its spokesmen was Josiah Strong, whose *Our Country* explored the effect that the frontier's end would have on the nation and its world relations. "There are no more new worlds," he wrote. "The unoccupied arable lands of the earth are limited, and will soon be taken."[45] Let the United States save those remaining for those who won them, not squander its dwindling resources on Europe's worthless outcasts. They had been welcome so long as the frontier cleansed the "depraved dregs of European civilization" and allowed the country "to digest almost everything sent us."[46] Now that cleansing agent was no more; immigration must be stopped. This was Josiah Strong's message, and it was echoed by many of his contemporaries during the 1880s.

With the increasing economic tensions of the 1890s the anti-immigrationists

44. An excellent discussion of the relationship between the closing of the frontier and the exclusion movement is in John Higham, *Strangers in the Land* (New Brunswick, New Jersey, 1955), pp. 133–41.

45. Josiah Strong, *Our Country*, pp. 160–61. Typical of the many articles arguing that the end of free lands justified immigration restriction was H. H. Boyesen, "Dangers of Unrestricted Immigration," *The Forum*, II (July, 1887), 634.

46. Richmond Mayo-Smith, "Control of Immigration," *Political Science Quarterly*, III (September, 1888), 418–19. Restrictionists used the closed-space argument to justify ending immigration far more widely after 1893 than before, suggesting that Turner's article greatly affected their thinking. This is discussed in Benson, "Historical Background of Turner's Frontier Essay," *loc. cit.*, 79–81.

multiplied in numbers and influence, and their thunders swelled in volume. Francis A. Walker, educator and statistician whose works were so admired by Turner, used his 1890 presidential address before the American Economics Association to warn that "alien breeds" were a menace to the nation since free lands could no longer absorb them.[47] He was joined by dozens of others from all walks of life. One was C. Wood Davis, tub-thumper for the Kansas farmers, who linked his favorite land-exhaustion theme with immigration and by 1891 was demanding its complete end. Another was Turner's Johns Hopkins friend, Albert Shaw, who became editor of the *Review of Reviews* in 1891 and saw to it that every issue of that influential magazine had at least one article dealing with the effect of a closed frontier on migration from abroad.[48] These spokesmen were representative; everywhere in the land the hue and cry was raised against aliens, with the exhaustion of the public domain the excuse to keep them from America. Even those sane enough to reject the racist argument saw the problems that newcomers would create in a frontierless land. "Reluctant as we are to recognize it," wrote one, "a labor-problem is at last upon us. No longer can a continent of free virgin lands avert from us a social struggle which the old world has known so long and so painfully." [49] That the "Immigration Restriction League" was formed in 1894, just months after Turner announced his hypothesis, suggests the degree to which the closing frontier burdened the national conscience.

The extent to which this propaganda shaped Turner's thought can never be known, but some evidence exists and some guesses can be made. We know, for example, that he was familiar with the *Review of Reviews* and a friend of its editor, Albert Shaw. We know that he was more than ordinarily interested in immigration and the problems it raised; in January 1893, probably while preparing his essay, he clipped from Chicago newspapers dozens of articles by leaders of the restrictionist movement, many of them stressing the closing of the frontier as the basis for their arguments.[50] At about the same time Turner prepared outlines for a portion of a course, labeling them "Immigration Syllabus—tentative." In them he listed the procedures necessary for a proper study of immigration: a statistical analysis of the composition of groups of newcomers, a survey of the causes that drove

47. Quoted in *ibid.*, 70–72.
48. The extensive magazine literature is described in *ibid.*, 70–76.
49. Francis A. Walker, "Immigration," *Yale Review*, I (August, 1892), 129–30.
50. These clippings are in HEH TU File Drawer 16D, Folder: Immigration.

them from their homelands, their mode of travel, their economic, social, and political adjustment when in the United States, their impact on the society. One major division would deal with the "free land period." [51] Turner also directed an undergraduate honors thesis on "The Effect of the Settlement of the Public Domain on Immigration," sending the student to many current magazines for information and working with him in the analysis of his material. Not only did Turner sign the thesis that resulted, but the arguments used suggest that the student was echoing his teacher's views.[52] Unquestionably Turner linked immigration with the closing of the frontier in his own mind, an association that had something to do—even though remotely—with the emergence of his hypothesis.

He must also have been aware of popular interest in the passing of the public domain, and of the alarmist theories that were freely voiced during the 1880s and 1890s. No sensitive young man with an exaggerated interest in the West could fail to respond. Whether or not he read the articles of E. L. Godkin and Hubert H. Bancroft, the novels of Jason Edwards and Hamlin Garland, the polemics of Josiah Strong and C. Wood Davis, or the racist assaults on the New Immigration from dozens of restrictionists whose propaganda was everywhere, he knew what they said and he realized the effect on them of the passing of the frontier. These writers simply publicized thoughts and prejudices that were generally held; they were spokesmen for beliefs that were part of the social atmosphere of that day. When Theodore Roosevelt complimented Turner after publication of his 1893 essay by saying that "you have struck some first class ideas, and have put into definite shape a good deal of thought that has been floating around rather loosely," he simply recognized that Turner's principal contribution was to give form and structure to beliefs then generally held.[53] Turner knew this; he wrote some time later that he claimed no exclusive priority for "an idea that would have evolved from the nature of growing American consciousness of itself." [54] If he had not welded those ideas into a useable thesis, he realized, someone else would have done so.

51. Two portions of this syllabus have survived, both in Turner's hand. They are in HEH, TU File Drawer 16D, one in a folder marked "Immigration," the other in one labeled "Immigration Syllabus."
52. Benson, "Historical Background of Turner's Frontier Essay," *loc. cit.*, 78–79.
53. Theodore Roosevelt to Turner, February 10, 1894. Frederick Jackson Turner Papers, The Houghton Library, Harvard University. Hereafter cited as Houghton: Turner Papers.
54. Turner to William E. Dodd, October 7, 1919. HEH TU Box 29. This letter is reproduced below, pp. 187–98.

To say this is not to minimize his contribution. History's greatest intellectual pioneers have been those who synthesized and popularized current thought; their contribution was to serve as channels through which generally-held ideas were defined and expressed in explicit language.[55] This was Turner's genius. He, alone in his generation, combined the attributes necessary to translate the vague beliefs of his time into a historical hypothesis that placed the entire past in new perspective.

55. This is the conclusion reached by Benson, "Historical Background of Turner's Frontier Essay," *loc. cit.*, 77–78, and James C. Malin, "Space and History: Reflections on the Closed-Space Doctrines of Turner and Mackinder," *Agricultural History*, XVIII (April, 1944), 68. Welter, "Frontier West as Image of American Society," *loc. cit.*, makes the point that later criticism of Turner's inexact definitions and loose language stemmed from his critics' failure to realize that he was using terms common in his day, and properly understood by readers to whom they were addressed.

CHAPTER V *The Intellectual Climate*

As Frederick Jackson Turner was formulating his frontier hypothesis, three events occurred—one in Brazil, another in London, and the third in Washington—that were apparently unrelated but that tell us something about the intellectual atmosphere in which he operated. In Brazil, during the summer of 1889, appeared a striking volume by a local historian, Capistrano de Abreu, bearing the formidable title of *Os Caminhos Antigos e o Povoamento do Brazil*, and advancing a theory that frontiering was responsible for that country's unique character. The movement into the *sertao*, or backcountry, its author argued, transformed the first settlers into near savages; then as the *sertao* climbed back toward civilization, so did they. They emerged as cultured citizens, but stamped with a new personality that accounted for the differences distinguishing them from their Portugese ancestors.[1]

While Professor Abreu's Turner-like book was enjoying its first popularity, an anthropologist in Washington fell to pondering the exhibit the Smithsonian Institution should prepare for the impending World's Columbian Exposition that was to open in 1893. As he did so, Otis T. Mason had an inspiration. Why not build a display on the biogeographic map of North America recently completed by Dr. C. Hart Merriam and published in 1892 by the Department of Agriculture? To show the effect of varying environments on Indian culture, Mason grouped the artifacts for display into "cultural areas," a principle as revolutionary in anthropological studies as the frontier thesis in history. Here was a concept significant in ethnology, but its broader implications shed light on the development of Turner's theory.[2]

1. Abreu's theory has been as influential in Brazilian historiography as has Turner's in the United States. His book and its importance are described in José Honório Rodrigues, "Capistrano de Abreu and Brazilian History," in E. Bradford Burns, ed., *Perspectives in Brazilian History* (New York, 1967), pp. 156–80.
2. John C. Ewers, *A Century of American Indian Exhibits in the Smithsonian Institution* (Washington, 1959), pp. 520–22. I am grateful to Dr. Ewers for calling my attention to

Mason realized that "cultural areas" differed one from another largely because Indian societies were shaped by the environment in which they existed; Turner saw the frontier environment as a force molding the traits and institutions of pioneers. Too, Mason developed his concept by studying a highly sophisticated map that related geographic and biological data; Turner visualized American expansion only after using maps of population distribution prepared by the Census Bureau. Without those visual guides neither he nor Mason would have reached the conclusions they did.

Only a few months after Mason's exhibit went on display in Chicago, a prominent British geographer, Halford J. Mackinder, speaking before the Royal Geographical Society in London, announced a theory as important to that discipline as the "cultural area" concept to anthropology and the frontier hypothesis to history. The era of expansion that began with Columbus, he told his listeners, was drawing to a close. For four centuries man had sought new worlds to exploit, new resources to stimulate the economy. Now he must adjust his life and institutions to a closed-space existence. With escape to new frontiers impossible, a mechanized, totalitarian society would emerge, with the state paramount and the individual merely an impersonal unit of manpower in the service of government. Mackinder predicted that the individual rights and democratic principles so treasured in the past were doomed with the passing of a global frontier.[3]

Were the publication of Professor Abreu's book on the Brazilian *sertao* in 1889, the decision of Dr. Mason to prepare a cultural areas exhibit in 1892, the reading of Turner's paper in July 1893, and the speculation of Mackinder on existence in a closed-space world in January 1894, purely coincidental? Perhaps. Or were all responding to changes in the global intellectual climate? This seems more logical. All began their speculations because they saw that the world's supply of exploitable land was dwindling as the "Age of Expansion" drew to a close. Others had made such an observation in the past, however, and had not been inspired to theorize on the effect of frontiering as did Abreu and Turner, or the future in a closed-space

the similarity between the views of Mason and Turner, and suggesting that both were products of the intellectual climate of the time. John C. Ewers to Ray A. Billington, September 25, 1962.

3. James C. Malin, "Space and History: Reflections on the Closed-Space Doctrines of Turner and Mackinder," *Agricultural History*, XVIII (April, 1944), 67–68, argues that the closed-space doctrine was part of the intellectual climate, and that both Turner and Mackinder responded. Actually Mackinder's views resemble those later expressed in Walter P. Webb, *The Great Frontier* (Boston, 1951), rather than those of Turner.

world as did Mackinder. They failed to do so because they found no stimulus in an intellectual climate that was little concerned with a far-distant day when expansion would end, and because scientific knowledge had not advanced to a point where their theories could be sustained on reliable authority.

Turner's good fortune was to live at a time when national and world attention was focusing on the closing frontiers, and when progress in a variety of disciplines assured him techniques needed for his investigations and theoretical foundations for his conclusions. He was equipped, as prior generations had not been equipped, to translate random speculations into scientifically-based theories. He was able, as others were not, to visualize the expansion process in the United States, and to appraise its role in shaping the American character because scholars laid the foundations on which he built and provided the intellectual atmosphere that would foster his theorizing. Advances in historical methodology, geography, biology, and statistical cartography made the frontier hypothesis possible no less than the nation's concern with the passing of its public domain.

All of these disciplines benefited from revolutionary changes during the 1880s and 1890s, but none more so than history. Here a threefold transformation paved the way for Turner's contributions. First, younger scholars launched a fatal attack on the dominant "Teutonic School" during the early 1890s, showing that institutions did not descend unchanged from their medieval "germs" but were the product of a variety of forces. Second, they recognized that human behavior was too varied to be understood solely through its political manifestations, and that man's total activities provided grist for historians. Finally, midwestern scholars in all fields were just at this time rebelling against eastern domination as they searched the records of their section to reveal cultural outpourings no less significant than those of Boston or New York—at least in their own eyes. Only by examining this triple revolution in historical thought and methodology can we realize the degree to which Turner benefited from the historical atmosphere in which he lived.

His first experience, while growing to manhood, was with the then-dominant "Romantic School" led by George Bancroft, Francis Parkman, William H. Prescott, and John L. Motley; all produced multi-volume histories that blended vivid narrative with glowing pictorial characterization, and all relied on imagination only slightly less than documentation for their subject matter.[4] By the 1880s the excesses of romanticism fostered the rise of the counter "Scientific School" that ruled the profession during Turner's apprenticeship. This borrowed its inspiration from two sources. From German scholarship as it had flowered under Leopold von Ranke (1795–1886) it accepted belief in complete objectivity; the purpose of the historian was to reveal exactly what happened, not to interpret or evaluate. From the findings of Charles Darwin and his fellow natural scientists the "Scientific School" adopted a methodology based on experimentation and inductive reasoning, and a concept of society as a continuously evolving organism, unfolding in response to changing pressures just as did the animal organisms that biologists were studying. This was a flattering association for the historians; they were linked now with the most glamorous of the sciences; they could talk of "organs" and "germs" and they could transform their seminars into laboratories where, as one put it, "books are treated like mineralogical specimens, passed about from hand to hand, examined, and tested."[5]

To conform exactly to the scientific tradition, historical scholars were expected to achieve complete objectivity. This meant that they must study critically the primary sources of the past and extract from them factual information to show what actually happened, just as a paleontologist would use fossil remains to reconstruct the precise truth about a phase of animal evolution. The facts must speak for themselves, unmarred by the prejudices or opinions of the investigator. Hypotheses were outlawed lest the user select evidence that would substantiate his prior beliefs. Interpretation was suspect as tainted with the views of the interpreter. The sole function of the historian was to pile fact on fact, arrange them in proper order, and allow a synthesis to emerge. This "scientific" historians believed to be the

4. The standard work on the "Romantic School" is David Levin, *History as Romantic Art* (Stanford, 1959). In the discussion of historiography that follows I have relied heavily on John Higham, *History* (Englewood Cliffs, New Jersey, 1965), a brilliant interpretation of the period. He summarizes his views in his essay on "The Construction of American History" in John Higham, ed., *The Reconstruction of American History* (New York, 1962), pp. 9–24.
5. Quoted in W. Stull Holt, ed., *Historical Scholarship in the United States, 1876–1901: As Revealed in the Correspondence of Herbert B. Adams* (Baltimore, 1938), p. 69, note 1. Excellent discussions of the "Scientific School" are in Higham, *History*, pp. 98–100, John H. Randall, Jr., and George Haines IV, "Controlling Assumptions in the Practice of American Historians," in Social Science Research Council, *Theory and Practice in Historical Study: A Report of the Committee on Historiography* (New York, 1946), pp. 23–34, Edward N. Saveth, "Scientific History in America: Eclipse of an Idea," in Donald Sheehan and Harold C. Syrett, eds., *Essays in American Historiography. Papers Presented in Honor of Allan Nevins* (New York, 1960), pp. 1–19, and W. Stull Holt, "The Idea of Scientific History in America," *Journal of the History of Ideas*, I (June, 1940), 352–62.

inductive method. To them history was the purest of all disciplines, for it alone rejected hypotheses, was built solely on inductive reasoning, and banned all interpretation that smacked of a "philosophy of history."

Given these rules of the game, historians in the 1880s outlawed narrative history as too prone to interpret and glorify individuals, and turned instead to the study of the institutions through which men governed themselves. Here was a tempting field, both because it could be approached with scientific objectivity and because it was suited to the use of evolutionary techniques. Societies could be examined as they evolved through the ages, just as biologists traced the alterations in life patterns in fossil remains. Historians could speak learnedly of "social organisms" and reveal the continuous, connected chain of events leading from past to present in the life history of each. They could present their discipline as a study that illuminated modern society by an understanding of its origins, and that revealed only the truth as it examined the endless sequences of causes and effects through which institutions progressed.[6]

This was a noble ambition but historians soon found that institutional studies of this sort were impossible; nature provided biologists with the succession of fossil remains needed to study the evolution of a species, but man's written records were too few and too recent to allow institutional beginnings to be traced to the remote past. Their ingenious solution was to adopt the "comparative" technique then used by philologists. Linguists knew that similarities in word forms offered a key to their common origin; why not assume that institutional similarities provided the same clue to their beginnings? Here was a fascinating new world for the historical investigator. He had only to compare a modern institution—a New England town, say— with an institution in the remote past—such as a medieval German *tun*—to prove that one descended from the other. If the similarities were sufficiently exact, there was no need to trace the evolutionary steps that led from past to present. This was the amazing reasoning that fathered the "Teutonic School" of the 1880s and early 1890s. Its members believed that before the days of Tacitus a "common primeval brotherhood" existed with its own language and institutions. When these Aryans eventually scattered, some went to Greece to lay the foundations of Grecian culture, others to Rome

6. Jurgen Herbst, *The German Historical School in American Scholarship* (Ithaca, 1965), pp. 99–104 is excellent on the German background of American history. The subject is also discussed in Higham, *History*, pp. 92–97, 158–60, and Cushing Strout, *The Pragmatic Revolt in American History: Carl Becker and Charles Beard* (New Haven, 1958), pp. 19–20.

to plant the seeds of civilization there, and the pick of the crop to Germany. There in the Black Forest these Aryo-Teutonic peoples developed the democratic institutions that were to be shared by Germany, Great Britain, and the United States.[7] The duty of the "Teutonist" historians was to link every American institution with its "germ" in medieval Germany.

The temple of the Teutonist cult was Johns Hopkins University and its high priest Turner's mentor there, Herbert Baxter Adams. His contribution was to link select New England town meetings with the tribal councils of primitive Germanic tribes. In those councils Teutons brandished spears to show assent or muttered their dissent; this was proof that they practiced democracy. Town meetings in New England also operated democratically. Therefore the town was a "survival" of the tribal council, the flowering of a germ that had lain fallow in Anglo-Saxon blood for a thousand years.[8] So wrote Adams in his monograph on the *Germanic Origins of New England Towns*. He also believed that the ancient Teutons had evolved in their *moots* "the seeds of parliamentary or self-government, of Commons and Congresses," the concept of a single head of state, the use of a small council, and the lodging of ultimate authority in "a general assembly of the whole people." In these practices "lay the germs of religious reformation and popular revolutions, the ideas which have formed Germany and Holland, England and New England, the *United States*."[9] "It is," declared Adams, "just as improbable that free local institutions should spring up without a germ along American shores as that English wheat should have grown there without planting."[10]

So long as such weird delusions governed American historians there was

7. Edward N. Saveth, "Historical Understanding in Democratic America," in Edward N. Saveth, ed., *Understanding the American Past* (Boston, 1965), pp. 12–13; Edward N. Saveth, "A Science of American History," in A. S. Eisenstadt, ed., *The Craft of American History* (New York, 1966), I, 120–22.
8. Herbert B. Adams, "The Germanic Origins of New England Towns," *Johns Hopkins University Studies in Historical and Political Science*, I (Baltimore, 1888), 23.
9. *Ibid.*, pp. 5–38. An excellent discussion of Adams' views is in Thomas F. Gossett, *Race: The History of an Idea in America* (Dallas, 1963), pp. 1–7, 108.
10. Adams, "Germanic Origins of New England Towns," *loc. cit.*, I, 1. Adams made no attempt to link American institutions with those of England, tracing them directly to medieval Germany. He believed that Anglo-Saxons were only one branch of the Teutonic race, and that both English and American institutions could be traced to their fountainhead in the Black Forest. Herbert B. Adams, "Saxon Tithingmen in America," *Johns Hopkins University Studies in Historical and Political Science*, I (Baltimore, 1883), 10–11. The persistence of the "germ" theory in later historical writings is traced in Gilman M. Ostrander, "Turner and the Germ Theory," *Agricultural History*, XXXII (October, 1958), 258–61.

no place for Turner and his doctrines. Fortunately those delusions were short-lived; by the time he was ready to advance his thesis they were already under attack. The excesses of the "Teutonists" proved their undoing, for monographs on the relationship between Saxon tithingmen and New England constables, the Teutonic basis for life in Salem, and the survival of the *folkmoot* in the form of a Kentucky Chautauqua, could not long be taken seriously. Edward Channing led the assault in 1891 with a small book on the *Genesis of the Massachusetts Town*. "Analogies," Channing pointed out, differed from "identities"; as well argue that New England towns evolved from Massai villages in Africa as from Teutonic *tuns* in Germany because both were surrounded by defensive walls.[11] Charles M. Andrews, Turner's fellow-student at Johns Hopkins, followed with an essay on "Some Recent Aspects of Institutional History" in the *Yale Review* in 1893. Neither man nor his institutions had evolved in the exact duplicate of their ancestral models, Andrews argued, for both exhibited local and ethnic divergences traceable to ethnological characteristics, climate, geographic forces, and economic pressures. Usually the differences between political and social behavior were more marked than similarities.[12] Channing and Andrews might attack from different directions, but they agreed that "comparisons" did not establish a direct evolution of traits or institutions from earlier forms. Their commonsense message made a deep impression. A whole new generation of younger historians was ready to reject the "Teutonic School" and return to a rational methodology.

Others among the young rebels of the profession were at the same time taking a fresh look at the content of history. The interest of the "Teutonists" in institutional continuity directed their attention solely to political forms; their dictum was that of Edward A. Freeman that "History is past politics and politics present history." This was an unacceptable definition for Turner's generation; all about them was evidence that man's conduct was shaped more by factories, labor unions, city bosses, and commercial enterprise than

11. Edward Channing, "Genesis of the Massachusetts Town," and "The Development of Town-Meeting Government," *Proceedings of the Massachusetts Historical Society*, 2nd Ser., VII (1891–1892), 388–89.
12. Charles M. Andrews, "Some Recent Aspects of Institutional History," *Yale Review*, I (February, 1893), 381–410. Andrews' views are expertly analysed in A. S. Eisenstadt, *Charles McLean Andrews* (New York, 1956), pp. 12–25, 37–60, 79–105. Andrews' rebellion against Adams' "germ" theory elevated him to the leadership of a new school of "Imperial Historians" who rewrote the history of colonial America. This is described in Higham, *History*, pp. 162–70.

by government. What was more logical than to ask whether these forces shaped human destiny in the past? The first man to do so was an Englishman, James E. T. Rogers, whose little book, published in 1889, on *The Economic Interpretation of History* argued that the past became real only if scholars investigated economic as well as political behavior. Two years later a second Englishman, J. Horace Round, advanced another step with a direct frontal attack on Freeman and his dictum. In two widely-read articles Round not only demonstrated that human behavior was far more complex than politics showed, but that Freeman was guilty of many factual errors in defending his position.[13] Turner was aware of these developments; he quoted approvingly Rogers' plea for an economic interpretation in his essay on "The Significance of History," and included an obvious travesty of Freeman's dictum by declaring that history was past literature, past politics, past religion, past economics.[14]

In taking this stand, Turner was moving with the tides, not against them. Everywhere younger historians were broadening their vistas as the complexities of the age heightened their distrust of simplistic explanations of the past. This Turner recognized; "the shift," he wrote later, "was part of the same general movement that is reflected in European history." [15] All about him were signs that this was true. In 1890 Alfred T. Mahan published his important *Influence of Sea Power Upon History, 1660–1783,* demonstrating that naval forces had altered the course of history and probably would do so again. The first volume of John Bach McMaster's *A History of the People of the United States* appeared in 1883, three years after John Richard Green completed his four-volume *Short History of the English People.* McMaster's work was poorly digested and awkwardly presented but it did range widely over aspects of the past neglected by Freeman and his political school.[16] Mahan, McMaster, and Green were unimportant in themselves, but they were significant as pioneers along a new frontier of historiography. Others were ready to follow, for the whole oncoming generation of historians

13. Robert E. Lerner, "Turner and the Revolt Against E. A. Freeman," *Arizona and the West,* V (Summer, 1963), 101–08. Round's essays were: "The Introduction of Knight Service into England," *English Historical Review,* VI (July, 1891), 417–43, and later numbers, and "Professor Freeman," *Quarterly Review,* CLXXV (July, 1892), 1–37.
14. Turner, "The Significance of History," in Frederick J. Turner, *The Early Writings of Frederick Jackson Turner* (Madison, 1938), p. 52.
15. Turner to Merle Curti, January 5, 1931. HEH TU Box 45. This letter is reproduced below, pp. 282–85.
16. Eric Goldman, *John Bach McMaster* (Philedlphia, 1943), holds this view.

recognized the errors of its teachers. "Our history is not in Congress alone," declared a Bureau of Education circular in 1887; "that is, indeed, a very small part of it. Our discoveries, our inventions, our agrarian interests, our settlements westward, our educational affairs, the work of the church, the organization of charities, the growth of corporations, the conflict of races and for races, at times in our history, are all sources for research." [17] Here was voiced a truth that the "Teutonists" never accepted, that behind political institutions lay not only race and continuity but the social and economic forces that altered man's behavior. A new era of historical investigation was beginning. Charles Francis Adams recognized the extent of the change when he noted that the "old history" was dying and that younger scholars could handle the "new history" better than he.[18]

These emerging views were ideally tuned to Turner's needs, for they coincided with his own interest in searching out the underlying forces that shaped the American past. One additional change in the intellectual climate was needed, however, to accelerate that quest: the assertion of midwestern independence from eastern domination. This would not come easily to a region that traditionally accepted the cultural supremacy of the seaboard and especially of New England. Nor was change possible until the people discovered a common identity and purpose by developing their own self-consciousness. Turner reached that point during his year at Johns Hopkins University when he staged a one-man revolt against eastern historians who ignored his section, but he needed reinforcements before he gained the self-confidence necessary to proclaim his freedom publicly.

He found them in the upsurge of regional expression that occurred just as his frontier thesis was being formulated. During the early 1890s mid-western scholars and writers, no less than midwestern business leaders, gained sufficient self-assurance to escape the shadow of the East and pro-claim pride in their own section. This cultural rebellion took many forms, but the revolt of Hamlin Garland was typical. A native of Wisconsin, a writer of vast reputation, and a loyal midwesterner, Garland was still so blinded by the glamor of New England that he moved to Boston as soon as circumstances allowed. There the smug rejection of all things western

17. F. N. Thorpe, "The Study of History in American Colleges and Universities," Bureau of Education, *Circular of Information*, No. 2 (Washington, 1887), 252.
18. This was the theme of Charles Francis Adams' presidential address before the Massachusetts Historical Society in April, 1899. *Proceedings of the Massachusetts Historical Society*, 2nd Ser., XIII (Boston, 1900), 81–119.

stirred his regional loyalty and led to a reaction not unlike that experienced by Turner in Baltimore. His *Crumbling Idols*, published just a year after Turner voiced his credo, argued that the West's slavish imitation of all things eastern deadened the emergence of a truly American culture. So long as westerners imitated easterners, and so long as easterners imitated British models, an "indigenous and democratic" native literature could not come of age. Garland urged his fellow writers to cease worshiping the crumbling idols of the past, to create rather than imitate, and to use the wealth of literary materials made available by the mingling of peoples in the Midwest. Only then would they express the "vivid and fearless and original utterances of the coming American democracy." [19] The emerging western nationalism that inspired Garland's message encouraged midwestern historians, Turner among them, to speak out against New England traditionalism in historiography.

Here he played a leading role, for there were few foundations on which to build. Western historical writing until his time had blended romance and antiquarianism to the virtual exclusion of sound exposition; the climax of its achievement was the plodding work on *The Old Northwest* by B. A. Hinsdale that appeared in 1891.[20] Now it must be recast to become a part of the national story, revealing the West's role as an integrated and essential ingredient in the emergence of the United States to greatness. This Turner was to do, but he did so only because his section was ready for a scholar to fulfill its emerging need for historical recognition. When he wrote, as he did a few years later, that "it is necessary to recognize that there is a New England vastly more extensive than that within her sectional borders, a New England that is part of an expanding nation," he was responding to an impulse that was part of the intellectual climate beyond the Appalachians.[21]

19. Garland's reaction is described in Richard Hofstadter, *The Progressive Historians. Turner, Beard, Parrington* (New York, 1968), pp. 49–50.
20. Turner's copy of B. A. Hinsdale, *The Old Northwest* (2 vols., New York, 1891), signed and dated 1892, heavily underlined and annotated, is in the Huntington Library, Accession No. 200222. Turner was apparently most interested in the post-Revolutionary period when the western political system was taking shape. He also owned and used Hinsdale's "The Right of Discovery," a reprint from the *Ohio Archaeological and Historical Quarterly*, II (December, 1888). This also is in the Huntington Library, Accession No. 246485. In it Hinsdale described the treatment of Indians by various European nationalities. Turner probably used it in preparing his colonization lectures.
21. This statement appeared in one of Turner's promotional pamphlets in behalf of the Harvard Commission on Western History. It is quoted in M. A. DeWolfe Howe, "Memoir of Frederick Jackson Turner," *Publications of the Colonial Society of Massachusetts, 1930–1933*, XXVIII (Boston, 1935), 493.

He was able to do so because he matured in a state where the historical library contained the finest collection of documents ever assembled for the study of the Midwest. If he had not, another scholar would have done so. This Turner recognized. "The ideas underlying my "Significance of the Frontier"; he wrote some time later, "would have been expressed in some form or other in any case. They were part of the growing American consciousness of itself." [22] His thesis, based on solid research among the documents assembled by Lyman C. Draper, responded to the emotional needs of his section by using the frontier to bring into coherent relationship the West and the nation.[23]

Changing historical currents gave Turner the background and incentive needed to develop his hypothesis, but more was necessary. He realized this as he read widely while preparing his lectures on "The History of Colonization." Visitors from abroad, he saw, recognized that easterners and westerners behaved in different ways and were developing differing institutions. Many were inclined to isolate traits they found along the frontier, and to label them as peculiarly "American." Turner realized that these characteristics resulted from the unique social conditions in forming communities on the hither edge of the wilderness, but a basic question must be answered before such an explanation could be sustained. *How* did life on the frontier change pioneers and their institutions? His fellow historians had no answers, for this was not the type of question with which they grappled. To find an explanation he must seek the help of practitioners of another discipline.

Turner was broadly enough educated to realize that help must come from the geographers. Since the fifth century before Christ when Hippocrates penned his work *On Airs, Waters and Places* scholars had believed that natural conditions altered human behavior. The physical environment was a molding force that shaped men and their institutions as they adjusted to the differing conditions provided by variations of climate, soils, and topography. This venerable theory, glorified now as environmental or geographic determinism, was gaining new importance as Turner grew to maturity. Darwin's evolutionary hypothesis was responsible. As biologists

22. Turner to William E. Dodd, October 7, 1919. HEH TU Box 29. This letter is reproduced below, pp. 187–98.
23. These points are discussed in Harry R. Stevens, "Cross Section and the Frontier," *South Atlantic Quarterly*, LII (July, 1953), 446–51, and Roy F. Nichols, *The Present State of Research on the American Frontier Problem* (London, 1959), pp. 62–63.

sought to account for the wide variety of species resulting from the evolutionary process, they found an answer in the differing physical environments that had molded life forms during the span of geological time. This was Darwin's own explanation, and a universal chorus of natural scientists sustained him. By the 1880s scientific opinion solidly supported the view that alterations in animal organisms as they evolved were the result of changing physical conditions.[24]

If the Darwinians accepted the principle of environmental determinism, this was only final proof that man as the supreme product of the evolutionary process was equally susceptible to geographic forces. To Turner this meant that the pioneers were altered by the unique physical and social conditions of frontier life. Proof was needed, however, and none were better equipped to offer this than the geographers. They were just emerging into respectability in the academic world of the United States, forming their own associations, defining the boundaries of their discipline, and finding posts in a dozen universities before the close of the century.[25] What was more natural than that Turner should turn to the literature of this subject to discover how frontiering altered the American character?

There he found proof in abundance, for geographers at this time stood in a solid phalanx behind the theory of environmental determinism. This was a universally accepted belief. France's outstanding student of the subject, Edmond Demoulin, after studying the great migrations of mankind, concluded that both the people and their institutions had been molded by the routes they followed and the natural conditions in their new homes. "Society," he pronounced, "is fashioned by the environment." [26] German geographic circles were dominated by the views of Friedrich Ratzel, whose system of "Anthropo-Geographie" was set forth in two fat volumes published in 1882 and 1891. Man, Ratzel believed, was governed by the physical forces surrounding him, and succeeded only to the extent that he adjusted himself to his environment. Differences in the modern world's populations

---

24. A brief discussion of the history of environmentalism is in O. H. K. Spate, "Environmentalism," *International Encyclopedia of the Social Sciences* (New York, 1968), V, 93–97, and a longer account in the essay by G. Tatham, "Environmentalism and Possibilism," in Griffith Taylor, ed., *Geography in the Twentieth Century* (London, 1951), pp. 128–47. Darwin's views on the impact of the environment are summarized in Henry F. Osborn, "The Present Problem of Heredity," *Atlantic Monthly*, LXVII (March, 1891), 356.
25. G. Tatham, "Geography in the Nineteenth Century," in Taylor, ed., *Geography in the Twentieth Century*, pp. 67–68.
26. Tatham, "Environmentalism and Possibilism," in *ibid.,* p. 129.

were the outcome of early migrations into a mosaic of regions, each isolated from the others by seas, rivers, or mountains, and each following a separate pattern of development dictated by physical conditions.[27] Ratzel was no environmental determinist; he recognized that human initiative was capable of transcending physical forces and that a "cultural diffusion" occurred as commerce and trade merged peoples of differing backgrounds.[28] But if Turner had read his books he would have found ample evidence that the environment did change those who came under its influence.

In the United States Ratzel's views were forcibly expressed by Nathaniel S. Shaler in a chapter on "The Physiography of North America" contributed to Justin Winsor's *Narrative and Critical History of America* and more fully in his own *Nature and Man in America* (1891). Shaler blended belief in environmental determinism with faith in Anglo-Saxon supremacy; the more favorable the physical conditions the higher the civilization. Europe's most stimulating environment was in Germany, which produced "the dominant people of the world" in the Anglo-Saxons. The United States offered a less favored climate for genius, but it did produce high moral and intellectual qualities "secured through the geographic variations which have been slowly developed through the geological ages." [29] Shaler's contribution was not only to popularize Ratzel's theories, but to identify the specific features of the American landscape—the coastal plains, Appalachian mountain system, interior river network, and arid western plains—that "explained" the nation's history.

His views, and those of Ratzel, were more widely spread by another geographer, Ellen Churchill Semple, whose beliefs were widely known long before 1903 when she published her *American History and Its Geographic Conditions*. Following Shaler's pioneering work, Miss Semple made a minute examination of the continent to show how each feature affected migration patterns and the subsequent social and economic development of

27. Friedrich Ratzel, *Anthropogeographie* (2 vols., Stuttgart, 1882–1891). Ratzel's influence on geographic thought is summarized in the excellent article by William Coleman on which I have leaned heavily in this discussion of the scientific atmosphere, "Science and Symbol in the Turner Frontier Hypothesis," *American Historical Review*, LXXII (October, 1966), 36–38, and in Tatham, "Geography in the Nineteenth Century," in Taylor, ed., *Geography in the Twentieth Century*, pp. 63–64; Thomas W. Freeman, *A Hundred Years of Geography* (Chicago, 1962), pp. 74–82, 174–75; and Gordon R. Lewthwaite, "Environmentalism and Determinism: A Search for Clarification," *Annals of the Association of American Geographers*, LVI (March, 1966), 10–11.
28. Lewthwaite, "Environmentalism and Determinism," *loc. cit.*, 9.
29. Nathaniel S. Shaler, *Nature and Man in America* (New York, 1891), p. 283.

communities. "If the tree planted by the fathers of the Republic has lifted its head high and spread its branches far," she wrote, "due must be given to the great, generous land which has nourished it and the seas which have watered its wide-running roots." [30] No nonsense here about European "germs"; Americans were a product of the land, and of the land only. Her principles were stated even more emphatically in 1911 when she re-stated and explained Ratzel's theories in her *Influences of Geographic Environment*. "Man," she made clear in her first sentence, "is a product of the earth's surface. The earth has mothered him, fed him, set him tasks, directed his thoughts, confronted him with difficulties that have strengthened his body and sharpened his wits." [31] Environment set the physical conditions that determined man's ability to survive, his racial and temperamental differences, the social and economic forces that governed his living patterns, and the topographical features that decided the direction of his migrations. [32] Miss Semple found a place for hereditary factors in her equation, but only a minor one; geography was determinative, operating persistently and relentlessly. Great men did not make their countries; their countries made great men. [33]

These were the evangelists, and their teaching was heard in every corner of the academic world. Under their influence geographic journals displaced their traditional narratives of explorers with articles glorifying environmentalism and illustrating its effect on man's history. "That man," declared one in 1889, "has been influenced in his development by his physical, climatic and social surroundings is well nigh indisputable." [34] Textbooks mirrored these

30. Ellen C. Semple, *American History and Its Geographic Conditions* (Boston, 1903), p. 435.
31. Ellen C. Semple, *Influences of Geographic Environment, on the Basis of Ratzel's System of Anthropogeography* (New York, 1911), p. 1. The origins of this book are described, and Miss Semple's influence analysed in J. K. Wright, "Miss Semple's 'Influences of Geographic Environment,' Notes toward a Bibliography," *Geographic Review*, LII (July, 1962), 346–61.
32. Semple, *Influences of Geographic Environment*, pp. 33–39.
33. *Ibid.*, pp. 2, 42. Miss Semple's acceptance of geographic determinism was duplicated in Albert P. Brigham, *Geographic Influences in American History* (Boston, 1903), and Harlan H. Barrows, *Lectures on the Historical Geography of the United States as Given in 1933* (Chicago, 1962). Barrows offered a pioneering course on "The Influence of Geography on American History" at the University of Chicago, beginning in 1904. His influence is described in H. Roy Merrens, "Historical Geography and Early American History," *William and Mary Quarterly*, XXII (October, 1965), 530–38.
34. Roland B. Nixon, "Notes on Anthropology," *Bulletin of the American Geographical Society*, XXXI (1889), No. 1, 60.

views. James D. Dana, revising his well-known *Manual of Geology*, ascribed the emergence of "superior races" to "favoring conditions in environment."[35] Newer books were even more emphatic. One declared its central purpose "to show how largely the progress of history, sites of settlement, natural products of rock, soil and water, lines of travel and boundary, were dependent upon geographical environment."[36] Another made its theme "Man in his relations to his physical environment"; still another taught that "the origin of temperament, diversity, genius, is hidden in the deeper science of Geography"; a third asserted that physical conditions "determined the pursuits, character, and total life of the people."[37] These were strong statements, and revealed the excessive degree with which geographers embraced environmental determinism.

With their fraternity standing shoulder-to-shoulder behind that theory, historians soon fell into line. The conversion of Lord Bryce was typical. By 1886 when he addressed the Royal Geographical Society he believed that man "was the creature of his environment" with his actions and ideals "largely determined and influenced by the environment of nature."[38] Men could occasionally alter the physical conditions in which they lived, but they were too puny to withstand nature's basic forces. Lord Bryce saw these operating in three ways: the configurations of the earth's surface shaped the character of nations and the course of commerce, the climate determined racial traits, and natural resources decreed the form of economic enterprise.[39] Nor were these idle phrases used to please the geographers to whom he spoke. When Lord Bryce revised his *American Commonwealth* in 1893 he added a chapter on the influence of environments on American history. "The variety of her resources," he wrote, "differing in different

35. James A. Dana, *Manual of Geology* (4th edn., New York, 1896), p. 1034.
36. Advance notice of W. M. Davis, *Physical Geography*, in *Bulletin of the American Geographical Society*, XXX (1888), No. 2, 167.
37. Redway and Hinman, *Advanced Geography*, and Trotter, *Lessons in Geography*. These textbooks, and many others, are described in an unpublished doctoral dissertation at Columbia University, 1967, by Henry M. Littlefield, "Textbooks, Determinism and Turner: The Westward Movement in Secondary School History and Geography Textbooks, 1830–1960." Dr. Littlefield has kindly provided me with a copy of his thesis and allowed me to quote from it.
38. James Bryce, "The Relations of History and Geography," *Contemporary Review*, XLIX (March, 1886), 426.
39. *Ibid.*, 427–29. Most of Bryce's address was devoted to an analysis of the principal nations of the world to show how internal and external developments were largely determined by geographic forces. *Ibid.*, 429–43.

regions, prescribes the kind of industry for which each spot is fitted." [40]

Not all historians in England or America followed Lord Bryce into the camp of the environmentalists; a few during the 1890s clung to the "germ" theory of the "Teutonic School" and a few more were too aware of the complexity of human motivation to label any one factor as determinative. Yet even the doubters gave credence to the physical environment as a molding force. "I would not say," declared Justin Winsor in his volume on *The Mississippi Basin* in 1895, "that there are no other compelling influences, but no other control is so steady." [41] So intimately did Winsor relate history to geographic forces that one reviewer accused him of creating the new science of "Histiogeography," and elevating it to the point where it could be used to predict the future. [42] This was no tongue-in-cheek observation, yet it seemed not at all absurd to historians of that generation. An International Congress of Geographers meeting in Chicago in 1893 devoted no less than five papers to geographic influences on history, [43] while a manual on *How to Study and Teach History* published that year concluded that physical conditions created civilizations, directed their development, and caused their downfall. [44] Scholars in the 1890s, whatever their discipline, accepted geographic determinism as an undisputable fact. No wonder that historians, casting about for a unifying theme based on scientific evidence, found it an admirable framework on which to build. [45]

That Turner embraced the doctrine as an explanation of the frontier's molding influence is not surprising under these circumstances. Just how far he went toward an extreme environmentalist position we can never know, nor can we identify the geographers who influenced his thinking on the subject. He apparently did not discover Ratzel until long after his hypothesis was formulated; his first contact came in 1895 or early 1896 when he

40. James Bryce, *The American Commonwealth* (3rd edn., 2 vols., New York, 1893–1895), II, p. 450.
41. From dedication to the president of the Royal Geographical Society, in Justin Winsor, *The Mississippi Basin* (Boston, 1895).
42. Review of Winsor, *The Mississippi Basin*, in *The Nation*, LXI (July 25, 1895), 67.
43. William Z. Ripley, "Geography as a Social Study," *Political Science Quarterly*, X (December, 1895), 536–55.
44. B. A. Hinsdale, *How to Study and Teach History* (New York, 1894), pp. 110–26.
45. Ripley, "Geography as a Social Study," *loc. cit.*, p. 639. For a discussion of the use of these theories by historians see Spate, "Environmentalism," *International Encyclopedia of the Social Sciences*, V, 94–96, Tatham, "Environmentalism and Possibilism," in Taylor, ed., *Geography in the Twentieth Century*, pp. 148–59, and Lewthwaite, "Environmentalism and Determinism," *loc. cit.*, pp. 1–23.

read an 1893 edition of the German's *Anthropogeographie*.[46] Turner was especially delighted with a chapter on "Space as a Factor in the United States," and reported to the American Historical Association in 1896 that Ratzel's conception might hold the key to the enigma of American development.[47] A few years later he hailed the geographer as "the forerunner in the path that American historians must follow who view their problems as those arising from the study of the evolution of society in the American environment." [48]

Evidence is also lacking to show Turner's familiarity with Shaler's views, although he almost certainly knew of the chapter on "The Physiography of North America" in the *Narrative and Critical History of America*, a work that he consulted frequently. He may also have known of Ellen Churchill Semple's theories; he later lauded her concern for the "physiographic basis of American development." [49]

Just what Turner read on geographic determinism, if he read at all on the subject before 1893, is unimportant; the ideas of Ratzel and Shaler and Lord Bryce were part of the intellectual atmosphere of that day and were inescapable. At a time when geographers were united in the belief that the physical environment influenced behavioral patterns and other social scientists accepted their judgment unquestioningly, no young scholar of Turner's perception could fail to know the way the wind blew. One of his closest friends on the University of Wisconsin faculty was Charles R. Van Hise, a pioneer in teaching structural and metamorphic geology, whose undergraduate course in 1892 explained "the geography of the continents; the effects of land relief, water areas and rivers upon the distribution of peoples." [50] Surely the two men talked of matters of such consuming interest to both of them during the hours they spent together. Almost certainly they discussed the degree of environmental influence on society as

46. Turner apparently owned no book by Ratzel; at least he gave none to the Huntington Library. He did have a copy of that author's pamphlet, *Die Lage im Mittelpunkt des Geographischen Unterrichts* (Berlin, 1900), which is in HEH TU File Drawer L4, Folder: Ratzel Die Lage. That Turner used this is doubtful; it is not underlined as were most of the things he read.
47. Turner, "The West as a Field for Historical Study," *Annual Report of the American Historical Association for 1896* (Washington, 1897), I, 283–84.
48. Turner, "Geographical Interpretations of American History," *The Journal of Geography*, IV (January, 1905), 34.
49. *Ibid.*, 37.
50. *Catalogue of the University of Wisconsin for 1892–1893* (Madison, 1893), p. 79.

they returned together from Chicago in 1893 after attending an International Conference on Geographical Sciences as official delegates of the University and listening to their former president T. C. Chamberlin urge teachers of history and geography to stress physical forces as basic in explaining the past.[51] Turner was surely aware that those best equipped to know—the geographers and geologists—stood as one in their belief that man's character and behavior were shaped by the natural conditions under which he lived.

Given this intellectual climate, the wonder is not that Turner believed environment to be a basic molding force, but that he did not succumb more completely to that doctrine. Neither at the time he prepared his 1893 essay nor afterwards was he a geographic determinist; time and time again he stated this explicitly. His faith was in multiple causation; no one influence— not even powerful nature—shaped human behavior. Turner saw the frontier not as coercive but as emancipating, freeing pioneers from the compulsions of tradition and allowing them to experiment with practices and institutions better suited to their needs. Such societies evolved under the influence of a number of forces, one the external environment, another the "germ" representing the hereditary factor; Turner wrote often of the contributions made by the "stock" to pioneer communities. This was a pragmatic conception of social evolution, based on the sound principle that societies were formed both by the resources available and the capacity of the people to utilize those resources. He was, this early, moving toward the explanations that were later to be given philosophical expression by John Dewey and practical example by Charles A. Beard and Carl Becker.[52] Yet Turner was human, and could not reject totally the universal belief that physical environments altered mankind. When he wrote that the unique physiographic conditions on successive frontiers created new behavioral patterns and institutional expression for the pioneers he expressed the belief of virtually every reputable scientist of his day.

Turner must borrow yet another concept from the sciences before he

51. T. C. Chamberlin, "The Relationship of Geology to Physiography in Our Educational System," *National Geographic Magazine*, V (January, 1894), 158. This subject is discussed in Coleman, "Science and Symbol in the Turner Frontier Hypothesis," *loc. cit.*, pp. 28–29, and Maurice M. Vance, *Charles Richard Van Hise: Scientific Progressive* (Madison, 1960), pp. 61–62.
52. The relationship between Turner and the rising school of pragmatism is discussed in Randall and Haines, "Controlling Assumptions in the Practice of American Historians," *Theory and Practice in Historical Study*, pp. 46–47.

could postulate his frontier hypothesis. This required two assumptions. One—that pioneers and their institutions were altered as they moved westward—he adopted from geographers who assured him that traits and behavioral patterns responded to changes in the physical environment. The other—that characteristics and practices acquired in this way were passed on to subsequent generations—he learned from biologists. Practitioners of this discipline were less certain that acquired traits were inheritable than geographers were of environmental controls; one group of traditionalists held to this belief while another took sharp issue with them. The latter group was eventually to prevail, but this was by no means certain in the 1890s. Turner had reputable scientific backing when he argued that traits acquired on the frontier were passed on to influence the American character down to the present day. He had, moreover, every opportunity to learn of this doctrine, for the battle between biologists over its validity attracted the scholarly world's attention just as he was formulating his thesis.

The conflict stemmed from the evolutionary hypothesis of Charles Darwin, just as did so many of the controversies that stimulated the physical and social sciences in the late nineteenth century. His findings, and those of the French zoologist Jean Baptiste de Money, Chevalier de Lamarck, supported the beliefs of the great body of traditional biologists that acquired characteristics were inherited. Lamarck rested his theory on the belief that animals had evolved over the course of centuries by adapting to changing physical environments. Thus the giraffe descended from a primitive antelope who browsed on leaves; as it stretched its neck, legs, and tongue to reach them, these parts were slightly elongated. These extended organs were passed on to the next generation, which stretched them still more. So the process went on until the giraffe emerged.[53] Lamarck's theories were substantiated by the observations of Charles Darwin. Darwin counted fourteen varieties of finches on the island of Galapagos, 650 miles from the Ecuador coast, and asked himself why such a large number. Surely no rational God would squander His creative powers so extravagantly. Darwin reasoned that each new species developed in response to changing food supplies; those finches able to eat larger seeds than the others, or tougher seeds, or insects, multiplied, while those not able to adapt were held in check by starvation. They, in turn, passed on their abilities to subsequent

53. Isaac Azimov, *A Short History of Biology* (Garden City, New York, 1964), pp. 40–41.

103

generations until a new species had evolved. By this process of "natural selection" life on the earth had branched into an infinite variety of forms.[54]

Scientists soon exposed a basic weakness in these theories. The earth, all agreed, had sustained life for only a few tens of millions of years; physicists knew nothing of nuclear fission and could not imagine chemical reactions that would generate the sun's heat for a longer period. This was too short a time to account for the slow evolutionary changes postulated by Lamarck and Darwin. Two questions must be answered: *how* did variations in species occur if not by the slow process of natural selection, and *why* did those variations take place? These were the basic problems facing the natural sciences in the late nineteenth century.

What seemed to be a logical answer to both was advanced by a Dutch botanist, Hugo de Vries, in the early 1890s. His experiments with fifty thousand primrose plants proved that new types suddenly appeared from older types; a standard primrose would produce a dwarf primrose as its offspring, and the dwarf primroses would breed true to produce only dwarf primroses. Obviously an existing species was able to produce a different species capable of maintaining itself and passing on its unique characteristics. This process de Vries called "mutation." [55] Scientists had no idea why these occurred, but they could now explain why countless varieties had emerged in the short life span of the earth. They also had additional proof that characteristics acquired through mutation were passed on to subsequent generations.

These comfortable conclusions were challenged just at this time by a German biologist, August Weismann of Freiburg. His experimental techniques were hardly sophisticated—he cut off the tails of white mice for a hundred generations with no effect on their offspring—but his conclusions rocked the scientific world. Acquired characteristics (in this case short tails on white mice) were not inherited. Instead determinants for all traits were present in every organism's germ plasm, the essential germinal element in germ cells. These were the sole transmitters of the heritage of the past. They were immune to any environmental forces then known; all traits were immutable and were passed on from one generation to the next without

54. *Ibid.*, pp. 60–65.
55. Bernard Jaffe, *Men of Science in America* (New York, 1944), pp. 386–88; Garland E. Allen, "Hugo de Vries and the Reception of the 'Mutation Theory'," *Journal of the History of Biology*, II (Spring, 1969), 55–65.

being altered by the environment.[56] Weismann's theory, announced in 1883, spread rapidly, and within a decade was commonly accepted by younger biologists in Europe and America. These "New Darwinians" as they called themselves, went beyond their master in denying environmental influences. All traits in every organism, they held, were biologically inherited at the time of conception. No characteristics could be acquired thereafter, through the influence of external forces or any other. Because traits could not be acquired, the inheritance of acquired traits was obviously impossible.[57]

This exaggerated statement was a red flag to traditionalists among natural scientists, and they over reacted in predictable fashion. If the "New Darwinians" held to the uninheritability of acquired characteristics, the "Neo-Lamarckians" (as they called themselves) would go to the other extreme and show that *all* traits were acquired and passed on to later generations. New species emerged in the evolutionary process, they argued, not by the slow steps envisaged by Darwin, but through a series of "leaps" forward. These "leaps" were the result of environmental pressures. Through them organisms acquired traits particularly useful to survival; they in turn speeded the growth of that organism and its ability to acquire other useable traits. As it passed on to its progeny the more advanced characteristics it had assumed, the whole course of evolution was speeded. This "acceleration," the "Neo-Lamarckians" believed, was matched by a comparable process of "retardation" in the growth of organisms that had acquired degrading characteristics. This would explain how so many species had evolved in the earth's short life span.[58]

These theories aligned the "Neo-Lamarckians" solidly behind the belief in the inheritance of acquired characteristics. Environment changed organisms, and these changes were passed on to progeny. This view they held to be "incontestable." [59] Wrote one in 1891: "If there is any principle in in-

56. Charles Singer, *A History of Biology to About the Year 1900* (London, 1959), pp. 553–57.
57. Hamilton Cravens, "American Scientists and the Hereditary-Environment Controversy, 1883–1940," pp. 9–13. This is an unpublished doctoral dissertation, University of Iowa, 1969. A copy was loaned me by the author, with the cooperation of the director of the thesis, Professor Stow Persons.
58. *Ibid.*, pp. 9–13; Edward J. Pfeifer, "The Genesis of American Neo-Lamarckism," *Isis*, LVI (Summer, 1965), 156–61.
59. Conway Zirkle, "The Early History of the Idea of the Inheritance of Acquired Characters and of Pangenesis," *Transactions of the American Philosophical Society*, N.S., XXXV (1946), Pt. II, 91–115. An excellent discussion of the subject is in George W. Stocking, Jr., "Lamarckianism in American Social Science: 1800–1915," *Journal of the History of Ideas*, XXIII (April–June, 1962), 239–41.

heritance which has appeared self-evident and not requiring any demonstration at all, it is that acquired characteristics *are* inherited." [60] A survey made at the time showed that nine of every ten scientists in Europe and America held to this belief.[61] To most this was the keystone of their entire theory concerning evolution. If ever a scientific principle was widely accepted, on the basis of sound scientific support, it was that organisms responded to environmental pressures and that the traits thus acquired were bequeathed to subsequent generations. This was the state of scientific knowledge when Turner was preparing his 1893 essay.

Social scientists stood as solidly as physical behind this belief. The pioneer in its application to human behavior was the English social philosopher, Herbert Spencer, whose voluminous writings were as well known in America as in his homeland. Spencer held that all traits were the product of differing environments, just as were physical peculiarities, and that they were passed from generation to generation, magnifying with each transmission. In this way national characteristics evolved; the people of some nations were nomadic, some sedentary, some warlike, some peaceful, some energetic, some slothful. His views were echoed in the United States by such respected figures as John Wesley Powell, director of the United States Geological Survey, and Lester Frank Ward, a pioneer sociologist. Both defended the inheritance of acquired characteristics in sociobiological terms, although assigning more influence to environmental forces than Spencer. They, and nearly all of their fellow social scientists, agreed that the "transmission of culture" through inheritance was a key factor in the formation of social organisms no less than physical.[62]

These Darwinian concepts were used to explain racial differences that seemed so important in that day of "Anglo-Saxon supremacy." These were laid to varying susceptibilities for "adaptation"; peoples able to "adapt" to one environment better than others acquired characteristics that were accentuated as they were bequeathed to later generations. Scholars of that generation spoke learnedly of the "French race" or the "English race," and agreed with the president of the American Association for the Advancement of Science when in 1895 he explained all racial differences as due to the

60. Henry F. Osborn, "The Present Problem of Heredity," *Atlantic Monthly*, LXVII (March, 1891), 354.
61. Henry F. Osborn, "Are Acquired Variations Inherited?" *American Naturalist*, XXV (March, 1891), 191–97, 215–16.
62. Stocking, "Lamarckianism in American Social Science," *loc. cit.*, 242–43.

"selection and survival of the best adapted."[63] This process of racial formation, one sociologist declared, went on "through the influence of the *milieu* and the diffusion of a common fund of beliefs, sentiments, ideas, and interests among a heterogeneous population brought by hap and chance into the same geographical zone."[64] Turner could not have defined the frontier process more exactly, although he would have used less cumbersome language. Little wonder that he believed a new "American race" was forming in the West, endowed with traits shaped by the unique environment, and capable of passing those traits on to their progeny and their progeny's progeny down to the present. Unimpeachable scientific evidence supported him.

Nor can his awareness of the latest trends in the biological sciences be doubted. His interest in natural science dated back to his undergraduate days when he elected courses in zoology, botany, physics, and chemistry. As a graduate student he listened to a series of lectures by his friend Charles Homer Haskins on physical geography that reflected the latest theories in that discipline.[65] During the months that he was formulating his thesis he was in daily contact with his friend and neighbor, Charles R. Van Hise, who kept abreast of the controversies that spread among geologists and biologists in the wake of Darwin's evolutionary hypothesis, and certainly talked them over with his colleague. As a member of the Wisconsin Academy of Sciences, Arts, and Letters Turner heard numerous papers by Van Hise and his fellow geologist, T. C. Chamberlin, all couched in environmental terms. There, too, he listened to the biologist E. A. Birge explain "Weissman's [*sic*] Theory of Heredity" in 1892.[66] He was certainly aware of the conflict between the "New Darwinians" and the "Neo-Lamarckians," for this raged in English journals in the early 1890s and spilled over into many American magazines that he regularly read. His own language suggests the extent of his borrowing from the scientists; Turner phrased his theories in evolutionary terms, and crowded his essays with biological metaphors such as "organism," "plastic," and "adaptation."[67]

63. *Ibid.*, 244–45, 248–49.
64. W. I. Thomas, "The Scope of Folk Psychology," *American Journal of Sociology*, I (January, 1895), 439.
65. Charles H. Haskins, "Lectures to Undergraduate Students on Physical Geography," *Johns Hopkins University Circulars*, VIII (1889), 28.
66. *Transactions of the Wisconsin Academy of Sciences, Arts, and Letters*, IX (Madison, 1893), viii. Turner joined the academy in 1887 when still a graduate student, and appeared frequently on its programs during the next years.
67. Coleman, "Science and Symbol in the Turner Frontier Hypothesis," *loc. cit.*, 24–25, 28–31.

This accounted for much of their appeal to his generation, its ears tuned to the Darwinian usages current in that day of conflict over evolution. When Turner wrote that the history of American institutions was not that of borrowing or imitation but "the history of the evolution and adaptation of organs in response to a changing environment" he spoke in a language the people could understand, as well as aligning himself with the "Neo-Lamarckians" and against the "New Darwinians" and their "germ-cell" concepts. He saw the constant evolution of social organisms as the key to continuity in history. He echoed the "recapitulation" theory of the biologists—that developing animal embryos "recapitulated" the stages through which the whole race ascended the evolutionary scale—when he described the growth of frontier communities through well-defined stages from hunting to industry.[68] These concepts and the words that clothed them meant more in the 1890s than they do today.

We know now that Turner erred in his application of some scientific beliefs, and that others he used were false. By 1910 biologists had proved that acquired characteristics were not inherited, and not long thereafter geographers and geologists concluded that the physical environment had less to do with altering physical and social organisms than other forces. These later findings should not cloud the fact that when Turner stated his thesis, he had sound scientific backing for two of the foundation stones on which it rested. He was fortunate to live at a time when geography and biology provided substance and understanding for his theories, and when historians were ready to receive them.

If Turner depended on these disciplines to provide a theoretical basis for his frontier hypothesis, he leaned on still another for the evidence on which it rested. This was the emerging field of statistical cartography. Without the efforts of a generation of statisticians and map makers who by the 1890s were able to depict the nation's expansion in graphic form, he probably would not have arrived at his thesis and certainly would not have visualized the frontier's advance exactly as he did. As it was, his familiarity with atlases, statistical tables, census bulletins, and the highly sophisticated maps that cartographers were producing at that time allowed him to picture that advance so accurately that his hypothesis followed naturally.

The father of the techniques that meant so much to Turner was a Prus-

68. *Ibid.,* 35–37.

sian cartographer, August Meitzen, who in 1871 published a monumental atlas that included twenty colored plates, one picturing population density by shades of coloration. Copies were sent to the Library of Congress prior to publication, and were probably seen by Francis A. Walker, superintendent of the 1870 census.[69] Walker realized their importance, and ordered the inclusion of maps and charts in the volumes being compiled. The result was the important *Statistics of the Population of the United States*, a fat work that bulged not only with tables and statistical graphs, but that included twelve maps showing the distribution of illiteracy, wealth, immigrants, and—most important—the density of population in six degrees of gradation. The techniques employed were primitive, but the basis had been laid and only refinement was needed to add the touches that would allow Turner to visualize the frontier's advance.[70]

This began with the publication in 1874 of *The Statistical Atlas of the United States Based on the Results of the Ninth Census, 1870*, an imposing volume edited by Walker. This work, which was pivotal in stimulating Turner's interest in the West, contained two features particularly useful to him. One was a series of maps showing population density for each decade from 1790 to 1870, shaded to indicate five degrees of concentration ranging from two to six per square mile at the edge of settlement to ninety or more in the thickly populated East.[71] These were effectively done, allowing a viewer to picture the flow of settlers westward, decade by decade. "The movement of population seems to take place under our very eyes," wrote one reviewer; "and it is a curious and instructive study to note in detail the progress of the human tide in its westward flow over the land from the Atlantic seaboard."[72] This was a fair judgment. The westward movement

69. Fulmer Mood, "The Rise of Official Statistical Cartography in Austria, Prussia, and the United States," *Agricultural History*, XX (October, 1946), 209–25. This is an excellent article from which I have borrowed frequently in the passages that follow. Fulmer Mood has also studied the rise of statistical techniques in Britain as they influenced map making in "A British Statistician of 1854 Analyzes the Westward Movement in the United States," *Agricultural History*, XIX (July, 1945), 142–51.

70. United States Census Office, 9th Census, 1870, *The Statistics of the Population of the United States* (Washington, 1872). This and other works on cartography and statistics that influenced Turner, are listed and described in Fulmer Mood, "The Concept of the Frontier, 1871–1898; Comments on a Select List of Source Documents," *Agricultural History*, XIX (January, 1945), 24–30.

71. The five density groupings used were: I 2–6 inhabitants to the square mile, II 6–18, III 18–45, IV 45–90, and V 90 or more. Francis A. Walker, *Statistical Atlas of the United States Based on the Results of the Ninth Census, 1870* (n.p., 1874), Pt. II, 4.

72. *The International Review*, II (January, 1873), 133.

was re-created; isolated communities were shown forming in the West, tiny at first, then expanding until they joined with the main body of population, at the same time darkening in color to indicate the increasing density. Turner could not escape their meaning as he turned the book's pages in the library of the State Historical Society. "Walker puts body of continuous settlement thus," he jotted on a small piece of paper as he read, "1790—83° W. Long[itude]. 1810—83°30'; 1830—95°; 1850—99°; 1870—95°45'.[73] He was picturing the westward movement in his own mind, ebbing at times, but steadily advancing.

A second feature of the 1874 atlas that impressed Turner was an essay on "The Progress of the Nation, 1790–1870" written by Walker.[74] Passages dealing with what Walker called "the line of continuous settlement" or "the frontier line," caught his eye especially. There he read that pioneers on the outer edge of settlement reverted to cattle-raising and other occupations suited to a sparsely settled region, that those just to their east practiced a primitive form of farming, that in the third zone where population ranged from 18 to 45 to the square mile agriculture was more technologically advanced. The final two divisions, with 45 or more inhabitants to the mile, Walker pictured as industrialized and urbanized, with professional and personal services available.[75] Walker's analysis was oversimplified and faulty in detail, but he used the term "frontier line" for the first time to designate the outer edge of settlement and he underlined the sequential evolution of western communities as they rose from primitivism to civilization.[76]

Whatever Turner learned from this essay was enlarged by his study of two others from Walker's pen, both published in the middle 1870s.[77] In them appeared language as well as concepts which suggested the metaphors that would reappear in the 1893 article. Walker described the flow of population

73. This notation on a 3 x 5 slip of paper, is in HEH TU 3 x 5 File Drawer No. 1, Section: Frontier. In his notebook, "American History I," probably used in 1887–1888 when he was teaching the basic American history course, Turner listed the books he asked his students to consult. One such notation read: "Walker's Atlas of US for maps showing facts as to nationality of population etc. of later history." HEH TU Vol. XIV (1). American History I.
74. Walker, *Statistical Atlas of the United States Based on the Results of the Ninth Census*, Pt. II, 1–4.
75. *Ibid.*, 3–4.
76. *Ibid.*, 2, used the phrases "line of continuous settlement" and "frontier line" interchangeably.
77. Francis A. Walker, "Growth and Distribution of Population," *Harper's Monthly*, LI (August, 1875), 391–414, and "Growth and Distribution of Population," in *The First Century of the Republic: A Review of American Progress* (New York, 1876), pp. 211–37.

through the passes of the Appalachian Mountains and across the central lowlands as resembling the overflow of a lake into a nearby level basin. The stream followed each depression, then spread across the lowlands, leaving small pools between the hills that it passed. With a second flooding higher areas were inundated and the pools widened; with a third still more of the high country was covered, and the ponds expanded into a great lake. By this time, even before the basin was filled, an overflow was seeking channels into the next lowland to the west, where the process would be repeated.[78] This went on over and over again as the center of population shifted steadily westward. "Even while we write," Walker went on, "it is pressing on with an equitable motion of seventy or seventy-five feet a day in a direction generally west, but also slightly north." [79] He noted that the advance followed latitudinal lines, with New Yorkers moving into Michigan and Wisconsin, Pennsylvanians into Ohio, and Carolinians into Alabama and Mississippi.[80] This was a bit of information that Turner was to use often.

The 1880 census, also directed by Francis A. Walker, produced a series of publications, each exhibiting improved techniques as cartographers evolved skills in graphic presentation. A special bulletin on "The Settled Area in 1880," unsigned but probably by Walker, first caught Turner's eye. Its population maps, now extending to 1880, were particularly impressive, for the westward movement was at its height during the 1870s and the contrast between the settled areas of 1870 and 1880 particularly striking.[81] Turner saw next the bulky official report of 1883, splendidly adorned with colored maps, and including an essay on "The Progress of the Nation" which for the first time called attention to the dwindling supply of free land.[82] Even more useful to him was an article by Henry Gannett, a geographer employed by the census bureau, published in the *International Review*. "An arbitrary line," Gannett suggested, "must be drawn somewhere beyond which the country must be considered as unsettled, although it may not be absolutely without inhabitants. Such a line may be properly taken so as to exclude

78. Walker, "Growth and Distribution of Population," *Ibid.* 394, 405–06.
79. Walker, "Growth and Distribution of Population," in *The First Century of the Republic*, p. 211.
80. *Ibid.*, p. 236.
81. United States Census Office, 10th Census, 1880, "The Settled Area in 1880," *Census Bulletin No. 269* (Washington, October 21, 1881), 1–5.
82. United States Census Office, 10th Census, 1880, *Statistics of the Population of the United States at the Tenth Census (June 1, 1880)* (Washington, 1883), Pt. I. The essay on "Progress of the Nation, 1790–1880" is on xi–xxxiii.

regions having less than two inhabitants to the square mile. All the country outside this line may be considered as unsettled territory, peopled, if at all, by a few scattered hunters, prospectors and cattle herders." [83] Here was a definition tailored to Turner's purposes; he could now think of a "frontier line" that had an exact meaning.

Each of these publications added a tidbit to Turner's knowledge, but none to the degree of *Scribner's Statistical Atlas of the United States*, prepared by Gannett and Fletcher W. Hewes, and issued in 1885.[84] From the time he encountered this thick volume it was his frequent companion, shaping his thinking as had the similar *Statistical Atlas of the United States* published in 1874. He urged it on his students, used it as his own reference work, parroted it in his writings, and almost certainly consulted it while preparing his 1893 essay for descriptions of each frontier line that he pictured.[85] This was understandable, for *Scribner's Atlas* admirably achieved its purpose—to present graphically all important statistical information on the physical, social, industrial, commercial, and political conditions of the United States.[86] Turner found within its covers excellent maps that vividly pictured the physical features of the continent, the advance of settlement, the coming and distribution of immigrants, the character and racial composition of the population, and the economic and political activities of the people. They spoke loudly to the young historian. Here are the United States in 1880, they said; now tell us why we are as we are.[87]

Turner's answer—his frontier thesis—took shape as he turned from the maps to the essays in the 1885 atlas. One on the progress of the nation was

83. Henry Gannett, "The Settled Area and the Density of Our Population," *International Review*, XII (January, 1882), 70–77. The lines quoted are on 70.
84. Fletcher W. Hewes and Henry Gannett, *Scribner's Statistical Atlas of the United States Showing by Graphic Methods Their Present Condition and Their Political, Social and Industrial Development* (New York, 1883). The volume was published by Charles Scribner's Sons because the publications fund of the census bureau was exhausted. It did not appear until 1885, although copyrighted in 1884. Accession records at the library of the State Historical Society of Wisconsin show that each census publication was purchased soon after publication, this one in 1887. Turner's notebook, "American History I," which he probably used in 1887–1888, lists among the books assigned his students "Scribner's Statistical Atlas." HEH TU Vol. XIV (1) American History I.
85. Fulmer Mood, "The Development of Frederick Jackson Turner as a Historical Thinker," *Transactions of the Colonial Society of Massachusetts, 1937–1942*, XXXIV (Boston, 1943), contains a detailed comparison of Turner's essay with the *Scribner's Statistical Atlas* and concludes that the latter was open on Turner's desk as he did his writing.
86. Hewes and Gannett, *Scribner's Statistical Atlas*, p. vii.
87. Mood, "Development of Frederick Jackson Turner," *loc. cit.*, 307–12 stresses the impact of the atlas on Turner, but does not mention the many other volumes in various fields that also influenced his views.

similar to those he had used in past census bulletins, but written with greater sophistication; here he read of the "westward movement" and of the "frontier line." [88] Another, probably prepared by Gannett, enlarged on the sequential nature of the westward movement. The Northeastern states were pictured as dominated by industrial and commercial enterprises needed to support their dense populations, the South Atlantic and South Central as in a state of transition from agriculture to industry, and the North Central between Ohio and the "frontier line of settlements" as harboring every type of farm settlement "from the very densely populated agricultural community to those which, in consequence of the excess of land at their disposal, raise from the soil far more than they themselves require for subsistence." [89] Here again was evidence that each frontier evolved from a primitive to a developed economy as its population increased and communications were established with the East. Turner's concept of economic growth, appearing often in his writings, probably owed something to Gannett's essay.[90]

This concept was sharpened when he turned to a pamphlet published by the census bureau in 1890 on *Population of the United States by States and Territories* as the first product of the enumeration of that year. "In the settlement of any new country," he read, "the industries commonly follow each other in a certain order." Hunters, trappers, and prospectors usually came first, then herdsmen, then agriculturists, then manufacturers, and finally, with the thickening of population, city dwellers. "We see in this country," the pamphlet stated, "all stages of this progress." [91] Here, clearly stated, was the "stages of civilization" progression that Turner had learned from Richard T. Ely at Johns Hopkins, applied now to the American frontier. This concept was so often reiterated, and so consistently accepted as unquestionable, that he must be pardoned for accepting it completely and

88. Hewes and Gannett, *Scribner's Statistical Atlas*, pp. xxxviii–xl. This is the usual essay on "The Progress of the Nation."

89. *Ibid*, p. xliv.

90. Turner may also have read at this time Townsend MacCoun, *An Historical Geography of the United States* (New York, 1889), a book favorably reviewed by Professor W. F. Allen in *The Nation*, XIL (July 25, 1889), 72. Turner bought a copy, probably in 1889, which is now in the State Historical Society of Wisconsin library. MacCoun used the "drainage basin" concept to divide the country into three parts, the Atlantic slope with its rivers and harbors "opening toward Europe, shut off from the rest of the continent by the Appalachian range," the Pacific slope, and the Great Interior Plain where a network of river systems "invited the coming of the nations." MacCoun, *Historical Geography*, pp. 3–4. Turner underlined these sections, as well as those dealing with expansion into Kentucky, Tennessee, and the Old Northwest.

91. United States Census Office, "Population of the United States by States and Territories, 1890," *Census Bulletin No. 12* (Washington, 1890), 5.

incorporating it in his writings. Not until he had spent much of a lifetime studying American history did he realize that the pattern was too orderly to reflect the complexity of the migration process.

Familiar as he was with the census bureau publications, Turner could hardly have realized that the story they told was to reach its climax in an unimpressive pamphlet that he read sometime between October, 1892, and the spring of 1893.[92] Four pages long, unattractively printed, and bearing a title designed to repel all but enthusiasts for statistics—*Extra Census Bulletin No. 2. The Increase and Decrease of Population, 1880–1890*—its most striking feature was a colored map showing the population of the United States in 1890 in six degrees of density, the first graphic presentation of the findings of the latest census. Turner may well have studied this first, marveling at the rapidity of expansion during the decade and the decrease in the extent of arable lands still open to occupation. If so, he may have wondered how long the westward movement would continue. As he reached the last page of the brief text he found an answer, for there he read the words that his essay was to make famous: "Up to and including 1890 the country had a frontier of settlement, but at present the unsettled area has been so broken into by isolated bodies of settlement that there can hardly be said to be a frontier line."[93]

92. This bulletin was published in April, 1891, and presumably reached the State Historical Society library not long thereafter. Apparently Turner did not read it at that time, however, for in his essay on "Problems in American History," published in *The Aegis* on November 4, 1892, and presumably prepared only a month or two before that date, he wonders what the "new frontier line" of the 1890 census will show. He also spent several days with Woodrow Wilson in December, 1892, and possibly read him a preliminary draft of the 1893 essay at that time. This meeting will be discussed in detail below, pp. 157–61. On the basis of their talk, and his reading of the article in *The Aegis*, Wilson prepared a review of "Mr. Goldwin Smith's 'Views' on Our Political History," *The Forum*, XVI (December, 1893), 495–97, which made much of the frontier in American history but did not mention its closing. On the basis of this evidence, Lee Benson, "The Historian as Mythmaker: Turner and the Closed Frontier," in David M. Ellis, ed., *The Frontier in American Development. Essays in Honor of Paul Wallace Gates* (Ithaca, 1969), pp. 8–15, concludes that Turner did not learn of the statement in the census bulletin until he read an article by Henry Gannett, "The Movements of our Population," *National Geographic Magazine*, V (March 20, 1893), 21–44, sometime in the spring of 1893. This was based on the 1890 census, and referred specifically to the closing of the frontier on p. 26. Benson points out that Charles R. Van Hise was a member of the society, and might have supplied Turner with a copy. Against this must be balanced the fact that by January, 1891, when Turner prepared his talk on colonization for the Madison Literary Club, his hypothesis was largely formulated, even to the extent of using terms that were to appear in his 1893 essay. For a discussion of this whole matter, see below pp. 156–61.
93. United States Census Office, Eleventh Census, 1890, *Extra Census Bulletin No. 2. Distribution of Population According to Density, 1890* (Washington, 1891), 4.

We can only speculate on Turner's thoughts as he read those lines. We know what he did; he wrote his name on the first page, labeled the pamphlet "Density," underlined a few passages—but not, strangely enough, the sentence he was to quote later—and filed it away among his notes.[94] As he did so, did all that he had learned from prior census bulletins suddenly appear in a new light? Did he hunt up the population maps for the years between 1790 and 1890 and realize that together they told the dramatic story of the peopling of the continent, a story now at an end? Did he recognize the ever-darkening areas as population thickened decade after decade as symbolic representations of the transition of a succession of communities from primitivism to civilization and realize that they duplicated in capsule form the whole history of man's progress? We can never know the answers to these questions.

Nor can we know whether the first feeling of disappointment that he felt at the passing of one era of America's past was displaced by elation as he sensed that here was a vast new field for historical investigation. The westward movement was now history, and could be subjected to sociological analysis to reveal its significance. This was an exciting prospect. He had learned from his study of census maps that pastoral pursuits sufficed for thinly settled areas, and the complexity and interdependence of economic activities intensified as population increased. He had learned from Richard T. Ely and others that social progress could be defined in terms of the degree of division of labor in any community. In Europe this evolved over the course of centuries, with each stage in the advance building on the progress of its predecessor. In the United States, on the other hand, the process was constantly taking place simultaneously in dozens of frontier settlements. Geographic, not chronological, time tables determined its rate; all stages of civilization existed side-by-side, following a set course as they emerged in the wake of the moving frontier. The United States was a laboratory where social processes could be studied firsthand. Here was a unique opportunity for the investigator, and here was the true significance of the frontier. When

94. Turner's copy of this bulletin is in HEH TU Black Box No. 9 (160–168), Item 164. With it Turner filed pp. xviii–xxxiv clipped from the United States Census Office, 11th Census, 1890, *Report on Population of the United States at the Eleventh Census, 1890* (Washington, 1895), Part I. This was the usual essay on "The Progress of the Nation," and described settlement during the decade. In it the sentence on the closing of the frontier was repeated from Bulletin No. 2. Turner has underlined the sentence in this copy; the rest of the essay is unmarked save for one line on p. xix where he underlined the words: "At this date settlements are almost entirely agricultural." HEH TU Black Box No. 9 (160–168), Item 163.

Turner wrote, as he did in 1893, that the nation "lies like a huge page in the history of society" he was revealing a basic truth taught him by the census data. He revealed it more exactly when he went on to say that "line by line as we read this continental page from West to East we find the record of social evolution." [95]

Before he could realize the true significance of his findings, Turner had to divorce himself from the census bureau's definition of the frontier as a "line" or narrow band where population varied from two to six persons to the square mile. To have a sociological impact it must be conceived as a broad zone in which the stages of society's evolution were observable, hunters and fur traders at the outer edge, herdsmen and small farmers and equipped farmers and primitive industrialists and town planters following. What happened to men and institutions within this belt? Were they altered by the unique environment? Were their habits and ideas different from those of the settled East where men lived shoulder to shoulder? These were exciting topics for investigation; they promised not only to shed light on the American past but to serve as case studies of the evolution of mankind. When Turner suggested, as he did in his 1892 paper on "Problems in American History," that here was "a life work, a work demanding the cooperative study of many students for generations," he was simply inviting the scholarly world to share in his discovery. [96] When he laid his thesis before that world, as he did a year later, he was doing little more than suggesting guidelines for the investigators and indicating the riches they would find. Turner's hypothesis, viewed in this light, was an invitation to historical adventurers, not a pronouncement of unchangeable truth, as some of his disciples believed.

Turner certainly had his frontier thesis well in mind by the time he read the 1890 census reports, but it was in skeleton form and would mean little until flesh could be added. He knew that men moved westward along predictable lines and that their western communities capsuled the history of civilization. But what was the significance of their migration in the total story of the nation's evolution? To answer that question he must determine whether the distinctive environments of the successive Wests altered the

95. Turner, "The Significance of the Frontier in American History," in Turner, *The Frontier in American History* (New York, 1920), p. 11. An excellent discussion of this aspect of Turner's thought is in Rudolf Freund, "Turner's Theory of Social Evolution," *Agricultural History*, XIX (April, 1945), 79–84.
96. Turner, "Problems in American History," in Turner, *The Early Writings of Frederick Jackson Turner*, p. 74.

character and institutions of the settlers. He would have to explore the effect of frontier abundance on the national economy and of frontier psychology on politics, and investigate the degree of change as institutions adjusted to an area with a low man-land ratio. Turner must, in other words, add meat to the bones of his theory before he could demonstrate that the westward movement was significant in the national sense that he used the word. He must turn investigator himself before he could tempt others into investigations.

CHAPTER VI *Reading and Speculating 1892–1893*

To flesh out the skeleton of the frontier theory that had formed in Frederick Jackson Turner's mind during 1891 and 1892 was no task to be undertaken lightly. Western historical writing was in its swaddling clothes; books about the West were almost nonexistent, and the few that were available were either romantic distortions of the truth or so packed with antiquarian details as to repel the serious scholar. To find out about life on the frontier and test his belief that it differed from life in the East he must read travel accounts, reminiscences of pioneers, guide books, diaries, newspapers, magazines—every fugitive scrap of writing where frontiersmen might reveal the alterations that occurred when they fled the settlements. He studied law books and compilations of statutes to probe the effect of the new environment on legal and governmental institutions. He mastered economic theory as a tool for interpreting statistics he might encounter on western trade and agriculture. Then, if this were not enough, he must immerse himself in political economy, historical philosophy, and political theory so that he could translate his scattered information into a logical pattern.

Time for such an ambitious reading program as this was lacking in the busy schedule of a college professor, but fortunately Turner had an incentive that transcended idle curiosity. In the autumn of 1892, just as his interest in the frontier was stimulated by the need to prepare his essay on "Problems in American History," he added a new course to his battery of offerings, and one dear to his heart. "The Economic and Social History of the United States," he called it; the advanced students who elected it would study "the origin and development of the social and economic characteristics of the country" from colonial times to the present. They would also investigate "the process of American settlement across the continent" paying particular attention to the relationship between its course and the physiography of the nation.[1] A year later expansion was even more stressed.

1. *Catalogue of the University of Wisconsin, 1891–1892* (Madison, 1892), p. 98.

119

"Particular attention," read the catalog, "will be paid to the spread of settlement across the continent and to the economic and social causes of sectional and national sentiment."[2] With these announcements, Turner was venturing into a totally unexplored field. His course was the first in the world to deal with the advance of the frontier; he had no textbooks, no outlines, no convenient bibliographies, to guide him. Now he had not only the need but the excuse to do the reading that would underlie his hypothesis. "It will be followed with great interest," reported the undergraduate newspaper.[3]

Neither Turner's notes nor those of his students have survived to tell us how much of his course was alloted to the study of expansion, but given his interests it probably received its fair share of attention. Certainly it attracted student attention, even to the point of inspiring what passed for jokes in those days in the college magazine:

"Turner: How did they formerly get from the Atlantic Coast to the interior?

"Miss Steenberg: By passes."[4]

More reliable evidence of the direction of his thinking was provided by Turner himself in a few notes on how to structure the course. One was typical: "Soc & ec U.S. Divide up into a series of *studies*. *Land*. History of land tenure. Am. problems. Comparative & historical study. *Agriculture*. Agrar. politik. Movement of population. Study historically."[5] The West, and the problems stemming from its occupation, were clearly to receive major attention in his new offering.

He could solve them only by haunting the State Historical Society library that 1892–1893 academic year. To retrace his steps as he read book after book, document after document, is to follow the trail that led him to his frontier hypothesis. Fortunately we can do so for he was in the habit of jotting notes on pages of the 3 x 5 pad that was always with him, then filing them in one of his numerous cases under "Social and Economic History." Most were fragmentary, and many have little meaning for today, but others provide clues to his interests and ideas. Some listed the books that he read or intended to read, others the thoughts that flashed through his mind when

2. *Catalogue of the University of Wisconsin, 1892–1893* (Madison, 1893), p. 61.
3. *The Aegis*, March 13, 1891.
4. *The Badger for 1893* (Madison, 1893), p. 230.
5. A number of these cards, written by Turner as he was preparing his course, are in HEH TU Box 54.

he stumbled on a statement that provoked a response. By following their trail, and by rereading the materials that interested him, we can gain at least a partial understanding of the steps that led him to his thesis.

The random notes recording his speculations on the nature of the frontier process offer particularly significant insights into his thinking. Some Turner jotted down when an idea occurred to him, probably at odd moments when his subconscious mind revealed itself without any particular stimulus. "Frontier," he wrote on one occasion. ". . . Note *war* as a characteristic. Boundary quarrels. Comparative study with e.g. Russian advance." On another, probably made after studying a census population map, he noted that the frontier line sometimes curved to run almost east and west rather than north and south.

The relationship between pioneer settlements and the occupied areas behind him inspired thought and comments. "Compare West to U.S., as New World to Europe," he wrote on one occasion, adding on another that the Atlantic Coast served as a "frontier of Europe" and wondering "was there a frontier to the Pacific States." Turner early recognized the nationalizing influence of expansion. "West," read one of his notes. "Influence on nationality"—then went on to list the Louisiana Purchase, internal improvements, and such western statesmen as Henry Clay as influences in that direction. Again he observed that the West "stands as a nation-making idea continuously—with the Great Lakes at stake there could not be quarrels between the states." [6]

More ideas occurred when a passage in a book he was reading set him to thinking about the influence of the frontier. Thus when studying a 1796 pamphlet advertising properties of the North American Land Company he found a description of frontier types—hunters, herdsmen, hunter-farmers, farmers, town-builders—and immediately picked up his pen. "Note," he wrote, "this process follows the evolution of society and at this date we have among Am[erican]s in diff[erent] localities, types of stages of economic growth." [7] Here was a basic concept in his hypothesis. Again a speech of Henry Clay's inspired: "Comment on it as expressing the growth of de-

6. These notes are in HEH TU 3 x 5 File Drawer 1, Section: Frontier.
7. *Observations on the North-American Land Company, Lately Instituted in Philadelphia* (London, 1796), pp. xv–xvi, 144. Turner's note is in HEH TU 3 x 5 File Drawer 1, Section: Frontier.

mocracy. Influence of West." [8] A sentence in James Schouler's *History of the United States* describing the liberalization of franchise laws between 1818 and 1821 brought from Turner: "Examine in newly adm[itted] states." [9] When he read in Goldwin Smith's *The United States* that American mechanics showed unusual ingenuity during the Civil War out came his 3 x 5 pad and down went the statement: "G. Smith says Am[erica] the 'most mechanical of nations.' Why? Frontier experiences!" [10] A passage in William Findley's *History of the Insurrections in the Four Western Counties of Pennsylvania* describing the journeys eastward made by frontiersmen to buy needed goods was copied onto one of Turner's pads and the comment added: "Westerners go east and so less provincial than easterners." [11]

As Turner read he not only experienced flashes of revelation but encountered ideas and interpretations that were worth preserving. Thus he recorded the words of a western writer in an 1889 issue of the *Unitarian Review:* "It is the singular advantage of a country like ours that we have not to go back in time, or many days journey in space, to come upon the rude beginnings of that social order which today we find so complicated. The beginning, middle, and end of that several thousand years' growth are spread out before us like a map or else foreshortened to our view in the perspective of our chronology." [12] From a learned article by the historian, Herbert L. Osgood, in an 1887 copy of the *Political Science Quarterly* Turner transcribed another suggestive passage: "No conditions are so favorable to the growth of individualism as frontier life. Each individual or family is there brought face to face with savage men and forced to depend

8. *Ibid.,* Charles A. Beard once suggested that Turner borrowed his thesis from Daniel Webster's speeches, pointing out that Webster made much of free land as a shaper of American government and institutions. Charles A. Beard, "The Frontier in American History," *New Republic,* XCVII (February 1, 1939), 361. This was an exaggeration, of course, but Turner was familiar with Webster's views, which probably influenced him. One of his notes in *ibid.* read: "Frontier. 'From the very origin of government these western lands and the just protection of those who had settled or should settle on them had been the leading objects of our policy.' Webster, III, 251."
9. *Ibid.*
10. Goldwin Smith, *The United States: An Outline of Political History, 1492–1871* (New York, 1893), pp. 278–79. Turner's comment is in HEH TU 3 x 5 File Drawer 1, Section: Frontier.
11. Turner's comment on the passage in William Finley, *History of the Insurrections, in the Four Western Counties of Pennsylvania: in the Year M.DCC.XCIV* (Philadelphia, 1796), p. 35, is in *ibid.*
12. "Frontier Conditions," *The Unitarian Review,* XXXII (September, 1889), 251. Turner wrote beside this comment: "cf European study of middle ages." *Ibid.*

on its own resources. Contact with civilized life ceases and union between settlers or communities becomes almost impossible. Society is atomized." [13] The concept of an atomized society, with individualism rampant, was to be basic in Turner's hypothesis.

If Turner's notes point to a few of the scattered sources from which he extracted ideas or information, they also help us learn something about the books he read and what they told him. He provided excellent signposts for those who would follow his trail, listing the volumes that he used, sometimes with page references to paragraphs that he deemed most important. To review some of what he surveyed in 1892–1893 is to realize the extent of his borrowing and the variety of works that he sampled. We can find in them the germs of most of the theories voiced in the 1893 essay—that the frontier was a seedground for nationalism, social and political democracy, individualism, inventiveness, and many of the traits distinguishing Americans from their European ancestors. We can realize that Turner's hypothesis came not in a flash of inspiration but by laboriously welding together masses of obscure demographic and historical data into a thesis that explained a phase of the nation's past. His genius was to see the relationship between the bits of information that he gathered, and to distill from them a meaning unrecognized by former historians. Latter-day critics who insist that the frontier hypothesis was lifted bodily from the works of Daniel Webster, or William Friedrich Hegel, or Lucius Q. C. Lamar, or E. L. Godkin, or Achille Loria (and a plausible case can be made for each) fail to realize that Turner accomplished something that they failed to do.[14] Each saw a segment of the frontier's role; he saw its entirety. This was his contribution. His creativity was the product of hard work, not a heaven-sent revelation.

13. Herbert L. Osgood, "England and the Colonies," *Political Science Quarterly*, II (September, 1887), 440–69. Turner took twelve pages of notes on this article, copying out in full the passage on individualism. He added his own note to the line "Society is atomized": "The West of our day relies on national gov[ernment] because gov[ernment] came before the settler, and gave him land, arranged his transportation, gov[ernment], etc. etc." HEH TU File Drawer E, Folder: Mass. Defense of Its Charter.
14. A case for Lamar has been made in Wirt A. Cate, "Lamar and the Frontier Hypothesis," *Journal of Southern History*, I (November, 1935), 497–501, and in the same author's *Lucius Q. C. Lamar, Secession and Reunion* (Chapel Hill, 1935), p. 458. Lamar's statement, which Cate believes Turner copied, had to do with the influence of the frontier on American nationalism. Joseph Schafer, one of Turner's staunchest defenders, answered this type of suggestion in his "Turner's Early Writings," *Wisconsin Magazine of History*, XXII (December, 1938), 224–25, by quoting Napoleon's aphorism: "The tools belong to him who can use them."

And hard work it was, for Turner's reading was as voluminous as it was varied. One would like to suppose that he went about his task systematically, using first the works of contemporary observers to discover how the West differed from the East, then the books of theorists to find out why. More likely he read haphazardly, mingling contemporary and modern authors, easterners and westerners, Europeans and Americans, travelers and commentators on what they saw. All of this would be sorted in his mind, rearranged in a meaningful pattern, and interpreted in terms of the national experience. We can best appreciate the magnitude of his problem if we recast the evidence that he gathered into the orderly pattern that it assumed in his mind, rather than leave it in the helter-skelter disorder in which it was accumulated.

In developing his hypothesis, Turner had first to show that frontier communities differed from those in the East and describe those differences. To do so he must read as widely as possible in the works of contemporary observers who were familiar with the West and westerners; he found that virtually all agreed that "shades of difference" distinguished East from West, and that these had been created "by causes and circumstances existing in the West." [15] He learned that newcomers to the frontier, even Europeans, were rapidly "Americanized," [16] and that they "developed by degrees a new type of character." [17] He reiterated his realization that expansion went on in well-defined stages, and that these capsulized the progress of civilization. Evidence on this point was more than ample; Turner found examples in such varied works as John H. Logan's *History of the Upper Country of South Carolina* (1859), Robert Baird's *View of the Valley of the Mississippi* (1834), John M. Peck's *A New Guide for Emigrants to the West* (1836), Victor Collot's *A Journey in North America* (1826), Francis Baily's *Journal of a Tour to the Unsettled Parts of North America* (1856), Achille Murat's *A Moral and Political Sketch of the United States of North America* (1833), Timothy Dwight's *Travels in New-England and New-York* (1821), and a half-dozen more. [18] Too many observers agreed that expansion duplicated the evolution of human society for the doctrine to be doubted.

15. Robert Baird, *View of the Valley of the Mississippi, or the Emigrant's and Traveller's Guide to the West* (Philadelphia, 1834), p. 100.
16. John M. Peck, *A New Guide for Emigrants to the West* (Boston, 1836), pp. 102–03.
17. Thomas Wentworth Higginson, *A Larger History of the United States of America to the Close of President Jackson's Administration* (New York, 1886), p. 421.
18. Baird, *View of the Valley of the Mississippi*, pp. 100–01; Francis Baily, *Journal of a Tour*

Turner's stable of contemporary writers also taught him that frontiering accentuated certain traits, and that these became imbedded in the national character. Nationalism was one; westerners, "wholly freed from that local attachment which arises from habit and long residence," looked to the central government for land, protection, and transportation facilities provided in the East by state governments.[19] "The West," wrote an author well known to Turner, "desired to enjoy at once the results which the old states had attained through two centuries of development, and there was no power that could gratify that desire except the general agent of all the states, at Washington."[20] Hence frontiersmen gave their allegiance to the federal authorities, not to their local rulers. This inclination was strengthened by their mobility, for as they shifted about in search of opportunity they lost attachment to any one place. This migratory instinct, Turner read in a traveler's reminiscences, "by continually agitating all classes of society, is constantly throwing a large portion of the whole population on the extreme confines of the state, in order to gain space for its development."[21] Turner's authorities might write in the stilted language of the nineteenth century, but they told him that mobility and nationalism were bred into Americans by frontiering.

Most of the writers that he read also pictured the West as fostering democratic practices. One saw the western states as "each a nursery of

in Unsettled Parts of North America in 1796 & 1797 (London, 1856), pp. 217–19; Victor Collot, *A Journey in North America* (2 vols., Paris, 1826), I, 109–14; John H. Logan, *A History of the Upper Country of South Carolina* (2 vols., Columbia, South Carolina, 1859), I, 149–53; O. Turner, *Pioneer History of the Holland Purchase of Western New York* (Buffalo, 1850), pp. 562–66; Achille Murat, *A Moral and Political Sketch of the United States of North America* (London, 1833), pp. 45–79; Timothy Dwight, *Travels in New-England and New-York* (4 vols., New Haven, 1821), II, 459–60; John M. Peck, *A New Guide for Emigrants to the West* (Boston, 1836), pp. 114–16; Theodore Roosevelt, *The Winning of the West* (4 vols., New York, 1889–1896), III, 208–11; P. P., "Uses and Abuses of Lynch Law," *American Whig Review*, XI (May, 1850), 460; Thomas B. King, "Review of the Report of Hon. Thomas Butler King on California," *American Whig Review*, XI (May, 1850), 446. All of these authors are listed by Turner in a note that he labeled "Western Classes." On it he wrote: "Examine texts to see how far one writer copied from another. Was the division simply traditional, or real, or both?" Under this he added another line: "The advance of the frontier is a sectional phenomenon." HEH TU File Drawer 7, Folder: Western Classes.
19. *Observations on the North-American Land Company*, p. 113.
20. Henry L. Nelson, "The Growth of Federal Power," *Harper's New Monthly Magazine*, LXXXV (July, 1892), 240–50. The quotation is from p. 245. Turner listed this article in his notes under Nelson's middle name, "Loomis."
21. Francis J. Grund, *The Americans, in their Moral, Social, and Political Relations* (Boston, 1837), p. 206.

freedom; every new settlement is already a republic *in embryo*." [22] Another argued that self-rule came naturally to peoples facing problems with which the East was ill equipped to grapple; hence they grew distrustful of absentee rule and set up their own claim associations to distribute land, built their own roads and schools, and punished criminals in their own rough way whenever a crime was committed. [23] Social democracy flourished on western soil no less than political. Class distinctions seemed unrealistic in a land where bountiful opportunity made all potential millionaires. "A pleasing feature of Western life," Turner read in an 1850 issue of *The American Whig Review*, "is the perfect social equality. . . . Strong arms and stout hearts their only wealth; all classes at last salute each other as brothers." [24] Money and lineage were alike unnecessary in a new country; the men respected there were those who could follow a forest trail, shoot unerringly, and fashion their own tools and dwellings. [25] This was true democracy.

Individualism, nationalism, mobility, equalitarianism—these were American traits because they were frontier traits. So a score of authors told Turner as he read his way through that winter of 1892–1893, piling note on note. Now and then he happened on a contemporary observer who played into his hands by pages-long disquisitions on the western character. One that pleased Turner particularly was Robert Baird, whose *View of the Valley of the Mississippi, or the Emigrant's and Traveller's Guide to the West*, published in 1834, cataloged a whole gallery of the traits "which may be said to distinguish the population of the West." These Turner ticked off in his notes: "a spirit of adventurous enterprise," "independence of thought and action," a roughness "which some would deem rudeness of manners." They were

22. *Ibid.*, p. 211.
23. One of Turner's notes read: "Frontier. Clash of newer regular authority with older ir-reg[ular] authority. Sherman's letters of Calif[ornia] Vigilantes. Macy, Institutional Beginnings etc. shows how local associations modified U.S. Laws in practice." HEH TU 3 x 5 Drawer 1, Section: Frontier. His reference was to Jesse Macy, "Institutional Beginnings in a Western State," *Johns Hopkins University Studies in Historical and Political Science*, II, No. 7 (Baltimore, 1884), 367, from which he copied the following on another slip. "The people of Iowa needed homestead laws; they organized claim associations and made for themselves homestead-laws in each neighborhood. They needed schools; they paid no attention to the elaborate system put into their statutes, they built for themselves school-houses and established schools better suited to their needs. They needed cart-roads, made them for themselves, constructed their rude bridges or provided ferries without regard to any general statute. Sometimes, though not often, a crime was committed and the little community administered such punishment as seemed fit."
24. "Western Prairies," *American Whig Review*, XI (May, 1850), 526.
25. P. P., "Uses and Abuses of Lynch Law," *loc. cit.*, 460–61.

products of life in thinly settled communities where men knew nothing of their neighbors' ancestry and lived in log cabins lacking the "external decorations" that symbolized social divisions in the East. "These circumstances," Baird wrote, "have laid the foundation for that equality of intercourse, simplicity of manners, want of deference, want of reserve, great readiness to make acquaintances, freedom of speech, indisposition to brook real or imaginary insults, which one witnesses among the people of the West."[26]

This was an impressive list, and Turner needed sample only a few more authors to make it complete. One gave him an additional clue; life in sparsely occupied areas where division of labor was unknown required each person to supply his own needs, often by improvising, and developed inventive skills unmatched elsewhere.[27] "More new tools, implements, and machines . . . have been invented in this new world," wrote one westerner, "than were ever yet invented in the old."[28] When Turner added inventiveness to his catalog of western traits he could boast an imposing collection: nationalism, individualism, social and political democracy, mobility, independence, rudeness, an adventurous spirit. He had the evidence that he sought to show that West and East differed, and he had in addition the gallery of frontier characteristics that he was to list in his 1893 essay.

A basic question remained to be answered. Turner's contemporary authors told him *how* westerners differed, but not *why*. What generative forces in the frontier atmosphere spawned nationalism, individualism, and democracy? What made the pioneers more mobile or inventive? These problems could be solved only by a sociological examination of the changes wrought in humans by migration and by life in developing areas. This would not be easy; sociology and anthropology were still infant social sciences, unable to supply him with ready-made answers. Instead he must turn to the handful of scholars in Europe and America who had interested themselves in the American frontier and asked themselves some of the same questions that he was trying to answer. Those who had done so offered a strange selection of bed-

26. Baird, *View of the Valley of the Mississippi*, pp. 101–03. Turner made little use of the best of the foreign observers, Alexis de Tocqueville. That this was not surprising is shown in Lynn L. Marshall and Seymour Drescher, "American Historians and Tocqueville's Democracy," *Journal of American History*, LV (December, 1968), 512–13. The authors demonstrate that Tocqueville was virtually unknown to American historians of that day. Turner first quoted him in 1901 in his essay on "The Middle West," and cited him often thereafter.
27. Peck, *New Guide for Emigrants to the West*, pp. 122–23.
28. *Observations on the North-American Land Company*, pp. viii–ix.

fellows: the French philosopher Emile Boutmy, the American tax-reformer Henry George, the French observer André Churillon, the English sociologist Walter Bagehot, the American geographer Francis A. Walker, and the Italian social scientist Achille Loria. All were read carefully by Turner, and each contributed something to the hypothesis that was forming in his mind.

Three played relatively minor roles. Emile Boutmy, whose *Studies in Constitutional Law. France-England-United States* appeared in English translation in 1891, saw the United States as "a huge commercial company for the discovery, cultivation, and capitalization of its enormous territory."[29] The conquest of its frontier had encouraged a spirit of enterprise and speculation, and altered the legal system to protect those who might over reach themselves in commercial ventures, but its principal importance was to foster democracy. In Europe, where a superabundant population was imprisoned within a narrow space, strict authority was necessary to maintain order but in the United States the use of force was rendered unnecessary "by the ease with which the needy classes could, instead of struggling for their share of the land with people already in possession, expand into those vast tracts of land which were without owners."[30] Universal suffrage originated in the less populous western states which could attract newcomers only by assuring them political freedom, and which lacked the aristocratic establishments which must be overthrown before democratic reforms were possible in older nations. Hence democracy was the "natural and necessary" government for America.[31] It would endure as long as those threatened by oppression could become free owners of the soil by moving a few miles westward. Boutmy provided Turner with a neatly packaged explanation of frontier democracy that he was to appropriate for his own use.

Another French observer, André Churillon, whose "American Life from the French Point of View" appeared in the *Review of Reviews* in the spring of 1892, helped convince Turner that pioneering fostered social democracy as well as political. In Europe, Churillon wrote, a caste-bound social order

29. Emile Boutmy, *Studies in Constitutional Law. France-England-United States* (London, 1891), pp. 127–28. One essay in this book, "The Sources and Spirit of the Constitution of the United States," dealt particularly with the frontier as a force shaping governmental institutions. Turner copied the passage cited for use in one of his essays. His note is in HEH TU File Drawer 15, Folder: Boutmy.
30. *Ibid.*, pp. 125, 128–29.
31. *Ibid.*, pp. 124–26, 131–32.

and a tradition-bound central government prevented men from rising above the level of society into which they were born. They had no choice but to perform the same tasks that had occupied their fathers, and their father's fathers before them. But in the United States where there was no "fixity of professions" every person "is ready for any work that may turn up, and has no hesitation in quitting one job for another—he may be in turn lawyer, farmer, journalist, engineer, and storekeeper." In the West especially there were no traditions to block progress from one level of society to another. There the social structure was fluid, changing rapidly as men rose or fell (but usually rose) according to their own abilities.[32] Churillon's observations, carefully copied or summarized by Turner, added another dimension to his understanding of the frontier's significance.

So did the writings of the American tax reformer, Henry George. This Turner refused to acknowledge; in his later years he insisted that he had not read George's *Progress and Poverty* until well after 1893.[33] Here his memory played him false. He heard George lecture while still a graduate student at Wisconsin and engaged in a lively debate at the Contemporary Club over his proposals for land reform.[34] He purchased a cheap copy of the 1882 edition of *Progress and Poverty* to use in Richard T. Ely's course in political economy at the Johns Hopkins University, and heavily underlined the sections assigned—the first seven chapters.[35] He also studied intensely an eight-page *Syllabus of 'Progress and Poverty'* that Ely recommended, using his pencil freely to indicate important passages and add marginal notes.[36] While at Johns Hopkins the historical seminar staged a

32. André Churillon, "American Life from the French Point of View," *The Review of Reviews*, V (May, 1892), 488.
33. Turner to Merle Curti, January 5, 1931. HEH TU Box 45. This letter is reproduced below, pp. 282–85.
34. Henry George spoke in Madison in the spring of 1887 on "Land and Labor." *Wisconsin State Journal*, March 23, 30, 1887. The Contemporary Club, in which Turner was active, devoted its next meeting to a discussion of his views. Turner participated, although apparently without too much enthusiasm, for he wrote his fiancée that after hearing the land question discussed for an hour, he decided that he would like to own a cabin on the shady part of Lake Mendota's shore. Turner to Caroline Mae Sherwood, May 11, 1887. HEH TU Box A. The Contemporary Club discussion was reported in the *Wisconsin State Journal*, April 28, 1887.
35. Henry George, *Progress and Poverty* (n. p., 1882). The volume is in the Huntington Library, Accession No. 152218. Turner wrote on the cover: "Copyrighted 1879 based on 'Our Land and Labor Policy,' San Francisco, 1871."
36. Louis F. Frost, *A Syllabus of 'Progress and Poverty'*, No. 1 (New York, January 19, 1889). Turner's copy is in HEH TU File Drawer 17D, Folder: Urban Land Values. Single Tax.

spirited discussion of George's social philosophy in which Turner joined.[37] Whatever tricks his memory played on him later, he was thoroughly familiar with the views of the American reformer when he prepared his 1893 essay. In all probability he consulted *Progress and Poverty* while that was being written; one of the several notes he wrote to himself at that time was a reminder to copy a passage from page 349 of his own edition.[38]

This passage, and others that Turner underlined, contained several useful ideas. Henry George was an unbending environmentalist; differences between communities in varying stages of civilization could be traced, he believed, not to innate differences between the individuals composing them but to the environment. "The influence of heredity which it is now the fashion to rate so highly," he wrote, "is as nothing compared with the influences which mold the man after he comes into the world." [39] George's principal importance to Turner, however, was to stress the role of free land as a transforming agent. In the best safety-valve tradition he ascribed to "unfenced land" the nation's "general comfort, the active invention, the power of adaptation and assimilation, the free independent spirit, the energy and hopefulness." The mere realization that unsettled areas lay to the west "permeated our whole national life, giving it generosity and independence, elasticity and ambition." [40] These were sweeping statements, but Henry George's stress on the importance of the public domain was not lost on Turner.

If he gained valuable insights from reading these three authors, he gained far more from another triumvirate: Walter Bagehot, Francis A. Walker, and Achille Loria. Walter Bagehot especially supplied him with ideas and

37. Johns Hopkins University Seminar Minutes, May 17, 1889. For a discussion of this point see Charles A. Barker, *Henry George* (New York, 1955), pp. 657–58.
38. One of Turner's notes read: "Be sure to get this note from George." This was almost certainly written in the fall of 1892, when he was reading the works of Achille Loria for the first time. The note is in HEH TU File Drawer 15A, Folder: Notes on A. Loria. Henry George's biographer, Charles A. Barker, points out that as early as 1868 George wrote in an editorial for a California newspaper: "When we cease to have cheap land we shall realize in full force the social evils which affect Europe." This was the basic concept developed in *Progress and Poverty*, and was to be used often by Turner. Barker points out that it was commonly accepted at that time, and expressed independently by George, Turner, Achille Loria, and many others. Barker, *Henry George*, p. 96. Eric Goldman, *Rendezvous with Destiny* (New York, 1952), p. 71, states unequivocally that *Progress and Poverty* "advanced much the same thesis about the significance of the frontier in much the same words as Frederick Jackson Turner."
39. George, *Progress and Poverty* (1882 edn.), p. 350. This is the note that Turner reminded himself to get from Henry George. See note 38 above.
40. *Ibid.*, pp. 387–88.

phrases that appeared in his 1893 essay. English banker, editor, man of letters, and political theorist, Bagehot wrote voluminously, but the book that helped shape Turner's thought was a fifteen-cent paperback edition of *Physics and Politics*, published in 1880, and probably purchased in 1888 or 1889 at the suggestion of Herbert Baxter Adams or Woodrow Wilson.[41] This volume, battered and badly worn, heavily underlined, and often copied as Turner read it again and again, must be ranked among the few works germinal to his thinking as he prepared his frontier essay.[42]

If we may judge from the marginal comments and extent of underlining, the passages that interested him most dealt with the formation of the American character. This was shaped, Bagehot believed, by the centuries-long struggle against the wilderness, a struggle so intense that it was the dominant concern of the people. Those who led the assault became the folk heroes; hence their ideas and practices were imitated by all. So it was that traits formed in the backwoods and developed by the conquest of the West soon became the nation's traits. "The eager restlessness," he wrote, "the high-strung nervous organization, are useful in continual struggle, and also are promoted by it. These traits seem to be arising in Australia too, and wherever else the British race is placed in like circumstances."[43] When Turner finished underlining that passage he reached for his note pad and recorded an idea that it suggested to him: "West. Infl[uence] on U.S.— Custom. It stood to East as the sea to Phoenicia, to Egypt, to Greece."[44] Here, in very rough form, was the phrase that would be used in both his 1892 and 1893 essays.

The characteristics that Bagehot saw emerging in the United States he ascribed not only to "colonial" conditions, but to the mingling in the West of men from many lands. This tended to create a fluid social order, weakening the pressure of traditionalism and making the national character receptive

41. A biographical sketch of Walter Bagehot by Norman St. John-Stevas is in the first volume of *The Collected Works of Walter Bagehot* (2 vols., Cambridge, [Mass.], 1965). St. John-Stevas has also edited a volume of Bagehot's *Historical Essays* (Garden City, New York, 1965), with a brief historical introduction. That Herbert Baxter Adams relied heavily on Bagehot and recommended him to his students is shown in Adams' introduction to J. R. Johnson, Jr., "Rudimentary Society Among Boys," *Johns Hopkins University Studies in Historical and Political Science*, II, No. 11 (Baltimore, 1884), 8.
42. Walter Bagehot, *Physics and Politics: An Application of the Principles of Natural Selection and Heredity to Political Society* (*Humboldt Library of Popular Science*, New York, 1880). Turner's copy is in the Huntington Library, Accession No. 124219.
43. *Ibid.*, p. 146.
44. HEH TU 3 x 5 File Drawer 1, Section: Frontier.

to change, as did the absence of a hereditary moral code or an established religion. "The old oligarchies," Bagehot wrote, "wanted to keep their type perfect, and for that end they were right not to allow foreigners to touch it." [45] Turner had only to substitute "frontier" for "colonial" to realize that the West fostered new traits through intercultural borrowings, just as it did by succumbing to environmental pressures. He thought that over, then scrawled at the bottom of the page: "Influence of West. It was the attractive force to immigration." [46]

Bagehot also believed that the American character was changing rapidly because its society was young and fluid enough to accommodate itself to major alterations. In the older "arrested civilizations" of Europe, India, China, and Japan customs persisted because they could not be peacefully dislodged. The problem, as he put it, was not to create a new social order, but to escape an old one, not of "cementing a cake of custom, but of breaking the cake of custom." [47] One phrase in that paragraph caught Turner's eye. He heavily underscored "breaking the cake of custom," then expanded on its meaning in a note on one of his 3 x 5 cards: "West. Influence on Am[erica]. Breaker of *custom*. The leavening power in U.S. hist[ory]. Always at the edge of civ[ilization] creating new needs, conditions, opportunities. See its economic power in determining rates of wages e.g. & developing Eastern manuf[actures] by rendering farms less productive." [48] Walter Bagehot had added substance to the theory shaping in his mind.

Still more was provided by Francis A. Walker. Statistician, political economist, prominent educator, and director of the United States census, Walker naturally attracted Turner's attention, even though he himself never grasped the frontier concept. Turner met his works first when at Johns Hopkins where Walker's texts on the theory of land and rent were headlined in Richard T. Ely's courses. From that time on Walker was part of Turner's required reading, but not until he came across a Phi Beta Kappa address on "The Growth of the Nation," delivered at Brown University in 1889, was a new dimension added to Turner's speculations. Somehow he obtained a copy of the Providence newspaper where the address was published in full, clipped it, pasted it on firm paper, added his underscorings

45. Bagehot, *Physics and Politics*, p. 147.
46. *Ibid.*, p. 147.
47. *Ibid.*, p. 150.
48. HEH TU 3 x 5 Drawer 1, Section: Frontier.

and marginal comments, and filed it away in his mind and cases.[49] This probably occurred when he was studying at Johns Hopkins in 1888–1889; a Rhode Island newspaper would be more readily available in Baltimore than Madison.

Walker, as might be expected of a director of the census, made his theme the nation's population growth and expansion—which he explained as due to the superiority of the country's agricultural classes—but his speculations on the probable results of expansion were more to Turner's tastes. Walker saw the "extraordinary progress of the population westward over new lands" as responsible for distinguishing features of the national character. One of these was inventive genius. "Invention is a normal function of the American brain," he wrote, "the American inventing as the Greek chiselled, as the Venetian painted, as the modern Italian sings." Living in a thinly-peopled land with much work to do they must fashion tools and devise techniques for greater efficiency; "to save time, to diminish labor, to cut corners and break down barriers in reaching an object, to force one tool to serve three or four purposes, and to compel refractory or inappropriate material to answer urgent needs; this was the daily occupation of our ancestors." Constant practice in "making do" bred the creative ability that was handed down from generation to generation as an enduring characteristic.

Pioneer conditions also fostered the extreme nationalism that was apparent everywhere in the United States, but especially in the West. "No one can doubt," Walker declared, "that both the increase of our population and its expansion over a continually wider territory, have been the chief causes of the remarkable development among us of that public spirit which we call patriotism." This emerged well after the Revolution, and only when population swept across the Ohio Valley. Not until come-outers from the "Old Thirteen" met and mingled in communities that had no history of their own, where there was no local pride to dim national loyalty, where nothing counteracted the spirit of unity, could the nation supersede the state in commanding the affection of the people. "This it was which made the fire of Americanism that had burned but slowly within the barriers of tradition and prescription, and that sometimes, alas, had but smouldered with a stifling smoke, to blaze forth with intense heat."[50] Turner's explanation of the

49. Francis A. Walker, "The Growth of the Nation," *Providence Journal*, June 19, 1889. Turner's copy is in HEH TU File Drawer 15B, Folder: F. A. Walker, PBK 1889.
50. Turner used a red pencil to mark this passage heavily.

133

influence of the frontier on nationalism was to be couched in fewer clichés and burdened with less extravagant metaphors, but it did little more than repeat what he had learned from Walker.

His debt to the third of the trio from whom he apparently borrowed generously is less easily defined. Achille Loria was one of Italy's most eminent political economists, a prolific writer, and a theorist of major importance. His most influential book, *Analisa della Proprietà Capitalista*, published at Turin in 1889, was more a monument to his industry than his originality, for it fused most of the beliefs then current to explain social evolution. As a rigid economic determinist, Loria saw human behavior governed by the relationship between man and the quantity of "free land" available to him. This determined the "stages" of civilization. To prove his theories, he focused his attention on "colonial" countries, for he shared the belief common among political economists that emerging cultures repeated in proper sequential order the steps by which social organization in older countries had progressed over the centuries. The first volume of his *Analisa* argued this theory; the second sought to demonstrate its truth by an analysis of the development of the United States.

Loria saw industrialism as the final stage of social evolution. This could not be achieved so long as "free land" allowed a laborer to change into a landed proprietor without expending capital. While this condition prevailed, workers would seek property rather than jobs, and neither interest nor profits could exist. The United States offered a splendid example. Loria pictured the first spread of population over "free lands," dispersing widely, and living comfortably with a self-sufficient economy. Eventually, however, repeated cultivation depleted the soil's fertility; this occurred after only a short time in the United States where intensive farming was impossible so long as laborers could move to more "free land" in the West. When this occurred, indentured servants and then slaves were introduced in an effort to offset declining yields. These were temporary expedients, so offensive to the moral sensitivities of the people that they had been discarded. With this step the nation stood on the threshold of its final evolutionary "stage." Agricultural efficiency was possible only by concentrating farm lands into giant estates; as these formed, laborers would be released from the land and could man the factories needed for the industrial era. Loria foresaw for the United States the social evils that were plaguing Europe; he predicted the end of economic freedom and democracy with the passing of "free lands," for now all would be at the mercy of the plutocrats in control of farming and industry. This was hardly a new theory, although Loria went beyond most political economists in linking social evolution to the man-land ratio.[51]

His views made their first impact on American academic thought in 1890. In December of that year a review of the *Analisa* in the *Political Science Quarterly* not only praised the book immoderately but summarized its "free land" thesis fully and accurately.[52] Turner almost certainly read this, for he regularly consulted that journal; if he did so he would have recognized Loria's views as pertinent to his own and be alert for any further publications. He may also have read an article by Loria on "The Landed Theory of Profit" in the *Quarterly Journal of Economics* when it appeared during the fall of 1891. This summarized the Italian's theories, repeating that "so long as there is free land which can be cultivated without capital, profit is impossible," and reiterating that no laborer would work for others when he could own his own farm. "Profit, then," Loria argued, "is only the corollary of the lack of free land, which takes away from the laborer all option and establishes economic servitude."[53] Statements such as these brought home to Turner the significance of "free land" for the nation, no less than for the West.[54]

51. Achille Loria, *Analisa della Proprietà Capitalista* (2 vols., Torino, 1889), is ably summarized in Lee Benson, "Achille Loria's Influence on American Economic Thought: Including His Contributions to the Frontier Hypothesis," *Agricultural History*, XXIV (October, 1950), 182–99.

52. E. Benjamin Andrews, "Review of Analisa della Proprietà Capitalista, by Achille Loria. Torino, 1889, 2 vols.," *Political Science Quarterly*, V (December, 1890), 717–19.

53. Achille Loria, "The Landed Theory of Profit," *Quarterly Journal of Economics*, VI (October, 1891), 109–11. The quotation is from p. 109. Ugo Rabbeno, "The Present Condition of Political Science in Italy," *Political Science Quarterly*, VI (September, 1891), 439–73, described Loria's work briefly, but not in sufficient detail to have influenced Turner. Turner almost certainly saw another article by Loria, "Economics in Italy," *Annals of the American Academy of Political and Social Science*, II (September, 1891), 203–24, for it appeared adjacent to one that he quoted, Francis N. Thorpe, "Recent Constitution-Making in the United States," *ibid.*, 145–201. In this, however, Loria scarcely mentioned his own theories.

54. Interest in Loria continued to mount in the United States. Two more articles analyzing his theories were published in 1892: C. A. Conigliana, "Professor Loria's Theory of Profit," *Quarterly Journal of Economics*, VI (April, 1892), 344–46, and Ugo Rabbeno, "Loria's Landed System of Social Economy," *Political Science Quarterly*, VII (June, 1892), 258–93. Turner may have consulted them, for both appeared before the autumn when he probably first learned of Loria's theory. The *Analisa* was not published in English translation until 1899 when an edition was edited by Lindley M. Keasby, *The Economic Foundations of Society* (New York, 1899). Keasby was the social scientist who most influenced the thought of a later frontier historian, Walter Prescott Webb. Walter P. Webb, "History as High Adventure," in Walter P. Webb, *An Honest Preface and Other Essays* (Boston, 1959), p. 198.

Such a sampling undoubtedly whetted his appetite for more. Yet the book that he needed for further enlightenment, the *Analisa della Proprietà Capitalista*, would hardly have been of the sort purchased by the State Historical Society, nor could he have read it if it had for he was innocent of knowledge of the Italian language.[55] Whence came Turner's knowledge of *Analisa*, and whence the quotation from it that he incorporated in his 1893 essay? Lee A. Benson, who has made a searching investigation of Turner's dependence on Loria, provides us with an ingenious answer.[56] He points out that Richard T. Ely, who joined the University of Wisconsin faculty in the fall of 1892, was thoroughly familiar with the *Analisa;* the first chapters of the revised version of his 1889 *An Introduction to Political Economy*, published in 1893 as *Outlines of Economics*, were virtually rewritten to incorporate Loria's system of land economics. These chapters were prepared for Ely by one of his graduate students, Harry H. Powers, who had studied in Italy after earning his Master of Arts degree in 1888 and was familiar with both Loria's works and the Italian language; Ely acknowledged that Powers' contribution to the volume was so extensive that it should be labeled a "joint product." [57] Turner read these chapters in manuscript at Ely's request, and there found passage after passage that stressed the national importance of land: "free land" rather than protective tariffs were responsible for high wages in the United States; "free land" tempered the impact of the class struggle; when "free land" was exhausted radical changes would alter the nation's economy unless new safeguards were provided by the government.[58] These theories were important to Turner, but they probably failed to satisfy his curiosity. He could not be happy until he had read the *Analisa*.

55. While traveling in Italy in 1900 and 1901 Turner twice wrote his mother that he was struggling unsuccessfully to learn Italian. Turner to Mary H. Turner, November 18, 1900, January 1, 1901. HEH TU Box F.
56. By far the best appraisal of Loria's influence on Turner is in Benson, "Loria's Influence on American Economic Thought," *loc. cit.*, pp. 182–99. Benson advances a highly ingenious and extremely persuasive argument to show that all of Turner's basic ideas were borrowed from Loria. In a later article he even writes of the "Loria-Turner frontier thesis." Lee Benson, "The Historian as Mythmaker: Turner and the Closed Frontier," in David M. Ellis, ed., *The Frontier in American Development. Essays in Honor of Paul Wallace Gates* (Ithaca, 1969), pp. 3–19. Logical as is Benson's argument, it was constructed without consulting Turner's own papers, which were not open to historians when he carried on his research. These indicate a reliance on many other sources of which Benson was unaware.
57. Powers' contribution is described in Richard T. Ely, *Outlines of Economics* (New York, 1893), p. 5.
58. In *ibid.*, p. v, Ely thanks Turner and Charles H. Haskins for reading the "early chapters" of his manuscript and offering valuable suggestions. For a typical example of Loria's influence on Ely see *ibid.*, p. 56.

That he fulfilled that ambition seems certain. In both his 1892 and 1893 essays he used concepts and phrases that too exactly duplicated Loria's to be coincidental. Thus Loria saw colonies as revealing the stages of social evolution to economists as mountains did to geologists; they allowed modern scholars, he wrote, to "read, in the book of the present, pages torn from social history." Turner used the quotation and the "mountain" metaphor in his 1893 essay, with a footnote to the *Analisa*, then paraphrased the next line to read that the United States "lies like a huge page in the history of society." [59] There could be only one explanation for such direct borrowing. Turner had read Loria's volume, either in a translation by Powers, or directly as Powers read aloud, translating as he went. He did so in September or October, 1892, for Ely did not reach Madison until late summer with Powers in attendance, while Turner's essay on "Problems in American History," which showed familiarity with Loria's theories, was published in *The Aegis* on November 4, 1892, and could not have been written after the end of October.[60]

The chain of reasoning that allows us to reach this conclusion seems convincing, but it fails to take into account other evidence that complicates the problem. Turner's copy of the 1889 edition of the *Analisa*, in Italian, has been preserved, but one turns the pages in vain when searching for the

59. Benson, "Loria's Influence on American Economic Thought," *loc. cit.*, 193–94, analyzes these similarities. Turner quoted the *Analisa* in his 1893 essay: "America has the key to the historical enigma which Europe has sought for centuries in vain, and the land which has no history reveals luminously the course of universal history," citing in a footnote "Loria, *Analisa della Proprietà Capitalista*, ii, p. 15." Turner then went on: "There is much truth in this. The United States lies like a huge page in the history of society. Line by line as we read this continental page from West to East we find the record of social evolution." Turner, "The Significance of the Frontier in American History," in Turner, *The Frontier in American History* (New York, 1920), p. 11. Benson points out that the "mountain" and "pages from history" metaphors are borrowed from Loria, who used them on page 8 of his *Analisa*, and that the sentence quoted by Turner is on page 15. He considers the sections between pages 8 and 15, "The Historical Revelation of the Colonies," as the part of the *Analisa* which most influenced Turner, and quotes it in translation in his article on "Loria's Influence on American Economic Thought," *loc. cit.*, 196–99.
60. *Ibid.*, 191–93. I am indebted to Professor Vernon Carstensen of the University of Washington, formerly of the University of Wisconsin, for a conflicting bit of evidence. In preparing the history of the university which he wrote in collaboration with Professor Merle Curti, Carstensen listened to a tape reminiscence of Professor Selig Perlman, who joined the economics faculty in 1916 and recorded his views in the 1950s. Perlman, who read Italian fluently, remembers that shortly after he reached Madison Turner asked him to translate portions of the *Analisa* that seemed to bear on his thesis. This was told me in October, 1963, by Professor Carstensen, who subsequently reported that he was unable to locate the tape to which he had listened earlier. Whatever Perlman's recollections, he could not have translated the *Analisa* for Turner in 1916; Turner left Madison for Harvard in 1910.

underlined passages and marginal comments that embellished every book that he read carefully.[61] Only one sentence in the two volumes is marked in red pencil—that quoted in the "Significance of the Frontier in American History" essay stating that "America has the key to the historical enigma which Europe has sought for centuries in vain." [62] Unless Turner varied his universal practice, the clean pages of his copy of the *Analisa* suggest that they were never read. On the other hand, evidence is abundant to show his familiarity with its contents. This is partly in the form of notes scattered through his files. Thus when reading a description of indentured servitude in colonial America he commented: "Note need of forced labor in the colonies owing to the attractions of free land—Loria." [63] Again he listed on a 3 x 5 card what he called "Loria's System" of social stages: "1. Primitive dis-association 2. Coercive association (Jamestown etc. New Eng[land] col[onies]. 3. Slavery 4. Serfdom 5. Wages and pauperism. cessation of free land 6. Ult[imate] revelation of col[onies]." [64] Obviously Turner knew Loria's theories well enough to cite them as evidence whenever he found opportunity.

One final bit of evidence obscures rather than clarifies his intellectual debt to Loria. At some time in his life, probably in the autumn of 1892, Turner filled six typewriter-size sheets with notes in his own hand to a twenty-two page passage in the *Analisa*, interspersing them with his own comments or reminders to look at this book or that mentioned by Loria.[65] If the portion that he chose to preserve contained the concepts and quotations that he later borrowed, or if it summarized the "free land" theories that were most influential to his frontier thesis, we would have additional evidence that Turner had read or listened to most of the second volume of the *Analisa* and had selected for use the most pertinent parts. Unfortunately for logic, it does not; the passage is distant in the *Analisa* from the sections usually cited as those influencing Turner and seemingly has less relationship to his frontier hypothesis than many others that he might have copied. Why did Turner

61. Turner's copy of Loria, *Analisa della Proprietà Capitalista* is in the Huntington Library, Accession No. 114780.
62. *Ibid.,* II, 15. Turner has underlined the last ten lines of this page.
63. HEH TU File Drawer 2B, Folder: 18th c. Colonies. Labor.
64. HEH TU 3 x 5 File Drawer 1.
65. These six pages, in Turner's hand, are in HEH TU File Drawer 15A, Folder: Notes on A. Loria. They show that Turner took notes on pp. 46–55 of volume II of the *Analisa*. I am indebted to Miss Josephine Colletti, a former graduate student at Northwestern University, for translating that section for me.

choose to save notes of such little apparent value? Two answers suggest themselves: these pages were a section of a complete summary of at least the second volume of Loria's work that has now disappeared, or they were considered sufficiently vital to deserve preservation.

If the latter, what did Turner find interesting in the sections which he summarized? To reread them today is to realize that they were rich in evidence of the transforming function of "free land." In them Loria argued that capital accumulation was impossible in a new country; so long as free land was available, settlers had no incentive to save money for the purchase of more tillable farms. "The first result of free land," he wrote, "is the stunted accumulation of capital." In such a primitive economy, currency circulated only for convenience as cheap paper money or "in the form of little balls, that they call *wampampeak*." Large profits were possible only through extra-legal devices; "speculation and search for unlawful profits break out like a national disease and spread their hurtful influences in the regions where the free land system prevails." This was a product of the environment, not of a dishonest population, and was due solely to the fact that free land excluded capital accumulation. Yet benefits were derived from free land as well; it converted the timid European into the daring cultivator of the Far West; it "infused a conscience of liberty and a feeling of well being among the people who lived extraneous to agricultural labor." In Europe the best seats at the banquet hall of life were already taken; in the United States free land endowed all people with a sense of security and independence of elasticity and ambition.[66]

These same conditions altered America's legal structure. In early colonial days English laws were universally used, but the settlers found them ill suited to their unique problems. Hence they discarded statute law for common law, changing this to meet local conditions. Its principal purpose was to provide protection for private property, for in America free land allowed all to be owners of farms or other tangible assets and to demand that the law guard their holdings. Well-protected property and land values that increased with the population underlay the prosperity of the colonies. Yet this stage of social evolution was short lived. Change was rapid; "just as the American man grows white hair earlier than the European man does, in the same manner the economic institutions grow old more rapidly in America than in

66. Loria, *Analisa della Proprietà Capitalista*, II, 41–45.

139

Europe, and the social evolution is accomplished more quickly."[67] The result was an alteration in the labor system.

This, too, Loria argued, stemmed from the abundance of free land. Collective labor was tried at first, but proved unworkable, just as did wage labor when workers could escape to farms of their own. The answer was slavery —"a mass of workers, who will remain in servitude despite every seduction of unoccupied lands." The slave system launched the colonies on the second stage of their economic growth, just as it had in ancient Europe when introduced there. Where slaves existed land values rose; where they were freed prematurely (as in Haiti) land prices fell to zero. This was because land prices were set by the value of the goods they produced; this depended entirely on securing slave labor, for non-slave agricultural workers could not be obtained so long as free land existed to the westward. Loria reported at length the plight of Scottish Highlanders in early Georgia who opposed slavery on moral grounds but were forced to forget their principles by economic pressures. He found the same progression of events in the pagan world of antiquity where free lands were as plentiful as in early America.[68] Free land determined the nature of the economy among all primitive peoples, whether in ancient Europe or colonial (or frontier) America; it held the key to understanding the evolution of any social order in its early stages.

These were the theories that Turner absorbed as he read (or heard read) the pages of the *Analisa della Proprietà Capitalista* which he singled out for particular attention. As he did so he interspersed with his notes a number of observations on topics of special interest. "First result of free land," he wrote, "—the accumulation of capital is slight—only accumulate to extend own cultivation." Loria's discussion of legal institutions inspired: "Free land—1) Cheating etc., 2) bravery, consciousness of liberty, sentiment of well being." A few pages later Turner added another speculation: "Free land an incentive to increase in population—note fecundity of the immigrants in America." As he read Loria's analysis of the labor problem he summarized the argument neatly: Slavery—formation. Pressure of pop[ulation]. Relative decline in productivity of land. Need of Association: Coercive labor on the basis of *individual* property. In this state of affairs slavery the *boon*."[69]

These were important realizations, but even more important were the

67. *Ibid.*, II, 46–54.
68. *Ibid.*, 55–65.
69. HEH TU File Drawer 15A, Folder: Notes on A. Loria.

further investigations suggested to Turner as he read. These he noted as he went along, usually as reminders to himself. Loria's description of cheating and speculation in early stages of colonial society brought forth: "Work up one part on colonial law. Frontier in 1765 regulators, etc." References to the colonial common law started a new chain of thought: "Too great stress has been laid on the democratic character of the immigrants to America. Free land is the explanation at bottom." Again when Turner read that slavery was necessary in primitive societies he added: "The dissolution of a wage society by free land. Antisocial tendency. Creation of economic inertia. Satisfaction in small agric[ultural] holdings. Lack of intellectual stimulus arising from contact." [70] Clearly Loria taught him much, but played an even more important role by stimulating his creative imagination.

To emphasize the fragments of information or inspiration that Turner received by reading the *Analisa*, however, is to obscure its major contribution to his emerging hypothesis. By the autumn of 1892 when he became familiar with Loria's work the cornerstone of his thesis was securely laid; he knew a great deal about the frontier process, he understood why men moved westward, he was familiar with the routes they followed and their methods of travel, and he had identified certain enduring results of the nation's frontiering experience in the form of character and institutional alterations. When he read the *Analisa* he saw for the first time, in all probability, *how* expansion changed the traits and institutions of the frontiersmen. Free land was responsible, Loria told him, and Turner accepted that judgment as the gospel. The abundance of opportunity in the form of resources that could be obtained almost for the asking determined the pace of society's evolution, recast British law into an American mold, underlay colonial prosperity, and decided the nature of the labor system. Loria dealt only with the colonies, but what he said applied equally to all new social orders. Free land was the

70. *Ibid*. In these notes Turner copied several of Loria's references to other authors whose views contributed to the frontier thesis. Thus he copied a reference to Edward G. Wakefield, *England and America. A Comparison of the Social and Political State of Both Nations* (2 vols. London, 1833), II, 10, which connected free lands with slavery in describing early Virginia. If Turner pursued Loria's footnote to Henry Brougham, *An Inquiry into the Colonial Policy of European Powers* (Edinburgh, 1803), I, 43–44, as he probably did, he learned that America was settled by "men of small capital, content with a living profit, attached to the soil, and entertaining no idea of removing from it. The smallness of their property excited their whole industry; and the part of their profits which arose from their labour, bore a great proportion to that part which came from their stock. They never thought of accumulating, unless to extend their improvements."

synonym for opportunity on frontiers, and the relatively greater opportunity for self-advancement there underlay the social changes that Turner had observed. This was a key point in his hypothesis, and while others stressed its importance, none brought the lesson home as forcefully as Achille Loria.

To assign Loria major credit, however, is to ignore the indisputable fact that the frontier thesis was a blend of many ideas voiced by many men and merged into a workable theory by Turner. Indeed a plausible case could be made that Turner's hypothesis would have been little altered if he had never read the *Analisa;* by the time he did so he was well stocked with information, and his interpretative skills would almost certainly have produced the "free land" explanation that he learned from Loria. He knew from Emile Boutmy that frontiering encouraged enterprise, altered the legal system, and laid the basis for democratic institutions that would endure only as long as space for expansion was available. André Churillon had taught him that the pioneering experience fostered social democracy by allowing each man to rise to a level set only by his own abilities. From Henry George he had learned that the move westward heightened the ability among Americans to adapt to unfamiliar situations, and stimulated their independence and ambition. Walter Bagehot had demonstrated that the West was a "breaker of custom," and that it had made the people more restless, more high-strung, more prone to move and experiment; he also showed Turner that traditional behavioral patterns were altered when people from many homelands mingled in new communities. From Francis A. Walker Turner became aware that pioneering bred disrespect for tradition, heightened inventive skills, and strengthened nationalism. Here were most of the ingredients for the frontier hypothesis, and Turner was familiar with them before he read the *Analisa.*

If we were to reconstruct a hypothetical timetable reproducing the steps that led to the essay on "The Significance of the Frontier in American History" we would realize that no single author—whether Achille Loria or Francis A. Walker or Henry George or Walter Bagehot, or anyone else—did more than stimulate Turner's imagination and supply him with a few facts or concepts that he could probably have obtained elsewhere. In essence, his hypothesis was the product of his creative ability; he borrowed from many and he was unusually sensitive to the social and intellectual climate in which he lived, but his own insights and his own skill in blending irrelevant ideas into a relevant whole played the essential role. This is clearly indicated by the chronology of events (so far as they can be dated) that led him to his hypothesis.

As early as the summer of 1889, long before he had read any authors considered significant save possibly Walter Bagehot, Francis A. Walker, and Henry George, Turner could write (as he did in his review of Theodore Roosevelt's *Winning of the West*) that the frontier was a major force in American development, that it produced a "new composite nationality," and that the study of expansion would reveal "the continuous progress of civilization across the continent." [71] In 1890 or early 1891 when he prepared the syllabus for his extension courses on colonization he was able to explain to his students "how European life entered America and how America modified that life"—how, in other words, the frontier environment altered behavioral patterns.[72] By this time Turner had probably read the Phi Beta Kappa address on "The Growth of the Nation" by Francis A. Walker and Walter Bagehot's *Physics and Politics;* he had certainly read Henry George's *Progress and Poverty,* but was unfamiliar with the *Analisa della Proprietà Capitalista.* He was in the same state of preparation in January, 1891, when he drafted his lecture on "The Colonization of North America" for the Madison Literary Club. By this time he was solidly committed to the belief that imported European customs and institutions were modified by contact with the frontier. "American history," he told his listeners, "is the account of how the environment was occupied by a new organization. It is the history of the application of men and ideas to the physical conditions." Turner was also aware, this early in his theorizing, that the "colonization" of the continent was "the key to American history," and that the occupation of the successive Wests had profoundly affected the social, economic, and political life of the East.[73] Most important of all, he incorporated a phrase dredged from the memories of his Johns Hopkins days, to use now and to use often in his later essays. He jotted this phrase down, probably in the spring of 1889 when he was reading Walter Bagehot's views on the frontier as a

71. Turner, "Review of Theodore Roosevelt, The Winning of the West (G. P. Putnam's Sons)," *The Dial*, X (August, 1889), 71–72.
72. Turner, *Syllabus of a University Extension Course of Six Lectures on the Colonization of North America* (Madison, n.d.,) first lecture.
73. Turner, "American Colonization," MS lecture before Madison Literary Club, February 9, 1891. HEH TU File Drawer 15A, Folder: Lecture. American Colonization. A note on the cover in Turner's hand states that it was prepared in January, 1891.

"breaker of the cake of custom." "West," Turner noted at that time. "Infl[uence] on U.S.—Custom. It stood to East as the sea to Phoenicia, to Egypt, to Greece."[74] Now the phrase appeared again, in more polished form: "What first the Mediterranean sea and later the new world were to the Aryan peoples, breaking the bond of custom, and creating new activities to meet new conditions, that the undeveloped West has been to American descendents of the Aryans."

That lecture on colonization ended Turner's writing on the frontier for some months; he was busy with his classes, his extension courses, his reading in the many books that would enlighten him on the course and results of westward expansion. Not until the fall of 1892 was he forced to record his views once more. We can imagine the circumstances; he had agreed some months before to prepare an essay for *The Aegis* on "New Aspects of the Early History of Wisconsin" to illustrate the work of the history department, but as usual writing had lagged. Now, in the fall of 1892, he was pressed for his contribution. In all probability he had been reading Loria's *Analisa della Proprietà Capitalista* and a local study of his state's history seemed less exciting as the theories that were to be molded into his hypothesis danced in his head. Why not experiment with setting these down? The result was his "Problems in American History," published on November 4, 1892, and almost certainly written only a few weeks before that date, for Turner was not the sort to finish a task long before it fell due.

This revealing essay showed the progress made in welding scattered concepts into a coherent thesis, and showed too that he had benefited from the extensive reading done that fall. Scattered through it were phrases that reflected firmly based conclusions, not tentative hypotheses: "American history up to our own day has been colonial history, the colonization of the Great West," "The ever-retreating frontier of free land is the key to American development," "The peculiarity of American institutions is the fact that they are compelled to adapt themselves to the changes of a remarkably developing, expanding people," "In the settlement of America we have to observe how European life entered the continent, and how America modified that life and reacted on Europe," and to conclude with that oft-used sentence, now further refined, "What the Mediterranean Sea was to the Greeks, breaking the bond of custom, offering new experiences, calling out new institutions

74. HEH TU 3 x 5 Drawer 1.

144

and activities, that the ever-retreating Great West has been to the United States directly, and to the nations of Europe more remotely." [75]

Here was a mature statement of the frontier thesis, needing only illustrative evidence to flesh out the skeleton outline, and additional examples of the manner in which frontiering altered the Americans and their institutions. Turner spoke now with an assurance lacking even in his lecture on colonization before the Madison Literary Club because he rested his case on the authority of such scholars as Francis A. Walker, Walter Bagehot, and Achille Loria. That he was partly familiar with the *Analisa della Proprietà Capitalista* by this time is suggested by his proposal to study the United States as one would a developing organism. "The institutional framework of the nation," he wrote, "may be likened to the anatomy of the body politic; its physiology is the social and economic life molding this framework to new uses." [76] That concept was familiar to Turner; it was basic to the instruction he received from Richard T. Ely and appeared often in his reading. But it may well have been strengthened when he read Loria's words: "The colonies really are . . . a political animal from which social psychology is able to garner treasures; they are for economic science what the mountains are for geology." [77] Biological metaphors were the stock in trade of most historians in that day, yet the similarity of the examples used by Turner and Loria seem to indicate a direct borrowing.

Whatever their relationship, one thing is abundantly clear. Turner did not rely on Loria, or Bagehot, or George, or any other author for the basic concepts of his thesis or even for the illustration that gave it plausibility. He had arrived at most of his conclusions by January, 1891, long before he read many of the writers who supposedly influenced him most. Viewed against this indisputable fact, his reading program in 1892–1893 can be seen not as a quest for a new interpretation, but as a search for collaborative evidence for an already accepted theory. He read western travelers and guide books and magazines not to learn that frontiersmen differed from easterners, but to discover *how* they differed. He consulted Bagehot and Loria and other

75. Turner, "Problems in American History," in Turner, *The Early Writings of Frederick Jackson Turner* (Madison, 1938), pp. 71–83. For the origins of this essay, see above pp. 56–59.
76. *Ibid.*, p. 73.
77. Loria, *Analisa della Proprietà Capitalista*, II, p. 8. This section of Loria's work appears in translation in Benson, "Loria's Influence on American Economic Thought," *loc. cit.*, pp. 169–99.

political economists not to find a new theory, but for an explanation of how his own theory operated. Turner's creative ability allowed him to provide unity and meaning to the thought about the frontier then current in the United States, and to fashion from it a tentative hypothesis. His further reading convinced him that his thesis was worth testing, and that it justified presentation to his fellow historians as a paper on "The Significance of the Frontier in American History." [78]

78. Turner once told Merle Curti that "a man does not make a fundamental discovery or effect a profound alteration in science after he is thirty." If he applied that rule to himself, he must have formulated his thesis before November 14, 1891, when he reached that age. Fulmer Mood, "Turner's Formative Period," in Turner, *The Early Writings of Frederick Jackson Turner*, p. 35, n. 37.

CHAPTER VII

The 1893 Essay and Its Reception

Probably by January, 1891, and certainly by October, 1892, Frederick Jackson Turner had developed his frontier hypothesis in all its essential details. Much remained to be done before it could be stated in final form. He had still to incorporate Achille Loria's theories concerning the role of "free land" as a principal creative force shaping the social environment in pioneer communities. He must add information on western traits and institutions—demonstrate the significance of the West to the nation as a whole. This meant more reading; as we have seen, much of the 1892–1893 academic year was spent poring over travel accounts, guide books, and the works of western writers in the alcoves of the State Historical Society library. It was a pleasant task, and one that he was reluctant to end until an unanticipated event forced him to begin writing the essay that was to bring him fame.

Before tracing Turner's progress between November, 1892, when his essay on "Problems in American History" set forth his hypothesis in semi-final form, and July, 1893, when he laid it before the members of the American Historical Association, one troublesome question must be answered. Why did Turner, rather than another young historian of his generation, advance the frontier thesis? Others were subjected to the social and intellectual climate created by the impending end of the era of cheap lands. Others read much as he read, for books on colonization were few and those on the theory of colonialism even fewer; anyone remotely interested in either topic could learn all that was to be known in a few months. Yet Turner, not one of his contemporaries, saw expansion as a major force in American history. What in his background, nature, and training allowed him to do so?

To seek an answer to that question we must ask the help of psychologists who investigate the nature of creative thinking.[1] They have written

1. The discussion of creative thinking that follows has been distilled from a dozen or so of the large number of books on the subject. I have found the following particularly helpful to

dozens of books and hundreds of articles on why and how men generate original thoughts or invent new gadgets, most of them more notable for their plausibility than for the evidence on which they rest. For this the psychologists cannot be blamed; the human mind and the human psyche do not lend themselves to empirical analysis and any investigations of their mysteries must be inconclusive. Yet the case studies that have been compiled and the few experiments conducted with people and animals shed some light on the creative process. To understand why Turner rather than some other historian reached his conclusions, and how he did so, some acquaintance with these findings is useful.

This must begin with an appraisal of Turner himself, for investigators agree that creative skills are found in some types of individuals and not in others. Intelligence is necessary, but a high level is not essential; many of the world's greatest inventors have been persons of modest intellectual attainment. More importantly the creator must not be overly practical; the most successful have been indifferent to details and have instead been concerned with broader meanings, implications, and symbolic expressions. He must be capable of visualizing "created images"—seeing an invented concept very much as a successful novelist sees his hero. This privilege is denied most of us, who fill our minds with "memory images" recalling things we have seen or read. The successful inventor thrives on mental disorder and confusion, and has little compulsion to set his thoughts in order. He inclines to nonconformity in the realm of ideas, refusing to be shackled by an established body of knowledge. He must be receptive to fresh perceptions and beliefs. Speaking physiologically, psychologists tell us, the inventor must possess a nervous system that allows a stimulus to be relayed to the brain without being distorted by preconceived notions. If he sees a pink tree he thinks "*This* tree is pink," not "this tree must be green because all trees are green." All of this is to say that creative thinkers are less rigidly bound intellectually than other mortals.

a layman unequipped with a psychologist's special vocabulary: Robert Thomson, *The Psychology of Creative Thinking* (Baltimore, 1959), D. M. Johnson, *The Psychology of Thought and Judgment* (New York, 1955), George Humphrey, *Directed Thinking* (New York, 1948), Jacques Hadamard, *The Psychology of Invention in the Mathematical Field* (Princeton, 1949), W. I. B. Beveridge, *The Art of Scientific Investigation* (New York, 1950), and A. P. Usher, *History of Mechanical Inventions* (New York, 1929), 8–31. A number of useful papers on the subject are assembled in Sidney J. Parnes and Harold F. Harding, eds., *A Source Book for Creative Thinking* (New York, 1962).

They are also more independent than their fellows and less prone to swing with the intellectual tides. The creative thinker puts less credence in the opinion of his contemporaries and more in his own judgment; he accepts an idea as good or bad because it is good or bad, and not because it has been criticized or praised by others. He must be intuitive, able to believe in possibilities as well as probabilities, and skilled at finding links between the known and the to-be-known. He must be imaginative yet able to control his imagination, for he must temper his fantasies with enough realism to cast his random thoughts into a controlled pattern when applied to a particular problem. He must be able to play with ideas, juggling them into wild hypotheses, toying with their meaning, arranging and rearranging them. He must be better able than most to select from a multitude of choices the one exactly suited to his needs, and know that he is right in doing so.[2]

To catalogue the characteristics of creative thinkers is to recognize that the process that leads them to their inventions is extremely complex. It encompasses a variety of mental and physical activities: how we memorize, how we acquire habits, how we develop skills, how we think, how we form concepts. It involves both the perceptional process and the process of motivation. In this sense invention—or "creative problem solving" as the psychologists put it—differs from analysis. Its purpose is not to bring order or meaning to known facts, but to add something new, something original. Its method is to create a unique set of conditions that will lead to a particular discovery. This may take the form of combining color and shape to create an oil painting, or arranging gears and wheels to form a new machine, or writing a novel, or advancing an original interpretation of the American past. The important fact is that the object or concept does not exist until the innovator creates it. This makes his task particularly difficult, for he has no structured pattern to guide him.

To add to his difficulties, the creative thinker must know a great deal about his subject, for he must have substantive basis for his mental explorations. He must at the same time avoid too much knowledge, lest he think in traditional patterns to the detriment of the innovative process. Thus a person who knows the alphabet recites it backward only with difficulty, while one who does not recites it easily. Too, many of the learned facts may be wrong, and this will further hinder his creativity. Achieving exactly the right amount

2. Carl R. Rogers, "Toward a Theory of Creativity," in Parnes and Harding, *Source Book for Creative Thinking*, pp. 64–72 is excellent on this subject.

of knowledge is only the first step, however. After that comes the equally difficult task of transforming and rearranging recognized facts so that they will apply to the problem he seeks to solve. Further to complicate the inventive process, acquired knowledge is often not sufficient to achieve a result. The creator must draw on experiences from his remote past that seemingly have little relevance. Often an inventor's firsthand experiences in boyhood (his "primary perceptions" according to the psychologists) interact with the information he has recently acquired through reading and formal instruction (his "secondary perceptions") to provide his solution. The path to creativity is strewn with many obstacles.

Not the least of these is the need to rearrange mental configurations into the exact patterns necessary to solve a particular problem. This requires three skills. First, the creative thinker must be able to recognize the need for a solution; he must see that a new gadget will perform a function not possible with existing methods, or he must realize that a new historical interpretation will correct the inadequacies of all previous interpretations of the events he is examining. Second, he must have the patience not to hurry to a solution; a leisurely pace will allow him to acquire the thorough knowledge that he needs, and to draw upon the total experiences of his past for relevant stimuli. Finally, the inventor must be able to utilize his experience and knowledge at the exact moment when some external stimulus stirs his creative imagination. Most original ideas occur to an individual when some unexpected and unsought stimulation—a sentence read in a book, a casual remark dropped in conversation, something observed on the street—serves as a bridge between his past experiences and the completion of the configuration which brings the act of creation to a close. If the creative thinker cannot respond to such a stimulus his prior training and speculation will be useless.[3]

Those endowed with this unlikely combination of virtues advance toward their discoveries in fairly well-defined stages. These must be understood before we can follow Turner's steps as he moved toward his frontier hypothesis. First comes a period of preparation when the creator is gathering facts, arranging them in his mind, sorting the relevant from the irrelevant, and analyzing his data. Hard work of this sort has laid the foundation for every act of creativity in human history. Next comes the incubation stage; the problem is pushed aside for long or short periods when the inventor does not

3. The importance of these three abilities is stressed in Usher, *History of Mechanical Inventions*, pp. 16–19.

150

seem to be thinking of a solution, let alone working toward it. Substantial progress is made during these "conscience lapses," however, even when the individual is asleep, for this is the time when data gathered during the period of preparation seem to sort themselves out below the range of consciousness. No one knows what happens during this phase of subconscious preparation, but it does occur, and progress toward a solution is rapid. Creative thinkers often emerge with the facts arranged to take on a new meaning, or with their perception sharpened. Sometimes they are so near a solution that they have an "almost there" or a "on-the-tip-of-my-tongue" sensation.

They are ready now for the third stage. This is the moment of illumination, when the significant idea, the defined hypothesis, the brilliant solution, suddenly presents itself. This usually occurs as a sudden revelation rather than through the short steps that normally establish connections between pairs of ideas. Psychologists call it the "leap forward" or the "Aha experience." More often than not it takes place when the creator is not consciously working on his problem, or even thinking of anything connected with it. It is, in other words, a product of the subconscious mind, and occurs when the subconscious, which has been laboring over the problem during the incubation stage, floods the conscious mind with its successful solution. Even now the task of the creator is unfinished. In the fourth stage of the inventive process he must verify his results; this means elaborating his conclusions, stating them in usable form, testing and revising, and finally presenting them to his colleagues in the form of a painting, a novel, an invention, or a historical interpretation.[4]

Modern psychologists recognize that these four steps do not necessarily follow one after the other in orderly sequence. A creative thinker may move so rapidly toward a solution that all four steps merge into one, or he may work in random fashion. Whatever the order of his four stages, all are aware of the final "leap forward" as the culmination of the inventive process. Dozens of inventors have testified to the exciting moment when the long-sought answer suddenly flashed before them. Charles Darwin remembered the exact location of his carriage on the road when the basic thesis of the origin of the species came to him during a ride; Goethe recalled that the

4. The steps in the creative process are especially well described in Hadamard, *The Psychology of Invention in the Mathematical Field*, pp. 21–63, Thomson, *The Psychology of Creative Thinking*, pp. 188–200, and Beveridge, *The Art of Scientific Investigation*, pp. 72–108. They were first identified in G. Wallas, *The Art of Thought* (New York, 1926).

theme of one of his major works occurred to him at the very moment when he heard of the death of a dear friend. Archimedes, rushing naked from his bath and shouting "Eureka," typifies the excitement of the creator as he experiences that insight coming "seemingly from heaven."[5] Yet hard work, not heaven, is responsible. The flash of revelation comes only to those whose preparation and experience has been thorough, and who have grappled with their problem for some time. Too, the inventor cannot capitalize on his find unless he has the patience and skill to cast his creation into usable form, explain its significance, and record it for others to use.[6]

Against this background of psychological theory, we can now ask ourselves: how well was Turner suited by background and training for his role as creative thinker? How exactly did he follow the steps usually followed in the inventive process? To answer those questions is to understand not only the reasons for his accomplishments, but the major contributions that he made to historical studies.

That Turner was well equipped for his part is unquestionable, for he was endowed by nature with the faults no less than the virtues that appear in exaggerated form in most inventors. His concern throughout his scholarly career was not with the minute details of history but with the broad patterns; his talent lay not in a well-documented page of narrative but in producing a hurriedly-penned essay or a sparkling interpretative paragraph. Unlike most "scientific" historians of his day he had little use for footnotes; the few that he used were rarely consistent, never complete, and often not very revealing. These are attributes of all creative thinkers, whose trademarks are indifference to detail, concern with overall configurations, and disorderly thinking. Turner shared with his fellow inventors, too, an ability to visualize concepts; his frequent poetical expression and constant use of metaphors and symbols indicated a mind more prone to imagery than most. The ideal creator is never caught in a strait jacket of conventional views that hinders his creative processes, nor was Turner, whose lack of formal training in American history freed him from the shackles of traditionalism. Had he followed Professor Allen into medieval studies he might have lived in slavish

5. These experiences are described in Humphrey, *Directed Thinking*, pp. 111–28, and in Ralph W. Gerard, "How the Brain Creates Ideas," in Parnes and Harding, eds., *Source Book for Creative Thinking*, pp. 116–26.
6. Humphrey, *Directed Thinking*, pp. 128–35, Thomson, *Psychology of Creative Thinking*, pp. 200–01, and Arthur Koestler, *The Act of Creation* (New York, 1964), pp. 119–20.

imitation of his master. Instead he found in the American West an area so unhampered by conventional scholarship that his mind could roam freely and widely as he sought to interpret its significance.

Thus the same human frailties that Turner revealed in his day-by-day affairs contributed to his greatness as a creator. He realized, almost from the beginning of his marriage in 1889, that he could never keep his business affairs in order or persuade his family to operate on a balanced budget. From that day on the Turners lived in a state of happy confusion and bank overdrafts. Had he fussed with time-consuming financial details, or insisted on a well-ordered checkbook, important ideas would have been crowded from his mind. Instead those that found lodgment there could be coddled and teased into producing significant theories. Turner's dislike of writing was another fault that plagued him throughout his career, but proved an asset in the long run. This was a near-fatal affliction with him; he would dillydally for days or months with an essay before some external pressure—usually a demanding editor or a looming lecture date—forced him to put pen to paper. Even then he was too late; his files bulged with speeches in which the first few pages were carefully prepared and typed, the next hurriedly written by hand, and the last even more hurriedly appended in rough outline form. Had Turner been a compulsive producer who allotted adequate time for each task he would have written more books, but put fewer ideas into them. Those hours of dawdling gave him time to juggle facts, rearrange ideas, and shuffle concepts into new patterns. He could also call on his vivid imagination for inspiration; like many inventors he loved to indulge in fantasies, embroidering his stories or indulging in imaginative byplay with a friend over the plot of a never-to-be-written novel.

If Turner's personality traits fitted him for a creative role, so did his background and training. Memories of his boyhood amidst the quasi-frontier conditions of Portage haunted him in later years and played an essential part in shaping his thesis. He was aided, too, by his lack of formal instruction in American history; as a newcomer to the subject he was better able to sense its incompleteness—the lack of meaningful explanations and interpretations—and free to read widely in unorthodox works as he searched for fresh viewpoints. A scholar better prepared in the field would have followed traditional paths already explored by generations of historians; one worse prepared would have lacked the foundations on which to build new explanations. Turner's excellent training in medieval history gave him the tools, but not the prejudices, needed for an original reappraisal of the American past.

That his background and preparation ideally suited him to the task was shown as he moved step by step toward the frontier hypothesis. His period of "preparation" lasted through his student days at Wisconsin and Johns Hopkins, where he read widely and discovered his instinctive interest in the American West. As he read ever more widely his mind stored fragments of information that formed no orderly pattern and suggested no new interpretation, but that were ready to respond to the proper stimulus. The "incubation" stage followed between 1889 and 1892 as he was required to evaluate the extent and validity of then-existing works on frontier history; as he prepared his review of Theodore Roosevelt's *Winning of the West* or hunted for information essential to his extension lectures or course on "The Economic and Social History of the United States," he realized the inadequacy of the factual materials and explanations then in use. Turner must think about interpretations now as he had not before. He was too busy to attempt an orderly arrangement of his ideas or to ponder the broader significance of the frontier, but his subconscious was operating steadily during this phase, sorting out details, forming experimental patterns, and perfecting linkages with his boyhood memories of life on the Portage frontier. By this time Turner was ready for the next step: the "leap forward" that would bring his hypothesis into focus.

We will never know when that moment of illumination came, or whether it came at all as it does to most creative thinkers. Two of his experiences during the latter "incubation" period seem most likely to have triggered such a response. One was the publication in April, 1891, of the census bulletin announcement that "the unsettled area has been so broken into by isolated bodies of settlement that there can hardly be said to be a frontier line." Did Turner, reading these words, experience a revelation that allowed him to realize the true significance of the frontier? Perhaps. But we must remember that he had his hypothesis well in mind in January, 1891, when he prepared his lecture on colonization for the Madison Literary Club. We must recognize that when he wrote his essay on "Problems in American History" for *The Aegis* in September or October, 1892—an essay that advanced his hypothesis in semifinal form—he probably had not yet seen the census bulletin with its fatal announcement. Had he done so, he would not have stated in that paper that "the map for the next census will show gaps filled in, and the process repeated on a new frontier line." [7] Evidence suggests that Turner did not read of the closing of the frontier until after November, 1892, when his hypothesis was already formulated.

If the census bulletin did not provide him with inspiration for the "leap forward," what of his reading of Loria's *Analisa della Proprietà Capitalista?* Did revelation flood his mind as he sat in an alcove of the State Historical Society library, listening to Ely's collaborator, Harry H. Powers, translate that work into English, and scribbling the notes that were to be preserved in his files? As he heard Loria's explanation of the manner in which "free land" altered the colonial economy did Turner suddenly comprehend *how* the frontier changed the people and their institutions? Did he recognize that abundant natural resources offered an unexampled opportunity for individual self-advancement, and that this in turn stimulated mobility, inventiveness, and materialism among frontiersmen, just as it heightened their individualism, nationalism, and faith in democracy? Did he awaken to the fact that most of the differences between East and West noted by travelers and guidebook authors could be explained by the man-land ratio? Possibly he did, but this seems most unlikely. Again we must recognize that Turner's thesis was well formed by January, 1891, and that he could not have read Loria's *Analisa* before September or October, 1892. We must also realize that Turner had already stumbled on most of the concepts found in Loria—including stress on free land as a transforming agent—in other books he read, even though not expressed in such persuasive terms.

This maze of conflicting evidence points to only one conclusion: that Turner experienced not one but a whole series of "leaps forward" as the frontier hypothesis took shape in his conscious and subconscious mind. This was natural, for his thesis comprised not one but several concepts. In all probability he recognized these one by one as he read and speculated on the nature of American expansion from 1889 onward. Henry George and Walter Bagehot brought realization that frontiering weakened customs and made pioneers more receptive to change. His friends in the science and geography faculties of the University of Wisconsin taught him that environment altered behavioral patterns and that acquired characteristics were transmitted to later generations. His reading of Theodore Roosevelt's

7. Turner, "Problems in American History," in F. J. Turner, *The Early Writings of Frederick Jackson Turner* (Madison, 1938), p. 75.

The Winning of the West sparked a rebellion against antiquarianism in western historiography and brought home the fact that expansion was significant in the political and economic development of the nation. His exploration of guidebooks and travel accounts awakened him to the differences between easterners and westerners and equipped him with a catalog of characteristics where these differences were most marked. His mastery of Loria's theories emphasised in his mind the place of free land in the transformation process. His discovery of the census bulletin's announcement of the frontier's closing suggested that one period of American history had ended, and was worth investigating. Each of these intellectual discoveries was a "leap forward" in his thinking, and each took its place in the total hypothesis that was gradually evolving in his mind.

That this was the pattern followed by Turner during his periods of "preparation" and "incubation" is further indicated as we trace his progress during the months that he was preparing his 1893 essay on "The Significance of the Frontier in American History." This, psychologists tell us, was the "verification" stage in his creative thinking; he must test the validity of the bundle of ideas that had accumulated and compress them into an orderly form for presentation. Just how and when this was accomplished is clouded in as many uncertainties as the steps leading to his thesis. Tangible evidence is lacking, forcing us to follow scant clues and add a great deal of speculation to the few facts available.

The trail begins in November, 1892, when he published his theory in *The Aegis* essay on "Problems in American History." What Turner next did must remain a mystery. Historians who have toyed with the problem believe that his imagination was now fired, and that he set to work immediately to add form and flesh to his tentative hypothesis. One of his students remembered that Turner radiated excitement during that 1892–1893 academic year; "Turner taught and lectured," he recalled many years later, "as only one could who had just written or was writing such an impressive organon." [8] Those who hold this view can point out that in early February the influence of free land occupied his thoughts, citing as evidence a talk before Madison's Contemporary Club. Although asked only to comment on the commercial policy of Europe, Turner strayed into a discussion of the

8. Joseph Schafer. "The Author of the Frontier Hypothesis," *Wisconsin Magazine of History*, XV (September, 1931), 96.

differences between Europe and the United States, tracing those to American "free land." This, said he, did away with the exhorbitant rents that made European agriculture so marginal and provided outlet for energies that in a landless nation would be diverted into industry.[9] Turner was not far from his reading of Loria's *Analisa* when he made those remarks, or from his own hypothesis either. Here was evidence that he worked steadily on his paper between November, 1892, and July, 1893, when it was delivered.

Supporting that viewpoint is an event usually cited as conclusive evidence that his essay was completed by December, 1892. At that time Woodrow Wilson visited Madison as a member of a committee of the National Educational Association entrusted with the perennial task of improving the teaching of history, civil government, and political economy in grammar and secondary schools.[10] Nothing would do but he must spend as much time as possible with his former student; hence Wilson elected to put up at the Turner home rather than with the university president, and to escape from committee meetings for long talks with Turner and Charles Homer Haskins, a boarder at the Turner home.[11] Wilson endured three strenuous days of meetings and tiring social events[12]—including a formal luncheon at the Turners' where the "tables were loaded with a tempting spread of edibles and beautifully decorated with choice cut flowers"[13]—but there was time also for long talks as the two sat about the fire in the "den" of the Gilman Street house. Supposedly one evening was devoted to listening to a draft of the paper Turner was to read that July, and to

9. *Daily Cardinal*, February 9, 1893. In April Turner discussed a paper given before the Contemporary Club by Charles H. Haskins on Edward A. Freeman. Unfortunately his remarks were not quoted in the press, but he probably quarreled with Freeman's political approach. *Wisconsin State Journal*, April 11, 1893.
10. *Daily Cardinal*, January 9, 1893.
11. Woodrow Wilson to Charles K. Adams, December 23, 1892. University of Wisconsin Archives. Presidents of the University. General Correspondence, C. K. Adams, 1891–1901. Series 4/8/1. Box 4, Folder: T-Z. Hereafter referred to as U. of Wis., President's File.
12. *Daily Cardinal*, January 12, 1893; *Wisconsin State Journal*, December 28, 1892. The committee met in the Fuller Opera House under the chairmanship of President Charles W. Eliot of Harvard University. Three men from the university—Haskins, Turner, and John B. Parkinson—were invited to sit with the committee and attended all meetings. Turner was asked on one occasion to address the group on the effort being made in Wisconsin's high schools to increase the amount of history instruction. The meeting is described, and the resulting report published, in Arthur S. Link, ed., *The Papers of Woodrow Wilson, VIII, 1892–1894* (Princeton, 1970), 61–73.
13. *Wisconsin State Journal*, December 31, 1892, January 10, 1893.

commenting upon it. Turner remembered years later that Wilson suggested one change; why not refer to the eastern fringe of the frontier as the "hither edge?" [14]

That Woodrow Wilson visited Turner that December is indisputable. But did Turner have a draft of his essay ready at that time? And did he read it to his house guest as they whiled away an evening? Those who maintain that he did advance several bits of evidence to substantiate their theory. They begin by citing Turner's own recollection of the event; in 1919 he wrote a friend that "I had read to Mr. Wilson, who was a visitor, as I recall it, at my house—though I am not at the moment sure where we met—the paper in manuscript, and he suggested the use of the word ' "*hither*" side of free land' for which I had been hunting." [15] They point out that Wilson left Madison imbued with enthusiasm for the frontier theory, and that he prepared a book review shortly thereafter that incorporated Turner's ideas so exactly that his biographer was inclined to believe that he originated the hypothesis. [16] Put these two facts together and they prove that Turner did read Wilson his essay. Thus it was completed by late December, 1892. [17]

But do they, and was the paper finished by that date, even in rough form? Let us first look more closely at Turner's recollection of the event as we try to answer those questions. In the rough draft of his 1919 letter where he reminisced about his visit with Wilson he wrote: "In 1893, summer, I revised and elaborated my 'Problems' paper into the Significance of the Frontier for the Chicago session (July) of the American Historical Association. . . . Mr. Wilson wasn't there [i.e. in Chicago] but he was at my house sometime within the year 1893 and I read it to him in manuscript." [18]

14. So Turner stated in a letter to William E. Dodd, October 7, 1919. HEH TU Box 29. For a copy of this letter, and an account of the circumstances that inspired it, see below, pp. 181–198.
15. *Ibid.* Two versions of this letter exist, one in rough draft in Turner's hand, the other in a revised, typed version. The latter has been published in Wendell H. Stephenson, "The Influence of Woodrow Wilson on Frederick Jackson Turner," *Agricultural History*, XIX (October, 1945), 249–53. Unfortunately it does not contain several references to preparing the paper in 1893 which are in the rough-draft form. Both letters are printed below, pp. 187–98.
16. Woodrow Wilson, "Mr. Goldwin Smith's 'Views' on Our Political History," *Forum*, XVI (December, 1893), 495–97.
17. This interpretation is admirably developed in Link, ed., *The Papers of Woodrow Wilson*, VIII, 61–73.
18. Turner to William E. Dodd, October 7, 1919. HEH TU Box 29. This sentence appears in the rough-draft copy of the letter, not in the typed version. Turner may also have discussed his essay with Theodore Roosevelt, who visited Madison in January, 1893, and stayed

He also recalled that he had sent Wilson a copy of his "Problems in American History" article in November, 1892; this would supply enough information on the frontier thesis to provide Wilson with ammunition for the review that he wrote sometime early in 1893. If Turner's memory is to be trusted, his essay was written not in December, 1892, but sometime in the summer of 1893, and read to Wilson after that date.

This seems probable in the light of still more evidence. Woodrow Wilson made a second visit to Madison, this time on July 29, 1893, seventeen days after Turner presented his paper at the Chicago meeting of the American Historical Association, and once more spent the night at the Turner home. This time his purpose was to persuade his former pupil to prepare volumes on Daniel Webster and Edmond Burke for the *Athenaeum Press Series in English Literature*, published by Ginn and Company, and edited by Wilson's friends Caleb T. Winchester and George Lyman Kittredge. Turner proved "stubbornly unwilling" to take on this assignment, pleading lack of familiarity with the subject and reluctance to commit himself to a publisher.[19] When Turner later wrote that "Mr. Wilson wasn't there but he was at my house sometime within the year 1893," he was remembering this visit, not that of December, 1892. This seems certain, for he also recalled that his paper was later printed by the State Historical Society of Wisconsin "as it was read in Chicago, except for 'hither'."[20] What happened that evening of July 29, 1893, can readily be reconstructed. Wilson recognized his inability to press the publishing commitment on his young friend and the two fell to talking of a subject dear to them both, the frontier theory. Perhaps he told Turner of the review that he had prepared or was preparing where he borrowed extensively from *The Aegis* article on "Problems in American History." Possibly Turner explained that he had at hand a more sophis-

at the home of Robert M. La Follette. On January 24 he spoke on "The Northwest in the Nation" to "a large and cultured audience including most of the prominent literary and educational leaders of the city." He also spent some time with Richard T. Ely, Turner's colleague. Turner would certainly have attended the lecture, and as an old acquaintance would probably have talked with Roosevelt either at the Ely's or at a reception given by La Follette for two hundred Madisonians. *Wisconsin State Journal*, January 24, 25, 1893.

19. Woodrow Wilson to Ellen Axson Wilson, July 29, 1893; Wilson to Caleb T. Winchester, August 17, 1893. Link, ed., *Papers of Woodrow Wilson*, VIII, 293, 312. In his letter to his wife Wilson told of staying with the Turners; in that to Winchester he described his attempt to sign Turner as an author.

20. Turner to Dodd, October 7, 1919. HEH TU Box 29. This phrase occurs in the revised typed version of the letter. It is printed below, pp. 193–98.

ticated version which would help Wilson with his review, and offered to read it then and there. We can picture his delight when Wilson responded with enthusiasm, and proposed the "hither edge of free land" phrase. Turner may well have inserted it in his manuscript at that time, to be used when he read the essay a second time to the State Historical Association of Wisconsin that December and in the published versions.

If this reconstruction is accurate, when was the paper on "The Significance of the Frontier in American History" prepared? There seems no reason to doubt Turner's memory when he wrote that "in 1893, summer, I revised and elaborated my 'Problems' paper." If he remained true to his character, his essay was written in the few weeks—or days, or hours—before it was due. As a habitual procrastinator he could never drive himself to complete any assignment until the last possible moment. This was illustrated time and time again during his career. In the spring of 1888, when as a graduate student at the University of Wisconsin he was invited to address the Madison Literary Club on the Wisconsin fur trade, the subject of his master's thesis, he dawdled away his time until two days before the meeting when he awakened to the fact that he had prepared only half his manuscript, and that in rough draft. "I feel," he wrote that day, "like a Freshman who is coming on with an essay and must write it at twelve o'clock the night before." [21] Maturity did not remedy his tendencies. Three days before he was to give an important paper to a historical gathering in St. Louis in 1904 he wrote his wife: "I am now about to try to write my paper," adding that if he accomplished the miracle he would get his check for fifty dollars. The check was his, for he could boast: "finished writing my paper at 9:30 this morning, delivered it at 10 to a small but select audience." [22] Again in 1914 he postponed preparation of a commencement address for the University of Washington until he arrived in Seattle only a day before the ceremony, then found that he had mislaid his package of notes and must rely on memory and imagination. [23] Turner was psychologically incapable of completing a task save under the whiplash of necessity.

Given this temperament, and given such evidence as we have available (including Turner's own memory which was far from reliable) we can

21. Turner to Caroline Mae Sherwood, May 12, 1888. HEH TU Box C.
22. Turner to Dorothy Turner, September 21, 1904; Turner to Caroline Mae Turner, September 25, 1904. HEH TU Box F.
23. Turner to Max Farrand, October 26, 1914. HEH TU Box 22; Turner to Charles H. Haskins, June 18, 1914. Firestone Library, Princeton University, Charles Homer Haskins Papers.

reconstruct events between November, 1892 and July, 1893, something as follows: With his essay on "Problems in American History" in print and widely distributed throughout the profession, Turner returned to the extended reading on the frontier required by his course in economic and social history. He was thus engaged between December 28 and 30, 1892, when Woodrow Wilson was a houseguest and the two discussed the significance of expansion as Turner had already described it in his paper in *The Aegis*. He was still thus engaged in late February, 1893, when he was invited to prepare an essay for the summer meeting of the American Historical Association in Chicago, and replied that he would speak on "The Significance of the Frontier in American History." [24] In all probability little if any had been written by the end of April, 1893; at that time he offered to withdraw from the program to make room for one of his students—a step hardly likely if Turner had finished his preparation. [25] Not until the last weeks in June and the first in July did he buckle to the task, using the brief period of leisure between the end of classes and the beginning of summer school teaching. As was customary with him, the last touches were not added until the day before it was given. [26] But as was also customary, this burst of last-minute energy resulted in a paper that was not only finished on time but that was expertly fashioned and delightfully written. Turner might compose only under pressure, but he composed well.

The invitation that forced him into this flurry of creative activity was not one to excite the nation's established historians. Its remote inspiration was the "World's Columbian Exposition," scheduled for Chicago during the summer of 1893 to commemorate the four-hundredth anniversary of the discovery of America. Chicagoans would be satisfied with nothing less than an exposition that would out-exposition every exposition in history, with more exhibits, more amusements, more cultural attractions, more fanfare and whoopla than in any world's fair known to man. Culture was especially important to show visitors that the western prairies could produce something more than corn and Populists. So it was that a series of "Auxilliary Congresses" were planned, on literature and the arts, each

24. Turner to Charles Kendall Adams, February 23, 1893. WSHS, Turner Papers.
25. See below, p. 164 for an account of Turner's effort to substitute Orin G. Libby for himself on the program.
26. See below, pp. 165–66 for the story of his attempt to finish his paper after he reached the Columbian Exposition.

packed with glittering stars of world renown. One would be the "World's Congress of Historians and Historical Students," arranged by local talent, but combining the resources of the American Historical Association which was invited to hold a special meeting in July. The program would be supervised by a committee of Chicagoans under William F. Poole, librarian of the city's Newberry Library, and a committee from the association under its perennial secretary, Herbert Baxter Adams.[27]

This proved a near-fatal arrangement, for Adams was as conscious of his own prestige as he was disdainful of the outlanders with whom he must work, and was determined to run his own show lest the Congress become a "pandemonium or an exhibition of cranks." "Every Chicago man," he complained, "wants the earth and proposes to dump everything into his lakeside show."[28] Adams' solution was to ignore Poole and the local committee entirely, assembling his historians at a quiet spot in Chicago for their own meetings where they would not be "dragged by chariot wheels of a world's historical congress with local historical management."[29] Not until President James B. Angell of the University of Michigan, himself a distinguished historian, made a special trip to Chicago was a compromise arranged. Dr. Poole and his local cohorts would retain their titles, but the program would be designed by the two members of his committee who were also members of the American Historical Association, working with a third member named by Adams. Invitations to speakers would be issued by the association. "In this way," wrote Herbert Baxter Adams with obvious satisfaction, "we can capture the historical congress."[30]

All of this squabbling took time, and not until late February and early March 1893, did the first invitations go out, just four months before the session would begin. Adams saw the initial list prepared by the committee in cooperation with Poole and President Angell and thought well of it, but was still skeptical. Few eastern notables would risk their lives by venturing as far westward as Chicago. Nor would the great of the profession

27. Clarence W. Bowen to William F. Poole, April 14, 1893. Newberry Library, William F. Poole Papers. Box: January–April, 1892. Hereafter referred to as Newberry: Poole Papers. Bowen was treasurer of the American Historical Association.
28. W. F. Poole to C. W. Bowen, November 28, 1892; Herbert B. Adams to C. W. Bowen, December 9, 1892. American Historical Association Papers, Library of Congress, Box 213, Folder: Treasurer's File, 1892. Hereafter referred to as L. of C., A.H.A. Papers.
29. H. B. Adams to C. W. Bowen, December 16, 1892. *Ibid.*
30. H. B. Adams to C. W. Bowen, December 30, 1892. *Ibid.*

be welcomed by the motley crew attracted by an exposition. "I fancy," he wrote, with masterful understatement, "people at the World's Fair will not care much about hearing historical papers." [31] One invitation Adams could approve. This was to Turner from President Charles Kendall Adams of the University of Wisconsin who was delegated the task of soliciting some of the speakers. On February 23, 1893, Turner replied; he was glad to accept and would read a paper on "The Significance of the Frontier in American History." [32]

Turner might accept with alacrity, but others were less willing. By March 20 Poole was assured only four participants, including Turner and J. Franklin Jameson, while the ten who had already declined included such dignitaries of the profession as Edward Eggleston, Henry Cabot Lodge, Hermann von Holst, and Albion W. Small. [33] This was hardly an impressive beginning; Justin Winsor thought it "a pitiful show," and predicted that the quality of the performers was so low that the committee was unjustified in "asking any reputable writer to take part in the Congress to the extent of reading a paper." [34] Despite these forebodings, the list grew steadily and sparkled with some names acceptable even to that crotchety Bostonian: Moses Coit Tyler, Edward Everett Hale, Ephraim Emerton, Frederic Bancroft, and the Honorable William Wirt Henry. Leavening these was a sprinkling of westerners judged inadequate by Winsor: Charles Homer Haskins, Reuben Gold Thwaites, James A. Woodburn, George E. Bourne, and of course Turner. [35] By June 1 twenty-seven had agreed to take part, [36] and even Herbert Baxter Adams admitted that "we have a large number of good papers and the literary success of the Congress is assured." [37]

Adams could not know when he wrote those words that the program was threatened with the loss of the one paper that gave it lasting im-

31. H. B. Adams to C. W. Bowen, March 4, 1893. *Ibid.,* Box 213, Folder: Treasurer's File, 1893.
32. Turner to Charles K. Adams, February 23, 1893. SHSW: Turner Papers.
33. H. B. Adams to C. W. Bowen, March 20, 1893. L. of C., A. H. A. Papers, Box 4, Folder: 1893A.
34. Justin Winsor to H. B. Adams, March 22, 1893 in W. Stull Holt, ed., *Historical Scholarship in the United States, 1876–1901: as Revealed in the Correspondence of Herbert B. Adams* (Baltimore, 1938), p. 199.
35. W. F. Poole to H. B. Adams, March 28, May 4, 1893; Poole to C. W. Bowen, March 25, 1893. L. of C., A. H. A. Papers, Box 5, Folder: 1898 Mc-P.
36. W. F. Poole to H. B. Adams, June 1, 1893. *Ibid.,* Box 5, Folder: Miscellaneous.
37. H. B. Adams to C. W. Bowen, June 3, 1893. *Ibid.,* Box 213, Folder: Treasurer's File, 1893.

portance. On April 25 Turner wrote Poole that he had two fine students—Orin Grant Libby who had prepared a thesis on the "Geographical Distribution of the Vote on the Ratification of the Constitution of the United States," and Albert Hart Sanford whose dissertation was on "The Judicial Interpretations of the Ordinance of 1787"—who deserved a role in the Congress. Could a place be found for their excellent papers? Poole was doubtful, and so informed President Adams. Turner was disappointed, for he believed Libby's paper especially worthy of the American Historical Association. Room must be made, even if he had to sacrifice himself. On May 10 he suggested to Poole that if there were doubt of a spot for Libby's paper, "kindly put it in place of my own paper on 'The Significance of the Frontier in American History.'"[38] Fortunately Turner's academic prestige was low enough that Poole was able to ignore his request, preferring to stud his program with professors rather than graduate students. Had he not done so, the world would have awaited a less auspicious occasion to learn of the frontier hypothesis.

No sooner was this matter settled than another crisis loomed. When Herbert Baxter Adams prepared the printed programs he pointedly failed to mention that the meeting was under the auspices of the World's Congress Auxilliary and did not bother to list Dr. Poole and his local committee. Proof reached Poole in time for him to express his outraged indignation and hurl a volley of threats Adamsward.[39] Once more President Angell was drafted as mediator, and once more a sectional compromise was arranged; Adams' program would go only to members of the American Historical Association as an invitation to attend, while an official program for distribution at the sessions would be printed by the Chicago committee.[40] This took so much time that association members did not receive their invitations until July 1, just eleven days before the meetings began.[41] Even these were not complete, for Poole was desperately seeking a few more performers to add lustre to his offerings. As late as June 23 he urged

---

38. Turner to W. F. Poole, May 10, 1893. Newberry: Poole Papers, Box: April–June, 1893. This letter has been published with an appropriate introduction in W. L. Williamson, "A Sidelight on the Frontier Thesis: A New Turner Letter," *Newberry Library Bulletin*, III (April, 1953), 46–49.
39. W. F. Poole to H. B. Adams, June 8, 1893. L. of C., A. H. A. Papers, Box 4, Folder: 1893 Mc-P.
40. W. F. Poole to H. B. Adams, June 10, 1893. *Ibid.*
41. H. B. Adams to C. W. Bowen, July 3, 1893. *Ibid.*, Box 213, Folder: Treasurer's File, 1893.

President Adams of the University of Wisconsin to read a paper, but without success.[42]

Despite these setbacks, the historical congress assembled on schedule. Turner and his wife arrived several days before the July 10 date when the opening session would be held, traveling by train from Madison with their friends the Reuben Gold Thwaites, the G. L. Hendricksons, and Charles Homer Haskins, and putting up at a University of Chicago dormitory near the fair where they had reserved modestly priced rooms.[43] Once unpacked the party joined the throngs gaping at the wonders of the Exposition—all, that is, but Turner. He spent the next days paying for his sin of procrastination by writing the last pages of his paper; "I am," he told a friend two days before it was to be delivered, "in the final agonies of getting out a belated paper."[44] His labors were interrupted on Monday night, July 10, when he joined his fellow-historians at Chicago's new Art Institute on the lake front at the foot of Adams Street for the formal reception that launched the meetings of the Literary Congresses. There Turner made his formal bows before the Committee on Historical Literature in Room 24, stopped briefly in the Hall of Columbus where Dr. Poole and a harp soloist greeted the assembled notables, and hurried back to the university dormitory to continue preparation of his paper.[45]

The Historical Congress began its sessions the next morning, meeting in Room 3 of the Art Institute. The meeting began auspiciously enough; a business session first to elect President Angell the presiding officer and Herbert Baxter Adams secretary, then a general assembly that listened to President Angell's address on "The Inadequate Recognition of Diplomatists by Historians." This over, guests settled for the first round of the special sessions that would continue through the next three days. Each was to last

42. C. K. Adams to W. F. Poole, June 23, 1893. U. of Wis. Presidents File, C. K. Adams, 1891–1901. Series 4/8/1, Box 5.
43. Wisconsin State Journal, May 16, 1893. Hendrickson was professor of Latin at the university.
44. Turner to Woodrow Wilson, July 16, 1893. L. of C., Wilson Papers, Ac. D. R. F303 F321, Box 6. Turner, writing shortly after delivering his paper on July 12, was explaining why he had not responded to a letter from Wilson received on July 10. In this Wilson asked Turner's advice on an invitation to prepare a history of the American people, similar to Green's *History of the English People*. Turner strongly approved, and promised to send Wilson a copy of the paper he had just delivered when it was printed.
45. These events are fully described in the *Chicago Tribune*, July 10, 11, 1893, p. 3.

two hours or more, mornings and evenings, with from three to five learned papers on every variety of historical topic, and only the afternoons free for sightseeing and relaxation.[46] "It will be seen," wrote the official chronicler of the Congress, "that amateur historians and sensational theorists had no place on the programme."[47] Professionals, accustomed to such a heavy diet, were numerous enough to fill Room 3 with one or two hundred persons at each meeting.[48]

Turner's turn came on the evening of Wednesday, July 12. The day was intolerably hot until a lake breeze cooled the air in late afternoon but the fair grounds were crowded with the usual thousands of visitors who milled about among the exhibits as they did all that summer.[49] Some watched the dedication of the South Dakota Building, others jammed the lake shore to welcome the replica of a Viking ship that arrived that day from Norway, more stood in silence as firemen raked through the ashes of a giant storage plant that had burned two nights before, searching for the bodies of fifteen firemen killed in the blaze.[50] Turner was not among them; he even resisted a special invitation to the historians to view Buffalo Bill's Wild West Show at the fairgrounds that afternoon. Those last precious hours were used to put the finishing touches on his paper.

So he was ready when the usual audience of some two hundred historians and curiosity seekers gathered in Room 3 of the Art Institute at eight that night. Listeners of that day were a hardy lot, but even the endurance of the most experienced convention-goers must have been tested by the procession of scholars who performed: Dr. George Kriehn on "English Popular Uprisings of the Middle Ages," Dr. George P. Fisher on "The Social Compact and Mr. Jefferson's Adoption of It," Professor Jesse

46. The opening sessions were described in *ibid.*, July 12, p. 2, and the *New York Times*, July 12, 1893, p. 8. The operations of the congress are well described in Johnson Rossiter, *A History of the World's Columbian Exposition* (4 vols., Chicago, 1894), IV, 169–73. A briefer description is in the annual report of the secretary of the American Historical Association, Herbert B. Adams, "Report of the Proceedings of the Ninth Annual Meeting of the American Historical Association," *Annual Report of the American Historical Association for 1893* (Washington, 1894), p. 6.
47. "The Auxilliary Congresses," *The Dial*, XV (August 1, 1893), 60. This unsigned article was written by Dr. William F. Poole.
48. Rossiter, *History of the World's Columbian Exposition*, IV, 169.
49. *Wisconsin State Journal*, July 12, 1893. In Madison the heat that day was so intense that farmers bringing eggs to sell in town arrived with chickens roasted in the shell—or so the local reporter maintained.
50. *Chicago Tribune*, July 11, 1893, p. 1; July 12, p. 2; *New York Times*, July 11, 12, 13, p. 1; *New York Herald*, July 11, 13, pp. 3, 4.

Macy on "The Relation of History to Politics," Dr. Reuben Gold Thwaites on "Early Lead Mining in Illinois and Wisconsin." Only after this solid fare was digested did Turner's turn come. The official reporter summarized his points one by one: "Up to our own day American history has been to a large degree the history of the colonization of the Great West. . . . This ever-retreating frontier of unoccupied land is the key to our development. . . . There are various kinds of frontiers that passed westward in successive waves. . . . Successive frontiers revealed the progress of society. . . . At the same time the United States could show the hunting stage, the pastoral stage, and the manufacturing stage, as the traveler crossed the continent from west to east." [51] Turner had spoken his piece, and a monumental piece it was.

More monumental, indeed, than the reporter indicated, for no audience could survive all of "The Significance of the Frontier in American History" after listening to four solid papers, and he probably took mercy on his hearers by summarizing only a portion of his essay. What remained unreported was as important as what was reported. Taking his cue from the census bureau's announcement that there "can hardly be said to be a frontier line" remaining, Turner announced his text: "the existence of an area of free land, its continuous recession, and the advance of American settlement westward, explain American development." The frontier was one of several vital forces lying behind constitutional forms "that call these organs into life and shape them to meet changing conditions." The nation's institutions owed their peculiarity to the fact that they had been "compelled to adapt themselves to the changes of an expanding people—to the changes involved in crossing a continent, in winning a wilderness, and in developing at each area of this progress out of the primitive economic and political conditions of the frontier into the complexities of city life." [52]

This perennial rebirth of civilization in successive Wests "furnishes the forces dominating the American character. The true point of view in this

51. The *Chicago Tribune*, July 13, 1893, p. 3, described this session as one in which "interesting" papers were presented. That by Dr. George Kriehn was summarized in two paragraphs by the reporter; the remainder were only mentioned by speaker and topic. The sole reference to Turner's paper was: "Prof. J. F. Turner concluded the evening's program with a paper entitled "The Significance of the Frontier in American History." The *New York Times*, July 13, 1893, p. 8, listed the papers read, but gave no details.
52. Turner, "The Significance of the Frontier in American History" in F. J. Turner, *The Frontier in American History* (New York, 1920), pp. 1-2.

167

country is not the Atlantic coast, it is the Great West." The frontier, "the meeting place between savagery and civilization," was the area of "most rapid and effective Americanization. Here new traits, new institutions, were born." There "the wilderness masters the colonist. It finds him European in dress, industries, tools, modes of travel, and thought. It takes him from the railroad car and puts him in a birch canoe. It strips off the garments of civilization and arrays him in the hunting shirt and moccasin. It puts him in the log cabin of the Cherokee and Iroquois and runs an Indian palisade around him." No one living on the frontier escaped this transformation, for "the frontier environment is at first too strong for the man." Those who survived were "a new product that is American." [53]

This took place in successive Wests as population marched across the continent. "At first the frontier was the Atlantic coast," the frontier of Europe. With each advance some of the cultural baggage brought from the Old World was discarded and more distinctly American traits added. This was because a social evolution took place on each new frontier, beginning with hunters who were mastered by the wilderness and ending with city-dwellers who had mastered their environment. "Stand at Cumberland Gap," Turner wrote, "and watch the procession of civilization marching single file—the buffalo following the trail to the salt springs, the Indian, the fur trader and hunter, the cattle raiser, the pioneer farmer—and the frontier has passed by. Stand at South Pass in the Rockies a century later and see the same procession with wider intervals between." Each frontier was built on the experiences of prior frontiers; the land system, or mining techniques, or Indian policy, or the state constitution was adapted from that perfected in the region lying just to the eastward. In this progression the whole history of mankind could be studied. "The United States lies like a huge page in the history of society. Line by line as we read this continental page from West to East we find the record of social evolution." [54]

Turner made clear that while each new West patterned its institutions on the East from which it emerged, "essential differences due to the place element and the time element" were noticeable. These differences distinguished American civilization, for "in the crucible of the frontier the

53. *Ibid.*, pp. 3–4.
54. *Ibid.*, pp. 4–11.

168

immigrants were Americanized, liberated, and fused into a mixed race, English in neither nationality nor characteristics." The result was "the formation of a composite nationality for the American people." The nationalizing force of the frontier was accentuated as the central government broadened its powers to care for its burgeoning settlements. "Loose construction increased as the nation marched westward," for Congress must deal with land sales, internal improvements, defense against Indians, tariff protection, and the acquisition of new territories. "It was the nationalizing tendency of the West that transformed the democracy of Jefferson into the national republicanism of Monroe and the democracy of Andrew Jackson." [55]

An even more important function of the frontier "has been the promotion of democracy here and in Europe." Pioneers, faced with unique problems, were inclined to rebel against rule by a distant government and to broaden the suffrage base within their own communities. This frontier democracy, "born of free land," was "strong in selfishness and individualism, intolerant of administrative experience and education, and pressing individual liberty beyond its proper bounds." It encouraged lawlessness, lax business honor, and harmful currency policies. This in turn alarmed the less democratic East, which sought to increase its political controls. These efforts always failed, but they helped explain the political history of the nineteenth century. [56]

Finally, Turner saw the frontier as a spawning ground for many of the social and intellectual traits distinguishing Americans from Europeans. "To the frontier the American intellect owes its striking characteristics:" coarseness and strength combined with acuteness and inquisitiveness; a practical, inventive turn of mind, quick to find expedients; a masterful grasp of material things but lacking in the artistic; a restless, nervous energy; a dominant individualism working for good and evil; and above all the buoyancy and exuberance that came with freedom. These were the traits of the frontier, and the traits bred into all Americans by the existence of a frontier. [57]

What would happen to the United States now that the frontier was

55. *Ibid.*, pp. 11–29.
56. *Ibid.*, pp. 30–35.
57. *Ibid.*, p. 37.

closing? Turner foresaw a major shift in national psychology. Since the days of Columbus "America had been another name for opportunity" as expansion went on into areas of untapped natural resources. Never again would nature's gifts yield their riches so generously. Never again would a stubborn environment help break the bonds of custom and imperiously summon mankind to accept its conditions. No longer would frontiers "furnish a new field of opportunity, a gate of escape from the bondage of the past." Now Americans must learn to live in a closed-space world. "What the Mediterranean Sea was to the Greeks," Turner concluded with his often-used metaphor, "breaking the bond of custom, offering new experience, calling out new institutions and activities, that, and more, the ever-retreating frontier had been to the United States directly and to the nations of Europe more remotely." Now, four centuries after the discovery of the continent, at the end of a hundred years under the Constitution, the frontier was gone, and with its closing had ended the first period of the nation's history.[58] So Turner ended one of the most germinal papers ever presented to an audience of historians.

That essay was to stir discussion for generations to come, but it probably had little effect on the faithful audience that remained when the session came to a close. Those who had not quietly departed or been lulled into indifference by listening to five lengthy addresses on a hot night were so tuned to the belief that the "germs" of American institutions germinated in the forests of medieval Germany that they simply could not comprehend a doctrine as radically different as that preached by Turner. One young historian who was present later recalled that the audience reacted with the bored indifference normally shown a young instructor from a backwater college reading his first professional paper; he remembered, too, that discussion was completely lacking.[59] Turner must have returned to his dormitory room that night burdened with a heavy sense of failure.

58. *Ibid.,* pp. 37–38.
59. This was the impression of Andrew C. McLaughlin, who attended the session, and many years later described the scene to his colleague at the University of Chicago, Avery Craven. Craven to Ray A. Billington, January 8, 1970. Personal letter. Another who attended, however, sensed the fact that "the Monroe Doctrine of American historical writing" was being pronounced. This unnamed historian is quoted in Avery O. Craven, "Frederick Jackson Turner," in William T. Hutchinson, ed., *Marcus W. Jernegan Essays in American Historiography* (Chicago, 1937), p. 254.

Nor was he heartened by the public reaction. Only one Chicago newspaper bothered to mention his address, and that in a small paragraph on page three.[60] Dr. Poole, who prepared the official report of the Congress for *The Dial* and *The Independent*,[61] found Reuben Gold Thwaites' dull chronicle of Wisconsin lead mining a notable contribution and praised another speaker so extravagantly that she gushed her thanks, but found no place for even a word about the significance of the frontier.[62] Even President Charles Kendall Adams, who was almost certainly in the audience, did not deem it worthy of mention five days later when he summed up Turner's historical qualifications for the editor of an encyclopedia.[63] Nor did Turner's father, who arrived in Chicago two days later and reported to the home folk that Fred was an admirable guide to the fair but did not feel his historical contribution merited even a sentence.[64] Three months later the student newspaper showed the same deplorable judgment when it published a pretentious article on the effects of the Columbian Exposition on historical writing without mentioning "The Significance of the Frontier in American History."[65] One can only speculate at the chagrin of these witnesses when, a few years later, they heard the paper hailed as the

60. *Chicago Tribune*, July 13, 1893, p. 3. The *New York Times*, July 13, 1893, devoted so much space to the arrival of the Viking ship that the historical congress was allotted only three lines. Turner had been similarly neglected in prior public announcements of the sessions. The *Chicago Tribune*, July 9, 1893, p. 12, contained a long article on the arts congresses, listing all participants and describing the arrangements. Turner's name was at the bottom of the list, which was not alphabetical. Similarly the *New York Times*, July 9, 1893, p. 12, in a sizable discussion of "American History at Chicago," listed the papers by Moses Coit Tyler, Frederic Bancroft, George P. Fisher, and William Wirt Henry—including even one by Miss Cora Stuart of Worcester, Massachusetts, on "The Historical Policy of the United States as to Annexation"—but did not mention Turner.
61. F. F. Browne, editor of *The Dial*, to W. F. Poole, July 18, 1893; Clarence Bouler, editor of *The Independent*, to Poole, July 13, 1893. Newberry: Poole Papers, Box: April–July, 1893.
62. "The Auxilliary Congresses," *The Dial*, XV (August 1, 1893), 60–61. The letter of thanks was from Mrs. Ellen H. Walworth of Saratoga, New York, who read a paper on "The Value of National Archives," a subject that would appeal to Poole as a librarian. Mrs. Walworth to Poole, July 26, 1893. Newberry: Poole Papers, Box: April–June, 1893. Poole also mentioned with approval a dull factual account of "Early Slavery in the Northwest" by Henry Smith of Lake Forest, Illinois.
63. Charles K. Adams to W. E. Appleton of *Johnson's Universal Cyclopedia*, July 17, 1893. U. of Wis. Arch., Presidential Papers, C. K. Adams, General Corr., Box 5.
64. Andrew Jackson Turner to Helen M. Turner, July 23, 1893. HEH TU Box E. The senior Turners left Portage on July 14, 1893, two days after their son delivered his paper. *Portage Democrat*, July 14, 1893.
65. *The Aegis*, VIII (November 3, 1893).

declaration of independence of American historiography. Perhaps their feeling was that of a young man who later became Turner's colleague and spent the rest of his life bemoaning the fact that he chose to see Buffalo Bill's Wild West Show that night of July 12, rather than journey downtown to learn about the true importance of the Wild West.[66]

The less-than-enthusiastic personal reaction to Turner's doctrine portended its fate in printed form. He was forced to wait some time for this verdict for Herbert Baxter Adams and William F. Poole were still feuding and neither found time to pry papers from their authors and arrange for publication.[67] This delay cost the American Historical Association the distinction of introducing "The Significance of the Frontier" to its members. Turner carried his paper back to Madison after a few days of relaxation and sight-seeing, had the pleasure of hearing it praised by Woodrow Wilson, added the phrase suggested by Wilson on "the hither edge of free lands," and probably tucked it away in his files.[68] Fortunately he had occasion to rescue it before too long. In October, 1893, it was presented again, this time to the university's Historical and Political Science Association,[69] and in December presented once more before the annual meeting of the State Historical Society of Wisconsin.[70] In this form it appeared in the annual volume of the society's proceedings, published early in 1894.[71] Not until February did Turner relinquish it to President Adams for submission to the American Historical Association,[72] and not until December was it printed in the annual report of that organiza-

66. Professor Max Otto in *Wisconsin State Journal*, October 1, 1938. Professor Otto makes this remark in a long review of *The Early Writings of Frederick Jackson Turner* which had just been published. A copy is in U. of Wis. Arch., Director's File, Folder: Turner, F. J.
67. Adams reported at the end of the year that he had not been able to "recover" the papers delivered at the July meeting, despite regular prodding of Poole and his committee. H. B. Adams to Charles H. Haskins, December 23, 1893. Princeton: Haskins Papers.
68. Despite Turner's hoarding tendencies, the original manuscript of his 1893 essay has not been preserved. He was in the habit of cannibalizing his own lectures, transferring pages from one to another. Hence it is possible that some of the pages exist as parts of papers that he delivered later, but these cannot possibly be identified.
69. *Wisconsin State Journal*, October 12, 1893.
70. *Ibid.*, December 13, 1893. Turner shared the program of the State Historical Society with another member who spoke on "Prehistoric Pottery." The local press reported that he gave a "very able and interesting lecture." *Ibid.*, December 15, 1893.
71. *Proceeds of the Forty-First Annual Meeting of the State Historical Society of Wisconsin, 1894* (Madison, 1894), pp. 79–112.
72. Turner to H. B. Adams, February 5, 1894. HEH TU Box 1. Turner told Adams to use his own judgment about retaining the subheadings that were sprinkled through his paper.

tion.[73] Following his lifetime custom he purchased reprints generously and broadcast them widely to the great and near great of the profession.[74]

The response was discouraging. Some who read it were skeptical, or totally misunderstood his purpose. Edward Everett Hale acknowledged "your curious and interesting paper," [75] while Theodore Roosevelt congratulated him on "striking some first class ideas" and putting "into shape a good deal of thought that has been floating around rather loosely." [76] Francis A. Walker judged "the mere title is a success in itself," [77] and apparently did not read farther. To Charles McLean Andrews it was "extremely interesting," but he envied Turner the "elements of romance" in his materials contrasted with the dry bones of the colonial period.[78] Even those who felt the paper worthy of faint praise did so because they saw it as an extension of their own contributions. B. A. Hinsdale, author of antiquarian works on the West, agreed that easterners needed to learn more about the region; [79] the distinguished German scholar K. C. Lamprecht found in the essay "a strong similarity in many respects with our colonizing pioneers," [80] and Achille Loria applauded the publication of a "learned substantiating piece" for his own theories.[81]

Turner, who thrived on praise, could find but faint solace in these offerings, but others gave him genuine satisfaction. John Fiske praised his "excellent, *admirable* essay," then cast cold water by saying that for some time he had been "working along toward the same *perspective*." [82] Friedrich Ratzel, the geographer whose books Turner was to admire, found it "a very im-

73. *Annual Report of the American Historical Association for 1893* (Washington, 1894), pp. 199–227. A bound copy of Turner's own offprint of this paper is in the Huntington Library, Accession No. 222535. In it Turner made a few corrections, all minor; thus he removed one "t" from Governor Spotswood's name and changed the date of the issue of *The Aegis* in which his "Problems in American History" appeared from November 8 to November 4. A word-by-word comparison of the several printings of this essay by Fulmer Mood is in Turner, *Early Writings of Frederick Jackson Turner*, pp. 275–92.
74. Turner to Public Printer, Washington, D.C., April 14, 1894. Turner ordered two hundred extra copies. L. of C., A. H. A. Papers, Box 5, Folder: 1894 S-W.
75. Edward E. Hale to Turner, April 21, 1894. HEH TU Box 1.
76. Theodore Roosevelt to Turner, February 10, 1894. Houghton Library, Harvard University, Frederick Jackson Turner Papers.
77. Francis A. Walker to Turner, January 31, 1894. HEH TU Box 1.
78. Charles M. Andrews to Turner, February 6, 1894. *Ibid*.
79. B. A. Hinsdale to Turner, September 28, 1894. *Ibid*.
80. K. C. Lamprecht to Turner, April 18, 1895. *Ibid*., Box 2.
81. Achille Loria to Turner, February 17, 1894. *Ibid*., Box 1.
82. John Fiske to Turner, February 6, 1894. *Ibid*.

portant work" and "an instructive example of the view of the state and its geographic origins." [83] Of all who passed judgment, only Talcott Williams, a Philadelphia editorial writer, wrote prophetically that "it seems to me the most informative and illuminating contribution to American history that I have read in several years." [84] Williams was virtually alone in his vision. Far more typical of the historical profession was the eastern professor who remarked to a friend that "Turner must be a very provincial type of historian." [85]

This reaction was inevitable and predictible. New ideas displace old ideas only slowly; man is a conservative creature and changes his mind as reluctantly as he changes his living patterns. Nor had Turner provided the tangible evidence needed to make his thesis convincing. This was not his purpose; he intended only, as he put it, "to call attention to the frontier as a fertile field for investigation," and "to suggest some of the problems which arise in connection with it." [86] In later years he frequently expressed his concern that an essay intended only to present a hypothesis to be tested should be accepted as the gospel by his less critical disciples. "It was really an attempt at interpretation," he told a friend shortly before his death, "rather than a piece of research." [87] This his critics recognized; his paper was dismissed as a wild theory that had not been and could not be substantiated.

For much of this reaction Turner himself was responsible. In his youthful enthusiasm, he claimed too much for such scant evidence as he did use. His examples were drawn from a small segment of the frontier—the eastern Mississippi Valley that he knew so well—yet he deduced from them a social process that "formed a huge page in the history of society" and revealed luminously "the course of universal history." He was equally in error when he awarded frontiering an exaggerated role in the historical process; to say that "the existence of an area of free land, its continuous recession,

83. A review written in 1895 and quoted in Murray Kane, "Some Considerations on the Frontier Concept of Frederick Jackson Turner," *Mississippi Valley Historical Review*, XXVII (December, 1940), 398–99. Ratzel was sufficiently impressed with Turner's thesis to incorporate much of it in his "Ethnographie und Geschichtswissenschaft to America," in his *Deutschen Zeitschrift fur Gesechichtswissenschraft* (Freiburg, 1897). A copy, underlined by Turner to indicate the passages referring to his work, is in HEH TU File Drawer 21C, Folder: Miscellany.
84. Talcott Williams to Turner [1894]. HEH TU Box 1.
85. Schafer, "The Author of the Frontier Hypothesis," *loc. cit.*, 69–70.
86. Turner, "Significance of the Frontier in American History," in Turner, *The Frontier in American History*, p. 3.
87. Turner to Maurice G. Fulton, October 12, 1931. HEH TU Box 46.

and the advance of American settlement westward, explain American development," was to fly in the face of common sense no less than the laws of human motivation. His assertions were too positive, his generalizations too sweeping, to convince historians who regarded themselves as exact scientists.[88] Their suspicions were heightened by Turner's lack of caution in defining terms or stating principles. He spoke of the "frontier" as a line, a region, a place, and a process. He found it a force for such opposites as idealism and materialism, nationalism and sectionalism, cooperative enterprise and individualism. Only if a reader looked beyond these exaggerations and inexact terminology could he realize the true significance of "The Significance of the Frontier in American History." Viewed as a cold, exact statement of immutable fact the essay had little appeal to that science-oriented generation.[89]

It offended, moreover, by disputing the value of the two schools of historical writing then in vogue. On the one hand, Turner asked for an understanding of the West vastly different from that of Francis Parkman and the "Romantic School." Let us, he was saying, abandon colorful writing, heroism and drama, heroes who are pure and villains who are evil, wars and glamor and excitement; let us substitute analysis and dull facts and impersonal interpretation. On the other hand, Turner cast doubt on the institutional history and racial determinism current among the "Scientific School." He did not openly condemn the "germ" theory that they espoused, but he did argue that "too exclusive attention has been paid by institutional students to the Germanic origins, too little to the American factors." Continuity and development, he argued, could be studied without going "to the prim little Townships of Sleswick." Turner might agree that only a "fit" people could

---

88. Turner was not long in recognizing that his extravagant statements slowed the reception of his thesis. "Of course," he wrote three years later, "there are some things in the paper that would be better modified, I think, but it expresses in a general way my idea of the place of the West." Turner to George P. Brett, March 28, 1896. HEH TU Box 2. His concern was also shown by the increased caution that marked his scholarly writings (although not always his public addresses) as the complexity of the historical process was driven home to him by further study. This change is discussed in Avery Craven, "Frederick Jackson Turner, Historian," *Wisconsin Magazine of History*, XXV (June, 1942), 416–18, and Max Farrand, "Frederick Jackson Turner: A Memoir," *Massachusetts Historical Society Proceedings*, LXV (May, 1935), 433. It is illustrated in a textual analysis of Turner's essays in Per S. Anderson, *Westward Is the Course of Empire: A Study in the Shaping of an American Idea: Frederick Jackson Turner's Frontier* (Oslo, Norway, 1956), pp. 20–49.
89. This point is made in Henry S. Commager, *The American Mind* (New Haven, 1950), p. 295.

respond to the democratizing forces of the forest, yet he moved far from a sole reliance of racial determinism.[90] Just how far can be realized by comparing his theories with those of his contemporaries who wrote of "hereditary fitness for self-government" or referred to mining camps as the "folk-moots of the Sierra."[91] Turner stood somewhere between racial and geographic determinism in 1893, although he still thought in institutional terms and still conceived the emergence of the frontier as a single organic process.[92] His quarrel with the institutionalists was not yet in the open, but they could sense that his theories doomed their interpretation of history.

If Turner kept one foot in the camp of the Teutonists, he still had moved far toward a modern understanding of historical processes, and had shaken older explanations to their foundations. He held that civilization was modified on entering the New World, partly by environmental pressures, partly by the mingling of peoples from many backgrounds in the "crucible of the frontier." He theorized that imported cultures were altered by the opportunity offered by free land, and that the distinctive features of American civilization—its democracy, individualism, and nationalism—were the product of a low man-land ratio. He listed a number of intellectual and social traits and argued that they were exaggerated in the national character by repeated westering. He believed that the interaction between the complex of sections left behind by the moving frontier held the key to understanding the nineteenth-century United States. And he proposed that the story of man's total evolution was capsulized in the rebirth of civilization on each frontier; there historians could study the interaction of forces that shaped universal history. Turner solved few problems, but he asked a number of very pertinent questions.

This was the significance of his essay. Neither his background, or the books that he read or the maps that he studied or the intellectual and social

90. For a discussion on this point see Gilman M. Ostrander, "Turner and the Germ Theory," *Agricultural History*, XXXII (October, 1958), 260.
91. Charles H. Shinn, *Mining Camps: A Study in American Frontier Government* (New York, 1885), p. 99. Shinn, like Turner, had been a student of Herbert Baxter Adams at Johns Hopkins University; unlike Turner, he was unable to rise above the teachings of his master. This point is made in H. C. Allen, "F. J. Turner and the Frontier in American History," in H. C. Allen and C. P. Hill, eds., *British Essays in American History* (London, 1957), p. 147.
92. Some time later Turner recalled that his frontier paper was "in some degree a protest against eastern neglect, at the same time, of institutional study of the West, and against western antiquarian spirit in dealing with their own history." Turner to Constance L. Skinner, March 15, 1922. HEH TU Box 31. This letter is reproduced below, pp. 205–16.

currents in which he lived, provided him with answers, nor did he expect them to do so. His purpose was not to close, but to open a chapter in the history of the United States. He offered the profession not a completed historical structure but a blueprint with which to build one, and he told his fellow craftsmen that if they built as he suggested they would understand a great deal about the *how* and the *why* of their country's past. Turner's true contribution was to lay down a challenge that occupied historical scholars for generations to come.

SECTION III Frederick Jackson Turner Remembers

In which Turner reminisces
about the genesis of his frontier
thesis and discusses his views of
history.

Frederick Jackson Turner's first opportunity to defend his authorship of the frontier hypothesis—and to speculate on the course of events that led him to the theory—came in the fall of 1919. By this time he was so deeply involved in his researches on sectionalism that he had little interest in the frontier, but he still took parental pride in his first-born and was willing to enter the lists against anyone who suggested prior authorship. Fortunately he did not have to do so on this occasion, but he was prodded into recalling circumstances long vanished from his memory, and he did add a few valuable words on the origins of his concept.

The associate who stirred these recollections was his fellow historian, Professor William E. Dodd, of the University of Chicago, a friend of many years. Dodd, born in North Carolina on October 21, 1869, educated at the Virginia Polytechnical Institute and the University of Leipzig, and baptized as a teacher at Randolph-Macon College before joining the Chicago faculty in 1908, was a pioneer historian of the South, and a remarkably good one. His sectional loyalties, no less than his devotion to the Democratic Party, interested him in Woodrow Wilson and led to a decision to prepare a biography of the President before he left the White House. Dodd devoted more than two years to preparation, talking at length with Wilson on three or four occasions, interviewing congressmen of both parties, and digesting the extensive printed sources. His purpose was not to tell the definitive story; this could only be done many years later when documentary evidence was available. Instead he sought to enlighten future biographers on the passionate faith that Wilson inspired among his followers. "A contemporary account of a great man or a great epoch," Dodd wrote, "if made in the spirit of truth and justice, may set somewhat the form of future history." [1] He wanted to assure the President's reputation by setting that form.

1. William E. Dodd, *Woodrow Wilson and His Work* (Garden City, New York, 1920), p. x. An excellent biography of Dodd is Robert Dallek, *Democrat and Diplomat: The Life of William E. Dodd* (New York, 1968).

While rereading Wilson's early publications, Dodd happened on a caustic review of a volume by Goldwin Smith, *The United States: An Outline of Political History, 1492–1871*, that appeared in *The Forum* in December, 1893. Wilson found much to criticize; Goldwin Smith's opinions were strictly traditional, even to seeing only two major forces shaping American development, "the one proceeding from New England, the other, which was in the long run to be discredited, from the south."[2] This affront to his beloved South Wilson could not tolerate, nor could he stomach the complete rejection of the West as a major influence in the past. He and Turner had talked too often on that subject for the significance of the frontier to be forgotten. His review voiced his indignation; Wilson vigorously defended the importance of the South and called on his memory of Turner's views to make clear that Goldwin Smith should have made the West, not New England, the primal force shaping American history.

This was the review that Dodd read, and as he read he came across phrase after phrase that had a Turnerian ring: "When the great westward migration began everything was modified. . . . Beyond the mountains, not only new settlements, but a new nation sprang up. . . . The formative period of American history . . . did not end in colonial times or on the Atlantic coast . . . nor will it end until we cease to have frontier communities. . . . That part of our history, therefore, which is most truly national is the history of the West. . . . Almost all the critical issues of our politics have been made up beyond the mountains."[3] These words had a familiar ring to one as well tuned to Turner's ideas as was Dodd.

2. Goldwin Smith, *The United States: An Outline of Political History, 1492–1871* (New York, 1893). Smith was English born and educated; he taught at the University of Oxford for some time before coming to the United States in 1868 to join the Cornell University faculty as professor of constitutional history.
3. Woodrow Wilson, "Mr. Goldwin Smith's 'Views' on our Political History," *The Forum*, XVI (December, 1893), 495–96. If Wilson had stolen any of Turner's ideas, Turner would have been justifiably angry when he read this review. Instead he was delighted. "The lucid and effective statement which you make, in the Forum, of the importance of the Middle Region, and the West, and the doctrine of American *development*, in contrast with Germanic *germs*," he wrote Wilson, "is very gratifying. It cannot fail to help toward a more rational study of our history. I am glad that you think I have helped you to some of these ideas, for I have many intellectual debts to repay you. The main point is to bring about the right view in these questions, and your article will fix attention on the subject." Turner to Wilson, December 20, 1893. HEH TU Box 1. This letter, and others exchanged by the two men during this period, are printed with complete documentation in Arthur S. Link, ed., *The Papers of Woodrow Wilson, VIII, 1892–1894* (Princeton, 1970), 417.

He knew that "The Significance of the Frontier in American History" was not published until early in 1894. Yet here were phrases and concepts anticipating it exactly, written by Wilson before December, 1893. Could it be that Woodrow Wilson was the true author of the frontier hypothesis, and that Turner had borrowed it from him?

There was only one way to answer that question. During Dodd's next visit to the White House he put it directly to the President. Wilson's answer set his mind at rest: the basic concept of the frontier and all its ramifications came directly from Turner. The two were close friends in their Johns Hopkins days and afterward, the President remembered, and often met to talk over their historical theories. "All I ever wrote on the subject," Wilson assured his questioner, "came from him." This generous tribute prompted Dodd to tell Turner of the conversation, knowing that his friend's respect for the President was as great as his own. At the same time he asked whether Turner remembered anything important about their companionship when he and Wilson shared a Baltimore boarding-house during the spring of 1889: [4]

University of Chicago
October 3, 1919

My dear Professor Turner:

I am writing a book in which I undertake to show what Woodrow Wilson has actually done and stood for in his life; and in gathering material for the work, I have had several conversations with the President. One thing I wish to say to you and it is the object of this to say it:

After reading all Wilson's writings I came to the conclusion that he advanced the idea of the importance of the West in the shaping of American ideals and even in the making of the nation contemporaneously with you. I refer particularly to his article in the Forum for December, 1893.[5]

Talking with him about this he promptly disclaimed all originality. He said, "Turner and I were close friends. He talked with me a great deal about his idea. All I ever wrote on the subject came from him. No, it

4. The letter is in HEH TU Box 29.
5. Professor Dodd had read Woodrow Wilson's review of Goldwin Smith's volume, described in note 2 above.

was in no sense a discovery of mine."[6] This attitude and the other highly complimentary things he said about you seemed very creditable to a man who was daily being charged with all the selfishness and ambition that man could be guilty of. I once talked with another very eminent public man, who had some and very high, standing in history, and he certainly did not disclaim anything.

In view of the President's condition and because we are all so prone to reserve our good opinions of our fellows till it is too late for the expression of them to have any good effect, I have felt like writing you. I seem to recall a conversation I had with you at your house in Madison about your relations with Wilson. It was in 1908. You then spoke of the very cordial relations between you in those student and young professional days.[7]

Possibly the passage of time and the tremendous effect of events have

6. When Turner was a graduate student at the Johns Hopkins University during 1888–1889 he had the good fortune to live in a boardinghouse much frequented by visiting historians and presided over by Mary Jane and Hannah Ashton. There Wilson also lived when he returned to Hopkins to teach in the spring term. "Dr. Wilson is here," Turner reported to his fiancée in February 1889, "homely, solemn, glum, but with the fire in his face and eye that means that its possessor is not of the common crowd." Turner to Caroline Mae Sherwood, February 13, 1889. HEH TU Box D. Their friendship ripened at once; they were drawn together by the common need to defend their sections—the South for Wilson, the West for Turner—against the dominant school of New England historians, just as they were by their mutual respect and liking for each other. Turner learned much in Wilson's course on "Administration," but he gained far more from their long talks as they walked about the Maryland countryside or sat far into the night in Miss Ashton's living room. "You remember, I suppose," Wilson wrote Turner the summer after they parted, "our talks in Baltimore on the growth of the national idea, and of nationality, in our history, and our agreement that the role of the west in this development was a very great, a leading, role, though much neglected by historians." Wilson to Turner, August 23, 1889. HEH TU Box 1. These conversations were both flattering and stimulating to young Turner. "I like to talk to him," he reported after one extended talkfest. "One is always sure that he must keep his wits about himself, or be voted commonplace, and besides he knows that if he does find an idea it will be readily seized by Wilson." Turner to Caroline Mae Sherwood, [March 6 or 8, 1889]. HEH TU Box D. Wilson was equally intrigued with Turner. When, a few years later, he again taught at Johns Hopkins and again lived at Miss Ashton's boardinghouse, his wife noticed that other boarders were seldom mentioned in his letters. "You have been ominously silent about them," she noted. "No more *Mr. Turners* I suppose." Wilson agreed that "there is no Turner among them." Ellen Axson Wilson to Woodrow Wilson, February 17, 1894; Wilson to Ellen Axson Wilson, February 18, 1894. Link, ed., *Papers of Woodrow Wilson, VIII, 1892–1894*, 491–92.

7. Turner's emphasis on his "cordial relations" with Wilson suggests that his secretary, Merrill H. Crissey, was wrong when he wrote that their friendship ended when Wilson took exception to an unfriendly review by Turner of his *A History of the American People* (5 vols., New York, 1902). Turner's judgments, Crissey remembered, "cut Wilson to the quick, and he was never able, apparently, to forget—perhaps even to forgive—them." Crissey speculated that Turner's refusal to review books in his later years was prompted by his de-

blurred those relations or the recollection of them. I know New England hates Wilson with a consuming hatred, except the *Republican* at Springfield.[8] During the summer I have sat in the Senate galleries in Washington, listened to the debates, or what passed for debates, and lamented that abiding sectionalism which underlies so much of the conduct of our public men.[9] I have thought of you and of Wilson's high esteem for you recently expressed and wondered how you felt about it all, you the keen and experienced historian and penetrator of men's motives. I hope you think as well of the President as I feel sure history will rate him. But this is another matter and I must not stretch out a letter to a busy scholar.

We have opened with large attendance and with students that seem to have some purpose in coming here. Of course this latter can only be determined after the passage of time. At any rate the great war has not dampened the

---

termination never to offend another friend. Crissey, "Notes on Frederick Jackson Turner," in HEH TU Box 35, Folder: Merrill H. Crissey. Drafts of Biographical Data. Actually Turner's review was by no means hostile; he wrote glowingly of the brilliant style, of the fusing of historical data into an artistic literary form, of the author's sound judgment. Turner did feel that Wilson was "more at home in characterizing political leaders and the trend of events than in dealing with the deeper undercurrents of economic and social change"—a charge levied against most books he reviewed at this time. Frederick J. Turner, "Woodrow Wilson, A History of the American People," *American Historical Review*, VIII (July, 1903), 762–65. There was no indication in their continuing correspondence that Wilson took offense at these statements; he realized that he had written a popular history to please the general public, not his professional colleagues. When Wilson was elected governor of New Jersey in 1910 Turner wired him: "Hearty congratulations. You are bringing Princeton into the nation's service." Turner to Wilson, November 9, 1910. Woodrow Wilson Papers, Library of Congress, AC 9712 Box 7. Turner's distaste for reviewing might have stemmed from an earlier unpleasantness. Shortly after a harsh appraisal of James Schouler's *History of the United States under the Constitution* (1895) appeared in *The Atlantic Monthly*, LXXVII (June, 1896), 837–44, Turner met the older man at a meeting of the American Historical Association. Years later Turner told Guy Stanton Ford that Schouler was "such a nice old man" that he greatly regretted offending him, and resolved to say nothing about a book unless something good could be said for it. Ford, "Reminiscences of Guy Stanton Ford," Oral History Research Office, Columbia University, p. 224. Copies of Dr. Ford's remarks on Turner were kindly furnished the Huntington Library by Louis M. Starr, director of the Oral History Research Office.

8. The *Springfield* (Massachusetts) *Republican* had a long record of political independence dating back to the editorship of Samuel Bowles III (d. 1878) and continued by his son, Samuel Bowles IV. The *Republican* was a low-tariff newspaper, and supported Democrats Grover Cleveland and Woodrow Wilson.

9. President Wilson laid the Treaty of Versailles before the Senate on July 10, 1919. Opposition to the League of Nations Covenant embodied in the treaty had been growing for some time and now burst in a bitter debate that lasted through the summer, with the initiative taken by opponents of the League and of Wilson. Dodd's reference to an "abiding sectionalism" was prompted by the fact that the leading "irreconcilables" who opposed the League in any form were such westerners as Hiram Johnson of California, William E. Borah of Idaho, and James A. Reed of Missouri. An excellent account of the debate is in Arthur S. Link, *Wilson the Diplomatist* (Baltimore, 1957), pp. 128–53.

ardor of some young men for education, or as much of it as one can get in a university.

Yours sincerely,
(s) William E. Dodd

Turner read these words with delight, and as he did so he scrawled two notes in the margins. One was designed to establish his prior rights: "My paper was read in July, 1893, and I read it in MS to Mr. Wilson before his Forum article." So he had, although Turner could not recall that Wilson had made two visits to his Madison home, one in December, 1892, the other in late July, 1893. Nor could he remember that he had, in all probability, used the latter occasion to read aloud the essay that he had presented two weeks before to the American Historical Association.[10] Yet one fact was clear; Wilson did hear the paper on "The Significance of the Frontier in American History" before he prepared his review for *The Forum*.

Turner's second marginal note, written to jog his own memory (or possibly for the guidance of a future biographer) expanded on his relationships with Wilson and made even clearer his prior rights: "See footnote to my "Significance of the Frontier" as published by Wis. Hist. Soc. Proceedings for 1893," he wrote, "and my article in *The Aegis* (Madison, Wis.) Nov. 4, 1892, VII, p. 48, which I sent Mr. Wilson. We never had any question on this point." Here Turner's memory was exact, for the first publication of the essay by the State Historical Society of Wisconsin early in 1894 did describe his relations with Wilson accurately, even to calling attention to the review of Goldwin Smith's volume. In the "footnote" to which he referred he stated that the "foundation" of his paper was his article on "Problems in American History" in *The Aegis* for November 4, 1892, and that it was read to the American Historical Association in final form on July 12, 1893. "It is gratifying to find," he added, "that Professor Wilson . . . accepts some of the views set forth in the papers above mentioned, and enhances their value by his lucid and suggestive treatment of them in his article in *The Forum*, December, 1893, reviewing Goldwin Smith's *History of the United States*." [11]

10. For an account of these visits, see above, pp. 157–61.
11. Turner, "The Significance of the Frontier in American History," *Proceedings of the State Historical Society of Wisconsin at Its Forty-First Annual Meeting* (Madison, 1894), n. 1, p. 79.

The record set straight, Turner went on to comment on Wilson's place in history, as Dodd proposed—a comment that filled eighteen handwritten pages and was later corrected, improved, and compressed into the six type-written pages actually sent. In this revealing document Turner tells us something of his political views, but a great deal more about his relations with Wilson, the genesis of his frontier thesis, and his views of history. Because the rough-draft and typed versions of the letter vary, each containing bits of information not in the other, both are reproduced here, the rough-draft version first: [12]

7 Phillips Place
Cambridge, Mass.
October 7, 1919

My dear Professor Dodd,

It was very good of you to write me your letter of October 3d when we are both saddened by the news of President Wilson's illness.[13]

There is no man who has been a more stimulating force in my life both in the matter of scholarship and of public affairs. It would be hard to overstate his influence upon my general conception of history and politics in the months of our intercourse in Johns Hopkins, when I learned to have affection as well as admiration for him. One of my friends, Colonel Cole (Jas. A.) USA has reminded me that I wrote him sometime about 1890 that I shouldn't be surprised if Mr. Wilson became President of the United States before many years.[14]

12. The original of this letter, in Turner's hand and filling eighteen pages, is in HEH TU Box 29.
13. Woodrow Wilson embarked on a strenuous speaking tour in September, 1919, to carry his case for the League of Nations to the people. At Pueblo, Colorado, on September 25 he showed such signs of complete exhaustion that his physician ordered him back to Washington. There, on October 2, he suffered a severe stroke with paralysis on the left side of his face and body. For a time his life hung in the balance, and he was not completely out of danger until the end of October. While his mind remained clear, he was thereafter physically feeble and emotionally uncertain. A lucid discussion of his illness is in Edwin A. Weinstein, "Woodrow Wilson's Neurological Illness," *Journal of American History*, LVII (September, 1970), 324–51.
14. James A. Cole, a boyhood companion of Turner who followed a military career after graduating from the West Point Academy, recalled that when Turner returned to Portage from Johns Hopkins in the spring of 1889 he was filled with enthusiasm for Wilson. "I remember," he wrote Turner in 1914, "your ending up your oration about him by saying 'By George, Jim, I bet that fellow will be President of the United States one of these days.'" James A. Cole to Turner, January 23, 1914. HEH TU Box 21.

I had forgotten that I had let my enthusiasm run into prophesy, but if this is a correct remembrance, I suppose I am one of the first "Wilson" men, and I am cordially in favor of his present policies. I cannot say that all of his presidential measures met my approval, for I had not the patience he displayed in dealing with Mexico, for example, in the days when Germany was forming an impression of how far she could deal with us as a pacific subordinate; [15] nor did I feel that he should have waited quite so long as he did before clearly calling upon Americans of foreign birth as well as natives to rally around him as the bearer of American rights and honor. [16] These were matters of judgment on the question of *when* to act, however, and in the event he gained strength by his very caution and patience, among those whose earlier support in a national cause, he hesitated to trust. I thought I knew the West well enough to dare to trust its response earlier. But I have studied the Congressional conditions of that period and later well enough to be con-

15. In April 1914, an unarmed party from the U.S.S. *Dolphin* went ashore at Tampico to buy supplies, and wandered into a restricted area. They were arrested by Mexican troops, despite the cover of their flag, and although they were promptly released with apologies, President Wilson took umbrage at their treatment. He demanded power from Congress to "obtain redress" from President Victoriano Huerta, by force if necessary. When this was granted, and word reached Washington that a German ship was approaching with munitions for the Mexicans, troops occupied Vera Cruz. War seemed certain, but Wilson accepted the offer of the ABC Powers (Argentina, Brazil, and Chile) to mediate. Their plan was rejected by the Mexican government, but its moral effect was so strong that Huerta left office, allowing the United States to withdraw its forces. The episode is described in Arthur S. Link, *Woodrow Wilson and the Progressive Era, 1900–1917* (New York, 1954), pp. 107–44. At first Turner supported Wilson's policy. In a commencement address delivered in June, 1914, he noted that "alien national interests lie threatening at our borders," but was pleased that "we take council with European nations and with the sisterhood of South America" rather than "sending armies of frontiersmen to settle our concerns." Turner, "The West and American Ideals," in Turner, *The Frontier in American History* (New York, 1920), pp. 295–96. Later he took a more belligerent stand. "I am not convinced," he wrote a friend in January, 1918, "that the Mexican policy, in spite of its good effect upon public opinion, did not encourage both Mexico and Germany to disregard our interests and discount our power and our determination." Turner to Edgar E. Robinson, January 19, 1918. HEH TU Box 28. This was his view at the time this letter to Dodd was written.

16. Turner was a strong interventionist between 1916 and America's entry into World War I, praising politicians who favored war, and damning those opposed. Wilson's cautious policies he found distasteful and due to uncertainty of mind rather than a well-planned program. "I have become convinced," he wrote in March, 1917, "that only by using this great national stress to strengthen our sinews and harden our tissues and learn our national lesson, shall we hereafter play an independent part in the world's affairs." Turner to Mrs. William Hooper, March 21, 1917. HEH TU-H Box 3. A year later his views had hardened into a dislike of Wilson's handling of public opinion, particularly when dealing with the "hyphenated Americans": "In his effort to hold the various foreign stocks in line for a cause that should appeal to humanity, he trusted less to the response to a sharp challenge of American rights and principles, than he might, and he postponed that call to the people longer than he should." Turner to Edgar E. Robinson, January 19, 1918. HEH TU Box 28.

vinced that no writer has yet sufficiently measured his service in disciplining his party, officered by men naturally opposed to his foreign policy, to follow him in what *seemed* to be a new path. I refer of course to men like Clark, Kitchin, Stone and Bryan.[17] He overruled the leaders of his party and defeated a large minority at least among the Republicans in enforcing his policy.

It has been one of the hardships of my recent years to have to antagonize my social companions in New England and risk my reputation for sanity not to say judgement in supporting Mr. Wilson.[18] If my health hadn't been such that the effort would have done as much harm as good to the cause, I should have tried to do more publicly. But in truth I have been, since the period of our war, on the edge of a breakdown, following an operation. Now I am better again.[19]

I agree with all you say about present partisan and sectional unfairness to Wilson; but as I am a democrat I suppose I'm liable to prejudice in the question of *partisan* motives. However the historian will have no difficulty in estimating such men as Henry Cabot Lodge.[20]

You would perhaps be surprised to find how much support the President has among men in the Harvard faculty in spite of what I have written above.

As to President Wilson's disavowal of priority in the matter of historical

17. Turner referred to Wilson's fellow Democrats Champ Clark of Missouri, Speaker of the House of Representatives, William J. Stone, chairman of the Senate Foreign Relations Committee, Claude Kitchin of Missouri, House majority leader, and William Jennings Bryan of Nebraska, secretary of state. All opposed Wilson's proposal of February 1916, to arm merchant vessels against submarine attack and other warlike measures of the President that Turner favored.

18. When Turner told a Harvard colleague, William Roscoe Thayer, as they walked together toward the polling place in November 1918, that he intended to vote a solidly Democratic ticket, Thayer was shocked that a "hard-headed man" could make such a statement. If Turner were right, he announced, he himself must be a crank. Then, on reflection, Thayer added that he probably was a crank, for crankiness ran in his family. President Charles W. Eliot's announced vote for a Democratic candidate for the Senate that year was looked on in Boston circles as a confession of senile dementia. Turner to Mrs. William Hooper, November 5, 1918. HEH TU-H, Box 4.

19. In June, 1917, Turner underwent a hernia operation at Harvard's Stillman Infirmary that invalided him for a month and left him so weak that he could do little for nearly a year. Turner to Dorothy Turner Main, June 13, 1917. HEH TU Box I.

20. "I still think," Turner wrote a few months later, "that Henry Cabot Lodge and the good Lord will have an unpleasant half hour if he ever climbs up for an interview." Turner to Mrs. William Hooper, January 16, 1920. HEH TU-H Box 5. Senator Lodge, a Massachusetts Republican, was Wilson's most effective opponent in the battle over the League of Nations. Turner, and most of the nation, believed that he was motivated by partisan ambitions rather than conviction, and that he was sacrificing the world's safety to better the Republican party.

exposition of the influence of the West in American development, I can only say that it was, as you say, an evidence of fairness and it was true. I am glad you first sought his own evidence. It would have been more than an unpleasant thing for me to contend for the parentage of my intellectual first born, dear as it is to me, and much as it means for my reputation. Nor have I the temerity to try [to] claim any exclusive property in an idea that would have evolved from the nature of the growing American consciousness itself. But for the form and time of my own expression of the idea I am naturally interested, and your letter leads me to try to recall some of the facts.

I couldn't say just when the thing took form. In a way it was involved in some of the underlying conceptions that shaped my thesis on the Fur Trade. Wilson's praise when I read it at a Hopkins seminary in 1888 or 1889 was very heartening to me.[21] I got a better conception of the South at JHU also, both because I had come to a new environment at Baltimore and also because I absorbed from Wilson an appreciation of its quality. My studies of sectionalism in the sense of Western, Middle, Southern and New England, rather than of North and South alone, began in that same time and were developments of the same general influences. I dare to believe that in this respect the conversations of President Wilson and myself had some historical results.[22] But that's another story.

By 1892 I put in print in a crude form some of these conceptions. Not, you will observe, immediately upon my leaving Baltimore. Mr. Wilson's Division and Re-union was published in March, 1893. I do not know that I had any definite influence upon the splendid first chapter of that model of a brief history.[23]

21. Turner's report to the Johns Hopkins seminar on February 15, 1889, was a summary of his dissertation on "The Influence of the Fur Trade in the North West from the Particular Standpoint of Wisconsin." His mentor, Herbert Baxter Adams, together with Richard T. Ely and Woodrow Wilson, were among the listeners. Johns Hopkins: Seminar Records, 1888–1889, February 15, 1889.

22. In his later reminiscences, Turner spoke often of the fact that he and Wilson, as westerner and southerner, felt outside the pale as they discussed the work of New England historians who dominated the profession. Because each felt that his section was misunderstood and neglected, Turner's awareness of the strength of sectional loyalties was increased. This, he recalled, helped to turn his attention to the sectional conflicts of the past and to make him realize that they were more important than the North-South division stressed by Civil War historians.

23. Woodrow Wilson, *Division and Reunion, 1829–1889* (New York, 1893), was the third of a three-volume *Epochs of American History* series edited by Albert Bushnell Hart. When writing this volume, Wilson asked Turner to substantiate his memories of their talks at Johns Hopkins, when they agreed that the extent of the West's influence in American history

Already, I had printed in the college magazine of Wisconsin (The Aegis) in November of 1892 (VII, 48) a paper on Problems in American History in which I had sketched some of my growing ideas and had sent a copy to Mr. Wilson. I think you would find this important in reaching a conclusion on the question, if the President hadn't already answered it. If it isn't easily accessible in Chicago I will lend you my copy. I sent various copies out at the time, but I don't know how many have survived.[24]

I had only the one year 1888–89 at Baltimore and during only a portion of that time was Mr. Wilson in residence, but it was one of the richest experiences of my life and I am very happy and very proud that he remembers me there. I had no correspondence with him on the themes we talked of in the next few years that would be helpful in tracing the genesis of my *Frontier*.

In 1893, summer, I revised and elaborated my "Problems" paper into the paper on the Significance of the Frontier for the Chicago session (July) of the American Historical Association. This did not appear in the *Report* until 1894. Mr. Wilson wasn't there but he was at my house sometime within the year 1893 and I read it to him in manuscript. I recall my gratitude to him for his general approval and for the word "hither" as descriptive of the eastern edge of the frontier! [25] I gave the same paper at the meeting of the Wisconsin Historical Society in Dec., 1893, and it was printed there in 1894 before the AHA *Report* was issued.[26] I haven't at hand the date of my talk with Wilson, but it was sometime before his Goldwin Smith article. If you have my paper in the Wis. Hist. Soc. edition, you will see that I refer in the footnote (first page) to his Dec. 1893 Forum article.[27]

I am setting forth these chronological facts because you may have a

---

had been neglected. Turner pleaded that he was too busy to undertake this assignment. Wilson to Turner, August 23, 1889; Turner to Wilson, August 31, 1889. HEH TU Box 1. Despite this refusal, Wilson incorporated many of Turner's ideas on the West in his volume, including the opinion that democracy and nationalism were intensified on the frontier. "Expansion has meant nationalization," he wrote, "and a distinctly American order of politics, begotten of the crude forces of a new nationality." This nationality was "distinctly new and buoyantly expectant." Wilson, *Division and Reunion*, pp. 4, 11.

24. In a marginal note at this point Turner wrote: "Sent him a copy under separate cover asking return."

25. Wilson's two visits to Turner's home in Madison in December 1892, and July 1893, are described above, pp. 157–61.

26. The paper first appeared in the *Proceedings of the State Historical Society of Wisconsin at the Forty-First Annual Meeting* (Madison, 1894). This small, paperback volume was apparently available by February, 1894, for Turner began distributing copies to his friends at that time.

27. For the wording of the footnote to which Turner refers, see above, p. 197.

historical interest in seeing some of the missing links that make it hard for the historian so often to reach a judgement on the basis of the accessible evidence. Mr. Wilson and I never had the faintest question of rivalry in the matter, of course.

In part it was the application to American history of a *mode* of historical thinking about institutional evolution which I learned from W. F. Allen, my Wisconsin historical master, in his lectures on Mediaeval institutions.[28] I saw even then the possibility of dealing with American history on similar lines in a new way. When Herbert Adams once told us, in Johns Hopkins, in effect, that his seminary having dealt with the American local institutions had exhausted the opportunities for new contributions in the field of U.S. history and would turn to European history for its next work, it was a challenge to me to work out my own ideas.[29] These ideas, I am sure, were broadened and enriched by Wilson's conceptions of *Politics*, in the large sense, and by his lectures and conversations on the evolution of institutions, on the Constitution "as a vehicle of life," on the realities behind the forms of institutions, on the present as a repository of the past and even more, on process idea of "breaking the cake of custom," as involved in Bagehot's ideas.[30] These seeds were planted in the soil of my own Western experiences and observations and in the soil of my studies of Mediaeval history, the evolution of new institutions or modification of old ones to meet new conditions. These general historical and evolutionary conceptions, however, I applied to U.S. and to the West myself.

28. Throughout his lifetime Turner repeatedly acknowledged his debt to Professor William Francis Allen, his mentor during his undergraduate and graduate years at the University of Wisconsin. Allen, educated at Harvard and in Germany, taught a sequence of courses in ancient and medieval history in which Turner enrolled, as he did in the one-term course in American history. Allen's "Class Books" for 1882–1884 when Turner was an undergraduate in his classes are in the SHSW: Allen Papers. A full account of his life is in a master's thesis prepared at the University of Wisconsin in 1955 by Owen P. Stearns, "William Francis Allen: Wisconsin's First Historian."

29. That Herbert Baxter Adams made this statement is questionable. It does not appear in the manuscript "Seminar Records, 1888–1889," nor did his continuing assignment of American history topics suggest that he was ready to abandon the subject. For a discussion of this point see above, pp. 27–29.

30. Turner refers to two books that influenced his thought on the frontier: Woodrow Wilson, *The State: Elements of Historical and Practical Politics* (Boston, 1889), and Walter Bagehot, *Physics and Politics: An Application of the Principles of Natural Selection and Heredity to Political Society* (New York, 1880). The former Turner heard just prior to its publication in the form of the twenty-five lectures in Wilson's course on "Administration" at Johns Hopkins. For a discussion of his use of Bagehot's volume, see above, pp. 130–32.

These somewhat disjointed recollections were apparently added, one after the other, as Turner continued to remember those distant days. He made no attempt to end his preliminary draft with the usual salutations, but probably used it to dictate the copy that was sent to Dodd: [31]

> 7 Phillips Place
> Cambridge, Mass.
> October 7, 1919

My dear Professor Dodd:

I cannot thank you sufficiently for your kind letter coming at a time when we have both been saddened and alarmed over the news of the President's illness. He means so much to us as a *man*, as well as a wise and far sighted leader in the world, that the feeling is both personal and American, and human!

For myself I may say that there is no man who has been a more stimulating force in both matters of historical thinking and in public affairs than Mr. Wilson. It would be hard to overstate either his influence upon my general conceptions of history or of policies during the months of our intercourse at Johns Hopkins and later. I have both affection and admiration for him now as I had before he became one of the great figures of the world.

A few years ago one of my friends, Colonel J. A. Cole, U.S.A., retired, wrote me reminding me that even in those days of the later eighties I had written him that I shouldn't be surprised if Mr. Wilson became president of the nation. I had forgotten this; but if his memory is right, I must have been one of the early "Wilson" men.

And I am now warmly in favor of his policies. I cannot say that I have approved every part of his course as president, for I hadn't his patience with Mexico, and believed that his course there encouraged German arrogance to us; nor did I think his *caution* in summoning German-Americans and all other Americans to rally around him in making an issue of American independence of German interference, was entirely justified. I believe that I understood the Middle West well enough to know that an adequate statement

31. This version of the letter to Dodd, taken from the William E. Dodd Papers in the Library of Congress, has been published in Wendell H. Stephenson, ed., "The Influence of Woodrow Wilson on Frederick Jackson Turner," *Agricultural History*, XIX (October, 1945), 249–53. The original is in HEH TU Box 29.

of the real conditions would win all its controlling elements to his support at an earlier period than he deemed prudent. But I can see, of course, that his delay strengthened his hand when finally he did raise the flag. The question was one of time simply and I did not attack but rather tried to explain to those of my friends hereabouts who were almost as pro-British or pro-French as they were pro-American in their criticism of him.

I have studied the situation enough also to see that no writers have yet adequately set forth the difficulties that confronted him, both in the labor situation—which but for his policies before the war would have been even more menacing—and in the control in Congress of Democratic leaders whom he had to overrule—men like Bryan, Stone, Kitchin, Champ Clark, and the other leaders of the party and chairmen of committees whose tendencies were all away from the line marked out by President Wilson. Nor am I ignorant of the serious situation created by the opposition of Middle Western and some Pacific Coast Republicans, who came dangerously near to holding a balance which would have turned the scale if the President's following had broken. His management of that critical situation was masterly and needs more adequate recognition than can perhaps yet be given to it with the approval of the President. But the later historian will see it; and he will see the difficulties to be met in confronting European statesmen, changing conditions there, and here, as well.

What you say of sectional misrepresentation and partisanship is all true. It made it hard often for me to get on with my New England associates. They were never ready to concede that a Democrat was President, or that there were other sections to consider than this corner of the nation. I have risked my reputation for sanity as well as for judgment in supporting the President, even with some who have since been converted! Neither my health nor my abilities permitted me to take the public position which I would gladly have taken on some of these issues. A man from the West, anyway, can hardly be of large public influence when he lives in a section that is accustomed to listening in preference to its own long-established leaders. I have sometimes wondered during the war if I could not have been more useful in the West. But after an operation early in the war I was practically out of commission and on the edge of a complete breakdown, from which I hope I am at least partly recovered.

The future historian will find no difficulty I trust in estimating the men

194

like Henry Cabot Lodge. But I ought to add that you would be surprised perhaps, at the number of men in University and other circles here, who take the side of Mr. Wilson.

As to the matter of the priority of the conception of the part of the western movement in the nation, it was indeed a fine and generous thing for the President to say what you quote in your letter. I am glad you consulted him before asking me.

Since you write me of your own conclusions prior to the interview with him, you may be interested in some of the chronology of the question. There never was any difference between President Wilson and myself about the matter and his words to you would make it unnecessary for me to say more than to thank you for repeating them. But you will perhaps let me tell you rather ingenuously of the thing as it lies in my mind.

I think the ideas underlying my "Significance of the Frontier" would have been expressed in some form or other in any case. They were part of the growing American consciousness of itself. What I shall write of is rather the time and form of my own attempt to express them.

In a way the ideas were involved in the point of view which I presented in my Fur Trade in Wisconsin. When I read this to the seminary at Johns Hopkins (1888–89), Mr. Wilson put new life into me by saying: "this is the kind of atmosphere in which we can breathe." His praise of the paper, which now seems not sufficiently warranted, heartened me to bolder attempts.

In part the paper came from attempts of mine to apply to American history the mode of treatment that I had learned from Professor Wm. F. Allen, in his courses on the evolution of society and institutions in the Middle Ages. There seemed to be a similarity in the problems that piqued my interest.

In part it was due to a reaction from a statement—loosely made—by Herbert Adams to the Hopkins seminary to the effect that the Hopkins men, having dealt with local institutional history in the United States, had thus explored the chief remaining opportunity for constructive work in American history and would next turn to European history for thesis topics—or words to that effect.

My own mind was warmed and stirred by the change from my more or less provincial life in the West to a new environment, where I could get a more detached view of the significance of the West itself and where I was challenged, in a way, to try to account for myself and my people, under conditions of a new audience.

But all my ideas and ambitions were broadened and enriched by Woodrow Wilson's conversations, and—though less so—by his lectures, expounding *politics* in a larger sense, discussing the evolution of institutions and constitutions as "vehicles of life," as expressions of society and human beings rather than as formal and dead things. It kindled my imagination. His emphasis upon Bagehot's idea of growth by "breaking the cake of custom" left a deep impression upon me when I came to consider what part the West had played. Mr. Wilson didn't apply the idea to the West, but he kindled my imagination by the general idea.

These seeds were planted in the soil I have already described.

Moreover I got new ideas of the South and its dynamic side in my talks— sometimes my arguments—with Mr. Wilson. I came to see, by a process of give and take, the larger meaning of sectionalism as a movement between New England, Middle, Western and Southern sections, rather than between North and South. I dare to think that these conversations had some effect upon the later history of the country as well as upon Mr. Wilson and myself. He was the older man and the riper scholar, and the greater mind. But I was bringing to him words from lands he didn't know, as he was giving me a new conception of the South, as well as a new outlook upon politics in general. But this is another story. We told each other that we were stimulated by these conversations over the right of secession, nullification, etc. And we talked of the power of leadership; he mentioned his ambition to get into political life, and his inability at the time to find the way [t]here, as he could have found it under such conditions as those in England; of the untested power of the man with literary ability in the field of diplomacy; of the need of reconstructing legislative procedure to make executive leadership useful and effective. Or rather Mr. Wilson talked of *these* things, and as I look back upon it he seemed to have set forth his own later programme. He even asked me what would happen if the German immigrants to the Middle West should sometime have to choose between Germany and the United States in case of war, and he seemed to doubt my confidence that they were assimilating so rapidly that there would be no real danger.

But to get back to the theme.

In 1892 in the student magazine of the University of Wisconsin, *The Aegis*, of November 1892 (VII, 48) I printed an article on "Problems in

American History" in which I outlined some of my ideas, and which I sent at the time to Mr. Wilson. As you will find this interesting, if you are interested in the evolution of my paper, I am loaning you my copy which I will ask you to return when you have read it as I should not like to lose it from my family furniture. It was not written until 1892, and my residence in Hopkins was in 1888–1889 (though I returned in 1890 for a week to take the examination for my degree).[32] It was therefore, in effect, the result of my consideration chiefly of what the western aspects of American history meant for me in my new chair.

Mr. Wilson's splendid first chapter of his Division and Re-union appeared in March 1893. I see only his own vision in its appreciation of the West.

My Aegis article I also sent to other students. Moran gave me the copy I'm sending you some years ago, for example.[33]

In 1893 I read at Chicago in *July* at the meeting of the American Historical Association there at that time my "Significance of the Frontier," not printed in the *Report* until 1894. But I also read it to the Wisconsin Historical Society in Dec. 1893 and it was first issued by that Society in its Proceedings. Meanwhile I had read to Mr. Wilson, who was a visitor, as I recall it, at my house—though I am not at the moment sure where we met—the paper in manuscript, and he suggested the use of the word ' "*hither*" side of free land' for which I had been hunting!

In the Wisconsin printing of the paper I referred to Mr. Wilson's article in the Forum (Wis. Hist. Society Proceedings for *Dec.*, 1893) in a footnote as reinforcing the ideas presented in my paper (July 1 [*sic.*], 1893)—which was printed as it was read in Chicago, except for "*hither*."[34]

But the important missing link is my Aegis article of Nov. 1892.

I am more than glad that you have in hand the important work of portraying the President. He is an abiding figure, worthy of the best you or

32. Turner intended to complete his doctoral work at Johns Hopkins in one academic year, 1888–1889, but was unable to pass the reading test in French and German required of all candidates. "The Hopkins instructor," he wrote that spring, "had hard work to keep a sober face when I read some French aloud at his request." Turner to Caroline Mae Sherwood, June 24, 1889. HEH TU Box D. Turner returned to Baltimore in May, 1890, to complete his examinations and win the degree.
33. Thomas F. Moran earned his doctorate at Johns Hopkins five years after Turner and taught at Purdue University thereafter. His interest in institutional and constitutional history as well as his Johns Hopkins connection made him a natural target for a copy of the paper that Turner sent him, and that he later returned.
34. Turner read his paper on July 12, not on July 1.

any man can put into such a work. May he be spared for further great service!

With renewed thanks
I am
Yours truly,
Frederick J. Turner

This long letter greatly pleased Dodd; it not only set his mind at rest concerning priorities on the frontier hypothesis, but inspired a few words of his own on history and historians. Most important of all, it allowed Dodd to express the feeling of indebtedness that Turner engendered; his gratitude typified the attitude of much of the profession in a day when Turner's interpretations were accepted unquestioningly as the proper key to American history: [35]

University of Chicago
October 14,19.

Dear Professor Turner:

I am greatly obliged for your full and painstaking letter. It made perfectly clear some points that were not clear in my mind. As I wrote you, I had come to feel that both you and Wilson came contemporaneously into the most interesting and important discovery in American historical writing. But Wilson very promptly disabused my mind. It was no very extraordinary thing for two great scholars to be working in the same direction. It has been so with many other important discoveries. I am sure you could not have felt that I, in the least, even in my mind, discounted the originality or importance of your famous paper. One thing, I had overlooked the fact that the paper was read in the summer, not in December.

So much for that. What you say about the new treatment of American history which must inevitably have come about. Yes and no. I wrote my Macon, or at least got the data first in order, in Goettingen and Leipsig; came back to North Carolina and put it into the form it now wears; and finally printed it in 1903.[36] I came frequently upon the fact of the bitter

35. The original of this letter is in HEH TU Box 29.
36. Dodd began his first book, *The Life of Nathaniel Macon* (Raleigh, North Carolina, 1903) while a doctoral candidate at the University of Leipzig and completed it at Randolph-Macon College, where he began his teaching career in 1900. He joined the University of Chicago faculty in 1908.

198

rivalries of West and East and realized that it amounted almost to civil war at one time; but the distressing fact is that my Macon was not influenced appreciably by it. I was never brought into touch with an American historian till 1901 at the first Washington meeting I attended, although I attended the Association's meeting in 1900 at Detroit.[37] Your influence began to count with me when I came to read your paper and devote special attention in my teaching to American history 1903 and 1904.

Thus I might have gone on all my life without realizing the greatest fact in our history, stumbling all about it all the time. You see historical writing is so conventional; men write from inherited points of view long after they think themselves wholly free; and in history, as in other lines of endeavor, men's minds are slow to see the whole significance of what they handle. Otherwise the race would long since have reached the ultimate knowledge. We grope and shall still be groping thousands of years hence. So, do not discount your own contribution by saying it must have been done about that time any how. At the same time you probably do say to your students— "Don't stop with my discovery."

I am returning your paper. It was of course new to me and it only removes one degree further any notion of a divided or contemporary authorship of the idea we have been discussing. Of course I should never have gone to print without writing or talking with you about the subject. And my talk with Wilson gave him a chance to reveal himself in a new light. History is certainly his dearest subject, even if his professional life took the turn it did. Although a hundred politicians and Irish agitators were clamoring for a word with him he sat quietly half an hour and talked about this subject and the historical side of the negotiations at Paris.

It is a pleasure to me to know that you feel as you do about Wilson. I think too he will rank as one of our great presidents. He narrowly missed being the greatest of all, in my opinion. A certain trait of character limited him.

Yours sincerely,
William E. Dodd

37. Dodd attended the annual meetings of the American Historical Association at Detroit and Ann Arbor in 1900, and at Washington in 1901.

Turner was greatly pleased by this exchange of views and intimacies. Here were letters worth preserving, not only because they set matters straight concerning his frontier hypothesis, but because they revealed a friendship with President Wilson of which he was immoderately proud. Such documents were worthy of special treatment. Instead of adding them to his files he carefully encased them in a manila folder, added a copy of *The Aegis* that contained his essay on "Problems in American History," and prefaced the lot with a typed note that no biographer could possibly miss:

> Letters from Professor W. E. Dodd to Frederick J. Turner regarding the origin of the idea of "The Significance of the Frontier in American History" with "Problems in American History," *Aegis*, University of Wisconsin, Nov. 4, 1892.[38]

Then, if this were not enough, Turner added still another note in his own hand:

> See further Dodd's Woodrow Wilson and His Work (N.Y., 1920), pages 27–28.[39] He overstates my influence on Wilson probably, but the reference to Wilson's conversation is important. I had read my paper on the "Significance of the Frontier" to Wilson *before* he wrote his *Forum*

38. Turner wrote on the front of this copy of *The Aegis:* "Contains first form of my doctrine of frontier. Prior to my paper in AHA 1893 I had not read Ratzel, or Godkin, or other writer who deals with this problem." This is in HEH TU Box 29. Turner referred to the German geographer, Friedrich Ratzel, a pioneer advocate of environmental determinism, and E. L. Godkin, editor of *The Nation*, whose "Aristocratic Opinions of Democracy," published in the *North American Review*, CCVI (January, 1865), 194–232, anticipated the frontier hypothesis. Turner was correct in this statement; he did not discover Ratzel's works until 1895 or 1896, and did not read Godkin's essay until three years after his own appeared. Then he chuckled, and remarked: "Godkin has stolen my thunder." See above, pp. 69–70, for a discussion of Godkin's essay.
39. The portion of Dodd's *Woodrow Wilson and His Work* to which Turner refers (pp. 27–28) described the way in which the two men met at Johns Hopkins and how each influenced the thought of the other. "Turner," Dodd wrote, "made Wilson realize how much the West and the ever-moving frontier had determined the course of American history. If Turner has never written a full history of the country, he has influenced the writing of that history more than any other man of his generation." Turner underlined these lines, and another reference to him on p. 20, in his copy of the book. This is now in the Huntington Library, Accession No. R200265.

review and before his "Calendar of Great Ams" etc.[40] This was at my house in Madison where he was my guest, prior to its publication. He suggested 'hither' side of free lands, but none of the ideas; merely helped me to an apt word.

Turner was taking no chances that posterity award him his just due as expounder of the frontier hypothesis.

40. Woodrow Wilson, "A Calendar of Great Americans," *The Forum*, XVI (February, 1894), 715–27, was a brilliant essay on Hamilton, Jefferson, Washington, and Lincoln, remarkable for its understanding and admiration of Lincoln. It clearly indicated that Wilson was under Turner's influence in relating the greatness of public figures to their attitude toward the West. Wilson continued to serve as a principal propagandist for Turner's views. In "The Proper Perspective of American History," *The Forum*, XIX (July, 1895), 544–59, and "The Making of the Nation," *Atlantic Monthly*, LXXX (July, 1897), 1–14, he explained the frontier theory and rated it of primary importance to an understanding of the American past.

CHAPTER IX *The Constance Lindsay Skinner Correspondence, 1922*

Constance Lindsay Skinner first attracted Frederick Jackson Turner's attention in 1919 when she published a small volume in Yale University's *Chronicles of America Series* called *Pioneers of the Old Southwest: A Chronicle of the Dark and Bloody Ground.*[1] A book on such a subject would naturally attract Turner, and as he read he found much that he liked. Because he believed in praise when praise was due, he sought out Dr. Allen Johnson, editor of the series, at the meeting of the American Historical Association that December to tell him how much he enjoyed the volume, calling it a "genuine contribution" and congratulating him on a genuine "find" in its author. Dr. Johnson was delighted, and so was Miss Skinner when the word was passed along to her. Dr. Johnson made clear that she had received a valuable benediction. "You can," he told her, "feel more than flattered by this interest on the part of America's greatest living historian." [2]

This was one of Miss Skinner's proudest moments, particularly when she recalled that she was neither a professional historian nor sanctified by a doctoral degree. Born in what she later described as the "Canadian Far North," of a Scottish mother and a fur-trading father, she spent her early years on one of the most rugged of all frontiers—an experience that meant as much to her as did Turner's Portage boyhood to him. As a young woman Miss Skinner drifted southward to British Columbia, where she served as political reporter and editorial writer on several newspapers. Posts as dramatic critic and feature writer on the *Los Angeles Times* and *Chicago American* followed before she finally reached New York. There she settled into an 11th Street apartment, and a career as novelist and free-lance writer.

1. Constance Lindsay Skinner, *Pioneers of the Old Southwest: A Chronicle of the Dark and Bloody Ground* (Chronicles of America Series, Allen Johnson, ed., New Haven, 1919).
2. Constance L. Skinner, "Notes Concerning My Correspondence with Frederick Jackson Turner," *Wisconsin Magazine of History*, XIX (September, 1935), 91–92; Constance L. Skinner to Max Farrand, April 15, 1935. HEH TU Box 52.

She was thus engaged when invited to prepare two volumes for the *Chronicles of America Series*, that on the Southwest and another on *Adventurers of Oregon*. Such slow-selling books were luxuries for an author who must live by her pen; once finished with them she abandoned history to settle into a novel-a-year routine, but still clung to her frontier interests. During the 1920s she produced such hair-raising tales as *Silent Scot, Frontier Scout* (1925), *Becky Landers, Frontier Warrior* (1926), and *Roselle of the North* (1927). She also dabbled in verse and plays to win a modest reputation as a popular writer.

Despite Turner's approval of her book on the Old Southwest she would not have had the temerity to strike up a correspondence with him had she not been commissioned by a publisher to compile a book of readings on the history of the frontier. Such a book would not be complete without portions of his 1893 essay; to reprint these she must have his permission. Off went a letter with such a request, followed almost at once by a flattering review of his 1920 volume on *The Frontier in American History* that she had prepared for the *Literary Review* of the *New York Evening Post*.[3] Her words of praise for that volume struck a chord with Turner, who thrived on flattery more than did most men. "The book," she wrote, "contains a fund of information, clearly reasoned, significantly and concisely expressed. It is readable, and it is suggestive."[4] Her one criticism was his failure to give proper credit to the Scots-Irish of Ulster and the Highlanders from Scotland for introducing the germs of democracy and individualism into the New World, and nurturing them to maturity in the forests of the Old West.

This intrigued Turner, and moved him to reply. In the amiable correspondence that followed Miss Skinner played the role of the professional Scot and Turner that of the gentle antagonist who made merry over her Scottish ardor and accused her of using "Scottish Metaphysics" to sustain her theories.[5] Inevitably he eventually put a question to her: whence came her enthusiasm for frontier history? He was delighted when he learned that she was frontier-born, and proudly boasted the same distinction for himself —with somewhat less reason. When he pressed her for details she responded with tales of her girlhood in the Canadian fur-trading post where she was

3. Skinner, "Notes Concerning My Correspondence," *loc. cit.*, 92.
4. *New York Evening Post*, December 4, 1920.
5. Apparently Miss Skinner failed to save these letters; they were not among the materials that she presented to the Huntington Library in 1935.

reared, winning him over completely. Turner was willing to trust someone possessed of the virtues bred of frontier life as he would not a lesser mortal.[6]

So it was that he responded favorably when she countered with a question to him: whence came his interest in the West and why his love affair with the frontier? She needed this information for the sketch of his career that must accompany his essay in the anthology she was editing. Would he mind replying fully? Reply fully he did on March 15, 1922, in no less than twenty-three pages filled with his bold handwriting. He began by recognizing her lack of academic training and suggesting a few reference books that might prove helpful: [7]

7 Phillips Place
Cambridge 38, Mass.
March 15, 1922

My Dear Miss Skinner:

I'm afraid I'm not equal to a brief *biography* of myself and my connection with Western history. You will probably find what you need—and a lot more—in these references:—

> "Who's Who," preferably the edition of 1922 to
>   appear this spring.
> National Cyclopedia of American Biography
> Harvard Bulletin XII. No. 7. Nov. 17, 1902
> World's Work, July, 1902, p. 2326
> Encyclopedia Americana, 19th edition S.V.
> "History" pp. 248, 249, 253 (col. 1), 256 (col. 1)

General Pol. Science Quarterly, Dec. 1921, XXXVI, 574, 584
Comments Daenell in Germanische-Romanische Monatsschrift, 1912,
>   p. 348 (Kiel).
> Huizinga, Mensch en Menigte in America, p. 144.[8]

---

6. Constance L. Skinner to Max Farrand, April 15, 1935. HEH TU Box 52.
7. The original of this letter is in the HEH TU Box 31, the gift of Miss Skinner to the Library. It has been twice published. For circumstances accompanying the first publication, see below, pp. 217–19. It appeared at that time as "Turner's Autobiographical Letter," *Wisconsin Magazine of History*, XIX (September, 1935), 91–103. Apparently Miss Skinner made the copy sent to that journal for publication, for it curiously omits the two German sources given by Turner as a source for information about himself, and contains other minor errors. An accurate version of the letter is included in Wilbur R. Jacobs, ed., *The Historical World of Frederick Jackson Turner* (New Haven, 1968), pp. 54–62. Neither published version provides annotation for the guidance of the reader.
8. Turner is mentioned in all of the reference works that he lists. *Who's Who in America,*

Bibliographies have been published in the Johns Hopkins University list of publications by their Ph.D's, edited by J. M. Vincent—not up to date.[9] The list is rather too long for your use. Perhaps my "Frontier in Am. Hist," "New West" and the reference to indexes of Am. Hist. "Review" and Am. Hist. Association for collected docu[men]ts & articles would do for the western end of it. But there is a western interpretation also in my article on U.S. since 1865,[10] in the Encyclopedia Britannica, (1910?), and in my part of the Guide to Am. History, 1912, by Channing, Hart, and Turner. I did the revision of western data, and the period since 1865. Also my articles on "Frontier," "Sectionalism" and "Western Politics" in McLaughlin & Hart's *Cyclopedia of Government*, embody western studies. My List of References in the History of the West (revised edition, Harvard University Press)

XII, 1922–1923 (Chicago, 1922), 3106, includes data from the 1920 edition, and adds his Litt.D. honorary degree awarded by the University of Wisconsin in 1921, the publication of his *The Frontier in American History* (New York, 1920), and his membership in the American Academy of Arts and Sciences, The American Council of Learned Societies, and the Association of American Geographers. A brief sketch of his career was published in *The National Cyclopaedia of American Biography*, XII (New York, 1906), 174-75. *The Harvard Bulletin*, XII (November 17, 1909), announced his appointment to Harvard and provided a short biography. His friend Henry Morse Stephens included Turner in a small group of historical scholars who were opening new vistas in an article on "Some Living American Historians," *The World's Work*, IV (July, 1902), 2316-27. The article on "History" in the *Encyclopedia Americana* (30 vols., New York, 1918-1920) referred flatteringly to Turner's theories. He was also obviously pleased with an article by Dixon Ryan Fox, "State History I," *Political Science Quarterly*, XXXVI (December, 1921), 572-85, which spoke warmly of his pioneer studies in sectionalism. Ernst Daenell of the University of Kiel in his article on "The Literature of the United States," *Germanische-Romanische Monatsschrift* IV (Heidelberg, 1912), favorably noticed Turner's work, describing him as a "pioneer" in western history. Turner often cited the book by the Dutch historian, Johan Huizinga, *Mensch en Menigte in Amerika, Vier Essays over moderne Beschavingsgeschiedenis* (Haarlem, 1918), p. 144. Huizinga, who described Turner as a leading contemporary historian, sent him a copy which he greatly treasured, as he particularly did all tributes from European scholars. Turner wrote on the flyleaf of Huizinga's book: "An interesting indication of method & attempt of a foreigner to comprehend Am. at present by its origins—spiritual as well as material." Turner's copy at the Huntington Library bears Accession No. 126360.
9. John M. Vincent, *Herbert B. Adams: Tributes of Friends with a Bibliography of the Department of History, Politics and Economics of the Johns Hopkins University, 1876–1901* (Baltimore, 1902), pp. 140-41, lists Turner's writings to that date.
10. Turner referred to his two published books: *The Frontier in American History* (New York, 1920), and *The Rise of the New West, 1819–1829* (*The American Nation: A History*, New York, 1906). He prepared the article on "The United States—History, 1865-1910," for *the Encyclopaedia Britannica* (Cambridge, Eng., 1911), XXIII, 711-35; this was a masterful survey of recent American history but with little emphasis on the West. He also contributed materials on western and recent history to the guide that was standard for a generation: Edward Channing, Albert Bushnell Hart, and Frederick J. Turner, *Guide to the Study and Reading of American History* (Boston, 1912).

might be mentioned.[11] It indicates a scheme of study, with books, etc. In the Am. Antiquarian Society *Proceedings*, Oct. 1919, XXIX, I published an article on "Greater New England in the Middle of the Nineteenth Century" —devoted to an estimate of the amount of the Yankee element in the West about 1850, and the reactive effects in New Eng[land].

I have given much attention to Western history, but rather as a process in American development in general, than as a region in itself. My early training was in medieval history, and the aspects of social and economic developments and expansions in that formative age, I probably carried over into my conceptions of how American history should be viewed—older society developing in or adjacent to the wilderness. A thesis in my junior year in the University of Wisconsin—on the Fur Trade in Wisconsin which was substantially like my doctoral dissertation in the Johns Hopkins University (Studies vol. IX 1891) indicates an interest in the frontier as a factor in American history and in the social and economic background, or foundations.[12] The address on the "Significance of the Frontier" was preceded by a paper 1892 on Problems in American History, (cited in my book p 1). But I had already published a little pamphlet of a few pages, "Outline Studies in the History of the Northwest" (Charles H. Kerr & Co Chicago) in 1888. This was a slight syllabus for club studies.[13] In the Chicago "Dial," I reviewed

11. Turner prepared three excellent articles for Andrew C. McLaughlin and Albert B. Hart, eds., *Cyclopedia of American Government* (New York, 1914): "Frontier in American Development," II, 61–64; "Sectionalism in the United States," III, 280–85; and "West as a Factor in American Politics," III, 668–75. His *List of References on the History of the West* (Cambridge [Mass.], 1922), was the fourth edition of a printed outline and reading list for the use of students in History 17, "The History of the West," at Harvard. The first edition appeared in 1911. In the 1922 edition for the first time Turner enjoyed the help of a collaborator, Frederick Merk.
12. Turner's memory played him false at this point. The paper that he prepared for his junior-year American history course with Professor William Francis Allen was on a French landholding in Portage, and was one of several assigned by Allen on the institutional beginnings of midwestern towns. It was published as "The History of the 'Grignon Tract' on the Portage of the Fox and Wisconsin Rivers," *Wisconsin State Register*, June 23, 1883, and made available to modern readers in Fulmer Mood and Everett E. Edwards, eds., "Frederick Jackson Turner's History of the Grignon Tract on the Portage of the Fox and Wisconsin Rivers," *Agricultural History*, XVII (April, 1943), 113–20. This bore little resemblance to Turner's master's thesis, accepted at Wisconsin in 1887, and published as "The Character and Influence of the Fur Trade in Wisconsin," *Proceedings of the Wisconsin State Historical Society*, XXXVI (Madison, 1889), 52–98, or his doctoral dissertation at the Johns Hopkins University, "The Character and Influence of the Indian Trade in Wisconsin: A Study of the Trading Post as an Institution," *Johns Hopkins University Studies in Historical and Political Science*, IX, Nos. 11–12 (Baltimore, 1891).
13. Turner's "Problems in American History" was published in *The Aegis*, VII (November

the first volumes of Roosevelt's Winning of the West, in August 1889, and suggested a different point of view for approaching the subject, and the need of a history of the continuous progress of civilization across the continent.[14] The Frontier paper was a programme, and in some degree a protest against eastern neglect, at the time, of institutional study of the West, and against Western antiquarian spirit in dealing with their own history.

The paper was regarded as a "curious" view by Edward Everett Hale, and some other correspondents; but John Fiske wrote me on February 6, 1894 (see his Old Virginia, 1897, II Chap. XV, p. 270 for the influence) that he was working toward the same perspective, and called the essay "admirable," so I "had faith in Massachusetts!"—remembering also Parkman and Winsor and Roosevelt, all of Harvard training,—though I wasn't a disciple of Harvard at the time, by any means.[15]

The Frontier made an appeal, oddly perhaps, to the editor of the International Socialist Review, of Chicago, which republished it shortly after (vol VI, 321), and to the "educators," especially to the Hebart Society, which republished it, with some additional matter by me, in the Fifth Year Book of the National Hebart Society; and to the economists (republished in Bullock's "Readings in Economics," and in Marshall's (Univ. of Chicago) volume of similar selections, etc.[16]

In the form of the "Problems of the West," restating many of the Frontier

4, 1892). His *Outline Studies in the History of the Northwest* (*National Bureau of Unity Club Leaflets*, No. 17. Chicago, 1888), was prepared as a study guide for extension work. On his copy of this pamphlet, now in the Huntington Library, Turner wrote: "My first publication." Professor Allen thought well of his pupil's effort. Allen to Turner, October 30, 1888. HEH TU Box 1.

14. Turner's review of the first two volumes of Theodore Roosevelt, *The Winning of the West* (New York, 1889), published in *The Dial*, X (August, 1889), 71–73, was one of the landmarks in the development of his frontier theory. It is discussed above, pp. 39–40.

15. For comments by Edward Everett Hale and John Fiske on Turner's paper on "The Significance of the Frontier in American History" see above, p. 173. In his *Old Virginia and Her Neighbors* (2 vols., Boston, 1899), II, 270–71, Fiske wrote that "until recently one of the most important factors in American history has been the existence of a perpetually advancing frontier," and predicted that its end would be "one of the foremost among the causes which are going to make America in the twentieth century different from America in the nineteenth." Turner was also "remembering" Francis Parkman, Justin Winsor, and Theodore Roosevelt, all historians of the West, and all Harvard trained.

16. The essay was published in the National Hebart Society, *Fifth Yearbook* (1899), pp. 7–41, with a number of additions designed to make it more useful to teachers, and in the *International Socialist Review*, VI (December, 1905), 321–46. It was also included in two books of readings: C. J. Bullock, ed., *Selected Readings in Economics* (Boston, 1907), pp. 23–59, and L. C. Marshall, C. W. Wright, and J. A. Field, eds., *Materials for the Study of Elementary Economics* (Chicago, 1913), pp. 66–73.

paper's interpretations, it was refused by Mr. Horace Scudder, of the Atlantic, but in 1896 at the request for an article by the late Walter Page, then the editor, I adjusted the paper to the Bryan campaign and he accepted it.[17]

Meantime out of a course on "The Economic and Social History of the U.S." (treating different periods, in different years) I evolved the course in the History of the West, the first, I think, in the country.[18] It seemed to "take;" and now something like half the states have such a college course, and many of the leading universities, east and west, include it in their curriculum. A considerable portion of the instructors were trained in my seminary.

In studying our social and economic development, and the frontier advance, I saw at once, that the frontier passed into successive and varied regions, and that new sections evolved in the relations between these geographic regions, and the kinds of people and society which entered them and adjusted to the environment; and that these sections interplayed with each other and reacted on the old East and on the nation, in economic life, political forms and legislation, and in social results and ideals as expressed in education, literature, religion, etc. In short the national spirit,—Uncle Sam's psychology,—was a complex, due to a federation of Sections. Behind the apparent state and nation type of federation lay the federation of sections, explaining manifestations of so-called State sovereignty, which are, more deeply, manifestations of sectional differences. This I had suggested in the paper on "Problems in Am. History," already referred to, and in the Hebart Society version of my "Frontier."

17. Turner's statement that Horace E. Scudder rejected his article for the *Atlantic Monthly* is too strong. Scudder wrote Turner in April, 1896, that he found great satisfaction in Turner's paper, felt that it had unity, and was pleased that "this beginning has been made." Scudder to Turner, April 10, 1896. Houghton: Turner Papers. Later that month Walter Hines Page wrote at some length, suggesting that the West persisted after the passing of the frontier, and stating that he would welcome an article on this theme. Page to Turner, May 29, 1896. *Ibid*. Again in July Page urged Turner to hurry the paper along, pointing out that the nomination of William Jennings Bryan by the Democrats on July 10, 1896, made the subject "immensely more timely." Page to Turner, July 14, 1896. *Ibid*. Apparently Turner's initial article had not been "rejected," but sent back for the type of revision that Page suggested. He completed it on July 29, 1896, and it was published as "The Problem of the West," *Atlantic Monthly*, LXXVIII (September, 1896), 289–97.
18. Turner's new course on "The Economic and Social History of the United States," introduced in the fall of 1892, included a discussion of "the progress of American settlement across the continent" and was the first college course in the nation to deal with that subject. *Catalogue of the University of Wisconsin, 1891–1892* (Madison, 1892), p. 98. Three years later, in the fall of 1895, he gave for the first time anywhere his course on "The History of the West." *Catalogue of the University of Wisconsin, 1895–1896* (Madison, 1896), p. 140.

I have kept at work on this companion piece to my Frontier in various regional or sectional studies, and quite a literature has resulted. See A. W. Small (Univ. of Chicago) *General Sociology*, 282–3 note. C. A. Beard, *Economic Interpretation of the Constitution*, 5, F. J. Turner, "Sectionalism in the United States," in McLaughlin and Hart's Cyclopedia of Am. Government, and ibid, Geographic Influences in American Political History, abstract, in Bulletin of the Am. Geographical Society, XLVI, 591. See also Barnes (Clark Univ) in Encyclopedia Americana (19th ed.) S.V. "History" 256, and especially his article in Journal of Geography, May, 1921, vol. XX, p 199 and p. *330* (Dec. 1921)[19]

The importance of regional geography in Am. History is also emphasized in my *Rise of the New West*, and in my forthcoming book on *U.S. and its Sections* 1830–50; and I have quite a mass of yet unpublished material on the subject, besides the chapters dealing with sections in my *Frontier* book.[20]

I am emphasizing it, because along with my *Frontier* interpretation, I should wish to be thought of in connection with investigations into *Sections*, as a means of understanding America. Not merely North and South, and East and West, but the many inter- and intra-state sections. From another angle, my frontier studies emphasized the amount of unworked material on the influence of the frontier upon *foreign relations*. I found it necessary to go behind the diplomat and the treaties of annexation to the frontier forces and sectional interests. Such studies as my articles in the American Historical Review on French Policy (AHR. X, 249) and Atlantic, XCIII, 676, 807, illustrate this interest,[21] I have published a lot of docu-

19. Turner collected words of praise as a bibliophile might collect books. Albion W. Small, *General Sociology. An Exposition of the Main Development in Sociological Theory from Spencer to Ratzenhofer* (Chicago, 1905), pp. 282–83, named him as a pioneer in the study of sectional forces, while Charles A. Beard, *An Economic Interpretation of the Constitution of the United States* (New York, 1913), p. 5, noted that "almost the only work in economic interpretation which has been done in the United States seems to have been inspired at the University of Wisconsin by Professor Turner." Turner also referred to two of his early essays on sectionalism, the article in McLaughlin and Hart, eds., *Cyclopedia of American Government*, III, 280–85, and one on "Geographical Influences in American Political History," *Bulletin of the American Geographical Society*, XLVI (August, 1914), 591–95. Harry Elmer Barnes, at this time a member of the Clark University faculty, commented favorably on Turner's work in his article on "History" in the *Encyclopedia Americana*, and another on "The Relation of Geography to the Writing and Interpretation of History," *Journal of Geography*, XX (December, 1921), 321–37.

20. The "forthcoming book" on *U.S. and Its Sections* was destined not to appear until three years after Turner's death, when it was published as *The United States, 1830–1850: Sections and Nation* (New York, 1935).

21. Two of several articles on diplomatic history published by Turner during the 1895–

mentary material on foreign relations, (with introductions and editorial work), from archives in this country, France, England and Spain, on the period of the administrations of Washington and Adams.[22] These can be reached by the index volumes to *Amer. Hist. Review,* and Am. Hist. Assoc. *Reports,* including the Reports for 1896, 1897 and 1903, II.—See H. J. Ford in *Chronicles.*[23] Similarly the evolution of *Government* on the Frontier interested me, and my papers in Am. Hist. Review, I on "State-Making in the West in the Rev. Era" are illustrations of this kind of study.[24]

So far my interest in *agriculture* and rural life has been more in evidence through the work of students like Taylor, Hibbard, Coulter, Trimble, Stine and Nils Olsen and others (who also reflect the influence of my colleague, Dr. Ely).[25] My interest in *Lands* likewise has rather stimulated studies by R. G. Wellington (Political and Sectional Influence of the Public Lands 1828–1842) (Boston 1914); Geo. M. Stephenson (Political History of the Public Lands, 1840–1862 (Boston 1917); Miss A. C. Ford, Colonial Precedents of our National Land System (Madison, 1910) and (in part) John

---

1905 period were: "The Policy of France toward the Mississippi Valley in the Period of Washington and Adams," *American Historical Review,* X (January, 1905), 249–79, and "The Diplomatic Contest for the Mississippi Valley," *Atlantic Monthly,* XCIII (May and June, 1904), 676–91, 807–18.

22. Turner edited a number of documents for publication in both the *American Historical Review* and the *Annual Reports* of the American Historical Association on the diplomatic contest for the Mississippi Valley during the administrations of George Washington and John Adams. His most ambitious undertaking was "Correspondence of the French Ministers to the United States, 1791–1797," *Annual Report of the American Historical Association for 1903* (Washington, 1904), I, 1–1110.

23. Henry Jones Ford, *Washington and His Colleagues (The Chronicles of America Series,* New York, 1919) referred flatteringly to Turner's work in diplomatic history.

24. Turner's first major research article was on "Western State-Making in the Revolutionary Era," *American Historical Review,* I (October, 1895, and January, 1896), 70–87, 251–69.

25. Henry C. Taylor, who earned his doctorate under Turner in 1902, was at this time Chief of the Bureau of Markets and Crop Estimates of the United States Department of Agriculture; Benjamin H. Hibbard, who also earned his degree in 1902, was professor of agricultural economics at the University of Wisconsin and a widely read author on agricultural topics; John L. Coulter, who took his doctoral degree in economics in 1908, served with the Census Bureau as an agricultural expert before becoming president of North Dakota Agricultural and Mechanical College; William J. Trimble, a doctoral candidate in 1909, was professor of history at this institution; Oscar C. Stine, who studied briefly with Turner at Wisconsin and then returned to complete his degree in 1921, was editor of the *Journal of Farm Economics* and an agricultural economist with the Department of Agriculture; Nils A. Olsen, recipient of two master of arts degrees under Turner's tutelage, one at Wisconsin in 1909 and one at Harvard in 1912, was Chief of the Bureau of Agricultural Economics in the Department of Agriculture. All, as Turner pointed out, were influenced by Richard T. Ely, professor of economics at Wisconsin.

Ise, Forest Policy, and other students than—printed in my own publication. These, except Ise's, were theses under my direction, suggested and worked out in my seminary.[26]

My interest in the *Indian*, helped (along with Dr. Thwaites' influence) to produce Miss Helen Blair's *Indian Tribes of the Upper Miss. Valley* (Cleveland, 1911) which she dedicated to me.[27]

The theme of discovery and the conception of the "Old West," influenced C. W. Alvord and Lee Bidgood in writing their *First Alleghany Explorations;* and Archibald Henderson, *Conquest of the Southwest.*[28] The conception of persistence of meaning, in American life, of the frontier ideals influenced Guy Emerson in his *New Frontier*. With the exception of the last named the books in this paragraph were also dedicated to me, as was also the volume, *Essays in American History dedicated to Frederick Jackson Turner* (N.Y., 1910).[29] They help explain how the life of the teacher of graduate students checks his own historical output, but furnishes compensations. The above are rather illustrative *types*, (and especially those related to my frontier interests), than complete statements of this side of my work. Since coming to Massachusetts the material available has tended to turn my seminary candidates for the doctorate rather to Mass. political history, but with emphasis upon economic and social *interpretations* of politics.

This is an outrageous kind of answer to your letter. But if you live through it, you will see that there is not the desire to exploit myself, but to give you a point of view in connection with my work—and a *point* can be reduced to the size of your pencil tip.

I was, as an undergraduate in Madison, given the freedom of the Draper

26. Turner was listing a series of well-known books by his former students: Raynor G. Wellington, who earned his master's degree at Harvard in 1903 and taught at the University of South Dakota; George M. Stephenson who received his doctorate at Harvard in 1914 and taught at the University of Minnesota; Amelia C. Ford, a Wisconsin doctor in 1908 and professor at Milwaukee-Downer College; and John Ise, professor at the University of Kansas, who won the doctoral degree at Harvard in 1914.

27. Emma Helen Blair, who completed her work for the master of arts degree with Turner in 1909, had served as an assistant editor when Reuben Gold Thwaites was preparing some of his documentary series. She died in 1911.

28. Turner's article on "The Old West," *Proceedings of the State Historical Society of Wisconsin*, LVI (Madison, 1908), 184–233, was a pioneer work in the study of the upland country on the western border of the colonies. Turner believed that it influenced Clarence W. Alvord and Lee Bidgood to prepare their *The First Explorations of the Trans-Allegheny Region by the Virginians, 1650–1674* (Cleveland, 1912).

29. Guy Emerson, a graduate of Harvard and a New York banker, corresponded extensively with Turner while writing his *The New Frontier. A Study of the American Liberal Spirit, Its Frontier Origin, and Its Application to Modern Problems* (New York, 1920). Turner was quoted often in this volume, and its thesis was adapted from his theories.

Collection (with limitations! I had only a third of one year in Am. history) and the other western manuscripts of the State Historical Society; and I enjoyed the friendship of Draper and my colleague, Thwaites at the same time that I was trained in European institutional history by Professor William F. Allen (A.M. Harvard), who taught me ideals of scholarship, even if he never made me the exact and critical scholar which he was himself.[30] These two things reacted upon each other in my mind, especially the Medieval History and the manuscripts of Western History. I saw American history somewhat differently than it was presented in the books I read. I was for a year a graduate student in Johns Hopkins, where Herbert Adams and R. T. Ely had an inspiring influence upon ambitious students, and where Woodrow Wilson gave a special lecture course. (See Dodd's *Wilson*, p. 20 (but I was not a fellow student, only a member of W's courses in Government)—and see *pp. 27–28 especially;*[31] also Wilson's comments on my "West as a Field for Historical Study" (Am. Hist. Asso. Report, 1896, I).[32] Wilson emphasized the neglect of the sympathetic study of the South, and I that of the West, in our conversations.

When I came back to Wisconsin I started a formal seminary in the library of the State Historical Society of Wisconsin, and began to study, by periods, the social foundations of American history. The Frontier and the Section were aspects of these interests. I recognized them as *parts* of Am. history— only parts, but very important ones. However, I have not conceived of myself as the student of a region, or of any particularly exclusive "key" to

30. For a discussion of Turner's relations with Lyman C. Draper, superintendent of the State Historical Society of Wisconsin, Reuben Gold Thwaites, his successor, and Professor William Francis Allen, see above, pp. 95, 15–25.
31. The influence of Herbert Baxter Adams, Richard T. Ely, and Woodrow Wilson on Turner during his year at Johns Hopkins University is described above, pp. 27–32. William E. Dodd, *Woodrow Wilson and His Work* (Garden City, New York, 1920), p. 20, states incorrectly that Turner and Wilson were fellow graduate students. Instead Wilson was teaching at Wesleyan University and returned to Baltimore to give one course in the spring of 1889. Dodd's biography, pp. 27–28, gives Turner credit for helping shape Wilson's historical concepts.
32. Turner presented a paper on "The West as a Field for Historical Study" at the meeting of the American Historical Association in December, 1896. Woodrow Wilson, who was one of the commentators, began by paying high tribute to him: "I believe he is one of those men who gain the affection of every student of history by being able to do what very few men manage to do; to combine the large view with the small one; to combine the general plan and conception with the minute examination of particulars; who is not afraid of the horrid industry of his task, and who can illuminate that industry by showing the goal to which it is leading him, and the general plan by which it should be done. Such men ought to be not only appreciated, but they ought to be loved and supported." *Annual Report of the American Historical Association for 1896* (Washington, 1897), I, 287–96.

American history. I have tried to make some changes in the perspective, and as a pioneer, with others, I have found it necessary to talk a good deal about these aspects. But it is in the *American processes* I have been interested.

I began my publication when Roosevelt and Winsor were active, and my colleague, Thwaites soon took up his editorial work. Roosevelt, though with a breadth of interests, was more concerned with *men* than with *institutions*, and especially with the strenuous life, and more particularly, the fighting of the frontier. Winsor approached the West as a cartographer and librarian. Thwaites' instincts were toward the romantic side, and toward editorial publication.[33]

The West appealed to me as a *factor* in interpreting American history and the life, ideals and problems of the present. And the West meant also various *sections* with their reactions. While the *great shadow* of the slavery struggle still cast itself over history-writing, even in the works of Rhodes and Von Holst, and while the epic period of the West fascinated Roosevelt, Winsor and Thwaites, I was trying to see it as a whole,—on its institutional, social, economic, and political side, its effects upon the nation as a whole, and I saw that there was a persistent pervasive influence in American life, which did not get its full attention from those who thought in terms of North and South, as well as from those who approached the West as a fighting ground, or ground for exploration history.[34] This was my opportunity. I was

33. Turner expressed his opinion of these men in reviews of their works. He appraised Theodore Roosevelt, *The Winning of the West* (New York, 1889–1896), in *The Dial*, X (August, 1889), 71–73; *The Nation*, LX (March 28, 1895), 240–42 and LXIII (October 8, 1896), 277; and the *American Historical Review*, II (October, 1896), 171–76; and Justin Winsor, *The Westward Movement* (Boston, 1897), in the *American Historical Review*, III (April, 1898), 556–61. He found that both overemphasized the romantic aspects of frontier life while neglecting the frontier's role as a major force in American history. On the other hand, Turner had only praise for his colleague, Reuben Gold Thwaites, when he reviewed the monumental collection of *Early Western Travels, 1748–1846* (20 vols., Cleveland, 1904–1908), for *The Dial*, XXXVII (November 16, 1904), 298–302, and XLI (July 1, 1906), 6–10.

34. In addition to the books of Roosevelt, Winsor, and Thwaites identified in footnote 33 above, Turner referred to James Ford Rhodes, *History of the United States from the Compromise of 1850* (7 vols., New York, 1893–1906), and Hermann E. von Holst, *The Constitutional and Political History of the United States* (7 vols., Chicago, 1876–1892). One of Turner's few direct attacks on a fellow historian was an address on von Holst's history given before the Historical and Political Science Association of the University of Wisconsin on January 23, 1894. *Daily Cardinal*, January 23, 24, 1894; *Wisconsin State Journal*, January 23, 24, 1894. Although he had a number of opportunities to publish this paper, Turner wisely refused lest he offend von Holst. It did not appear in print until edited by Wilbur R. Jacobs in his *Frederick Jackson Turner's Legacy: Unpublished Writings in American History* (San Marino, 1965), 85–104. The manuscript is in HEH TU File Drawer 15A, Folder: Essay on History of U.S. by von Holst.

interested in economics, as well as in institutional history, and I soon (though an instructor) went into the Geological course (physiography) of Professor Van Hise, and tried to get a scientific geographical foundation.[35]

I spent my youth in a newspaper office in contact with practical politics, and in a little town at "The Portage," Wis. over which Marquette had passed. There were still Indian (Winnebago) tepees where I hunted and fished, and Indians came into the stores to buy paints and trinkets and sell furs. Their Indian ponies and dogs were familiar street scenes. The town was a mixture of raftsmen from the "pineries"—(the "Pinery road" ran by my door), or Irish (in the "bloody first" ward), Pomeranian immigrants (we stoned each other), in old country garbs, driving their cows to their own "Common"; of Scotch, with "Caledonia" nearby; of Welsh (with "Cambria" adjacent); with Germans, some of them university-trained (the Bierhalle of Cark Haertel was the town club house); of Yankees from Vermont and Maine and Conn. chiefly, of "New York-Yankees," of southerners (a few relatively); a few negroes; many Norwegians and Swiss, some Englishmen, and one or two Italians.[36] As the local editor and leader of his party, my father reported the community life, the problems of the farmer, the local news, (which I helped to "set up"), went as delegate to state and national Republican conventions, assigned the candidates of his party to the varied nativities and towns of the county, as chairman of the Board of Supervisors, harmonized the rival tongues and interests of the various towns of the county, and helped to shepherd a very composite flock.[37] My school fellows were from all

35. During the autumn term in 1898, when Turner's interest in sectionalism was mounting, he enrolled in a class on "General Geology" offered by his friend and neighbor, Charles R. Van Hise, professor of geology. The first half of the course was advertised to deal with the geology and physiography of the United States, with each province studied in turn. *Daily Cardinal*, October 4, 1898. The notes kept by Turner, dated October and November, 1898, are scattered through his files, and may be found in HEH TU File Drawer 12C, Folder: Van Hise Course; 14D, Folder: Lecture Physical Geography U.S.; and 15A, Folder: Notes on Van Hise's Lectures.
36. See above, pp. 9–15, for a discussion of the ethnic composition of Portage and the frontier atmosphere that persisted there during Turner's boyhood. The subject is further discussed in Ray A. Billington, "Young Fred Turner," *Wisconsin Magazine of History*, XLVI (Autumn, 1962), 38–48.
37. Andrew Jackson Turner was editor and publisher of the Portage newspaper, the *Wisconsin State Register*, during most of Turner's boyhood. He was also a prominent Republican politician, serving as mayor of Portage, in various capacities in the county government, as a member of the state legislature, and as delegate to several national nominating conventions. An account of his political career is in Donald J. Berthrong, "Andrew Jackson Turner, Workhorse of the Republican Party," *Wisconsin Magazine of History*, XXXVIII (Winter, 1954), 77–86.

these varied classes and nationalities, and we all "got on together" in this forming society. Occasionally some fortunate youth went out to Montana or Colorado and returned to tell of mines and ranches. I rode on the first railroad into the pine forests of northern Wisconsin and fished along rivers and lakes in the virgin pine woods, where French names made real the earlier frontier, and followed Indian trails.

Is it strange that I saw the frontier as a real thing and experienced its changes? My people were pioneers from the beginning of the seventeenth century—though they did not go back to Scotch or Irish moors and highlands! One of my ancestors was the Rev. Thomas Hanford who early went to the frontier town of Norwalk, Conn. His parishioners complained that he called them "Indian Devils"—a horrid thing to the Puritan pioneer. But Cotton Mather tells us that what he really said was that "Every *Individual* was in danger of Hell fire," and having defective teeth, he had been misunderstood. My people on both sides moved at least every generation, and built new communities—from Conn. to central and western Mass., to Vermont, to the Adirondacks, to the Dela. Valley in N.Y. and to western N.Y. to Mich. and Wisconsin, and others of the family to Nebraska and to Alaska.[38] My father was named Andrew Jackson Turner at his birth in 1832 by my Democratic grandfather, and I still rise and go to bed to the striking of the old clock that was brought into the house the day that he was born, at the edge of the Adirondack forest. My mother's ancestors were preachers! Is it strange that I preached of the frontier?

Very sincerely and very apologetically

Yours

Frederick J. Turner

P.S. Of course this is for your personal information and not for publication. Don't smile, please—

As Miss Skinner turned the pages of this remarkable letter she realized that she held a document of genuine significance in American historiography, for this was Turner's first venture into speculating on his past and the forces

38. In his later years Turner developed a mild interest in his family's history and carried on a few investigations. On one occasion he filled nine sheets of paper with information. These are in HEH TU Box K, headed "Material on Turner and Hanford Families." He also saved copies of a printed pamphlet on *Turner Genealogy, 1628–1919* (n.p., n.d.), p. 1–7, and of the *Turner Family Magazine*, I (January, 1916). These are in HEH TU Box 62, and are heavily underlined by Turner.

that shaped his historical concepts. She realized that it was a very personal document as well; his remarks on the lack of Scottish or Irish ancestors in his own family tree were prompted by her boast that she was three-fourths Scot. Too, she took seriously Turner's injunction against sharing her new treasure with others. So she filed the letter away in a nail-studded trunk that came to America with her mother when she migrated from Scotland. Other correspondence followed, some of it related to an overambitious project of Miss Skinner's to write a book on how rivers had influenced men through all history. Would Turner look over her outline and offer advice? He would, reluctantly, if she would tell no one, for once the word was out he would be plagued by similar requests from his many friends and students. His criticism was sound; such a book would take a lifetime of investigation. Could not she narrow the project to something more practical? Miss Skinner recognized the good sense of this suggestion; the alternative plan that she finally developed was for a collaborative series of books on the "Rivers of America." That idea she sold to the publishing firm of Farrar and Rinehart, Inc., which launched its highly successful series under that title.[39] She managed to lose Turner's letter containing his advice, but his autobiographical letter remained locked in her nail-studded trunk.

There it stayed until just after Turner's death in the fall of 1932, when two unrelated events brought it to light once more. One was the Huntington Library's campaign to assemble all of Turner's letters and papers. An appeal to his students and friends brought a slow response—most reread their letters with such nostalgia they were reluctant to part with them—but gradually the collection mounted. All were eagerly read by the Library's director, Max Farrand, a lifelong friend of Turner, and by Turner's secretary, Merrill H. Crissey. One or two contained mention of an autobiographical letter he had written to one Miss Skinner. Acting on this clue, a request went off at once; did that important document still exist, and if it did would she allow the Library to make a copy?[40] Miss Skinner would do more than that. "It will be a pleasure,—more, a sort of grateful, reverent joy—," she answered, "to search through a mound of unfiled letters for whatever letters I have of Dr. Turner's so that the Huntington Library may preserve them."[41]

Search she did, with happy results, but before she could send it on its way

39. Skinner, "Notes Concerning My Correspondence," *loc. cit.,* 92–93.
40. Merrill L. Crissey to Miss Skinner, December 10, 1934. HEH TU Box 51.
41. Miss Skinner to Crissey, December 25, 1934. *Ibid.*

a second event occurred that delayed her action. A book arrived at her apartment to be reviewed, a book that annoyed her mightily. Dixon Ryan Fox was its editor, *Sources of Culture in the Middle West* its imposing title, and an essay by Benjamin F. Wright called "Political Institutions and the Frontier" the source of her annoyance.[42] Miss Skinner could not know, as she read, that this was one of the first of a whole battery of charges to be levied against the frontier thesis during the 1930s and 1940s. She knew only that her beloved Dr. Turner was under attack; young Dr. Wright, a political scientist, no less, had the audacity to say that democracy did not originate in the forests of America but that it advanced across the country from east to west. For a time Miss Skinner amused herself with appropriate epithets that might be included in her review—she toyed with saying something about the impossibility of a duet between an eagle and a mole—but common sense prevailed. Why not use Turner's autobiographical letter to confound this upstart critic? This she did, quoting several lines to refute Wright's charge that he was "narrow and provincial." [43]

This experience set Miss Skinner to thinking. If she could use Turner's letter so effectively to confound an attacker, others might find it equally valuable. Surely it should be published where it would be available for his defenders. The one man who could arrange this most effectively was Joseph Schafer, superintendent of the State Historical Society of Wisconsin, former student of Turner, and his most vocal supporter. The Huntington Library would preserve her precious document safely, but it would become a museum piece there. Joseph Schafer would make it live. This decided, a copy was sent him at once, to use as he wished.[44] What Schafer wished was to publish the letter in the *Wisconsin Magazine of History*; it was, he assured Miss Skinner, the nearest approach to an intellectual autobiography that Turner had ever written, and both he and the members of the history department agreed that it deserved a wide audience. Would she consent? [45] Miss Skinner was "happy to tears" at the prospect, and not only gave her permission but agreed to prepare an introductory note that would explain why the account was written.[46] This she did; "Turner's Autobiographical Letter," properly

42. Benjamin F. Wright, "Political Institutions and the Frontier," in Dixon Ryan Fox, ed., *Sources of Culture in the Middle West* (New York, 1934), 15–38.
43. Miss Skinner to Joseph Schafer, March 5, 1935. Wisconsin State Historical Society, Joseph Schafer Papers. MSS IL.
44. Schafer to Miss Skinner, March 5, 17, 1935. *Ibid.*
45. Schafer to Miss Skinner, March 14, April 2, 4, 1935. *Ibid.*
46. Miss Skinner to Joseph Schafer, April 9, 1935. *Ibid.*

introduced, was featured in the September, 1935, issue of the *Wisconsin Magazine of History*.[47]

With justice assured her idol, Miss Skinner was ready to send her treasured document to the Huntington Library. She did so in the sincere belief that hers was a unique account, never to be duplicated. Turner shared his intimacies with her because they shared a common frontier background. "He wrote me so fully because I would *understand*," she explained to Max Farrand. "We *knew* the same life at first hand. I mean to make clear that he was responding to eager requests for data about himself. He was curiously un-egotistical and unselfish about his work. I am sure that the personal details wouldn't be in the letter unless another bold and eager 'frontiersman' had asked for them specifically."[48] This was a pleasant thought to harbor, but Miss Skinner misjudged her man. Turner during his later years would have been less than human had he not realized his importance in American historiography, and determined that posterity should give him the credit he deserved. He was willing to share his "intimate views" with any trusted colleague likely to give them proper circulation. He did so on three more occasions, the first with a quiet scholar who was hardly suited to the role of "bold and eager frontiersman," Carl Becker.

47. "Turner's Autobiographical Letter," *Wisconsin Magazine of History*, XIX (September, 1935), 91–103. The paper was published without annotation, and with the omissions noted in footnote 7 above.
48. Miss Skinner to Max Farrand, April 15, 1935. HEH TU Box 52.

CHAPTER X *The Carl Becker Correspondence, 1925–1927*

When Howard W. Odum, a University of North Carolina sociologist, laid his plans for a volume of essays on *American Masters of Social Science*, his first task was to establish guidelines on the selection of those to be included. The rule that he finally adopted was both simple and logical; he would choose only scholars whose careers spanned the late nineteenth and early twentieth centuries, a period that had witnessed "such a development in the social life and culture of man as had not occurred in all previous history." And he would select in each social-science discipline the two or three individuals whose teaching and research best illustrated those changes.[1] Using these criteria, Odum named nine for inclusion: John William Burgess, Lester Frank Ward, Herbert B. Adams, William A. Dunning, Albion W. Small, Franklin H. Giddings, Thorstein Veblen, James Harvey Robinson, and Frederick Jackson Turner. All had lived during the years of change, all contributed significantly to research in their specializations, and all had trained loyal graduate students, some of whom could be drafted into preparing the essays that Odum wanted.

That Carl Becker should be asked to write on Turner was almost inevitable, for he stood head and shoulders above the other graduate students of Turner's Wisconsin period. Born in 1873, reared in the small-town environment of Waterloo, Iowa, Becker entered the University of Wisconsin in 1893 and earned his undergraduate diploma three years later. Two years of graduate work under Turner followed, then a year at Columbia University, before Becker settled into a precarious career as college teacher. Precarious it was for him, for while Turner recognized his potential brilliance and did his best to find a post worthy of his talents, Becker was shy and aloof, to a degree that students rebelled against his instruction and colleagues mistook his introspection for disdain. Turner spent many hours during the early years of the century on letters of recommendation for Carl Becker, but with un-

1. Howard W. Odum, ed., *American Masters of Social Science* (New York, 1927), p. v.

satisfactory results. He taught brief and disastrous stints at Pennsylvania State College and Dartmouth, then considered leaving the classroom for a business career before finding a relatively safe harbor at the University of Kansas in 1902. From there he returned to Madison at Turner's insistence to complete his doctoral degree in 1907. This was the turning point, for his published dissertation awakened the historical world to the rising of a new star. As his reputation spread, he moved to the University of Minnesota in 1916, then after only a year to Cornell University where he spent the rest of his career.[2] By the time Odum sought his services as author of a biographical sketch of Turner, Carl Becker was one of the nation's most eminent historians.

He was also one of Turner's most ardent disciples. The world began for Becker when he entered Turner's classroom in the fall of 1894. "Until then," he testified, "I had never been interested in history; since then, I have never ceased to be so." He learned few facts, and those that he did remember were incidental to the course but inseparable from the teacher. "To me," he wrote his former teacher in 1910, "nothing can be duller than historical facts; nothing more interesting than the service they can be made to render in the effort to solve the everlasting riddle of human existence. It was from you, my dear Professor Turner, more than from anyone else, that I have learned to distinguish historical facts from their use."[3] To Carl Becker, Turner was not a knowledge peddler, not a guide along well-worn trails, but a fellow explorer who was always ready to venture into the unknown, side-by-side with his students. He inspired rather than led, for he shared with them the thrill of looking beneath the surface for the hidden forces that operated to shape the course of society. Turner, if he taught them anything, taught them to look for meaning; suggest any chance collection of dry facts to him and he could throw out a fresh interpretation that gave them significance and vitality. So Becker believed; he adored Turner as the greatest of teachers, a man who challenged the imagination of his students at the same time he spurred their

2. Burleigh T. Wilkins, *Carl Becker: A Biographical Study in American Intellectual History* (Cambridge, [Mass.] 1961), is an excellent biography. A briefer account of Becker's life is in Charlotte W. Smith, *Carl Becker: On History & the Climate of Opinion* (Ithaca, 1956), while his intellectual contributions are appraised in Cushing Strout, *The Pragmatic Revolt in American History: Carl Becker and Charles Beard* (New Haven, 1958).
3. Carl Becker, "Tribute to Frederick Jackson Turner," in "The Red Book." HEH TU Vol. 1. Red Book. This is a collection of manuscript letters presented to Turner when he left Wisconsin for Harvard in 1910.

industry. His own industry, such success as he had enjoyed, he laid at Turner's door. To him there was only truth in the remark of a fellow student: "Whenever I have ten minutes to talk with Professor Turner, I feel that I ought to go home, take off my coat, and get down to business." [4] Becker shared that feeling when asked by Odum to write about his mentor. Of course he would, and gladly. He was all ready to take off his coat and get down to business.

But first he wanted to have something to say that would be worthy of his subject. Becker knew Turner somewhat better than most students know their masters, but when he started to tot up his knowledge he found that he had precious little. Of course he could describe his teacher's performance in classroom and seminar, and of course he had read the few books and articles that embodied Turner's ideas. But whence came those ideas? What did Turner really think about the significance of the frontier, and why? What was the genesis of his theories? What was his philosophy of history—and of teaching? Here was a vast area waiting exploration, and there was only one source that held the answers. Faced with this situation, Becker did a very sensible thing. He wrote Turner an apologetic letter explaining the assignment he had accepted, and asked for aid. Could Turner supply him with some of that dull factual information that he abhorred but that could not be omitted? Would he speculate a bit on the origins of his historical concepts? Would he be willing to read the resulting manuscript when it was completed, and make needed corrections? [5]

Turner was delighted, as who of modest ego would not be when ranked among the masters of social science? He made this clear in the first of several letters that he was to write Becker over the next months, letters that provided the foundation for Becker's essay and that offer us an intimate glimpse into Turner's mind as he sought to reconstruct the past and appraise his own views of history: [6]

4. Carl Becker, "Frederick Jackson Turner," *Wisconsin Alumni Magazine*, XI (January, 1910), 143–44.
5. Apparently Turner did not save this letter from Becker; it is not among his papers at the Huntington Library.
6. This is a typed letter, replete with the many inaccuracies that always appeared when Turner did his own typing. It has many penciled revisions, and the second postscript has been added in pencil. A version is in the Carl Becker Papers, Collection of Regional History and University Archives, Albert R. Mann Library, Cornell University. The copy from which this transcript was taken is in HEH TU Box 34.

Hancock Point
Maine

October 3, 1925

Dear Becker:

I had not heard of the new social science project—in its biographical aspect at any rate—nor that I had become a *maestro!* It is a piece of good luck to fall into the hands of a man who can write and whose capacity to use the dissecting knife may be restrained by old associations and present friendship! I think I have sent you everything I have monographed, the latest being the address to the Wisconsin Historical Society on "The Significance of the Section in American History"—if you did not receive this, please let me know.[7] I am finishing up a book on the period 1830–1850, in which I try to sketch the characteristics and development of the leading sections during those decades, and briefly to indicate in two or three chapters—possibly four—the intersectional aspect of political history in those years.[8] It will be a book on the border zone between regional geography and history. If you would let me send you a chapter for your criticism it would be a real kindness to me, though I suspect that it would not be to my advantage so far as the proposed social study goes, for I find that I do not write to the satisfaction of my franker friends any longer. The book will leak statistics, but I really think the maps will exhibit the correlation between physical geography (especially topography and soils), land values in 1850, illiteracy, party politics, and culture, have a real merit in the line of showing the interdependence of the social studies.

Although my work has laid stress upon two aspects of American history—the frontier and the sections (in the sense of geographic regions, or provinces, as Royce called them)[9]—I do not think of myself as primarily either a

7. Turner retired from Harvard University in June, 1924, to settle in a small home in Madison next to the larger house of his daughter Dorothy and her husband, John S. Main. As soon as it was known that he was returning to Wisconsin he was invited by Joseph Schafer, Superintendent of the State Historical Society, to address that body at his earliest convenience. Turner to Schafer, March 26, April 5, 1924. HEH TU Box 33. Turner thought of the occasion as comparable to that when he delivered his paper on the frontier to the society in 1893; hence he prepared a careful essay on "The Significance of the Section in American History," which he delivered on January 15, 1925. It was published in the *Wisconsin Magazine of History*, VIII (March, 1925), 255–80.
8. Turner's "finishing" took some time; the book was not published until three years after his death. It was entitled *The United States, 1830–1850: The Nation and Its Sections* (New York, 1935).
9. Josiah Royce, philosopher and Harvard colleague of Turner until his death in 1916, de-

western historian, or a human geographer. I have stressed these two factors, because it seemed to me that they had been neglected, but fundamentally I have been interested in the inter-relations of economics, politics, sociology, culture in general, with the geographic factors, in explaining the United States of to-day by means of its history thus broadly taken. Perhaps that is one of the many reasons why I have not been more voluminous! Professor Allyn A. Young, of the Economics department in Harvard (who was once in my seminary), at the farewell dinner in Cambridge which my students offered me, said some things along this line which he might be willing to repeat to you.[10] They were—as such speeches are bound to be—too kind to me, but they hit things which I have *wished* to do, at any rate. Prof. Theo. C. Smith said some things about my teaching! [11]

It seems to me that I should not read what you say in advance of publication, both because of my own reluctance to have seen the friendly things you may wish to say before they are put out, and because you might be restrained from saying some things you ought to say from the same fact. Let us suppose that the chapter is written some years after I have left this terrestrial sphere. Some one may happen to remember me that long. If that happens I shall be

fined a "province" or "section" as "any one part of a national domain which is, geographically and socially, sufficiently unified to have a true consciousness of its own unity, and to feel a pride in its own ideals and customs and to possess a sense of its own distinction from other parts of the country." Royce used this definition in a Phi Beta Kappa address on "Provincialism," given at the State University of Iowa in 1902. This was first published in a small pamphlet as *Provincialism* (Iowa City, 1902), and later in a volume by Royce on *Race Questions, Provincialism, and Other American Problems* (New York, 1908), pp. 57–108. The definition copied by Turner is on p. 61. Turner apparently did not own a copy of this book, but he did possess a copy of the original pamphlet in which he underlined Royce's definition. When he copied that definition to use in his essay on "The Significance of the Section in American History," *loc. cit.*, he inadvertently omitted the words: "of its own unity, and to feel a pride in its own."

10. Allyn A. Young, who earned a doctorate at Wisconsin in 1902 under Turner and Richard T. Ely, was at this time professor of economics at Harvard. When Turner's students honored his retirement from teaching with a gala dinner at Boston's Harvard Club on May 24, 1924, Young was one of the speakers, representing Turner's friends on the faculty. His remarks were not preserved, but Becker wrote asking him to recall the occasion. Young replied at length, saying that he made two points: (1) Turner's belief that the principal value of history was to illuminate the present, and (2) Turner could best be understood as an artist rather than as a scientist. Allyn A. Young to Becker, October 9, 1925. HEH TU Box 34A.

11. Professor Theodore Clark Smith of Williams College, who had served as a teaching assistant under Turner in 1894–1895, spoke at the banquet as representative of his Wisconsin graduate students. The banquet was described in the *Boston Herald*, May 25, 1924, and *Christian Science Monitor*, May 26, 1924. Clippings from both papers are in HEH TU Box 33.

written up with no chance to protest any way,—"ultimately, why not *now*," as the *ads* say.

I learned only recently that you had been ill. It is a great relief to hear that you are again in fit condition. The domain of History needs you, for scholarship and for literature—both of which belong there.

With warm good wishes and appreciation

Yours sincerely

Frederick J. Turner

Apropos of my *sections*, there is among the files of the Yale Review a letter from an Austrian, Dr. Redlich, if I recall, regarding my article in that magazine for October, 1922, which I wish you could read, as it shows how an intelligent scholar and publicist thought I had presented a new conception of the United States to European readers, at least.[12] I had a copy of it in a collection of reviews and letters regarding my Frontier and this article on the Section, but in moving I seem to have lost them both. I am sorry, because the collection contained letters from Lord Bryce, and others, which I thought that my family might want to keep. Perhaps it may turn up later.[13]

There is no one whom I would sooner leave such a chapter to—if it is to be done—than to yourself.[14] Your review of Barnes' *New History* interests Haskins and myself deeply.[15]

12. Turner's article, "Sections and Nation," *Yale Review*, XII (October, 1922), 1–21, inspired favorable comment not only from friends, but from editorial writers and scholars in many fields. One of the letters that pleased him most was from Joseph Redlich, an Austrian professor at the University of Vienna, who called it a "really marvelous essay," and "one of the most thoughtful and original essays on the nature of the United States that I have ever seen." He also thought that "the whole essay is amazingly full of new information, recent points of view and experiences of American life unknown, I daresay, also to such old students of things American as I am one." Redlich to Wilbur L. Cross, editor of the *Yale Review*, November 10, 1922. Cross sent the letter to Turner; it is in HEH TU Box 31. Turner replied that he was "glad to have so flattering a comment from so distinguished a publicist." Turner to Miss McAfee, *Yale Review*, January 23, 1923. Frederick Jackson Turner Papers, Beinecke Library, Yale University.
13. Apparently the lost was found, for the letters mentioned by Turner, including one from Lord Bryce expressing extravagant praise for Turner's contributions to history, were later given to the Huntington Library. James Bryce to Turner, March 8, 1921. HEH TU Box 31.
14. This brief paragraph is handwritten in pencil at the end of the letter.
15. Turner and his colleague, Charles Homer Haskins, were interested in the review by Becker of a recent book by Harry Elmer Barnes, *The New History and the Social Studies* (New York, 1925). The review was published in the *Saturday Review of Literature*, II (August 15, 1925), 38.

1844 Kalorama Rd., N.W., Washington
[1925. October]

Dear Turner:

Thanks for your letter with its permission to go ahead. I accept your suggestion about not sending you the ms. I will write as of the year 1975, with a "standard" edition of a "standard" historian before me. The fate of a standard history is to be more celebrated than read—as Laguét said of the *Encyclopedia*, and my function will be to remove the heavy burden of that "standard" from your sainted shoulders! But I shall probably say less about your works than about you. Your works will remain in cold print to be read by any one and everyone who cares to read them. But that intangible thing called personality lives only in the minds of those who knew you, and I hope to get something of that down for the benefit of those who do not know you. However, I should be more than glad to see as much of your forthcoming book as you care to send me. Your last article, on the Significance of the Section, I have. Frankfurter, who was in Cornell this summer, was immensely pleased with it. Live, and lovely, wire, Frankfurter! [16]

I am here in Washington for three or four months—sabbatical—trying to write a text book for schools.[17] Miserable job in every way. Don't tell Haskins!

Sincerely yours,
Carl Becker

2214 Van Hise Avenue
Madison Wis.
Nov. 16, 1925

Dear Becker

I have just received from a former student of mine at Harvard a copy of his thesis, prepared under me at Harvard, and published by the Yale Press, with a dedication to me, and this reminds me that you may possibly have some reference to this matter of dedications in your chapter.[18] Therefore I

16. Felix Frankfurter, professor of law at Harvard and later justice on the United States Supreme Court, was a good friend and staunch admirer of Turner.
17. Becker was apparently working on a high school textbook that did not appear until several years later: *Modern History: The Rise of a Democratic, Scientific, and Industrialized Civilization* (New York, 1931).
18. The book mentioned by Turner was Arthur B. Darling, *Political Changes in Massachusetts, 1824–1828* (New Haven, 1925).

enclose this list, which may omit some items, as my library is largely in my Maine home. I am not suggesting that you use it, but that if some are mentioned all should be referred to.

I have quite a mess of letters about my leaving Wisconsin and leaving Harvard and about my books and articles which might do for an obituary!

Cordially

Turner

Archibald Henderson [Professor University of *North Carolina*] *The Conquest of the Old Southwest*

Homer C. Hockett (Professor in State University of *Ohio*) *Western Influences on Political Parties to 1825*

Raynor G. Wellington (Professor in the University of *South Dakota*) *Political and Sectional Influence of the Public Lands.*

Arthur B. Darling, (Professor in *Yale* University) *Political Changes in Massachusetts 1824–1828.*[19]

I should like to have my work in Diplomatic history mentioned. An appreciation of it is in Bemis, *Jay's Treaty*—bibliog.[20]

2214 Van Hise Avenue
Madison, Wisconsin
November 23, 1925

Dear Becker:

Such a nice letter;[21] but I can answer one question that you ask,—or suggest(?). If I ever did anything as a *teacher*, it was because I didn't conceive of myself as a teacher at all. I was enamoured of my subject; I saw how much remained to be done on it, by stressing the economic and social aspects of it

19. Archibald Henderson, an amateur historian and professor of mathematics at the University of North Carolina, was a friend and admirer of Turner. His book, *The Conquest of the Old Southwest* (New York, 1920) was one of several he wrote on that subject. Homer C. Hockett completed his undergraduate degree with Turner in 1903 and his doctorate in 1916. His *Western Influence on Political Parties to 1825* (Columbus, 1917) was his dissertation. Raynor G. Wellington graduated from Harvard in 1902 and earned a master of arts degree there in 1903. Turner erred in listing him here; his book on *The Political and Sectional Influence of the Public Lands, 1828–1842* (Cambridge, [Mass.] 1924) was dedicated to his wife, although he spoke warmly of Turner in the preface.

20. Samuel F. Bemis, *Jay's Treaty* (New York, 1924), listed all of Turner's articles and edited documents on the diplomacy of the Washington-Adams era, then added: "They are most ably edited, and the introductions are most valuable. Indeed, these pithy prefaces, and Professor Turner's articles in the *American Historical Review* remain the best account of the relation of the West to American diplomacy." Bemis, *Jay's Treaty*, p. 358.

21. Turner failed to preserve the letter from Becker asking about his theories of teaching.

and the geographic aspects of it, and this led to a realization that, aside from narrative history, and annexation-of-territory history the *West*—the land beyond the Alleghanies, was almost virgin soil, and that the *frontier process* began with the coast; and that the South also—indeed all the *sections*—needed re-study objectively. Institutional history also had not received its proper study in America.

Now with this enthusiasm for the opportunities of my subject, and with a devotion to research and re-interpretation in the light of research, and some capacity, perhaps, for correlation, I realized that the field was too big for one investigator and for one historian! *That*, with a genuine liking for my graduate students, and for advanced men of the undergraduates, led me to a desire to interest men in my subject to urge them to "carry on." I sensed (because I had no conscious theory or plan in the matter) the fact that a rubber stamp of my own on these men would crush out their initiative. That too harsh criticism would produce inhibition also.

So *I tried most of all not to be a teacher,* and I was blessed with an historical progeny of which I am proud—(C.L.B. among the large stars!) They were my friends and colleagues—not my pedagogical products!

Gildersleeve once, at a Chicago Convocation resented the introduction of himself as "an educator" and professed a willingness to be "a radiator." [22] I have the antipathy to being an educator without, I suppose, the distinction of being "a radiator"—but I know that such success as I may have had with men like yourself was due to love of original research; to the spirit which Kipling has portrayed in his *Explorer* (read it, if you haven't it already by heart!); to the realization of undiscovered countries "beyond the edge of cultivation." [23] I was, as it happened, for some of you, the porter at the gate; the keeper of the keys, that I had received from Allen, and a man with an explorer's instinct, who had enough common sense to keep out of the way of you men who were willing to blaze trails of your own. [24]

22. Basil L. Gildersleeve, professor of Greek at Johns Hopkins University since 1876, was one of the most famed members of that school's distinguished faculty.
23. Kipling's "The Explorer" was one of Turner's favorite poems, and was quoted several times in his essays as well as used in his classes. It described in ballad form a man who could not settle down because his conscience whispered:
> "Something hidden. Go and find it. Go and look behind the Range—
> Something lost behind the Range. Lost and waiting for you. Go!"
The poem is in *The Five Ranges* (*Collected Works of Rudyard Kipling*, New York, 1908), pp. 51–57.
24. Allen is of course Professor William Francis Allen, Turner's undergraduate teacher, whose influence is discussed in a later letter of this series.

I admit that I tried not to spare punishment when my seminarians got lost, or soldierd!

But, please, Becker, do not drop me down to posterity as a teacher (by intention at least!) I had no interest in the "shooting" of the "young idea." I was interested in history, and in the companionship of men like yourself. [Privately I have the idea that that's the only way to teach!] [25]

The book chapters are not worth bothering you with now. They will do to reconcile people who read my obituary!

Pamphlet goes again. This time to Washington.

Cordially,

Frederick J. Turner

[P.S.] I am doubtful about Ann Arbor—I may and I should love to see you. You kiddies ought to go anyway! I may try to be both there and here—geographers—in the same wk. if my health permits it.[26]

So far as I know, *Who's Who's* correct. I am now "Fellow of the Historical Society of Wisconsin," an honorary position.[27] My *legal* residence is Hancock Point, Maine, where I live about half the year.[28] I sent in some additions—which I do now recall!—to the pub[lisher]s [of Who's Who] for their forthcoming volume.

1844 Kalorama Rd., N.W.
Washington, D.C.
[Nov. 1925]

Dear Turner:

Your letter has bucked me up on my job, because what I have written is I think little more than an elaboration of what you say about your being a teacher. So far I have been trying to convey the impression you made on a

25. The brackets are Turner's.
26. The American Historical Association was scheduled to meet in Detroit and Ann Arbor on December 26, 1925. Turner did not attend.
27. When the State Historical Society of Wisconsin learned that Turner was to return to Madison after his retirement, the Curators created a new honorary post of "Fellow of the State Historical Society of Wisconsin," and named Turner as the first fellow. This entitled him to an office in the society's library, where he worked for the next two years. Joseph Schafer to Turner, June 9, 1924. HEH TU Box 33.
28. After his retirement from Harvard in June, 1924, Turner planned to spend the winter months in his small home in Madison and the spring, summer, and fall at his summer home at Hancock Point, Maine.

green, shy observant undergraduate in the Junior Course—an undergraduate who had never before had the slightest interest in history; and you know the whole point of it is just that I was gradually made aware that this man Turner wasn't a "teacher" at all. It almost seemed that he wasn't "teaching" us at all but was himself studying history up there behind the desk before our eyes, for our benefit no doubt, but just continuing the labors of the morning. And history came to seem to me not a convention agreed upon to be learned by rote—a thing I could never do, and can't now—but just an aspect of life itself to be looked into, searched, questioned and written about. All this I sum up by saying "From the moment Turner ceased to figure in my mind as a "teacher," I began to learn something." Needless to say I entirely agree with you about teaching. You were a great teacher for me because I seemed always to be watching an independent and penetrating intelligence at work on its own account, and not merely rehearsing for the benefit of others.

The second part, which I am now working on, will deal with the graduate work, your methods, attitude towards students and the more fundamental influences I received from you—the impression briefly that you accepted the universe and the people in it, never pronounced judgment on God or his handiwork, but were always engaged, with an independence and objectivity rarely equalled, in trying to *understand* just what was going on and why.

The third part will deal with your work—approach to the problems of history, interest in geographic, economic and social influences etc., and something about the immense difficulty of writing your kind of history—difficulties illustrated I think in your book in American Nation Series.[29] If one conceives of history in terms of governments merely and their activities it is easy enough to construct a narrative which goes forward and shows a kind of evolution or development in time. You have your "thin red line of heroes" and they go gaily marching on. But what you want to do is first to generalize, on the basis of a minute and difficult examination, the conditions, varying according to sections or localities, which create a type of society. Here you are dealing not so much with a concrete series of events as with types and generalized statements of immeasurable concrete facts. How these generalizations spread out over space; but how to make the damn things march forward in time—that is a great difficulty.

29. Becker refers to Turner's *Rise of the New West, 1819–1829* (*The American Nation: A History*, XIV, New York, 1906).

Well, I begin to see my way through this business, which I find much pleasure in doing, and I think it will not be too bad. But it is a slow and painful business for me to write. To get one page really done, I throw on an average of about eight or ten in the basket. But if I can put down on paper a fairly correct and adequate idea of what you have tried to do and have done and the profound and enduring influence you have had on your students, I shall be satisfied.

Sincerely yours,
Carl Becker

P.S. Of course I shall have something to say about the "Frontier" idea. Impossible to tell your story without the "Frontier," as it would be to tell of Jack Horner's without the plum. But I think the Frontier idea is an aspect of something larger—the conception of American history as having, not more or less importance than European, but a *peculiar* importance, due to the fact that it is relatively a new country, a splendid virgin field where one can study the evolution of society from relatively primitive conditions, a process repeated often as population spread to the West. I sometimes think, and I wonder if it is true, that some of your pupils have missed this, have followed in "your steps" indeed, but so literally and with so little independence that their lesser and lighter leagued boots have made no mark.

Well, I hope you will like it. If you don't it will be my fault, for it is being done in the most honest and affectionate spirit in the world. It will be my fault I mean because I shall have failed to convey what I have in mind to convey.

2214 Van Hise Avenue
Madison
Wisconsin
Dec. 1, 1925

Dear Becker:

I surely am blessed in my friends. Your letter makes me feel very unworthy of the kind things you say. To have had an influence upon your life as an historian and as a writer; and to have you take valuable time to tell about me—or what you graciously remember me to have been!—is quite sufficient to reconcile me to the name of "teacher," especially since you agree with me in the matter!

I am really deeply moved by your letter, and I think the statement of what I have *tried* to do is admirable.

Beyond the "frontier" was a dynamic America shaping itself into social, economic, and political sections, and reacting upon Europe too!

The "frontier" process is one which applies to certain portions of Old World history, as well as to that of the New, and sometime it will be worked out thus. And beyond all this is the conception of history as a complex of all the social sciences. The conception of the One-ness of the thing. As you intimate, this is a rather paralyzing conception. I didn't consciously fashion it as a guide-book to begin with (and I can't claim authorship of it)! But it does help to know that these subjects are tied together and to deal with a phase of the whole, realizing that it is only a phase.

Yes, I think that some of my students have apprehended only certain aspects of my work and have not always seen them in *relation*. But perhaps they have done better work *for that very reason!*

I really feel guilty, as well as proud, that you are doing this, for you must not neglect to continue your own work and your own exploration in order to say kind things of your predecessors. But I realize what a lucky man I am in having you as my friend and exponent.

Please put what you say in such a way that other men in the field will not feel that I am unduly shoved into lime light. I think that the attitude of a student doing a portrait of his older friend and "teacher" may be the way out of the difficulty and may save me from seeming unduly promoted. For I realize only too deeply how little in volume of historical writing I have done as compared [with] the distinguished group of my colleagues. Almost I want to put my head under the bed-clothes! But I *am* interested in having the historical points of view which you present, brought out; and I have no right to determine the choices of others, I suppose.

With deep appreciation and with affection, I am

Unworthily yours,

Frederick J. Turner

Becker's reply to this letter of Turner's was not saved, but its contents may be surmised from Turner's reply. Becker obviously inquired about the circumstances that led to the frontier hypothesis, thus setting Turner's memory to working, and leading to another of his informative excursions into the past:

233

2214 Van Hise Avenue
Madison, Wisconsin
December 16, 1925

Dear Becker:

Two or three years ago, Miss Constance Skinner, asked me that question. You may remember her as a New York newspaper woman who did some good work for Allen Johnson in his *Chronicles*, and who essayed a general history of the world which I think fell under the scalpels of both you and me. She wanted to publish extracts from my frontier in a volume of reprints, which, so far as I know, didn't appear.[30] All this to say that like most men who have passed the sixty mark, I have various replies to that question on record and I am taking big chances on adding another. Perhaps Miss Skinner (whose New York address I haven't at hand—possibly Johnson has it—or *Who's Who?*) might in view of your purpose be willing to show you the letter—or may be you and she are of incompatible temper!

1. Like most things, I suppose the frontier idea came from a complex.

a. I was educated under Allen (W. F.) and also under H. B. Adams to an interest in institutional history as related to society in general, in the fields of ancient and mediaeval history.[31] When one tries to apply this way of looking at history to America, he drops the purely narrative type, and sees the importance of the American factors that condition American development. At least I thought that *I* did.

b. H. B. Adams told the seminary (this is my present memory) while I was there, that American institutional history had been well *done*. That we would better turn next to European institutions! The frontier was pretty much a *reaction* from that due to my indignation. You may have seen a paper I did in *The Aegis*, a student publication of the U.W., Nov. 4, 1892, which was the first form in which I stated the need of a new way of attacking American history (See footnote to my *Frontier*). Dodd had the idea that Wilson might have preceded me, in framing the formula. But in fact I had read my paper in *MS* on the "Significance of the Frontier" to him at my house before he wrote his review of Goldwin Smith, mentioned in that foot-

---

30. Turner's letter to Constance L. Skinner is reproduced above, pp. 205–16.
31. For a discussion of the influence of Professor William Francis Allen on Turner during his undergraduate and early graduate years see above, pp. 15–26. His relations with Professor Herbert Baxter Adams during his graduate year at the Johns Hopkins University are described above, pp. 27–29.

note, and he told Dodd that I had the priority.[32] In moving from Cambridge, I lost a portfolio of reviews of my frontier, with this Dodd letter, and letters of Bryce, Parkman Fiske etc.[33] But in Dodd's life of Woodrow Wilson you will find that he states the thing substantially, if I recall. Possibly Dodd could show you a copy (if he kept one) of his letter but don't ask for it unless you need it! I may have placed it—or a copy—in a folder of letters to me from Wilson, Roosevelt, and Walter Page, which I gave to Harvard University Library, with the requirement that permission to see them must be given by Haskins and the head of the Library.[34] I had retained photostats, which I can't now find,[35] so I suppose the photostats were lost in transit, as one of my crated files was broken open and the contents partly lost. I supposed the contents were unimportant until I looked in vain for this case—(I have a half-memory that I gave a copy of Dodd's letter to my friend Mrs. Wm. Hooper, of Manchester, Massachusetts, and I will ask her for it, if it doesn't give her trouble.)[36]

I had had to tell Wilson about the neglected West, as he told me about the neglected South. Some of the stimulus to writing the article may have come from my attempts to put the case in those days. He was *not* a fellow student, as Dodd supposed, but was lecturer at the J.H.U the year I spent there, 1888–9. He discussed local governments—(in substance he gave us "The State" as it later appeared (i-e. the local gov't part).[37] The Johns Hopkins atmosphere was friendly to new ideas. Men like Commons, Charley Andrews, Haskins (then quite a youthful person!) as well as Wilson called out one's

32. These matters are discussed in the exchange of letters between Turner and William E. Dodd reproduced above, pp. 183–99.

33. The portfolio was found later, for Turner deposited these letters in the Huntington Library.

34. Turner presented these letters to the Harvard University Library at the time of his retirement. They are currently classified as Frederick Jackson Turner Papers, Houghton Library, Harvard University. At the time he retired, his close friend Charles Homer Haskins was Dean of the Graduate School of Arts and Sciences.

35. These photstats were also found, and are now in the Turner Papers at the Huntington Library.

36. Turner did loan a copy of Dodd's letter to his good friend Mrs. Alice Forbes Perkins Hooper, patron of the Harvard Commission on Western History. Turner to Mrs. Hooper, February 19, 1921. HEH TU-H Box 5. This letter, together with several hundred others exchanged between Turner and Mrs. Hooper, are printed in Ray A. Billington, ed., *Dear Lady: The Letters of Frederick Jackson Turner and Alices Forbes Perkins Hooper 1910–1932* (San Marino, 1970), 331–32.

37. See above, pp. 30-31, for Turner's relations with Woodrow Wilson when both were at Johns Hopkins during the spring of 1889.

best and challenged one's originality.[38] But I got absolutely nothing of suggestion on either frontier or fur trade from H. B. Adams, or so far as I can recall, regarding frontier, from any one, unless it be from Gannett's census maps and the description of the frontier line in its successive eras and some of the Guides I quote in my Frontier Essay.[39] I applied historical data and interpretation to those maps, with Mediaeval historical processes as a more or less conscious guide. [What I got from Adams was a sympathetic expectation that I should accomplish good things. He encouraged me] [40]

2. As to the influence of the fur trade on the frontier idea I am not conscious of just how or if it came in—but there is an evolutionary conception in each. I also have lost my copies of the fur-trade paper, but it might interest you as a critic to notice what changes I made in that paper between its presentation (*in absentia*), to the Wis. Hist. Soc. and its publication in the J H U Studies.[41] It was published first in the W.H.S.—*Collections or Transactions*, probably the latter (see collected index to the first series).[42] What I now recall about it is that I talked more about the Phoenician fur trade (!) in the J H U form than in the Wisconsin form of the paper.[43]

38. John R. Commons, Professor of Political Economy at the University of Wisconsin, Charles McLean Andrews, Yale University's distinguished historian of colonial America, and Charles Homer Haskins, a medievalist who taught at Wisconsin before moving to Harvard University, were all graduate students during 1888–1889 when Turner was at Johns Hopkins.
39. One of the most important books shaping Turner's concept of the frontier was Fletcher W. Hewes and Henry Gannett, *Scribner's Statistical Atlas of the United States Showing by Graphic Methods Their Present Condition and Their Political, Social and Industrial Development* (New York, 1883). Its influence on him is discussed above, pp. 111–13.
40. The brackets are Turner's.
41. Turner twice presented a paper on the fur trade of Wisconsin, drawn from his master's thesis, in Madison. The first occasion was a meeting of the Madison Literary Club on May 14, 1888. *Wisconsin State Journal*, May 15, 1888. Turner's second talk, to which he apparently refers here, was to the State Historical Society of Wisconsin on January 3, 1889. He was in Baltimore at the time, and his paper was read for him by Reuben Gold Thwaites. It represented a revised version of his master of arts thesis, but had not yet assumed the form that it took for his doctoral dissertation. *Ibid.*, January 4, 1889.
42. The thesis was first printed, apparently in the form read to the Society in January, 1889, as "The Character and Influence of the Fur Trade in Wisconsin," *Proceedings of the State Historical Society of Wisconsin*, XXXVI (Madison, 1889), 52–98. Submitted in revised form as his dissertation at Johns Hopkins, it reappeared as *The Character and Influence of the Indian Trade in Wisconsin: A Study of the Trading Post as an Institution* (*Johns Hopkins University Studies in Historical and Political Science*, IX, Baltimore, 1891, 1–94).
43. Turner's revision of his master's thesis largely took the form of fitting it into the institutional framework popular at Johns Hopkins. He began by tracing the trading post as an institution back to the Phoenicians, and speculated that Roman traders blazed the trails

The fur trade came about this way. Allen assigned me, in one of his classes, a thesis on the subject "Common lands in Wisconsin." He had found in the Public Lands vol. of the Am State Papers docs showing that the French villages at Prairie du Chien and Green Bay gave evidences of common fields etc. which interested him in connection with his study of that general subject in New and old England.[44] I soon saw that it wasn't a subject which would get me far, and while I was looking over the material, Dr. Draper happened in the library (then in the State capitol) and looking over my shoulder said that I might be interested in some old French fur traders' letters from those villages.[45] Of course I was glad to see them, and he let me loose on a box of paper, waterstained, tied in deer skin thongs, written in execrable French which, however, did me no harm, for I was guiltless of any knowledge whatever of French. This proved a blessing, for the instructor in French to whom I appealed was so worried by the writing, the spelling, and the grammar, that I found I could, with a dictionary get on more rapidly myself.[46] So I learned Kanuck French, and fur trade history from these manuscripts and the French and English printed documents that seemed pertinent, and a minimum of the history of the region in secondary accounts.[47] Thus, while a Junior, I

followed by the great "Migration of the Peoples" that influenced Teutonic society. *Ibid.,* pp. 87–89. He lived to regret this venture into fantasyland, ascribing it to his desire to "conform to the institutional side of the Hopkins papers." Turner to Joseph Schafer, October 14, 1931. HEH TU Box 46.

44. Turner refers here to the paper on the Grignon Tract prepared for Professor Allen during his junior year. For a discussion of this paper see above, pp. 21–22.

45. This may or may not be an accurate statement. Lyman C. Draper, former director of the State Historical Society library, was in ill health, and spent most of that winter in New York. On the other hand, Turner did have a pleasant talk with him in the library in October, 1887; he described him to his fiancée as a "little thin voiced and thin bodied man." Turner to Caroline Mae Sherwood, October 16, 1887. HEH TU Box B. He saw him again in July, 1888, when they talked together of editing some documents from the Draper collections. Turner soon gave this up, finding him "a great procrastinator," who "will hardly come to any conclusion." Turner to Caroline Mae Turner, July 6, 1888. HEH TU Box C.

46. He reported in December, 1887: "I saw the pretty French teacher at the library Saturday and she tried to read some French mss. for me with very poor results. I must learn French myself or I despair of going through those papers." Turner to Caroline Mae Sherwood, December 4, 1887. HEH TU Box B.

47. Turner's memory played him false, for his glib statement that "I learned Kanuck French" mightily stretched the truth. He made valiant efforts over the next year, as he regularly reported to his fiancée, but with little success. Thus he wrote in April, 1888, as the thesis was nearing completion: "I must learn to read French fluently this summer." Turner to Caroline Mae Sherwood, April 22, 1888. HEH TU Box A. His failure cost him the chance to earn his doctorate at Johns Hopkins in one year, for he was unable to pass the reading test in French.

did the thesis, which in substance, I later turned in for my doctoral dissertation. It was my own idea—by accident.[48]

I cant tell you just *how* the *"how"* instead of the *"what"* came to appeal to me. Probably I owe my interest to history as not merely narrative to William Francis Allen, trained in Harvard and in Germany. He had taught economics (using Roscher) by the historical method at Wisconsin, (before I came so that I didn't take that subject with him) while most other—if not all—American Universities were basing instruction in that field upon such manuals as Wayland—Chapin etc.[49] He gave a course of three successive years in history—viz

1. Territorial and Dynastic, covering the world—by topical method

See W F Allen's [50]   e.g. 800—Charlemagne
History Topics   subheads of ty & dynastic changes &c&c
(Ginn?)   Each boy had to lecture on one topic

2. Institutional
      a Roman Institutions (& Greek too)
      b Mediaeval Institutions
      c English Constitution

3. Hist of Civilization
      Classical
      Guizot &

[I had only one term (⅓ yr), two three times a week, in American history at Wis—and practically none at J H U][51] (He was also Professor of Latin and

48. Turner's memory failed once more. The paper prepared for Professor Allen on the Grignon Tract of Portage had nothing to do with the thesis on the fur trade that he began three years later. See above, pp. 25–26, for a discussion of this point.

49. Francis Wayland (1826–1904) and Aaron L. Chapin (1817–1892) were well-known authors in the field of political economy during the nineteenth century. Wayland, a minister and president of Brown University, produced a textbook, *The Elements of Political Economy* (Boston, 1840), which taught generations of students that economic change was the result of God's will rather than man's volition. These views were challenged by Wilhelm Roscher, professor of political economy at the University of Leipzig and founder of the so-called "Historical School" of political economy. His views began to be known in the United States about 1875, and two years later his textbook, *The Principles of Economics,* appeared in an English translation. Allen was well abreast of his times in accepting Roscher's historical approach when he did. These developments are discussed in Joseph Dorfman, *The Economic Mind in American Civilization* (3 vols., New York, 1946–1949), II, 758–70, and III, 88–92.

50. Turner referred to William F. Allen, *History Topics for the Use of High Schools and Colleges* (Boston, 1883). Turner remembered correctly, for the publisher was Ginn & Company.

51. The brackets are Turner's.

a recognized classical scholar.) I guess the order isn't correctly given but the idea is there! First the dry bones of geography & tables of kings &c Second the political institutions, by retracing the same field, using lectures on the basis of mimeographed documents—(Latin & Anglo-Saxon) which he put in our hands: laws, &c &c—Then finally the world of ideas, culture &c &c—It worked well for those who lived to the end. He made me realize what scholarship meant; what loyalty to truth demanded. I never had, in Hopkins or elsewhere his equal as a scholar and a simple sincere *acute* mind. He wrote political articles and reviews of all kinds for The Nation. See the memorial volume entitled Monographs and Essays by W F Allen, edited by Frankenburger. I did the bibliography.[52] In Pyre's History of the University of Wisconsin, he says (p.   ) that I got my idea of the Frontier from one of these essays entitled "The Northwest in American History," but I can't see it, and I doubt if Pyre ever read the Frontier.[53] But I got something better— the idea of scholarship and the love of exact truth, even if I couldn't practice it as Allen did.

Possibly my birth at Portage (the portage) on the Fox-Wisconsin river had an unconscious influence upon my western studies and my conception of history. I don't think I ever realized while a boy that Marquette & Jolliet went that way, or that the portage meant history. But my father was a newspaper editor, and a kind of Thurlow Weed in Wisconsin politics, and I lived, so to speak on the inside of things political, learned to contrast the outcome, the ostensible thing and the inner history of how it came about.[54] Around me were all kinds of nationalities. There was an Irish ward, into which we

52. William F. Allen, *Essays and Monographs by William Francis Allen: Memorial Volume* (Boston, 1890), was edited by Allen's colleague, Professor David B. Frankenburger. It contained many of Allen's more important essays, as well as a bibliography of his works, unsigned, but prepared by Turner.

53. James F. A. Pyre, *Wisconsin* (New York, 1920), is an uncritical history of the University of Wisconsin written by a long-time professor of English there. Allen's essay, "The Place of the Northwest in General History," was prepared for the Washington meeting of the American Historical Association in December, 1888. Allen was unable to attend, and Turner, who was in nearby Baltimore, read it for him. There is nothing in the paper to suggest the frontier theory; Allen wrote a sweeping survey of the European background of colonization and said very little even about the Nothwest. The paper is printed in *Papers of the American Historical Association* (New York, 1889), III, 331–48.

54. Turner's father, Andrew Jackson Turner, purchased the Portage *Wisconsin State Register* in 1861 and served as publisher and editor until 1878. He was also active in Republican politics, serving as mayor of Portage, as a member of the state legislature, and for many years on the Board of Supervisors of Columbia County. For his political career see Donald J. Berthrong, "Andrew Jackson Turner, Workhorse of the Republican Party," *Wisconsin Magazine of History*, XXXVIII (Winter, 1954), 77–86.

boys ventured only in companies. There was a Pomeranian ward where women wore wooden shoes, kerchiefs on their head, red woolen petticoats &c and drove their community's cows to a common pasture in the marsh lands which these people bought. Their dikes and drains made homesites on a neighboring marsh, which was almost a lake in my boyhood. There were Norwegian settlements, Scotch towns, Welsh, and Swiss communities in the county.[55] Father shepraded these new people in the county-board meeting; lectured them on politics and farming in his editorials, and was followed by them very wonderfully. In the city itself we had all types from a negro family named Turner, to an Irish "keener" who looked like a Druid and whose shrill voice could be heard over impossible spaces when an Irish soul departed. But I must not try to tell you all about my boyhood town. There was a sort of club in the local beer saloon where a very able and intelligent German sold his brew; in it gathered an ex opera singer, who had grown too fat to sing, but who had a university train'g; a cooper ditto &c &c. It was a town with a real collection of types from all the world, Yankees from Maine & Vermont, New York Yankees, Dutchmen from the Mohawk, braw curlers from the Highlands, Southerners—all kinds. They mixed too. And respected and fought each other. When I went to Europe, it was familiar. I had seen it in Portage. When I went to Harvard I found that I had met the Puritan in the flesh long years before.

What goes to make up a man is pretty varied. I cant unravel the threads. Here is some of the tangle!

Best wishes
Frederick J. Turner

I daren't re-read this, perhaps you can't even *read* it. After it I don't think you need Miss Skinner's unless to save me from two conflicting answers?

P.S. Dec 18 '25 [56]

Still trying to answer your question about the frontier—perhaps it was in the blood. Both my father and my mother descended from pioneer stock. I knew little of this until my father "researched" the family tree in his later

---

55. The ethnic composition of the region adjacent to Portage is described above, pp. 9–15.
56. Turner wrote this postscript in pencil at the end of his letter.

years, but I did know that both the Turners and the Hanfords started in Connecticut with the first migrations—both families apparently (the Hanfords certainly) having landed in Massachusetts and then settled in Conn. Almost every new generation pioneered a new town; up through Conn and Mass into Vermont and into New York, west of L[ake] Champlain in the Plattsburg region; thence my father went to Michigan, then to Wisconsin; an uncle went to Nebraska as one of the pioneer surveyors, two cousins went to Alaska, &c &c.[57] My mother's ancestor, Thomas Hanford appears in an amusing light in Mather's Magnalia, I 394 ff (edition?). He was the first preacher at Norwalk, Conn. (His mother, who also came to America was Eylin Hatherly Sealis Hanford, a sister of the Timothy Hatherly who figures in Bradford's History.)[58] Once Rev. Hanford's congregation demanded that he be disciplined because he had called them "Injun devils." Being on the frontier, they wouldn't stand for it. However, he showed his manuscript to his brother ministers, and it turned out that what he said was that "every *individual* of you is in danger of hell-fire," or some such thing. Having bad teeth it got across as *Injundevils*." "Thus," says Cotton Mather "much smoke cometh from a little fire"![59]

This branch went also wandering via Delaware water gap, I suppose, into Delaware county, N.Y., at (?), & at Walton, and then to Allegheny County at (old) Friendship when it was new,—thence as a community to (New) Friendship Adams County, Wisconsin, where my father met my mother and married her.[60] So when I went back to Massachusetts (having I may tell you

57. Humphrey Turner, the first of the family to reach America, arrived in Massachusetts in 1634. His descendants moved first to Connecticut, then to Vermont. Turner's grandfather, Abel Turner, pushed on to western New York after the War of 1812, settling at Schuyler Falls. One of his twelve children was Andrew Jackson Turner, Turner's father, who was born in 1832, migrated to Michigan in 1853, and pushed on to Wisconsin two years later, living in Madison, Portage, and the small town of Friendship before settling permanently in Portage in 1860. *Turner Genealogy, 1628–1919* (n.p., n.d.), pp. 1–7; F. J. Turner, handwritten MS "Material on Turner and Hanford Families." Both are in HEH TU Box K. His father's reminiscences, which contain much family history, are in the *Wisconsin State Register*, February 8, 1890.
58. Timothy Hatherly was one of the merchant adventurers who helped finance the Pilgrim migration to Plymouth. He came to Massachusetts in 1623 and settled permanently at Scituate in 1632. William Bradford, *History of Plymouth Plantation* (Boston, 1898), pp. 319–29, 334–35, 360, 439.
59. Cotton Mather, *Magnalia Christi Americana* (2 vols., London, 1702), appeared in its first American edition, also in two volumes and published at Hartford, in 1820.
60. Mary Hanford's father, Samuel Hanford, was one of the founders of Friendship, Adams County, Wisconsin. There she met Andrew Jackson Turner, and there they were married in 1860. Turner, "Material on Turner and Hanford Genealogies." HEH TU Box K.

confidentially declined to be considered at Yale—I had already accepted Harvard and declined California—) [61] it was a good deal like taking the back-track and when afterwards I found myself President of the Colonial Society of Massachusetts it seemed rather complicated for a frontiersman whose ancestors were open to Cotton Mather's reproach as having "gone beyond the hedge" (my *Frontier* p 64).[62] The Rev. Hanford married as a second wife Mary Miles Ince (widow of the "New Haven scholar" Jonathan Ince). My mother's side included Gen. John Mead, the Eels—one of whom was a representative of Mass. in England, commander of the garrison at Dartmouth in King Philips war &c &c [His son Rev. M. married Hannah North, aunt of Lord North] [63] I suppose this is also the Oregon missionary Eels family.[64] On my father's side were Nathan Beman, who piloted Ethan Allen into Ticonderoga, & who always insisted that what he said was not, "Surrender in the name of the Continental Congress and the great Jehovah" but "Come out of this you damned old rat" jerking the commander out of bed! Such is frontier family tradition in contrast with polite society's version.[65] The Mayhews missionary at Nantucket, &c, were ancestors of the

61. Turner resigned from the University of Wisconsin faculty in 1909 in the hope of awakening the regents to the danger of their attacks on humanistic research. His first intention was to accept an offer from the University of California. When his friend Charles H. Haskins, Dean of the Faculty of Arts and Sciences at Harvard, learned of this he immediately engineered a similar offer from Harvard, which Turner accepted. His friend Max Farrand also tried to get him to come to Yale at this time. This story is told in Ray A. Billington, "Frederick Jackson Turner Comes to Harvard," *Proceedings of the Massachusetts Historical Society,* LXXIV (1962), 51–83.

62. Turner was fond of quoting from Cotton Mather's *The Short History of New-England: A Recapitulation of the Wonderful Passages which Have Occur'd, First in the Protections, and Then the Afflictions, of New-England* (Boston, 1694), p. 45, the passage that read: "Again, Do our *Old* People, any of them *Go Out* from the Institutions of God, Swarming into New Settlements, where they and their Untaught Families are Like to *Perish for Lack of Vision?* They that have done so, heretofore, have to their Cost found, that they got onto the *Wrong side of the Hedge,* in their doing so." The passage to which he refers was in his essay, "The First Official Frontier of the Massachusetts Bay," in F. J. Turner, *The Frontier in American History* (New York, 1920), p. 64.

63. The brackets are Turner's.

64. John Mead served as Brigadier General of the Fourth Brigade, Connecticut Militia, during the latter part of the American Revolution. Samuel Eels of Milford, Connecticut, as an officer in King Philip's War, arranged for the surrender of a group of Indians at Dartmouth, near New Bedford, then protested bitterly when they were sold into slavery by the authorities. He later moved to Hingham, where he was elected a representative in 1705. He died in 1709. Turner did not seem to realize that the Oregon missionary, the Reverend Cushing Eells, spelled his name differently from the Connecticut Eels.

65. Both versions of Ethan Allen's remark were written some years after the surrender of Fort Ticonderoga, one by Allen, the other by a soldier present at the time. Turner's remembrance of the latter quotation was slightly wrong; Allen was reported to have said: "Come out of there, you damned old rat."

Bemans—So you see I might well have been a minister (There were 22 Rev. Eels-) if the children hadn't split up into frontier builders and preachers. Perhaps I fell between the two stools!

All this may not interest you, but since you asked the question I have tried to canvass the situation. What I was *conscious* of, was that father had come of pioneer folk, that he loved the forest, into which he used to take me fishing. I have polled down the Wisconsin in a dug-out with Indian guides from "Grandfather Bull Falls," through virgin forest of balsam firs, seeing deer in the river, —antlered beauties who watched us come down with curious eyes and then broke for the tall timber, —hearing the squaws in their village on the high bank talk their low treble to the bass of our Indian polesman, —feeling that I belonged to it all.[66] I have seen a lynched man hanging to a tree as I came home from school in Portage,[67] have played around old Fort Winnebago at its outskirts,[68] have seen the red shirted Irish raftsmen *take* the town when they tied up and came ashore,[69] have plodded up the "pinery road" that ran by our house to the pine woods of Northern Wisconsin,[70] have seen Indians come in on their ponies to buy paint and ornaments, and sell their furs; have stumbled on their camp on the Baraboo, where dried pumpkins were hung up, and cooking muskrats were in the kettle, and an Indian family were bathing in the river—the frontier in that sense, you see, was real to me, and when I studied history I did not keep my personal experiences in a watertight compartment away from my studies. Early I got hold of Droysen's dictum that history is the self consciousness of humanity, and conceived of the past as the explanation of *much* of the present —not *all* of it, however, thank God.[71] But possibly this capacity to see relations between past and present may explain much of me.

66. "Big Bull Falls" consisted of a series of rapids and small waterfalls on the Wisconsin River at present-day Wausau. Both the Wisconsin and Baraboo rivers were favorite camping spots for the Indians, who still clung to their hunting grounds near Portage when Turner was a boy. For an account of his contacts with them see above, pp. 12–13.
67. Two lynchings occurred in Portage in 1869, when Turner was seven years old. They are described above, pp. 10–11.
68. Fort Winnebago was built in 1828 on the right bank of the Fox River, two miles from the Wisconsin River, to guard the portage between those two streams. It was abandoned in 1845 and was crumbling into ruins when Turner played about its walls in the 1860s.
69. Great lumber rafts, formed of several "cribs" loosely held together, regularly passed Portage on the Wisconsin River, bound from the northern pine forests to markets on the Illinois and Iowa prairies. If the raftsmen "took" the town on occasion, the event was not considered important enough to be mentioned in the local newspapers.
70. The "Wisconsin pineries" were world famous at this time, supplying lumber used for building all along the Mississippi Valley.
71. Turner owned two copies of Johann G. Droysen's principal work: *Grundriss der*

This is too, too much *Turner*—I feel a bit sick as to my stomach at the amount of it and I am, with respect

Very humbly your servant

Me

Frederick J. Turner

I am glad to talk with you this way, nevertheless, just as a man might wish to "look pleasant" when he sat to a famous portrait painter.

Cornell University

Ithaca, New York

[Dec., 1925]

Dear Turner:

Many thanks for your two biographical budgets. It will help me a good deal. Much of it only confirms what I have already suspected. I am glad to know where you got the "self-consciousness of humanity"—for I recall your quoting that in class. I didn't suppose you got your idea from Johns Hopkins —in fact I had about figured out from your writings that Johns Hopkins gave you so stiff a dose of "German Mark" and "germ" theory, and inheritance of institutions, and the like, that you probably sickened and spewed the stuff up. Well, I am on the last lap now and I see my way through pretty well.

I am going to Ann Arbor after all. Hamilton got me to give two talks at the Brookings School of Economics and much to my surprise a substantial check came, which my wife said I must use to go to Ann Arbor. One reason I want to go is to talk with Phillips and Lord and others, discriminating pupils of yours about this business.[72] I already have letters from Phillips and Allen Young—nice letters which would burn your ears a little maybe.[73]

Historik (Leipzig, 1882) and *Outline of the Principles of History* (Boston, 1893). The first he purchased in 1890, the second in 1893. In the latter he marked several passages in which the concept was expressed that "history was the self-consciousness of humanity." Both are in the Huntington Library.

72. Walton H. Hamilton, an economist who had taught at the University of Michigan and Amherst College, had since 1923 been professor of economics at the Robert Brookings Graduate School of Economics in Washington, D.C., where Becker had lectured. Becker wanted to attend the meeting of the American Historical Association at Detroit and Ann Arbor later in the month, to talk with Ulrich B. Phillips and Robert Howard Lord, one Turner's colleague at Wisconsin, the other at Harvard. What he learned from them we will never know, but Phillips had already written Becker a long letter about Turner and his skills. U. B. Phillips to Becker, October 13, 1925. HEH TU Box 34A.

73. Phillips' letter to Becker of October 13, 1925, is mentioned in n. 72 above; Allyn A.

Well, you laid a kind of magic spell on us, and I have to fight it now in self defence.

Thanks ever so, and best wishes,
Carl Becker

Becker's task was time-consuming, made more so by the avalanche of materials sent his way by Turner. But by February 11, 1926, he could write that he was nearing the end. Could he ask one more favor? A complete list of Turner's publications should be included; he was sending a separate sheet with all the titles that he knew, but was not sure whether or not some might have been missed? Would Turner mind looking it over, and making additions when necessary? Turner added a few titles to Becker's compilation and starred those he thought most important. Beside the title of his doctoral dissertation he wrote: "My doctor's thesis—done in substance in my under-graduate junior year." This misconception restated, he was compelled to begin another letter, indicating this time the contributions that he considered most important, and adding a few observations about items in his work of which he was particularly proud: [74]

2214 Van Hise Avenue
Madison, Wisconsin
February 13, 1926

Dear Becker:

I fear that you must loathe my name by this time! But I wish to ease up the job as much as I can, so long as I am "in for it."

Let me say right off that I am fearful that I included Raynor Wellington in the list of dedications. I have just noticed that he dedicates to his wife and that I confused his kind words in the introductory note with the dedication.[75]

I enclose various titles and—to save your time—I return with jottings, your own list.

Young, a former student and later a colleague at Harvard, also wrote at length about Turner's qualities as historian and teacher. Young to Becker, October 9, 1925. HEH TU Box 34A.

74. This handwritten letter by Turner is in HEH TU Box 35. The bibliographical materials have not been included here; a better bibliography of Turner's writings is in Everett E. Edwards, comp., "Bibliography of the Writings of Frederick Jackson Turner," in F. J. Turner, *The Early Writings of Frederick Jackson Turner* (Madison, 1938), pp. 233–68.

75. See above, p. 228.

I'd rather like to have the diplomatic stuff go in as this side of western and American history engaged a lot of my time, and has led to a good deal of writing of diplomatic history. See, e.g. Bemis' *Jay's Treaty* the bibliographical comments and the use made of the monographs and introduction and notes to Bassett, Federal System, and to Henry J. Ford's volume on the period in the *Chronicles* series.[76]

The *Yale Review* article on "Sections and Nation" should go in. I may quote you *confidentally and not for publication*—since I am baring my nakedness to you!—these words from a letter of Prof. Jos. Redlich, the Austrian scholar and publicist who wrote the "Problem of the Austrian State and Empire," lectured at the Institute at Williams, 1922, etc.

He wrote to Cross, the editor of the Yale Review: [77]

"I wish to speak only of that *really* marvellous essay of Professor Turner on Sectionalism in the United States. It is one of the most thoughtful and most original essays on the political nature of the United States I have ever read. Late Lord Bryce would have liked and admired it as much as I do. . . . The whole essay is amazingly full of new information, recent points of view and experiences of American life unknown, I dare say also to such old students of things American as I am one."

I have been so generally classified as limited in my scope to the West, as a geographic area, rather than as a factor and phase of American life, that these words of praise from an eminent European public man pleased me not so much from the side of vanity—as from the side of feeling that I had at least made my goal clear to a European authority.

I sometimes wonder if after all I have not been simply, rather blindly, trying to explain America to myself instead of writing history!

or writing agriculture

or   geography

or   diplomacy

76. Turner forgot that he had mentioned the favorable remarks made by Samuel F. Bemis about his diplomatic studies in a letter to Becker written on November 16, 1925. See above, n. 20. John S. Bassett, in *The Federalist System, 1789–1801* (*The American Nation: A History*, XI, New York, 1906), 306, praised Turner's edited documents on the foreign policy of George Washington and John Adams as "essential sources" for the study of the period. He was similarly praised in Henry J. Ford, *Washington and His Colleagues* (*The Chronicles of America Series*, New Haven, 1918), p. 228: "New light has been cast upon Genet's mission causing a great change in estimates of his character and activities by materials drawn from the French archives by Professor F. J. Turner."

77. Turner again forgot that on October 3, 1925, he wrote in full to Becker of the praise he had received from Joseph Redlich. See above, n. 12.

or   economics—land transportation etc
or   literature
or   religion

I have a goodly list of students who write me that I got them going on the American phases of the history of these fields, and to a rather surprising degree they have become the pioneers in their fields. I am not philosopher enough to be a "maker" of social sciences but I have had a lot of fun exploring, getting lost and getting back, and telling my companions about it. And I have learned a heap from my fellow seminarians.

No there's no science of history. Sometimes I doubt if there is a real science (in the sense that cuts out history) of anything.

'Nuff sed.

Yours cordially
Frederick J. Turner

This was Turner's last letter; Carl Becker was on his own now, left to grapple with the formidable task of compressing the volumes of information that he had received into a short essay while leaving enough space for his own observations and interpretations. Turner, his obligations to his student fulfilled, settled into his own researches in Madison, working hopefully toward completing his volume on sectionalism and the nation. Progress was slow, particularly because Wisconsin's frigid winters sapped his strength and made him vulnerable to a succession of colds that left him weak and miserable. His wife, knowing that his heart could not endure such torture, finally persuaded him to seek a warmer clime during the winter of 1926–1927. The Turners left for New Orleans in January, 1927, then worked their way westward with stops at Tucson and Claremont before they finally arrived in Pasadena—and what was to be a new chapter in their lives.

Its author was Turner's old friend, Max Farrand, who had just been named director of research at the Henry E. Huntington Library and Art Gallery, then newly opened to public use. Farrand was in the East at the time, but he saw his opportunity; no one, he knew, was better equipped to offer advice on building a library in American history than the dean of the nation's historians. The letters and telegrams that he hurried westward to the Library's trustees and staff accomplished their miracles; Turner was persuaded to accept a month's appointment as Senior Research Associate to appraise the collections and recommend the direction of growth. He blossomed during those weeks, basking in the warm sunshine of Southern

California and enjoying his excursions into the treasures that Mr. Huntington had assembled. Fred, his wife reported to a friend, had undergone a real "resurrection." [78] Nor did he alone benefit. The reports that he prepared proved of such value to Farrand and the trustees that they would be satisfied with nothing less than having him as a permanent member of the staff.[79] No commitments were made that spring, but Farrand was confident and Turner so satisfied with his stay that his favorable decision seemed certain.

So it was that the Turners were in a happy mood when they left Pasadena that May of 1927, bound for their summer home at Hancock Point, Maine, with a few weeks' stopover in Madison on their itinerary. One item in the bundle of mail awaiting them at their Van Hise Street home mightily intensified their happiness. Carl Becker had sent them an inscribed copy of his page proofs.[80] We can imagine that Turner waited no longer than to greet his daughter and grandchildren in their house next door before he settled in the easy chair in his study to enjoy the first pen portrait of himself that he was to read in his lifetime. His reaction was immediate and enthusiastic, as the letter he wrote the next day amply demonstrated: [81]

> 2214 Van Hise Ave.,
> Madison, Wisconsin
> May 14, 1927

Dear Becker:

We returned yesterday noon from our winter in the Southwest, chiefly California, and I find among the printed mail your proof-sheets and the book, which my daughter had been holding for me during our wanderings. So, I fear, you will doubt—or will have doubted, rather—my appreciation of the portrait you have drawn, with such fascinating brush work, of your unworthy sitter.

But I do appreciate most deeply your chapter. If, at times, I feel that you

78. Caroline Mae Turner to Mrs. William Hooper, [May, 1927]. HEH TU-H Box 6.
79. These reports, entitled "Memoranda," are in HEH TU File Drawer 15. Some have been published in Wilbur R. Jacobs, "Frederick Jackson Turner's Notes," *Southern California Quarterly*, XLVI (June, 1964), 161–68.
80. An inscribed copy of these proofs was presented to the Huntington Library by Turner. They bear Accession No. 138067.
81. The original of this letter, like others in the series exchanged between Becker and Turner in 1925, is in the Becker Papers, Cornell University. The originals of the letters from Becker to Turner are in the Turner Papers, Huntington Library. Copies of all are in the latter collection. This letter is in HEH TU Box 36.

are writing your youthful enthusiasms *over finding history*, rather than painting the man as he really is, (or was), I—and my family!—seem to see the young and ardent adventurer "beyond the edge of cultivation," and I get a real thrill from the evidence that, at least, I had a part—a too generously recognized part—in shaping such careers as yours, and by companionship, not by school master's drills.

In a word,—it seems to me that you have done the best possible with the subject; and that if I am admitted by the readers into the group of "Masters" framed in the volume, it will be quite as much because of your skill as an artist, as because of anything I have done, or been, to deserve the things you believe of me.

You have hit the essentials of my way of looking at history, of my efforts, and my incompleted conceptions. I understand myself better—(barring the parts where your youthful enthusiasms as a student idealize my personal qualities and influence), from your analysis. And even here, I am inwardly much cheered up, and in danger of becoming vain.

Did you ever hear the story of the man who visited Oliver Wendell Holmes, in his last days, and said to him, "what a pity you can't read your obituary," and Holmes told him of the family who became so poor that they had to cook and eat the pet dog Fido? As the last morsels disappeared, the young daughter of the family burst into tears, and exclaimed: "How Fido would have loved these bones."—I am more fortunate than Fido!

As yet I haven't done more than finger the pages of the other chapters dealing with old and loved friends in many cases, but I am impressed with the fact that through them all runs the thread of emphasis on personal influence, and independent ways of looking on the subjects with which the mean have dealt. There is really little effective teaching that is not vitalized by research and by realization of the interconnection with other fields.

In the matter of the frontier you are right of course in saying that complex urban industrialism has brought the frontier process toward its end. But I have been dealing with the *past* processes that made American history, and although urban development has always been one of those processes, its form and quality have been deeply affected—to a large extent shaped—by the westward movement into unoccupied spaces and resources. Much as I should love to start all over and investigate more in detail the eastern aspects, and the reasons for the America, say of the year 2000, I shall have to leave that to you younger fellows.

California was a boon to us, and I have taken a renewed grip on life after our winter there. The Huntington Library, where I worked for some six weeks, is, naturally, as yet a collectors library of rarities, but in buying them Mr. Huntington laid his hands on whole libraries where he wanted items, so that I was agreeably surprised to find the breadth as well as the unexampled collection of placer mines in his Anglo-American manuscripts and books. Farrand has a real opportunity to make it a center of historical research, considering what is already there, and the funds provided for its adjustment to future needs. But the work will be one of years.[82]

I am thinking very seriously of transferring my hearth fire and library to some Southern California place. Madison winters to a man of forty are quite different to one of over sixty five. I found that it took too large a percentage of my vitality to merely meet the climatic severity here. The Pasadena region is the home of lovers of art, literature, music, and such scientists as Hale and Millikan of the Wilson Observatory and California Tech.[83] It is, with Los Angeles, building up a new center of civilization in America, and is "carrying on" with the initiative and energy of the historic "West." [84]

We leave about June 1 for Hancock Point, Maine, where I wish I could see you, and hear about yourself and family

Yours affectionately

Frederick J. Turner

Little wonder that Turner was pleased with his portrait, for Carl Becker's essay was a masterpiece of expression and understanding.[85] Few teachers in our history have been favored with pupils who could diagnose their techniques so accurately and delightfully; few research scholars have found disciples capable of such a penetrating analysis of their theories. Becker's

82. An account of Farrand's successful effort to create a great research library out of the priceless rare books and manuscripts collected by Henry E. Huntington is in Ray A. Billington, "The Genesis of the Research Institution," *Huntington Library Quarterly*, XXXII (August, 1969), 351-72.
83. George Ellery Hale was a prominent astronomer associated with the Mt. Wilson Observatory near Pasadena. He was also a trustee of the Huntington Library and influential in persuading Turner to accept a place on its staff, as was Robert A. Millikan, president of the California Institute of Technology in Pasadena.
84. The Turners did move to Pasadena in the fall of 1927, where he was named Senior Research Associate at the Huntington Library. He retained this post until his death in March, 1932.
85. Carl Becker, "Frederick Jackson Turner," in Odum, ed., *American Masters of Social Science*, pp. 273-318.

pen sketch can be enjoyed today as it could be when Turner's fame was at its height; it remains one of the most brilliant gems produced by an author notable for the brightness of his writings. Yet Turner had earned those plaudits, and more that were to come. For even as he was congratulating Becker, a younger scholar was preparing himself for a second portrait of his master that would rival Becker's in comprehension and appreciation.

CHAPTER XI *The Merle Curti Correspondence, 1928–1931*

That Carl Becker should be the first to subject Frederick Jackson Turner's historical contributions to expert analysis was singularly appropriate, for Becker ranked at the top among students trained by Turner during his early teaching years at the University of Wisconsin. That the second historian to undertake such an analysis should be Merle Curti was equally appropriate, for Curti was the brightest star among the many who entered his seminar during his final teaching years at Harvard University. Born in rural Nebraska in 1897, Curti graduated from Harvard College *summa cum laude* in 1920, earned his master of arts degree there a year later, and in 1927 added the doctorate. His teaching career began at Beloit College in 1921, but in 1925 he moved to Smith College, where he was an associate professor of history when the following correspondence began. He later advanced to a professorship at the Teachers College of Columbia University, and finally to the University of Wisconsin where he was the first recipient of the Frederick Jackson Turner Professorship in American History, a distinction that he retained until his retirement in 1969.[1]

While a graduate student at Harvard University Curti fell under Turner's magic spell and remained an ardent—although not an uncritical—admirer. He found Turner not only a guide into an exciting new world of intellectual adventurers, but a warm friend and sympathetic companion. "You will, I know," he wrote during his third year of graduate study, "forgive me the unconventionality when I tell you that you are the only one whom I have idealized and for whom I have been constantly forced to widen and enrich my ideal. Quite apart from the intellectual side, your kindness, your sympathy, strength and loveableness have given me something I cannot even try to measure."[2] Turner reciprocated in kind; he skillfully directed his young

1. Professor Merle Curti has graciously given his permission for the publication of these letters, which he presented to the Huntington Library after Turner's death.
2. Merle Curti to Turner, January 30, 1923. HEH TU Box 32.

admirer through the academic maze, helped him select a doctoral dissertation subject, and arranged for his study in France and Germany in 1924 and 1925. When Curti returned to Cambridge his mentor had retired, but an equally skilled successor awaited in the person of Professor Arthur Meier Schlesinger. Schlesinger judged the thesis on which he had labored abroad was too diffuse for a dissertation, and that Curti had compounded the problem by writing a series of essays in social and literary criticism rather than a connected narrative. He must discard "The Young America Movement of 1852" and start afresh. This meant three years of wasted work, but Curti had his own doubts about what he had done and turned to the subject suggested by Professor Schlesinger—a study of the peace movement in the United States—with enthusiasm, earning his degree two years later.[3] In him Turner was assured a well-trained and sympathetic interpreter.

His opportunity to play this role was provided by the Social Science Research Council. This interdisciplinary organization had since its inception in 1922 debated means of acquainting its varied members—historians, sociologists, economists, political scientists, anthropologists, and the like—with a common body of knowledge that would allow all to utilize the aims and methods of the social sciences. Preliminary investigations led to the creation in 1926 of a Committee on Scientific Method which, after more months of considering the many devices that might be employed, settled on a "case book" that would demonstrate the actual techniques used by specialists in the various disciplines. More planning followed, an editor was designated, consultants were drafted, and the form and nature of the book agreed upon. One major problem was the selection of the social scientists whose methods were to be subjected to analysis; this was resolved by asking each of the professional associations represented on the Council—the American Historical Association, the American Anthropological Association, and the like —to name a committee of three to designate the scholars who had made the most significant contributions in each discipline. It was also agreed that the methodology and purposes of each would be analyzed by a thoroughly competent investigator in the same field of study. These recommendations were laid before the Social Science Research Council in April, 1928, and enthusiastically approved.[4]

3. Curti to Turner, September 26, 1925. HEH TU Box 34A.
4. Stuart A. Rice, "History and Organization of the *Case Book*," in Stuart A. Rice, ed., *Methods in Social Science: A Case Book* (Chicago, 1931), pp. 731–39.

254

The special committee nominated by the American Historical Association to name the historians whose methodological concepts were worthy of study was headed by Professor Sidney B. Fay of Smith College. Those it singled out for analysis were largely Europeans who had pioneered in the use of new techniques: Jules Michelet, Ernest Renan, Henri Pirenne, Georg von Below, Ernest Troeltsch, and Voltaire. Only one American was felt worthy of joining this distinguished company: Frederick Jackson Turner. This settled, the search for another historian capable of analyzing his methods and contributions began. This proved difficult. Two well-known scholars were invited, but forced to refuse because of other commitments. Then Professor Fay had a brilliant idea. Why not invite his younger colleague at Smith College, Merle Curti? He was young, enthusiastic, superbly endowed with intelligence, and familiar with Turner's teaching techniques and theories, yet sufficiently critical not to prepare a laudatory essay. Curti was asked but tried to refuse, modestly considering himself incapable of such an important assignment. When he finally accepted, the American Historical Association was assured an excellent analysis of its leading member, and Turner a scrutiny of his place in history that would be just, as well as objective.

No sooner had Curti agreed to undertake the assignment than he faced the same problem that had confronted Carl Becker a few years before. How could he learn enough about Turner's ideas and methods to subject them to the type of methodological analysis required? He reacted just as had Becker, and in August, 1928, wrote a frank letter explaining the circumstances of his appointment and asking for help:[5]

105 Prospect Street
Northhampton, Massachusetts
August 8, 1928

Dear Professor Turner:

In June, it was about Commencement time, Mr. Fay rang me up, and asked me to write a brief article on the significance of your work for the methodology of the social sciences. I had been teaching historical method at Smith, and had talked a good deal with Barnes about methodology in relation to the social sciences, and without much reflection, said I would be happy to do it.[6]

5. This letter, and others in this series, are in HEH TU Box 40.
6. Harry Elmer Barnes, historian and sociologist, was at this time a colleague of Curti's on the Smith College faculty.

Mr. Fay sent me a brief prospectus, from which it appears that a survey is being made of the methodology of outstanding sociologists, political scientists, economists, and historians. The project seemed to me much more important than Mr. Fay's rather casual manner had suggested, and I decided it was worse than absurd for such a novice as myself to attempt such a task. I had come down to Worcester to teach in the Summer School, and I wrote to Mr. Fay that I had changed my mind.[7] I put it on the ground that your work was much too important to be handled by anyone save a master, and that in fairness to you I must ask to be released. I had no letter from Mr. Fay, and supposed that another arrangement had been made, as I suggested the names of some of your students, and reminded Mr. Fay that I was among the least distinguished of the people that had worked with you.

Now I find that two really distinguished historians had been asked, but were unable, because of other engagements, to undertake the sketch. Mr. Fay was so persuasive yesterday when I saw him, that I finally consented to do it. I should have refused, except for the fact that the articles must all be in by September 25, and I feared that with Mr. Fay's tendency to delay and with people away on vacations, it might be difficult to get at people quickly.

It would be a labor of the greatest love if I felt at all equal to it. But I feel terribly inadequate, and am very wretched. Will you be good enough to help me? I shall devote all of my time to it, and I know there will be questions I shall want to ask you.

I hope you will understand how I feel about it.

Sincerely,
Merle Curti

Will you make suggestions, cautions?

Turner reacted to this request as he had to Carl Becker's initial inquiry three years before; nay, he overreacted to the extent of a handwritten letter twenty-three pages long, followed almost immediately by another of twenty-one pages. More were yet to come, most of them the result of Curti's skillful probing; his astute questions stirred Turner's memory into revealing events and ideas that he had forgotten himself. Much that he said duplicated what he had told Dodd, Miss Skinner, and Becker, but a great deal more was added.

7. Curti taught that summer at Clark University, Worcester, Massachusetts, where Barnes had previously served on the faculty.

The remarkable series of letters that follows contains more on Turner's historical concepts, and the basis for those concepts, than anything else from his pen.

Not for publication   Hancock Point, Maine
    or quotation!   Aug. 8, 1928

Dear Curti:

I am not in the least surprised that you find it difficult to write of my "methodology," for I shouldn't know what to say myself. If I have one, I don't know what it is! I have never formulated a philosophy of history, or of historical research, or of pedagogy. Once Giddings said to me that I behaved like a sociologist, not a historian; I answered that I didn't care what I was *called*, so long as I was left to try to ascertain the truth, and the relation of the facts to cause and effect in my own way.[8] One of my Harvard students (undergraduate) was overheard to say that what I was doing in the classroom "might be all right, but it wasn't history." Nevertheless, I think I am a historian, tho' I have been dubbed by the Socialists an economic determinist (which I'm not!); by geographers as a geographer, etc.

I early responded to the suggestion of Droysen in his *Historik* that History was the self consciousness of humanity—in other words the effort of the present to understand itself by understanding the past;[9] and I, as you perhaps recall, valued Chamberlin's paper on the Multiple Hypothesis, which I have aimed to apply to history as he to Geology.[10]

Perhaps at bottom the belief that all the social sciences were one, and related to physical science has influenced my work. The need of dealing with

8. Franklin H. Giddings began teaching sociology at Columbia University in 1891, and was revered as one of the pioneers of his discipline.
9. Turner was quoting Johann G. Droysen, *Grundriss der Historik* (Leipzig, 1882). This was a judgment which, as he repeatedly testified, underlay his whole concept of history.
10. Thomas C. Chamberlin was professor of geology and later president of the University of Wisconsin when Turner taught there. His famed paper, "The Method of Multiple Working Hypotheses," *Journal of Geology*, V (November–December, 1897), 837–48, urged the use of multiple hypotheses to avoid the danger of bias inherent in a single hypothesis. Turner embraced Chamberlin's teachings, although his stress on the frontier and section as primary shapers of American society has subjected him to the accusation that he did not always practice what he preached. Actually he did so; he recognized the importance of economic forces, the class struggle, cultural influences, hereditary factors, and others, but emphasized the frontier and section because he felt they had been neglected. To this he testified frequently in his writings. This is discussed in Wilbur R. Jacobs, "Turner's Methodology: Working Hypotheses or Ruling Theory?" *Journal of American History*, LIV (March, 1968), 853–63.

economic, political and social (in the largest sense, including Literature, Art, Religion etc.) fields has shaped my conception of historical research.

My first historical training, under Professor Wm. F. Allen, Wisconsin, a Harvard man who began as a Latinist, but changed to a Historical scholar, of an ability and breadth of view not adequately recognized by students of historiography (probably because his work was done in a University not then recognized as later).[11] He was especially interested in mediaeval history— especially English history—and his breadth of interest in social classes, economics, and cultural factors, was ahead of his time in this country. His use of sources in seminary methods with his upper classmen anticipated the seminary method in the United States, I think, though C. K. Adams is usually credited with priority in this method.[12]

At any rate I was led to approach American history in the spirit of Mediaeval historians who had to deal with institutions in the formative period. I had, under Allen, been encouraged to *creative* research rather than to memorize narrative history in the fashion then prevalent.

Because my original work was done in the field of "Western" history, some undue emphasis has been laid upon my attention to that field. But, as you know, the "West" with which I dealt was a *process* rather than a fixed geographical region: it began with the Atlantic coast, and it emphasized the way in which the East colonized the West, and how the "West" as it stood at any given period affected the development and ideas of the older areas to the East. In short, the "frontier" was taken as the "thin red line" that recorded the *dynamic* element in American history up to recent times.

In studying this factor it became clear to me almost from the beginning that the advance of settlement required a study of the Atlantic coast sections and an understanding of their make up—their people, institutions and ideas; and an understanding of the geographic provinces into which they moved—

11. For a discussion of Professor William Francis Allen's influence on Turner see above, pp. 15–25. Turner is right in saying that Allen was a classicist most of his life; he was not made professor of history until 1886, when Turner was well on his way to his degree of master of arts.

12. Professor Charles Kendall Adams is generally credited with launching the nation's first seminar in history at the University of Michigan in 1869. He later became president of the University of Wisconsin during Turner's early teaching career there. Allen used the "topical" method of instruction in most of his courses, requiring students to prepare papers based on investigations in sources, then present their results to the class. This was Turner's reason for crediting him with originating the seminar technique.

the new environments and conditions which modified these colonists as well as the contributions which the colonists made.

Thus I had to have some knowledge of American physiography, I had to know something of demography, as well, and I had to recognize that these changes and inter-relations affected American social life and characteristics in general: its literature, art, religions, ideals. Thus the *frontier* in this larger sense,—considering what went on behind the *frontier*, and what the frontier zone of pioneer settlement meant in American life, reactivity on the East as well as in itself and the *section* in its sense as the geographic province, rather than the mere North and South of the current usage when I began my work led me naturally into a conception of American history which differed from that of my contemporaries. My work, whether good or bad, can only be correctly judged by noting what American historians and teachers of history (see college and Univ. catalogues of the later eighties) were doing when I began. I am saying these things to you in confidence, of course, and with some pain! The attitude toward Western history was at the time largely antiquarian or of the romantic narrative type devoid of the conception of the "West" as a moving process—modifying the East, and involving economic, political and social factors. (See my paper, "A Plea for the Study of Western History" or some such title, in the Am. Hist. Asso. Report, for some date in the middle nineties.[13]

Recurring to the matter of my interest in various fields, and in all the sections—rather than in the West alone (which seemed to me the most neglected part of our history) I may help you to understand my work better if I sketch the way my seminary etc. worked. My undergraduate courses were naturally as a beginner in general American history, which my make-up didn't permit me to take conventionally. I had had but one-third of a year in American history under Allen in Wis. When I went to Johns Hopkins U. for a year of graduate work (1888-9) the only American history I had was a brief seminary with Small (later Professor of Sociology in Chicago, but at the time an older fellow graduate student at JHU) who for two or three months conducted an enquiry by a group of us into the question of what

---

13. In December, 1896, a paper by Turner on "The West as a Field for Historical Study" was read at a meeting of the American Historical Association. It was published in the *Annual Report of the American Historical Association for 1896* (Washington, 1897), I, pp. 281-87.

powers were given by the various states or colonies to their representatives in the continental congresses.[14]

So I had a lack of general American history training which in some ways was a handicap—requiring much hard study on my part—but which in other ways was an advantage in that I hadn't been fitted into the mould of the teachers of the usual successive courses in American history. I had to work out my own salvation!

In my graduate and upper classmen seminary on my return to Wis. in 1890, I conceived the idea of gaining an independent and thorough knowledge of American history by taking up in successive years, successive periods of American history, beginning with Virginia colonization.[15] This plan I followed down to my last course in Harvard in the period around 1876 to the present, in 1924.[16] I seldom used the seminary to study the West per se. I omitted seminaries on the Civil War period—as pretty well covered.

In an upper class undergraduate course, I had a course on the Economic and Social History of U.S. at different period.[17] In this I assigned different

14. Albion W. Small was a professor at Bowdoin College before enrolling as a graduate student at Johns Hopkins University. During Turner's year in residence, 1888–1889, he was drafted to present a course on "The Growth of American Nationality," in which Turner enrolled. Each member of the course analyzed early state documents to determine the degree to which power was surrendered to the national government during the period in which the constitution was being drafted. Turner's notes in the course are in HEH TU File Drawer 15A, Folder: Notes on A. W. Small. Small later published an article based on materials accumulated during the course: "The Beginnings of American Nationalism," *Johns Hopkins University Studies in Historical and Political Science*, VIII (Baltimore, 1890), 7–42.

15. This was Turner's ideal when he began teaching, but he failed to remember that it was seldom realized. His first seminar was on "The History of the Old Northwest," not on the early settlement of Virginia; his second on the period from 1830 to 1840. His seminar topics varied with his own interests; when he was preparing his volume on *The Rise of the New West* (*The American Nation: A History*, New York, 1906), his seminar studied the period 1819–1829 with him, and he even gave a lecture course on the subject. His teaching career at the University of Wisconsin may be followed in the instructional reports that he submitted each term. These are in the university archives.

16. During his last term at Harvard, in the spring of 1924, Turner offered a course he had never given before on "The United States, 1880–1920." His opening remarks, which explain why he spent a whole term preparing an offering he would never give again, are in HEH TU Box 56. Many of his lecture notes are in HEH TU File Drawer 22B, Folder: Notes and Other Materials, 1880–1920.

17. Turner introduced his course on "The Economic and Social History of the United States" in the fall of 1892, planning to alternate it with the "Constitutional and Political History of the United States." Its purpose was to survey "the origin and development of the social and economic characteristics of the country" from the colonial period to the present; among the topics considered was "the spread of settlement across the continent." *Catalogue of the University of Wisconsin, 1891–1892* (Madison, 1892), p. 98. He offered "The History of the West" for the first time in 1895. *Ibid., 1895–1896* (Madison, 1896), p. 140.

fields to different members of the class, sometimes a single field to a group. These fields were intended to cover all the larger interests, such as Agriculture, Immigration and Migration, Banking, Finance, including Tariff, Land, Internal Improvements and Transportation, Slavery, Literature, Religion and Churches, etc. etc.

The members of the classes were allowed to choose their field, in the seminary and in these courses; and were expected to hand in papers on some limited topic in their own field, and a correlation paper summarizing the reports of their fellows and relating it to their own field.

In the class discussions I tried to serve as listener, correlator, and interpreter of the class reports and I aimed to knit together these contributions to show how they supplemented or corrected conventional histories and thus the class came to conceive of itself as engaged in creative work.

In dealing with these reports, I tried to criticize, by Socratic type of questioning, but keeping in the back ground. I was accustomed to ask the reporter "how he knew" that such and such a statement was true. If he had relied on secondary sources, I called for comparison with the original source, and cultivated the critical attitude toward previous writers. But I did not aim to produce too cocky or scornful an attitude toward the men who had built before, and I demanded wide reading in standard histories, at the same time that I demanded an independent study of the subject.

As a result of this optional choice of fields, I have had students, for example, who became eminent in railway transportation history, like Meyer of the Interstate Commerce Commission, Johnson of the U. of Penn., Haney etc.; in agriculture men like Taylor, formerly of the Dept. of Agr., whose students are now shaping much of the work there; and Hibbard, Olsen, Stine, Trimble; Schmidt (Iowa) etc. Coulter, who was at the head of the agricultural division of the Census office one year was for a time in that course.[18]

18. Balthasar H. Meyer earned the doctoral degree under Turner and Richard T. Ely in 1897 and became a prominent economist who was serving at this time as a member of the Interstate Commerce Commission. Emory R. Johnson received his graduate degree in 1891 and went on to become professor of economics and dean of the Wharton School of Finance and Commerce of the University of Pennsylvania. Lewis H. Haney was awarded the doctorate in 1906, served as professor at the University of Texas, and was at that time professor of economics at New York University. Henry C. Taylor, having completed his degree with Turner in 1902, became Chief of the Bureau of Markets and Crop Estimates of the United States Department of Agriculture and was at this time professor of economics at Northwestern University. Benjamin H. Hibbard, another doctoral candidate in 1902, was professor of agricultural economics at the University of Wisconsin. Nils A. Olsen earned two degrees of master of arts under Turner, one at Wisconsin in 1909 and the other at Harvard in 1912,

In the field of diplomatic history were a number of men, including Shafer of Wis., Merk etc. Bemis did some work with me and Whitaker dedicated his recent book to me. I have had dedications also from editors like Thwaites, Miss Blair, and Alvord in Western history; and from Henderson the writer on the "Conquest of the S.W." [19] The writers on Public Land policy, such as Miss Ford, Stephenson, Hibbard, Wellington etc. illustrate how the field became developed by men or women who chose this field—their work in my classes. [20] Writers on Am. literature have shown similar tendencies—but I mustn't try to list all my jewels!

I have intended merely to point out that by allowing the student to choose, by encouraging as well as by criticizing, some original work in fields such as these (and in several others) eg Hansen in immigration has been promoted. [21] Possibly I had something to do with stimulating their investigations and in guiding their work; but much was due to "salutary neglect" and to an

<hr />

then became Chief of the Bureau of Agricultural Economics in the Department of Agriculture. Oscar C. Stine, who studied briefly with Turner at Wisconsin, was an economist in the same bureau, and editor of *Agricultural History*. William J. Trimble, after receiving his degree in 1909, was professor at North Dakota Agricultural College. Louis B. Schmidt studied with Turner during the 1905 summer school at Madison; he later completed his graduate work and became professor of agricultural history at Iowa State College. John L. Coulter, who took his doctorate in economics in 1908, was currently president of the North Dakota Agricultural College after serving with the Division of Agriculture of the Census Bureau between 1910 and 1914.

19. Joseph Schafer earned his doctoral degree with Turner in 1906 and was at this time Superintendent of the State Historical Society of Wisconsin. He wrote widely on the diplomatic history of the Pacific Northwest. Frederick Merk, Turner's successor at Harvard, received his degree in 1920 and was studying the diplomacy of the Oregon Boundary Dispute. Samuel F. Bemis submitted a thesis on Jay's Treaty for his 1915 Harvard doctorate; he was at this time professor of history at George Washington University but was shortly to move to Yale University. Arthur P. Whitaker, one of Turner's last doctoral students in 1924, dedicated his book on *The Spanish-American Frontier, 1783–1795* (Boston, 1927) to Turner. Reuben Gold Thwaites, Superintendent of the State Historical Society of Wisconsin until his death in 1913, was a prolific writer, producing well over one hundred volumes. Emma Helen Blair dedicated her *The Indian Tribes of the Upper Mississippi Valley and Region of the Great Lakes* (Cleveland, 1911), to Turner. So did Clarence W. Alvord and Lee Bidgood their *The First Explorations of the Trans-Allegheny Region by the Virginians, 1650–1674* (Cleveland, 1912), and Archibald C. Henderson, *The Conquest of the Old Southwest* (New York, 1920).

20. The former students to whom Turner refers, and their books, were: Amelia C. Ford (Ph.D. Wisconsin, 1908), *Colonial Precedents for Our National Land System* (Madison, 1910); George M. Stephenson (Ph.D. Harvard, 1914), *The Political History of Public Lands from 1840 to 1862* (Boston, 1917); Benjamin H. Hibbard (Ph.D. Wisconsin, 1902), *A History of Public Land Policies* (New York, 1924); and Raynor G. Wellington (MA Harvard, 1903), *Political and Sectional Influence of the Public Lands, 1828–1842* (n.p., 1924).

21. Marcus Lee Hansen was one of several students who completed the doctoral degree with Turner in 1924. He went on to pioneer the study of immigration history, and was at this time professor of history at the University of Illinois.

attitude of hopeful expectation on my part. Usually, I delayed severe criticism until the student had acquired some confidence in himself.

It is also a point to be noted that I have been more interested in studying a leader's environment, the society in which he lived, the lesser men whose support he needed and whose opposition modified his policy, than in *minutiae* of his personal life.

It has seemed to me important both to gather details however—to dig deeply—and then to reject immaterial or subordinate details. This process of elimination, however, cannot well be done safely until the field had been surveyed in sufficient detail to reach a conclusion on the important and un-important, so in some of my seminaries, I have probably given to the student the impression that I laid too much stress on detailed research; but this was designed to cultivate critical thoroughness, and to furnish a safe basis for elimination and for reaching conclusions.

I lay stress in my own mind also upon the geographical, regional, interpretation of American politics, by the use of such mappings by counties and by congressional districts as you have seen. This method came out of my seminary, with the start by Libby in his "Ratification of the Constitution." [22] Morison has somewhere criticized this method under the misapprehension that I failed to see the fact that powerful minorities often underlay the majority color.[23] Of course preponderances, tendencies, and a very significant geographical pattern of these preponderances was all I aimed to show. When cultural and economic data are similarly mapped, there are significant and important relationships revealed.

I don't know how much light these numerous pages may cast on your problem; nor how far they treat of methodology. Mine, if I have any, has

22. Orin G. Libby was one of Turner's earliest doctoral students, completing work for his degree in 1895. His dissertation, a ground-breaking work in mapping public opinion, was published as *The Geographical Distribution of the Vote of the Thirteen States on the Federal Constitution, 1787-8* (Madison, 1894), 1-116. His contributions are appraised in "Orin G. Libby: His Place in the Historiography of the Constitution," *North Dakota Quarterly*, XXXVI (Summer, 1969).

23. If Samuel Eliot Morison, Turner's student and later colleague at Harvard, made this statement, he did so in conversation, and not in writing. Morison did, however, poke impish fun at Turner's compulsion to map everything from early congressional votes on the tariff to current divisions on the St. Lawrence Seaway. After Woodrow Wilson defeated Charles Evans Hughes in the election of 1916 he remarked: "I suppose Professor Turner will now proceed to plot out a map of the election and show us how the New Englanders supported Hughes and how the West broke away from the leadership of the conservative East"—then added that Turner would have difficulty bringing in the limestone ridges this time. Thomas P. Martin to Turner, November 9, 1916. Harvard University Archives. Harvard Commission on Western History, Correspondence, Box V, Folder: Turner, F. J.

263

been largely unconscious, as I have said—the search beyond the skyline for new truth, and the use of such methods of getting there as the immediate need and resources permitted. I may add that my practical experience in newspaper work, and in contact with politics through my father probably gave me a sense of realities which affected my work and my influence upon students. I *had* to see the connections of many factors with the purely political. I couldn't view things in the purely "academic" way.

My interest has been less in the pedagogy of my work, than in the subject which I was studying with the aid of student companions. I have not tried, nor have made a body of followers in my own special mould. I have been a porter at the gate, rather than a drill seargent.

Becker's chapter in Odum's book on *Masters of the Social Sciences* will give you the reactions of one of my earlier students.[24] Your own contact with my classes in Harvard will be helpful. Men like Bullock, Allyn Young (but I believe he is abroad) and T. C. Smith (Williams) could tell you of my Wisconsin period. Merk and Baxter could help you on the Harvard phase.[25]

Becker stresses my work as teacher more than I do, and no doubt draws too flattering a picture of my "personality." I enjoyed my companionship with students, but I do not think of myself so much as training young men as I do in working on a subject with a pleasant *comitatus*.

Barnes has written too generously of my contributions and you may get some suggestions from him.[26] I have written thus voluminously and hastily at once, because if I delay I shall not write at all, and I would gladly respond with a treatise on Methodology in Am. History, if I knew how. I may say that the amount of available original material in recent, and perhaps especially in American history makes the problem of methods here different from that of the student of Ancient or Mediaeval history who must reconstruct from scanty materials. The truth of historical details used by Ancient or Mediaeval historians has always worried me, and my own work emphasizes

24. Carl Becker, "Frederick Jackson Turner," in Howard W. Odum, ed., *American Masters of Social Science* (New York, 1927), pp. 273-318.
25. Charles Jesse Bullock earned his doctorate at Wisconsin in 1895, doing much of his work with Turner, then went on to become George F. Baker Professor of Economics at Harvard. Allyn A. Young followed a similar course, winning a Wisconsin degree in 1902 and becoming professor of economics at Harvard. Theodore Clark Smith, professor of history at Williams College, completed his doctoral work at Harvard in 1896, but served as Turner's assistant at Wisconsin in 1894 and 1895.
26. Turner's presentation copy of Harry Elmer Barnes, *The New History and the Social Studies* (New York, 1925), with the many passages mentioning his work heavily underlined, is in the Huntington Library, Accession No. 139510.

tendencies, institutions, mass movements rather than the exact truth as to details of events, motives of an individual etc.

Please do not quote from this letter or indicate that you are interviewing me or speaking with the authority of this letter. You may use *as your own* any part that seems to fit your own impressions and judgements of my "method," but not as from me. The letter is a confidential confession to you personally and much of it isn't germane.

I'm sorry for you!

Yours with regard,
Frederick J. Turner

105 Prospect St.
August 13, 1928

Dear Professor Turner,

Yes, how generously you give! Your letter is invaluable, of more help than I can begin to tell you. Of course I shall not quote from it, nor in any way indicate that you supplied me with information; though, with your permission, I should like to make indirect use of a considerable part of it. In fact, I find very little in it that is not extremely relevant. Since the work of your students is inseparable from your own (I think this is certainly true) a description of your seminary method seems to me most appropriate. I am glad you spoke again of Chamberlin's multiple hypothesis idea. I had not forgotten it; in fact, the way in which you constantly, and I think unconsciously, applied it in the seminar impressed me more deeply than any single experience that I had as one of your students. I was telling, some weeks ago, a young historical friend about this, and I said I felt that your application of this idea to historical methods was, in fact, a very great methodological contribution. He (a student of Becker's) replied that this seemed to be a fairly general attitude of historians, though they might not think of it in Chamberlin's terms. I wonder. I had two other seminaries at Harvard, and in neither was I made conscious of this concept.

Becker has rightly said that you cannot be "tagged." I shall not try to do so! I know too well how often you have pointed out that no single factor is determinative in explaining causes, even proximate causes. You have emphasized the influence of climate, geographic soils, stocks, inherited ideals, personal leadership. It is this very catholicity, this synthetic quality, which makes your methodology superior, it seems to me, to that which selects and emphasizes any single factor, whether it be economic, geographic, social, intellectual. In surveying American historiography I cannot find that anyone before you did anything like this in a scientific way.

Schlesinger has said that you were "the first historian who perceived the importance of economic influences on American history," and that your "chief importance to American historical thinking has, in the last analysis, been (your) elucidation of the part played by economic group conflicts in our history." [27] Some of the old Federalists and Hildreth appreciated and even emphasized somewhat the importance of economic facts in their relation to political facts.[28] But certainly, from say 1865 to your time, American historiography seems chiefly concerned with constitutional and political theorizing. Of course Weeden and a few others were working in the field of economic history, but they seldom saw the political and constitutional implications of economic facts.[29] It seems to me, therefore, that you led in the work of analysing economic data and seeing their relationship to political action. Am I going too far? (Please discount modesty in the interest of truth!!)

Beard, in his review of THE FRONTIER IN AMERICAN HISTORY, suggests that you have over-emphasized the influence of free lands and the frontier in explaining American development, and that you have not sufficiently emphasized conflicts between organized capital and labor.[30] Much as I value Beard's work, this seems a little unfair. Certainly in History 17 you elaborated the idea that the contest between "the capitalist and the demo-

27. This remark appears in Arthur M. Schlesinger, *New Viewpoints in American History* (New York, 1928), p. 70.
28. Richard Hildreth, *The History of the United States of America* (6 vols., New York, 1877–1880), was an old-fashioned, New England-oriented history, but it did stress economic forces more than most of its contemporaries.
29. William B. Weeden, *Economic and Social History of New England, 1620–1789* (2 vols., Boston, 1890).
30. Charles A. Beard, "The Frontier in American History," *New Republic*, XXV (February 16, 1921), 349–50, was strongly critical of Turner's 1893 essay on the grounds that it neglected the class struggle and industrialism as formative forces shaping American development. Curti, when preparing his essay, asked Beard about the review and the causes of his dissent. Beard answered that he disagreed only with the "extreme view" that free land and the westward movement "explain American development." "They partly explain it," he went on, "but only partly. Mr. Turner felt somewhat wounded by my review, I fear, and perhaps it was sharper than I should have made it, in view of the great service he has rendered to American history. In my opinion (and you may quote this if you like) Mr. Turner deserves everlasting credit for his services as the leader in restoring the consideration of economic facts to historical writing in America. . . . It was Mr. Turner who led in putting history on a scientific plane." Beard to Curti, August 9, 1928. HEH TU Box 39. Turner wrote Beard when the review appeared, protesting some of his statements. This letter has not been found, but Beard's reply, defending some of his criticisms and backing down on others, is in HEH TU Box 31. Beard to Turner, May 13, 1921.

cratic pioneer" could be traced from the earliest colonial days. Certainly in your address as president of the American Historical Association you emphasized the far-reaching implications of the industrial revolution.[31] I believe that Beard, recognizing the great importance of industrial capitalism in our own day, has possibly let his interpretation of our earlier history be colored by a kind of an ex-post-facto industrial bias. Until the newly settled areas were fairly well filled in, there were of course few class conflicts within the areas; most of the economic conflicts were with the older areas. No one has pointed this out with more clearness than you. And also, you have emphasized the fact that as the newer areas became dotted here and there with cities, that class and economic conflicts arose within the area, and that as a consequence it often spoke with a divided voice. I suppose there is a grain of truth in the concept that the East was never a section in the same sense that the West was, for the upper classes, even after the democratic waves from the West, retained more power of speaking and acting for the "section" than was true, perhaps, in the West.

As to your emphasis on sectionalism, and especially the papers in the Journal of American Sociology, the Yale Review, and the Encyclopedia of American Government.[32] It seems to me that you have made in this concept a very significant contribution. Until your work, sectionalism was too restricted, narrow a concept to be very pregnant as a hypothesis. I take it Dodd and others have been much influenced by you in the emphasis they have put on sectional bargains, ententes, alliances.[33] Even the Beards in their RISE OF AMERICAN CIVILIZATION make much use of the sectional concept, though so far as I remember they do not credit you with it.[34] Just how did you come to this concept? I ask because you were apparently not influenced by Ratzel, for in your paper of 1896 (The West as a Field of Historical

31. Turner's presidential address was printed as "Social Forces in American History," *American Historical Review*, XVI (January, 1911), 213–33.

32. The articles by Turner to which Curti refers are: "Is Sectionalism in America Dying Away?" *American Journal of Sociology*, XIII (March, 1908), 661–75; "Sections and Nation," *The Yale Review*, XII (October, 1922), 1–21; and "Sectionalism in the United States," in Andrew C. McLaughlin and Albert B. Hart, eds., *Cyclopedia of American Government* (3 vols., New York, 1914), III, 280–85.

33. Professor William E. Dodd of the University of Chicago, a pioneer student of the history of the South, often testified the extent to which Turner had influenced him. See Dodd to Turner, October 14, 1919, reproduced above, pp. 198–99.

34. Charles A. and Mary R. Beard, *The Rise of American Civilization* (2 vols., New York, 1927), relied on the sectional concept in analyzing political factors in pre-Civil War history, but made no mention of Turner. His name appeared only twice in the two volumes, each time as a pioneer in the study of the frontier whose followers in their enthusiasm for a long-neglected subject "have pressed their argument too far." *Ibid.*, I, 516, II, 764.

Research) you speak of very recently having seen Ratzel's American Geography.[35] Did Shaler mean much to you?[36] I half suspect you gave the geographers as much as they gave you. One of the few impressively concrete things in Hulbert's paper on THE INCREASING DEBT OF HISTORY TO SCIENCE, is mention of your work in pointing out the historical significance of the limestone pathways leading from the old granary of America, Pennsylvania, southward to the limestone oases of Tennessee and Kentucky and the relation of these limestone areas to transportation etc.[37]

Ought Royce be mentioned in connection with your work on cultural sectionalism? [38]

I believe students have not sufficiently appreciated your work in what one might call our intellectual history. I know very little about statistics, but your paper on CHILDREN OF THE PIONEERS seems to me important. I am going to study it more carefully, as well as the article on "Greater New England." [39] Certainly your emphasis on the origin of typical American assumptions, ways of doing things, ideals, needs to be brought to the attention of social psychologists, even more than it has been. I remember that as an undergraduate I called Allport's attention to the significance of your work for his interests, and I believe that his group at the Syracuse School of Citizenship might, in its research, go more deeply into this field.[40]

35. Turner repeatedly denied that he had read the works of the German geographer, Friedrich Ratzel, a geographic determinist, before preparing his 1893 essay. His first contact with Ratzel was in 1895 or 1896. In his paper on "The West as a Field for Historical Study" read to the American Historical Association in December, 1896, and published in the *Annual Report of the American Historical Association for 1896* (Washington, 1897), I, 283–84, Turner quoted extensively from Ratzel's chapter on "Space as a Factor in the United States"; this first appeared in English translation in 1893 and was probably not discovered by Turner until more than a year later.

36. Nathaniel S. Shaler was an early American counterpart of Ratzel in preaching geographic determinism. For a discussion of his influence on Turner see above, pp. 97, 101.

37. Archer B. Hulbert, "The Increasing Debt of History to Science," *Proceedings of the American Antiquarian Society for 1919*, XXIX (Worcester, 1920), 29–42. Turner's study of the influence of limestone pathways on the routes of early roads is on pp. 35–36.

38. For Turner's use of Josiah Royce's views on sectionalism, see above, Chapter X, n. 9.

39. Turner's article, "The Children of the Pioneers," *Yale Review*, XV (July, 1926), 645–70, was based on a statistical analysis of *Who's Who in America* and similar works, and demonstrated that the second and third generation of midwesterners made significant contributions to American culture. His "Greater New England in the Middle of the Nineteenth Century," *Proceedings of the American Antiquarian Society for 1919*, XXIX (Worcester, 1919), 222–41, was also based on statistical techniques; in it Turner traced the expansion of New England and the impact of New Englanders on other sections of the country.

40. Floyd H. Allport, a professor of social and political psychology, was at this time head of the Syracuse University School of Citizenship.

You speak of your interest in demography. Did you come to it pragmatically, as it were? That is, your analyses of statistics in the Census Reports? Did you, by a sort of trial and error method, come onto pitfalls in the use of such statistical materials which might be mentioned? If so, I think it would be well to include something about it. Possibly some of your students who worked especially with statistics feel quite definite methodological obligations to you. My colleage, Faulkner, was asked last year to write an article on the use of statistics in historical research, and could find scarcely no guides. I told him what I knew of your use of statistics, and we compared this, as best we could, with the usages of such students as Lybyer.[41]

You speak of Morison's criticism of your use of plots and maps. I never heard Morison make this criticism, but it is to be found in Allen Johnson's HISTORIAN AND HISTORICAL EVIDENCE, though your name is not mentioned.[42] I think that if you had used only a few maps, the criticism might be just. But when, as in your case, there were scores of maps, with the same significant pattern recurrences, then it seems justifiable to deduce tendencies and point out correlations. In fact, this method-device seems an important contribution. As I understand it, it came out of your seminary and Libby's work on the ratification of the constitution was the first example of it.[43] Do you remember how the idea suggested itself to you?

41. Harold U. Faulkner was Curti's colleague at Smith College, teaching courses in the economic history of the United States. Albert H. Lybyer was a professor at the University of Illinois, specializing in Near Eastern history.

42. Allen Johnson of Yale University, in his book on *The Historian and Historical Evidence* (New York, 1926), pp. 161–62, wrote that in election mapping "no account is taken of opposing election returns, which are often only slightly less than a majority through a period of years. The tabulator has taken only the majority vote of a district and then has recorded the vote in Congress of the representative chosen by that majority. Can it be affirmed confidently that physiographic conditions controlled the political action of a district of two hundred thousand voters when ninety-nine thousand voters were in opposition?" Curti wrote Johnson asking him for the basis of his criticisms. Johnson's reply made clear that he exempted Turner from his charges, which were instead levied against "some of his disciples and imitators who lack his philosophical outlook and his discrimination." Johnson to Curti, August 26, 1928. HEH TU Box 40. Turner was well aware of the deficiencies of his mapping techniques, and spent much of his life trying to perfect a method that would allow a graphic representation of election returns as they reflected determinant forces. On one occasion he listed five areas in which the method he was using failed to provide accurate representation. Among these he included his inability to reflect the extent and influences of minorities. These criticisms, filling several sheets of paper, are in HEH TU File Drawer 10A, Folder: US 1830–50. New England Politics.

43. Orin G. Libby's pioneering use of mapping votes originated in Turner's seminar. Curti's reference is to his *The Geographical Distribution of the Vote of the Thirteen States on the Federal Constitution, 1787–8.*

I think something should be made of your work in editing diplomatic documents. I have looked over the diplomatic monographs previous to your work, and it seems to me that American diplomatic studies were one-plane affairs, without reference to geographic and economic conditions. I am asking Bemis and Merk if, in their judgment, this is correct.[44]

Gidding's remark as to your sociological behaviour is interesting. But the sociologist, with far less data, far less research, would have deduced laws as to the relative importance of social inheritance and environment, I believe. You very rightly admit that only the future can disclose how far frontier characteristics, institutions, assumptions, will persist in an environment greatly different. The sociologist tends to want mathematical conclusions which the historian avoids. Thus, so far as I know, you did not try, in a one-two-three way, to say just *how* much environment, or just *how* much social inheritance explained things. Did you ever apply your concepts of the frontier process to Australia, Canada, or Russia?

I do not think Barnes' estimate of your significance too sweeping, tho' I confess, much as I admire and like him, I sometimes find his statements too sweeping. I should quarrel with him only for having, it seems to me, over-emphasized Robinson's work in developing the concepts of the so-called "new history." Your presidential address showed that you had the leading concepts of the "new history": the purpose of history, its relation to the present; the sciences as allies of historical study; and the importance of synthesis.[45] But do not worry, I shall not claim for you the perhaps dubious honor of "founding" the new history!

One more question occurs to me. You may feel your whole work is the best answer. You have emphasized the necessity of gathering data, more data, plowing deeply. Then you rejected immaterial or subordinate details. I take it the criterion of elimination was the perspective, or pattern of the forest, which you unconsciously acquired by discovering trees, describing, analysing them. This achieving of a criterion for elimination is a subtle thing. Some of the newer German historians would say that with the limitations of the mind, with the "tricks" which the unconscious plays, there can be

44. Samuel F. Bemis, who earned his doctoral degree in 1916 at Harvard as a student of Turner, was a well-known diplomatic historian. Frederick Merk, also one of Turner's students and his successor at Harvard, was engaged in studies of the diplomacy of the Oregon Boundary dispute.

45. Curti was correct in stating that Turner's presidential address before the American Historical Association in 1910 on "Social Forces in American History" anticipated much of the viewpoint later popularized in James Harvey Robinson, *The New History* (New York, 1912).

no real objective criterion. Anything you might say on this would be very helpful.

These are some of the considerations that have been on my mind. You may want to give cautions in respect to some of them, or correct me if you think I am in error. I hope you will, though it seems a shame to impose any further on your good will and generosity. You ought to be enjoying Maine and all it offers rather than bothering with me.

Most sincerely,
Merle Curti

The Moorings
Hancock Point, Maine

Aug. 15, 1928

Dear Curti,

I don't think it wise to try to help you in the matter of priorities; and particularly on the question of relating economic and social data to American history. Henry Adams for example does much in the first volume of his history with that sort of thing, though he doesn't do it in my way.[46] The tendency was to deal with such topics in one or two separate chapters and then turn, without knitting the two together, to political and diplomatic history. I tried to keep the relations steadily in mind, but it isn't an easy job, and the effort is sometimes conducive to unwritten books! But all I can say is that in class work, seminary, and essays I emphasized these connections, and as to how far I was original you must decide by running your eye over the work of men like my contemporaries and predecessors in the treatment of American history. But do not create enemies for me by creating jealous rivalries and criticism.

I think Beard did not pay sufficient attention to essays in my frontier volume, other than the title essay, and I agree with your criticism, but I shouldn't feel it necessary to deal with him by name.[47]

---

46. The first volume of Henry Adams, *History of the United States during the Administrations of Thomas Jefferson and James Madison* (9 vols., New York, 1889–1891), followed much the pattern that Turner employed in his *Rise of the New West, 1819–1829* and *The United States, 1830–1850*, first describing the intellectual and social climate of the nation and its regions, then analyzing the effect of this climate on political and economic developments.
47. Turner might excuse Beard for his criticisms, but his daughter, Dorothy Turner Main, did not. She took such violent exception to Beard's review of *The Frontier in American History* that her father addressed her as "Dear Fighting Peggy," then went on: "I'm thicker skinned than you are, and I enjoyed Beard's review, though I am writing him of some points of doubt about his microscope. He read the first essay at least, and that is more than can be

Re sectionalism, I dealt with that subject in the Wisconsin Magazine of History (date?) and in the Annals of the Association of Am Geographers for 1926, as well as in the articles you cite, and I think I added something in each.[48] Dodd heard my lectures in the University of Chicago, on the relation of political sectionalism to economic and social data, illustrated by maps. How far they influenced him, I don't know, but I emphasized the points you mention.[49]

If you can get hold of the paper on Significance of the frontier in Am Hist published in the Fifth year book of the Hebart Society you will note that I emphasized sectionalism in that form of my paper, which is somewhat enlarged from the form in which it was first published.[50] I reached the idea naturally, as I indicated in my other letter, by seeing how the geographic (regional especially) factor was involved in the settlement of the continent. I was not influenced by Ratzel or Shaler. I gave an address before a Chicago geographical society by request of Professor Salisbury long before I knew much of geographers, and Barrows now Professor—U. Chicago came one year to listen in to my course on the History of the West, in Wis.[51]

---

expected of most reviewers, and his reactions are interesting and have a real point to them. Only, as you hint, there is something besides the urban side of the case. But at present (30 or so years after the 1st essay) the capital and labor side has an importance which I think emphasizes the importance of the *ending* of the frontier, while he thinks the movement was all along more important than the frontier. The truth is both are related. See my forthcoming (?) book." Turner to Dorothy Turner Main, February 18, 1921. HEH TU Box I.

48. Turner referred to two of his articles: "The Significance of the Section in American History," *Wisconsin Magazine of History*, VIII (March, 1925), 255–80, and "Geographic Sectionalism in American History," *Annals of the Association of American Geographers*, XVI (June 1926), 85–93.

49. That William E. Dodd heard Turner's lectures at the University of Chicago seems improbable. Turner taught there during the summer of 1898 and again in the autumn of 1899 when he substituted for Professor Hermann von Holst, who was ill. Dodd, after graduating from the Virginia Polytechnical Institute in 1895, taught as an instructor there until 1897, when he left to spend three years at the University of Leipzig, which awarded him a doctoral degree in 1900. Dodd remembered that he first met Turner at a meeting of the American Historical Association in December, 1901. See above, p. 199, for his recollection of this meeting. Turner did give occasional individual lectures at the University of Chicago, and Dodd may have heard one or more of these after he joined the faculty there in 1908.

50. "The Significance of the Frontier in American History" was reprinted in the National Hebart Society, *Fifth Yearbook* (Chicago, 1899), pp. 7–41. This edition, designed for the use of teachers, contained advice on the use of maps as well as greater emphasis on the importance of sections than in the earlier printings.

51. Turner was repeating a point made in all his reminiscences, that he was influenced by neither Friedrich Ratzel nor Nathanial S. Shaler, both proponents of geographic determinism. Rollin D. Salisbury was professor of geography at the University of Chicago after 1891. His invitation was probably to lecture at the Geographical Society of Chicago, which was formed in 1898. Turner's notes for this lecture, undated, are in HEH TU File Drawer 14A, Folder:

Royce did not influence me on cultural sectionalism.[52]

No, I didn't read up on "demography" before writing on it. Having seen the importance of the subject I have since tried to see how the authorities treated it, and I came upon the name thus.

Yes, the map method came out of my seminary and Libby was the first of my students to map votes, but how far I saw the larger significance of his maps for general use, and applied them, and how far the idea of mapping came from Libby, I can't say. Giddings used it in analyzing the maps in Scribner's Atlas for presidential elections.[53]

I have forgotten who did these maps, or which had priority. What I did was to knit together the cultural and economic mapping with the political. This I really think I made an instrument widely used. But the mapping is a natural device. I think my work was in extending its use, and in emphasizing the relations of political mapping to physical geography and cultural and economic data more generally than would be indicated in such papers as Libby's. You may be interested in knowing (but don't use the fact) that I did a good deal of editing of Libby's paper on the Ratif. of the Const., and that I added the quotation from Hildreth.[54] Schaper's paper on on S C

Influence of Geography upon the Settlement of the United States. Harlan H. Barrows, professor of geography at the University of Chicago after 1906, was a graduate student at that university between 1903 and 1906. He may have spent part of one year in Madison listening to Turner's lectures, but this is not revealed in available records.

52. For a discussion of Turner's reliance on Josiah Royce for his views on sectionalism, see above, Chapter X, n. 9. His statement to Curti suggests that he had forgotten that he owned a copy of the Phi Beta Kappa address that Royce delivered at the University of Iowa in 1902: *Provincialism* (Iowa City, 1902). In it he underlined the definition of sectionalism that he later incorporated in his essay on "The Significance of the Section in American History," *loc. cit.* He also failed to remember that he was aware that the essay had been reprinted in Royce's volume on *Race Questions, Provincialism and Other American Problems* (New York, 1908), pp. 57–108; he made a note to this effect, together with the call number of the volume in the library of the State Historical Society, on his copy of the pamphlet. On the other hand, he apparently did not cite Royce as an authority until 1918, when he made two references to him in his Lowell Lectures in Boston. HEH TU File Drawer E1, Folder: Lowell Lectures, 1918.

53. Franklin H. Giddings, Columbia University sociologist, was an early user of statistical methods and a fellow of the American Statistical Association. His article on "The Nature and Conduct of Political Majorities," *Political Science Quarterly*, VII (March, 1892), 116–32, to which Turner probably referred, analyzed election returns from 1888 and 1890 in terms of voting patterns.

54. Turner's "Editorial Note" prefacing Orin G. Libby's *Geographical Distribution of the Vote of the Thirteen States on the Federal Constitution* contained a long quotation from Hildreth's *History of the United States*, I, 415–16, dealing with the effect of internal divisions within the states on Federalist-Republican election conflicts. Turner added that he found this example of political divisions (or class divisions as they were to be called later) influential in determining the results of elections only after Libby's paper was completed.

sectionalism was *begun* in my seminary but was really done in Columbia.[55] Phillips was a student in my classes one year at Chicago—see the reference in his Sectionalism in Georgia;[56] also McCarthy's Antimasonic Party shows the sort of thing that my graduate students were led to do, in this line.[57]

Bemis refers to my diplomatic papers in a complimentary way in his bibliog. in his Jay's Treaty.[58]

I started off men like Robertson, U. of Ill., on his diplomatic studies, and my paper on 1790 diplomatic situation (AHR) probably started Manning's interest in Nootka Sound, perhaps not.[59] Carter and I. J. Cox were for a time in my classes and others.[60]

55. William S. Schaper was a graduate student under Turner at Wisconsin in 1895–1896. That he began working then on the topic later submitted as a doctoral dissertation at Columbia University is indicated by the fact that he spoke in April, 1896, to the Contemporary Club on "Some Aspects of Sectionalism and Representation in South Carolina." *Wisconsin State Journal*, April 16, 1896. He attended Columbia on Turner's urging and there completed his thesis, which was published as "Sectionalism and Representation in South Carolina," *Annual Report of the American Historical Association for 1900* (Washington, 1901), pp. 237–463. In his "acknowledgments" Schaper paid high tribute to Professor Franklin H. Giddings, who directed his work at Columbia; but he failed even to mention Turner, who suggested his topic and carried him well along toward its completion.

56. Ulrich B. Phillips, who joined the Wisconsin faculty in 1902, completed his graduate work at Columbia University, but attended a summer session at the University of Chicago when Turner was lecturing there. In his doctoral dissertation, *Georgia and State Rights* (n.p., n.d.), p. 5, Phillips wrote: "As a result of listening to a very suggestive lecture by Dr. F. J. Turner upon American sectionalism, I set to work some years ago to study the effects of nullification upon Georgia politics."

57. Charles McCarthy, a graduate of Brown University, earned his final degree at the University of Wisconsin in 1901 with a thesis on "The Anti-Masonic Party." This was published in the *Annual Report of the American Historical Association for 1902* (Washington, 1903).

58. Samuel F. Bemis, *Jay's Treaty* (New York, 1923), said of the diplomatic documents edited by Turner: "They are most ably edited, and the introductions are most valuable. Indeed, these pithy prefaces, and Professor Turner's articles in the *American Historical Review*, remain the best accounts of the relation of the West to American diplomacy. They are gems of historical writing."

59. William Spence Robertson, professor of history at the University of Illinois, was a student of Turner in 1899 and 1900. Turner believed that his own article on "English Policy toward America in 1790–1791," *American Historical Review*, VII (July, 1902), 706–735, and VIII (October, 1902), 78–86, had influenced another diplomatic historian, William R. Manning, to prepare his article on "The Nootka Sound Controversy," *Annual Report of the American Historical Association for 1904* (Washington, 1905), pp. 279–478. Manning completed his doctoral work at the University of Chicago in 1904, and was at this time an economist with the Division of Latin American Affairs, Department of State.

60. Clarence E. Carter earned a master of arts degree wth Turner in 1906, taught at Miami University, and became the first editor of the *Territorial Papers of the United States*. Isaac J. Cox worked with Turner in 1902–1903 before going on to earn his doctoral degree at the University of Pennsylvania in 1904. He was at this time professor at Northwestern University; his Albert Shaw Lectures at Johns Hopkins University had been published as *The West Florida Controversy, 1798–1813* (Baltimore, 1918).

But it would not be fair to the men, or to me, to give the impression that they merely worked out my ideas. I may have suggested the opportunities unused in some of these fields.

My paper at the St. Louis Exposition (published in its proceedings) on fields of investigation and problems in American history may offer a picture of how I was thinking at the time.[61] If I had a copy of my paper in a U. Wis. magazine "The Aegis," containing a discussion of "Problems in American History" (referred to in my "Frontier") you would see how early (1890?) I outlined my life work.[62] But I gave my remaining copy to the Huntington Library. There may be one in Harvard.

The matter of elimination is, of course, one of personal judgement, and therefore affected by the psychology of the individual. I know of no historian who can be really and absolutely free from the personal equation. But to preach the importance of reaching conclusions on relative importance of facts, and the need of dealing with relations, the causal element and with results, is the only way to avoid mere dumping of brick and mortar for another's use. And the way is left for our wiser successors to correct to reconstruct and to be reconstructed!

Please remember above all in dealing with me that "comparisons are odious"—and difficult too, unless the student has had contacts with the men compared.

But, if I recall, my paper on Social Forces and Robinson's paper propounding some of his "new history" were at the same meeting of the AHA, and as you intimate, there is need of caution in discarding old for new lamps in history.[63]

Anyway, don't claim so much for me that you start a row!

Yours cordially,
Frederick J. Turner

61. Turner's paper on "Problems in American History," presented in 1904 before the International Congress of Arts and Science in St. Louis, was first printed in Howard J. Rogers, ed., *International Congress of Arts and Science, Universal Exposition, St. Louis, 1904* (Boston, 1906), II, 183–94.

62. See above, pp. 56–61, for a discussion of the 1892 version of Turner's paper on "Problems in American History," in which he first set forth in print his frontier thesis.

63. Turner remembered correctly. His presidential address on "Social Forces in American History" was given at the 1910 meeting of the American Historical Association. So was a paper by James Harvey Robinson on "The Relation of History to the Newer Sciences." This was published in his book on *The New History and Other Essays in Modern Historical Criticism* (New York, 1912). His paper is described in the *Annual Report of the American Historical Association for 1910* (Washington, 1912), pp. 40–41.

No, I haven't tried to apply my frontier idea in any detail to other nations, though I have seen that it applied, and have said so in class room. Fish has a paper on the subject and Thompson of U. of Chicago has applied it to German expansion; Belaunde (AHA) to South America, and some students of Classical history have told me it applied there.[64] I think it should be tried out generally.

Smith College
Northampton, Massachusetts
Department of History

August 25, 1928

Dear Professor Turner:

You are the last person in the world about whom there ought to be a row! Certainly your modesty and generosity should be sufficient safe-guards against jealousies and rivalries. I shall be very careful not to create what your own personality has avoided, and I shall try to write of you as you would want to be written about. I did not mean to give the impression that it was necessary to establish, meticulously, priorities. But if the work of a historian is to be written about in relation to historical writing it is necessary to point out fields and methods in which he has been a pioneer and a pathfinder.

Woodrow Wilson, in his discussion of your paper on "The West as a Field for Historical Study" caught, I believe, one of the significant aspects of your technique.[65] He said that you combined the large view with the small one, the general plan and conception with the minute examination of particulars. Though you rigorously insisted on exactness you were interested as you have said, in the last analysis, in tendencies, institutions and mass movements, rather than in the exact academic truth as to details of events, motives of individuals and the like. How the leader's environment condi-

---

64. Turner referred to Carl Russell Fish, "The Frontier a World Problem," *Wisconsin Magazine of History*, I (December, 1917), 121-41; James Westfall Thompson, "Profitable Fields for Investigation in Medieval History," *American Historical Review*, XVIII (April, 1913), 490-504; and Victor A. Belaunde, "The Frontier in Hispanic America," *Rice Institute Pamphlets*, X (October, 1923), 202-13.

65. Woodrow Wilson was one of several historians who discussed Turner's paper on "The West as a Field for Historical Study" when it was delivered at the 1896 meeting of the American Historical Association. Their remarks are in the *Annual Report of the American Historical Association for 1896* (Washington, 1897), I, 287-96.

tioned his behaviour, how he made concessions to the men whose support he needed, how he came to agreements with other leaders—these were the problems that concerned you. Did you, in your historical thinking, put much emphasis on what seemed to be sheer accidents or the results of personality? To the scientist, of course, what seem sheer accidents and the fortuitous whims of personality have their explanations, even though the data be too scanty to achieve explanations. In other words, to the scientist we live in an orderly universe which has laws, even though we don't understand them. In reading some historians—Dodd for example—I am impressed by the emphasis placed on fortuitous circumstances, which play an important part in their scheme of causation. Though you insist that you never formed a philosophy of historical research, I am sure you have pondered this problem. I should say your attitude here was that of the scientist, who rests content with proximate explanations, rather than that of the speculative philosopher.

One of the things that made 17 and the seminary so rich and abundant was your historical imagination, which was always so disciplined, yet never hurt by the discipline! [66] This is probably to be explained, in part, by your own inheritance and environment.

Was it not the fashion for some historians, though by no means all, to refrain from finding any implications or significance for the present from their study of the past? Or at least, were they not very guarded and hesitant in expressing them? Robinson, to be sure, insisted that one of the chief purposes of historical study was to make us less conservative,[67] to make us more intelligent in our attitude towards change. You have spoken, again and again, of the relationship between our inheritance of pioneer ideals and the problems of the present. These ideals, you hoped, might be spiritual guides in attacking these problems. You recognized that the environment which made these ideals was fast passing away, and that there was an open question as to how effective they would be in a technological, industrial society. Becker seems to find an inconsistency here. To him your emphasis on environment as the factor which made America different from Europe does not square well with the belief—or hope—that in a new environment these

66. "17" was, of course, Turner's History 17, "The History of the West," given regularly by Turner after he joined the Harvard faculty in 1910.
67. This was one of the points made by James Harvey Robinson in his volume on *The New History*.

offspring of the old environment will endure.[68] One might also feel that legislation was an inadequate means of preserving these ideals, since legislation is responsive to changing economic and other interests. It would seem to me that you were here not inconsistent, but only throwing out another hypothesis—which the future will test. That hypothesis involves diffusionism versus effusionism. It may be that social inheritance will give these older frontier ideals permanence—it may be otherwise. I think it is a fine tribute to your scientific mindedness that, recognizing the possibility that environment is not *always* as important as it was in our earlier frontier history, you are willing to admit the possibility, and to let the future prove it true or false. It is this tentativeness which makes your work meet the best canons of science. Which does not mean for a minute that within definite time and space limits which you studied, the frontier environment and process was not the most important single factor in explaining how we have come to be what we are. I wish you would tell me what you think of my analysis of this problem.

Whether or not personal hopes and faith have any part in the discussion of a man's methodology, it was your faith and hope and belief in what America stood for that gave to me a sense of value in living. Of how many others the same thing is true, none can say. But that reverts to your personality and pedagogy, which Carl Becker has done as no one else, I suspect, could.

Ever,
Merle Curti

Hancock Point, Maine

August 27, 1928

Dear Curti:

I have never formulated any theory or philosophy regarding "sheer accidents or the results of personality." But my studies—especially those where

68. Carl Becker, despite his admiration for Turner, realized that his master's belief that frontier traits would persist after the closing of the frontier was based on hope rather than reason. He said so, gently, in his essay on Turner in Odum, ed., *American Masters of Social Science*, pp. 273–318, and far less gently in a letter to Charles Beard. There was, he believed, "a fundamental inconsistency in Turner's general philosophy," and particularly in his belief that the environment shaped man's ideas and institutions. "If so," Becker went on, "the conclusion would be that as these conditions of a new country disappeared and came to resemble those of older civilizations, the peculiar ideas and institutions would be modified and perhaps disappear altogether. But Turner, although never explicitly drawing this conclusion, never

I went as thoroughly into details as I could—convinced me that much of what was regarded as "sheer accident," "fortuitous circumstances" and "personality" was really dependent upon preparatory conditions, deep-laid tendencies released by the special circumstance or man, rather than the extemporized work of accident or individual. Nevertheless, I am also convinced that personality and accident play a very real part in history; but I am not sure that in the long run, taking a considerable period into consideration, the effects of fortuitous circumstances and unusual leaders have not been exaggerated by historians and by biographers. The personality usually colors, rather than determines, the direction of the flow of history. That doesn't prevent a man like Lincoln or Roosevelt, for example, from shaping by his personality and leadership, the events of a limited era or from requiring the skilful pen and understanding of the historian of a period or even of a nation. I would not wish to stand for a purely social or determinative view of historical processes. The individual has a real part and *sometimes* his leadership creates public opinion, and, within limits, opens new channels of tendency. I cannot see that history is either the "lengthened shadow of the great man," or the result of economic determination in which the leader doesn't count. Natural science and social science do not *yet* seem to me to have the same "laws," but, as I said before, I have never speculated much on these things. It is too early at least. Science itself now deals with a much more mysterious universe than in the days when I was a college student. Yes, "proximate explanations," rather than "speculative philosophy" represent my "attitude."

Yes, I think history, in the days when I began to study it, was deeply affected by Rancke's school who aimed to determine the fact "exactly as it was," rather than to stress its significance, to narrate rather than to interpret, but there were eminent exceptions, especially among historians of institutions; and even narrative history had perforce to partake of the color of the man's time and of his own prepossessions. No one need flatter himself that these limitations no longer exist, whether by unconscious interpretation, selection, emphasis, or by conscious, but unsuccessful interpretation, selection and emphasis. "We're all poor critters," especially FJT.

Environment includes both geographical and social factors, and the physi-

---

liked explicitly to admit it either." Undated fragment of a letter from Carl Becker to Charles Beard, probably about 1921, when Beard wrote his hostile review of *The Frontier in American History*. A copy is in HEH TU Box 52.

cal environment itself is changed by changing economic processes and interests. The fur trading area of Lake Superior was the same area in part as the later lumber area and the present day iron mining area; tomorrow the water powers of the region may be utilized to create another type.

I like to believe that inherited ideals persist long after the environmental influence has changed; but the environment does change, and society changes —otherwise no history! And the past rather than the future or even the immediate present, seems to me the legitimate field of the historian. But the present, and its tendencies do cast light upon historically significant events, institutions, ideas, which the man who shuts his eyes to the present and deals with the past without the light cast on its meaning by the present may fail to use in his study and thereby miss important factors which to the time of which he is the historian may have seemed of trivial importance—as I tried to say in my "Social Forces" address.[69] And if I didn't believe that history helps us understand the present I should not have the interest in it which I have.*

But now I must get out and enjoy the sunshine that has been denied us for several days.

Yours cordially,
Frederick J. Turner

* But I think the idea wasn't so new. Perhaps it wasn't used in the same way by teachers in this country, as applied to U.S. History.

Of course you needn't be told that I do not think that such reasons for historical study as: "history repeats itself," or similar sayings, apply to the relations between past and present in their relation to history. Differences are usually at least as important as resemblances between the two; on the other hand I have been impressed by Renan's remark to the effect that truth lay in the delicate distinctions (*les nuances*).[70] This was borne in upon me by the way examination papers in History 17, especially, would go me, not "one" but many, better when I generalized!

Armed with this harvest of material from Turner, amply supplemented by information solicited from his friends, and having read all that had been written by and about his subject, Curti set to work to meet the November

69. "Social Forces in American History," see n. 63 above.
70. Joseph Ernest Renan (1823–1892) was a historian and theological writer in France, and a follower of Auguste Comte.

deadline, now less than three months away. He succeeded, as he was to succeed through his lifetime, but only by nudging the space limitation of 4,000 words placed on him upward to 4,500 words. Excessively modest, he was thoroughly dissatisfied with the finished product, feeling himself incapable of doing justice to the theories and methods of a scholar of Turner's greatness. Only after the essay had been read and praised by Carl Becker, and only after a special trip from Northampton to Worcester, where it could be judged by his good friend James Blaine Hedges (another of Turner's Harvard doctors of philosophy), was Curti ready to relinquish it to the publisher.[71]

He had labored to complete his paper on time, but now the usual delays began. The editors must make their corrections and send it to the usual readers, who took an unusual amount of time to say that they approved. By the time this interminable process was concluded, two years had passed and those responsible, anticipating that authors might have changed their minds or discovered new materials, returned all essays for a final revision. This nearly proved fatal for Curti, for as he reread he was overwhelmed with doubts once more. Was his effort really worthy of Turner? Three of his friends on the Smith College faculty—Sidney Fay, Harry Elmer Barnes, and Harold U. Faulkner—were required to reassure him. This done, a new doubt beset Curti. Would not the essay be improved with a series of maps demonstrating Turner's correlation of social, economic, and political data in graphic form?[72] Those that he selected—published originally in the March, 1908, issue of the *American Journal of Sociology* to illustrate an article on "Is Sectionalism in America Dying Away?"—aroused Turner's immediate objections. They had been drawn many years before, he pointed out, were inaccurate in many details, and were far too crude to represent the more refined map-making techniques he had developed since that time. He preferred that they not be published.[73] That ended that; the article went off to the publishers with no maps added.

Curti's effort needed no embellishments, for despite his disclaimers he had written a masterful analysis of Turner's contributions and methodology. It appeared early in 1931, buried deep within a massive volume bearing the title *Methods in Social Science: A Case Book*, as part of a section pretentiously designated, "Interpretations of Temporal Sequences with Consider-

71. Curti to Turner, November 21, 27, 1928. HEH TU Box 40.
72. Curti to Turner, August 15, 1930. HEH TU Box 44A.
73. Turner to Curti, August 21, 1930; Curti to Turner, August 30, 1930. HEH TU Box 44A.

ation of Special Types of 'Causation.' " [74] Despite this formidable label, Turner was immensely pleased when his copy reached him early in January —although he did have a few qualifications. He said so at once: [75]

January 5, 1931

Professor Merle E. Curti
105 Prospect Street
Northampton, Massachusetts

Dear Curti:

I had ordered the *Methods in Social Sciences* from the University of Chicago and have just received it. As I wrote Becker after his paper, I feel in reading it very humble and very grateful that I have such loyal friends as you and he. [76] I should feel that I was taking myself very seriously if I accepted all the good things you say of my work and its influence on historical writing. I notice that Edwards, in his "Bibliography of the History of Agriculture in the United States" (U.S. Dept. of Agriculture, Misc. Pub. No. 84; Washington, 1930), uses (p. 5) language much like yours in regard to "rewriting American history;" but Edwards was also a member of my class in "The West" at Harvard, so that you both have probably been more generous than your critics may be in this matter. [77] However, I have received some similar comments in past years from others. But on the whole I am inclined to think that the shift was a part of the same general movement that is reflected in European history; as it is indicated in the Rice volume, and that, if I had not pushed the subjects, someone else would.

What you write of Henry George is interesting. I never saw his earlier

74. Curti, "The Section and the Frontier in American History: The Methodological Concepts of Frederick Jackson Turner," in Stuart A. Rice, ed., *Methods in Social Science* (Chicago, 1931), p. 353–67. Turner's copy of this book at the Huntington Library has not been underlined, a sad commentary on the fact that it reached him when his failing health curtailed his normal practices. It has only one marginal note, in the handwriting of Turner's secretary, adding A. C. Stine of the United States Department of Agriculture to the list of students in economic history trained by Turner. This is on p. 360.
75. Turner to Curti, January 5, 1931. HEH TU Box 45. Both the original of this letter, which Curti presented to the Huntington Library, and Turner's own carbon, have been preserved.
76. Turner to Carl Becker, May 14, 1927. This letter is reproduced above, pp. 248–50.
77. Everett E. Edwards was a student in Turner's class and seminar, completing his work for the master's degree in 1924. The comment to which Turner refers appeared in his *A Bibliography of the History of Agriculture in the United States* (Washington, D.C., 1930), where he said of the essay on "The Significance of the Frontier in American History": "It caused all students of American History to reshape their views of the meaning of American history and has had a dominant influence in all American historical writing since its appearance."

essays and think that I never read his *Progress and Poverty* before writing the "Frontier." [78] Since reading your chapter, I have read the *Progress and Poverty* discussion of the public domain and its influence upon the question of labor and capital. It is clear that, so far as the land question and legislation on its taxation goes, he had the idea before my "Frontier;" but the single-tax conception never met with my assent. And, in general, I think it is true, as you indicate, that my use of the presence of the frontier spaces touched more aspects of American society and culture than the one to which he gave almost exclusive attention. At any rate, the idea did not seem to have been influential upon the historical brethren until after I had urged it.

I am very grateful to you for emphasising the fact that, not alone the frontier, but the whole of America interested me in my seminary and class work; and for presenting so friendly a view of the reception of the attempts which I made to deal with the economic, political, and social subjects in relation to history and American geography and by a method of using the sciences and scientific method. I cannot claim to be a scientist, but I have realized the importance of understanding their point of view and methods.

I think that you have presented my work and methods as I would wish to have them thought of—barring the question of the importance of their influence upon the writing of American history. This latter question I have not the ability to determine nor the willingness to assent to your very friendly view and that of some others; but I should like to have my contributions as a whole seen in the way that you present them, aside from the question of influence. This is not a criticism but merely a personal disclaimer, for I think you have done a real and effective presentation of my seminary and writings.

One or two questions have arisen in my mind. For example, I do not recall just why you think that I influenced Pelzer. I have a good opinion of his work; but I confess that I do not now recall that he was ever in my classes.[79] Since you mention James as one of my students, he should also,

78. Turner's memory tricked him at this point. While still a student at the University of Wisconsin he heard Henry George speak and took part in a discussion on his theories. As a graduate student at Johns Hopkins he bought and read most of *Progress and Poverty*. For evidence on these points see above, pp. 129–130.
79. Turner was right. Louis Pelzer, a historian of the frontier and editor of the *Mississippi Valley Historical Review*, was educated at the Unversity of Iowa, where he enrolled in 1903 and completed his doctoral work in 1909. "Louis Pelzer, Scholar, Teacher, Editor," *Mississippi Valley Historical Review*, XXXIII (September, 1946), 201–16. Curti had listed Pelzer among those who had studied the significance of sectionalism under Turner. Curti, "The Section and the Frontier in American History," *loc. cit.*, p. 364.

perhaps, be mentioned in the group of diplomatic historians, because it is in that field that he has made contributions as well as in his *George Rogers Clark*.[80] E. E. Robinson, of Stanford, has written importantly on American political history, and he was one of my men.[81] But most of the American-history people of the Pacific Coast are also former students of mine and it would be too much to try to enumerate them all. Men like Professor Parish, of the University of California at Los Angeles, and Stephenson, at Claremont College, were not students in my work but have been good enough to say in public that I had influenced their views.[82] Parish, by the way, has just been presenting a paper on the frontier, before the Pacific Coast Branch.[83]

The movement to Oregon was influenced by the wheat crisis as well as agricultural depression in general; but the movement to Texas belonged rather to cotton depression than to wheat.[84]

What you say of the movement of wheat-raising and its influence on the tariff is, I think, the result of your notes in my class lectures, without realizing that the work of Chester W. Wright on *Wool Growing and the Tariff* was cited at the time, or mentioned in connection with the lantern-slide charts, as were also the maps of H. C. Taylor showing the location of sheep decade by decade (by the dot method). On page 85 of my *References* I cite Wright.[85] However, it is possible that I had not sufficiently empha-

80. Curti listed Frederick Merk, Samuel F. Bemis, Isaac J. Cox, Joseph Schafer, W. S. Robertson, and Arthur P. Whitaker as students of Turner who made their reputations in diplomatic history. Turner wanted to add to the list James Alton James, who graduated from Wisconsin in 1888 and was encouraged by Turner to continue his doctoral work at Johns Hopkins. James was the author of biographies of George Rogers Clark and Oliver Pollock, both dealing with Revolutionary War diplomacy in the West.
81. Edgar E. Robinson graduated from the University of Wisconsin in 1908, served as a fellow in the history department for two years, and completed work for his master of arts degree in 1910. He was at this time professor of history at Leland Stanford University, and one of Turner's most devoted students.
82. John C. Parish, a distant cousin of Turner's wife, earned his doctor's degree at the State University of Iowa in 1908, and was at this time professor of history at the University of California at Los Angeles. Nathaniel Wright Stephenson, a well-known historical writer, was professor of history and biography at Scripps College, Claremont, California.
83. Parish's paper before the Pacific Coast Branch of the American Historical Association was entitled "Reflections on the Nature of the Westward Movement." In it, and in other essays of his reprinted in his *The Persistence of the Westward Movement and Other Essays* (Berkeley, 1943), pp. 25–45, he paid high tribute to Turner as the fountainhead of all frontier studies.
84. Curti wrote on p. 359 of his essay on Turner: "By employing statistics in the study of wheat prices between 1840 and 1850, it was found that agricultural hardship in the wheat areas explains in part the migration from these regions to Oregon and Texas in this period."
85. Turner's copy of Chester W. Wright, *Wool-Growing and the Tariff* (Boston, 1910), heavily underlined and with some marginal comments, is in the Huntington Library, Acces-

sized the sources of these remarks on sheep in that general undergraduate class on the "History of the West." But I would guard against seeming to absorb the work of others without proper credit if your sentence is ever questioned.

Again thanking you for your presentation, and for putting it as the reaction of one who had been in my seminary, I am

Cordially your friend,

Frederick J. Turner

Curti was delighted with this approval, although embarrassed at his failure to credit Professor Wright with the materials Turner borrowed from him; his class notes, he reported, indicated no source, but he should have consulted the *Syllabus*. He did take amiable exception to Turner's hint that he had glorified his subject because of his own loyalty as a student. This, Curti stoutly maintained, was not true; he had labored for complete objectivity and had not let his friendship or admiration color his judgment in any way. That he had succeeded was proved by the fact that his three colleagues who read the essay—Sidney Fay, Harry Elmer Barnes, and Harold U. Faulkner —none of whom was a Turner student, agreed that he had not exaggerated the importance of Turner's contributions one iota.[86]

This verdict secretly pleased Turner a great deal, and well it might. He was, as he confessed to a friend, immeasurably proud that Curti was courageous enough to present a picture that others might not recognize, but that was basically accurate.[87] He was even more explicit when he wrote to his daughter. "Don't get too set up over your POD [Poor Old Dad]," he cautioned. "Not that I don't appreciate the loyalty of Professor Curti, for aside from the place he gives me, I think that he has set forth my ideas and aims very well."[88] That Merle Curti had. Turner had been well treated by two of his favorite students, and had told posterity much about his historical beliefs in the process.

sion No. 139897. It contains a chart showing the number of sheep by sections for each decade from 1840 to 1900. Turner has pasted in the back of this book a number of maps showing by dots the number of sheep in each state for the period 1840–1890. These he clipped from an article by Henry C. Taylor, "Place of Economics in Agricultural Education and Research," *University of Wisconsin Agricultural Experiment Station, Bulletin No. 16* (July, 1911). He referred to the chart in Turner and Frederick Merk, *List of References on the History of the West* (revised edn., Cambridge [Mass.], 1922), p. 85.

86. Curti to Turner, January 17, 1931. HEH TU Box 45.
87. Turner to Mrs. William Hooper, Januray 2, 1931. HEH TU-H, Box 8.
88. Turner to Dorothy Turner Main, January 18, 1931. HEH TU Box K.

CHAPTER XII *The Luther L. Bernard Correspondence, 1928*

Both Merle Curti and Carl Becker sought Frederick Jackson Turner's aid when asked to evaluate his contributions and methodology for volumes demonstrating the interrelationship of the social science disciplines. His last autobiographical effort was inspired by a similar project. This originated during the 1920s, when rapid strides in the study of society were being made by historians, sociologists, economists, political scientists, anthropologists, psychologists, and other social scientists. As their knowledge of mankind and society increased, so did their realization that their progress was slowed by the watertight compartmentalization of their individual disciplines. Man as a social animal followed such complex behavioral patterns that no one approach sufficed; he could be understood only by cooperative studies in which all joined. Only a multidirectional approach would allow the better analysis and comprehensive synthesis needed to give meaning to the incomplete and provisional findings of the separate sciences.

A call for such an effort was issued by the American Sociological Society in 1923, and met an immediate favorable response. Within a year six of the professional associations representing the social sciences established a joint committee to investigate means by which their members could cooperate in their investigations. This committee, after considering a number of alternatives, concluded that their goal could best be attained by a comprehensive publication showing the interrelationship of the social sciences, and that this should take the form of an encyclopedia through which each discipline could share the methods and findings of all others. When this plan was approved by the cooperating societies and by the Social Science Research Council the project was fairly launched; when by the end of 1927 necessary financial backing was obtained and a staff assembled under the editorship of Edwin R. A. Seligman, its success was assured. A ten-volume encyclopedia was projected, with articles written by recognized authorities in each field, to provide up-to-the-minute information on all aspects of the behavioral sciences. This decided, boards of editors were named, advisors selected, topics and authors agreed upon, and work began.[1]

One author chosen to prepare several major articles was Luther Lee Bernard, a well-known sociologist. Born in 1881 and educated at the University of Chicago, where he earned the doctoral degree in 1910, Bernard had held important posts in teaching and research at home and abroad before accepting a professorship at the University of North Carolina and membership in that university's Institute for Research in Social Science. He was there when the invitation from the editors reached him. Could he prepare an article on "The Social Sciences as Disciplines in Latin America and the United States?" And could he have the completed work in the hands of the publishers in just two months? Bernard was self-assured enough to accept this formidable assignment, but he soon found that help was necessary to complete the task on time. His solution, not unusual among sociologists of that day, was to distribute wholesale a three-page mimeographed questionnaire asking each recipient to send within ten days lengthy answers to twenty-six questions.[2] Most of these had to do with the manner in which the social sciences were taught at various universities, but some probed more deeply than others into concepts and methods.

If Bernard had been abreast of the times he would have realized that Turner had retired four years before and now lacked the university connections needed to answer most of his questions. Fortunately he was not; his questionnaire went off to Turner at Harvard University and was forwarded to the Huntington Library, where it arrived with the two-week deadline already at hand. With it went the usual mimeographed note: May I ask your kind cooperation with regard to the items mentioned in the enclosed or any other data you can send me? Not much time will be required, and I shall be glad to have whatever you can give me within two weeks. In Turner's case Bernard added a personal note that helped shape the nature of the reply: "I am sure that there are most interesting origins to your work, which I should be most fortunate to get at."[3] Ignoring the

1. Edwin R. A. Seligman, "Preface," *Encyclopedia of the Social Sciences* (New York, 1930–1935), I, xvii–xix. When the encyclopedia was in the planning stage, the editors were so impressed with the quantity of material that must be included that they increased the size from ten to fifteen volumes.
2. A copy of this questionnaire was enclosed in Luther L. Bernard to Turner, November 14, 1928. HEH TU Box 40.
3. *Ibid.*

questionable syntax and the fact that most of the questionnaire required a university connection, Turner answered at once, pointing out that Bernard's letter had been routed from Chapel Hill to Cambridge to Madison to San Marino, taking so much time that he would miss the two-week deadline. He would, however, write at greater length in a day or two.[4] At the same time he wrote Merle Curti, suggesting that Bernard be supplied with any information that could safely be loaned without breaking confidences.[5] Curti was delighted to comply, sending off a thick packet of notes at once.[6] This reached Bernard simultaneously with the lengthy reminiscences that Turner dispatched in his direction on November 24, 1928: [7]

November 24, 1928

Professor L. L. Bernard
Institute for Research in Social Science
University of North Carolina
Chapel Hill, North Carolina

Dear Professor Bernard:

I should certainly be glad to furnish the information requested in your letter of November fourteenth if it were possible. I am spending the year here as Research Associate in the Huntington Library, away from material I should need to use in answering the queries; and I am under obligations, I think, to devote my time to the undertaking for which the Huntington Library is furnishing the means.[8] I am trying to complete a study of the United States in the period 1830 to 1850, with reference to the characteristics and development of the different sections—New England, Middle Atlantic, South Atlantic, South Central, North Central, and Far West—in those years, to be followed by chapters in the same book on the interplay of these different sections in the debates and legislation of Congress in those

4. Turner to Bernard, November 23, 1928. *Ibid.*
5. Turner to Curti, November 27, 1928. *Ibid.*
6. Curti to Turner, November 27, 1928. *Ibid.*
7. Turner to Bernard, November 24, 1928. *Ibid.*
8. Turner enjoyed his six weeks at the Huntington Library in the spring of 1927 so greatly that he was ready to accept when Max Farrand, the director, offered him a permanent post as Senior Research Associate at a salary of $5,000 a year. This arrangement was authorized at a special meeting of the Board of Trustees in June, 1927, and Turner began his new assignment in the fall. He remained at the Huntington until his death in March, 1932. Minutes of a Special Meeting of the Board of Trustees, June 25, 1927. HEH, Minutes, Board of Trustees, Book B, 94. His coming was reported in the *Pasadena Star-News*, June 28, 1927.

years.[9] This is a continuation of a study which seems to me of practically as much importance as my earlier study of the significance of the frontier.

Looking over your queries, I do not see how it would be possible for me to answer them without such investigation as I have not the means of making here, nor the requisite time at my disposal. I can see the importance of them for dealing with the subject you have in hand, but I can also see that you are a bit optimistic in thinking that "not much time will be required for complete answers."

Professor Carl Becker, who did me the honor of a sketch in Professor Odum's *American Masters of Social Science*, may have accumulated notes and material that he might be willing to lend you for your purpose; and Professor Merle Curti, of Smith College, Northampton, Massachusetts, informs me that he is doing a similar sketch for a work to appear on methodology in the social sciences.[10] I do not know the exact title. It may be that he, also, has gathered notes that would serve your purpose and that he might be willing to loan. Possibly proof sheets may be available, but I do not know.

As my department has been History, in both the University of Wisconsin and Harvard University, I suppose your study of the "History of Sociology in America" means that your queries do not relate to that department directly. So far as my work has been in the direction of Sociology, I should say that it was influenced first by the teaching of Professor William F. Allen, in Wisconsin (see his *Monographs and Essays*).[11] Allen was a classical scholar, who had also studied in Germany in the fields of History and Economics and who was perhaps the first to give a course in Economics from the historical point of view in this country.[12] While he was no longer

9. Turner confidently believed that with all of his time available for writing, the study of sectionalism on which he had labored for two decades would be finished within a few months of moving to the Huntington Library. Instead the riches that he found there lured him into further research, and "The Book," as his friends called it, was not finished at the time of his death. It was published three years later as *The United States, 1830–1850: The Nation and Its Sections* (New York, 1935).

10. For the correspondence that led to the articles by Carl Becker and Merle Curti see above, pp. 281–85.

11. William F. Allen, *Essays and Monographs by William Francis Allen: Memorial Volume* (Boston, 1890), was a compilation of some of his essays, published by his friends after his death. Turner compiled a bibliography of Allen's writings for the volume. For a discussion of their relationships, see above, pp. 15–25.

12. Allen was among the first teachers in the country to use the historical techniques and textbook of Wilhelm Roscher, the German founder of the so-called "Historical School" of economists. His views began to be known in the United States about 1875, and his textbook, *The Principles of Economics*, was published in English translation in 1877. Joseph Dorfman, *The Economic Mind in American Civilization* (3 vols., New York, 1946–1949), III, 88–92.

giving this course when I was a student in Wisconsin, his interest in the field was very obvious in the courses he gave on Institutional History, especially in the fields of Medieval and English History. These studies, of medieval institutions particularly, left an impression on my mind that undoubtedly influenced the mode of treatment that I tried to apply to American History. A study of the period when populations were moving, new geographic provinces being occupied, and institutions plastic and forming, probably gave a background to my own conceptions of American History.

In the Johns Hopkins University, where I did a year of graduate work and took my doctor's degree, Professor Herbert B. Adams was a stimulating force. Perhaps even more stimulating were Woodrow Wilson, who gave a course in local governments, and Doctor Ely in the field of Economics. My association and discussions with fellow students like Professor Charles H. Haskins (now of Harvard) had an influence in the emphasis upon the importance of critical scholarship.[13] I also was a member for two or three months of a graduate seminary conducted by Professor Albion W. Small (later Professor of Sociology at the University of Chicago), who gathered a little group of us to give co-operative study to the question of the instructions and powers of the representatives from the colonies, and later the states, to the various Continental Congresses, with a view to casting light upon the question of sovereignty in the United States. Small at that time, however, simply acted as a quasi-chairman of the group, and little or no sociological suggestions were made by him.[14] It was purely a study of the sources for the period and the subject. I had previously been inducted into the use of sources by the seminary method in my work under Allen (who, I think, has not been sufficiently recognized as a pioneer in this country in the employment of this method).

Possibly my interest in the frontier was caused by the fact that I was born in Portage, Wisconsin, at a time 1861 when the region was in the later stages of a frontier community. My father was a newspaper editor, and I was brought up in the printing office and found my schoolmates among representatives of many nationalities and many American sections who were

13. Turner's intellectual debt to his instructors at Johns Hopkins University during his year there in 1888–1889—Herbert Baxter Adams, Woodrow Wilson, Richard T. Ely, and Albion W. Small—is discussed above, pp. 27–30. Charles Homer Haskins, later an outstanding medievalist and dean of Harvard College, lived in the same boarding house with Turner and became his closest friend. Turner brought Haskins to the University of Wisconsin, and Haskins played a leading role in attracting Turner to Harvard in 1910.
14. For a description of his course under Albion W. Small, later an outstanding sociologist, see above, pp. 29–30.

settled in the little hamlet and the region thereabouts. I had, therefore, without any special consciousness of the subject, a background of youthful experience when I began my studies in American History following my earlier training in Medieval History. I may say that my undergraduate instruction in the University of Wisconsin included only about one-third of a college year in American History and that the Johns Hopkins, during the year I was there, afforded no formal course in American History, aside from the occasional reports made in the gatherings of the graduate students and in the work with Small that I have already mentioned.[15] This, of course, was in some respects a handicap, but I have never felt sure that it may not also have been a distinct advantage to me in the way in which I had to "work out my own salvation" and in the fact that I was not under the discipline of a series of formal courses which might have made it less necessary for me to think out my own conceptions of what American History meant and my own methods of handling it.

My study of the frontier should be understood as not a study of the frontier *per se*, but as a study of the movement of population into unsettled geographic provinces, thus creating a dynamic force in American History and influencing the East by the economic, political, and social development of these new lands. I mention this because some recent critics have seemed to think that whatever I have said regarding the frontier was based purely upon the more or less raw outer edge of this movement. It has rather been my intention to use the term as something like the record traced on a chart by the barometer or thermometer of the scientist for a general symptomatic condition. Obviously, "mental ability," "literary skill," etc., would not proceed from the outer edge of civilized society, and I have never for a moment thought of such things as the "basic premise" of my essays on the frontier.[16] Nevertheless, the way in which Eastern developments progressed

15. Turner's one-term course in American history, taken during his junior year at the University of Wisconsin, was a hurried survey taught by Allen. Johns Hopkins University normally offered instruction in the subject, but Professor J. Franklin Jameson, who taught the American history courses, was on leave during the year that Turner spent in residence.
16. The principal attack on Turner's frontier thesis did not begin until after his death in 1932, but by 1928 one critical article had appeared. This was by a Stanford University sociologist, John C. Almack, "The Shibboleth of the Frontier," *The Historical Outlook*, XVI (May, 1925), 197–202. Almack adopted his own definition of the frontier as "an isolated and sparsely settled area, where the primary process of occupation is going on," then on the basis of this definition argued that the frontier had little impact on American traits and institutions. Turner quite properly pointed out that this was not his own definition of the frontier, and that his thesis was valid. His friends, and most of the profession, agreed with

in the fields of industry, political institutions, and political thought, and in cultural and social directions was, I think, deeply influenced by the fact that there was a frontier of settlement which continually opened up new fields for social development and continually presented in its rear a society transforming both by the fluidity of its outer edge and by the changes that the advancing waves of density of population, industrial life, and cultural life brought to its eastern edge.

In this movement of peoples and institutions into the wilderness, new geographic provinces were encountered, occupied, and developed. My interest in the geographic aspects of American History was, therefore, an actual outcome of the fact that in dealing with the occupation of these different provinces, I found it necessary to consider the relations between the physiographic conditions and the society that formed in the various regions and sections. It became very obvious that sectionalism was not a phenomenon of North and South, as was commonly considered by the historians of the period when I was a young man. It was a much more complicated thing, involving not only a moving West against East, but a complex of sections making up the "North" and the "South," the "East" and the "West." For definiteness, I have used in my own work the Divisions of the United States Census. These seem to me to have a real basis, both in physical geography and in the human element. Within these various sections, however, I have found it necessary and informing to recognize the geographers' *regions* as limitations upon sectional unity and as important in themselves.

I have dwelt upon this matter because, so far as my relations to sociology are concerned, the frontier and the section will probably be regarded as the

---

him. Professor Arthur Meier Schlesinger put the case for the defense well when he wrote Turner: "It is the best case I have ever known of putting up a straw man and knocking him down." Schlesinger to Turner, May 2, 1925. HEH TU Box 34. Turner was less angry than disturbed at being misunderstood. "As you say," he wrote Frederick Merk, "he has been demolishing a man of straw, but I don't quite enjoy being fashioned into that kind of a scarecrow for exhibit to teachers who haven't read what I really wrote. The only thing that I take to heart is the fact that I could have written anything capable of such distortion in a reader's mind. . . . Of course the Frontier paper is open to criticism and would have received it anyway. It is no credo, sacrosanct, unalterable. But the job could have been better done! The idea that I was attributing all that was good in American civilization to the Frontier and the backwoodsman in his cabin and that a statistical demonstration that education and ability existed in the east was needed by a Stanford man gives me pain as it shows how ineffective my mode of statement must be." Turner to Merk, May 6, 1925. HEH TU Box 34.

two things in which I may have had an influence in the field of social studies. I should add, however, that the attempt to *correlate* the economic, social, and political factors was at the beginning of my studies and of my instruction in the historical field. As I said once to Professor Giddings, when he raised a question as to what my field was, "It is the subject that I am interested in, and I don't particularly care what name I bear." [17] I have always regarded the interdependence of all the social studies as fundamentally important and, while I realize that there must be also a division of labor, I think that the division has been so sharply made in the past that there has been a loss to students of economic history, political science, and literary, religious, and other cultural history, as well as to history itself, from the water-tight compartments in which the social sciences have previously been divided. Perhaps I may refer in this connection to my "Social Forces in American History," published in my volume on the *Frontier* (Henry Holt & Company). [18]

Referring to your Query No. 22, I have never distinctly placed before myself the aim of training students for teaching. [19] I have rather thought of them as a group of companions interested in the solution of problems by gathering source material for criticism and consideration of its significance. It has been an interest in the subject rather than a pedagogical purpose that I have followed.

So far as possible, it was my practice to select a particular period or field for research in the seminary as given in different years and to allow and encourage individual students to select the particular field or phase of the subject in which they were interested, for their investigations. As a rule, I asked them to prepare a paper upon some very limited portion of the field they chose, but also to give a more general examination to the field during the whole period and to attempt to consider it in the light of the investigations and reports made by their companions. The results of this, I think, have been rather fruitful, for among the graduate students who picked special fields were men whose important contributions to agricultural history, the history of the public lands, the history of diplomacy, the history of

17. Franklin H. Giddings was professor of sociology at Columbia University.
18. Turner's presidential address to the American Historical Association in 1910 on "Social Forces in American History" was the first read before that body to urge an interdisciplinary approach.
19. In the list of questions submitted by Bernard in his mimeographed questionnaire, Item 22 asked: "How do you train students for teaching? For research?"

political parties, the history of transportation, and the history of the westward movement into the back country of the North Atlantic, of the South Atlantic, in the Middle West, and in the Pacific Northwest, have been the result of their having chosen these particular fields as the ones in which they were to work in the seminary. Salutary neglect of minute direction of their work; encouragement of the graduate student to be responsible for his own field; refraining from stamping him with a particular impress—these have been among the methods that have seemed to me useful in my own experience. In other words, I have felt that my function was that of "the porter at the gate." I believe this has resulted in more productive scholarship on the part of the men of my seminary than would have been yielded by a different method.

With regard to Queries 8 and 9,[20] I have known rather intimately such men as James Ford Rhodes, Schouler, Woodrow Wilson (see the first volume of Ray Stannard Baker's "Life of Wilson"; index, under my name), Walter Hines Page, Robert M. LaFollette, Balthasar Meyer, William Roscoe Thayer, Reuben G. Thwaites, and Worthington C. Ford, and, less intimately, Theodore Roosevelt.[21] I have also numbered among my friends practically all of the academic men who were important in the field of History during my active years. I have already mentioned some of the men who were my

20. Question 8 on Bernard's list read: "Please give me similar facts about outstanding public or private individuals not in academic positions working in your field whom you have known more or less intimately." Item 9 read: "Please give such facts about any outstanding teachers or other associates in the social sciences whom you have known well, whether these men were connected with the institution where you now teach or not."

21. Turner was obviously doing some name dropping. James Ford Rhodes and James Schouler were prominent historians of an older generation. Woodrow Wilson was a close friend from the day they met in Baltimore in the spring of 1889; his views altered Turner's thinking, just as Turner's shaped Wilson's opinions on the influence of the West. Their relationship is described in the second, not the first, volume of Ray Stannard Baker, *Woodrow Wilson: Life and Letters* (Garden City, New York, 1927), II, 124–25. Walter Hines Page was editor of the *Atlantic Monthly* between 1896 and 1899, then of *World's Work* from 1900 to 1913 before he became President Wilson's ambassador to England. Turner had known Robert M. La Follette since their undergraduate days at the University of Wisconsin, and was the Wisconsin senator's staunch admirer until they parted over American entry into World War I. Balthasar H. Meyer, a student who earned his doctoral degree with Turner in 1897, was a member of the Interstate Commerce Commission. One of Turner's Harvard friends was William Roscoe Thayer, author and editor of the *Harvard Graduates' Magazine* between 1892 and 1915. As director of the State Historical Society of Wisconsin during Turner's years on the university faculty, Reuben Gold Thwaites became one of his close friends. He met Worthington C. Ford at the Massachusetts Historical Society, where Ford was director of publications. Turner's acquaintance with Theodore Roosevelt was based on his reviews of Roosevelt's *The Winning of the West*, and apparently did not progress beyond the corresponding stage.

instructors. Among the younger men, I have the pleasure of numbering among my former students men in leading positions in many, if not most, of the important universities from the Atlantic to the Pacific. In Sociology, I had an early intimate acquaintance with Professor Giddings, Professor Small, and Professor Ross; [22] in Economics, I have known well Professor Ely and his associates in the University of Wisconsin, and Professor Taussig, Bullock, Young, Carver, and Ripley, of the Harvard faculty—also Professor Davis R. Dewey, of the Massachusetts Institute of Technology.[23] I have also had friends among the leading authorities on Political Science in the United States. In the field of geography, I learned much from my associations with Thomas C. Chamberlin, Charles R. Van Hise, and Rollin C. Salisbury.[24]

Droysen's *Historik* had a particular influence upon my conception of history.[25]

In addition to the discussions in Becker and Curti, you may care to know of the *Essays in American History* dedicated to me by various of my students and published by Henry Holt & Company in 1910.[26]

With reference to the suggestion regarding possible material in the notes of Professors Becker and Curti, please do not ask them to attempt to answer the questionnaire. They would not be able to furnish the information desired without labor that it would be unwarrantable to ask.

Very sincerely yours,
Frederick J. Turner

22. Turner's sociologist friends included Franklin H. Giddings of Columbia University, Albion W. Small of the University of Chicago, and Edward A. Ross, who joined the University of Wisconsin faculty in 1896.
23. Richard T. Ely taught Turner at Johns Hopkins University, then served with him on the University of Wisconsin faculty; Frank W. Taussig, Charles J. Bullock, Allyn A. Young, Thomas N. Carver, and William Z. Ripley were his colleagues at Harvard. Bullock and Young were his students at Wisconsin, taking their degrees in 1895 and 1902. Davis R. Dewey taught at the Massachusetts Institute of Technology after completing his doctorate at Johns Hopkins University in 1886 and was a well-known writer on financial topics.
24. Turner misspoke when he termed these friends geographers. Thomas C. Chamberlin and Charles R. Van Hise were geologists; each served as president of the University of Wisconsin during Turner's tenure there, and Van Hise was one of his closest Madison friends and neighbors. Rollin D. Salisbury died in 1922; he had been professor of geography and dean at the University of Chicago since 1892. He and Turner met when he taught briefly at Wisconsin in 1891–1892.
25. As Turner often testified in these letters, Johann G. Droysen, *Grundriss der Historik* (Leipzig, 1882), was a book that greatly influenced his views on history when he was a young man.
26. Turner's students honored him on his election to the presidency of the American Historical Association by preparing a book of essays to be presented on that occasion. Guy Stanton Ford, ed., *Essays in American History Dedicated to Frederick Jackson Turner* (New York, 1910).

When Luther Bernard received this voluminous letter, to be followed at once with a thick bundle of notes from Merle Curti, he must have felt that he knew considerably more about Frederick Jackson Turner than was necessary. His purpose, after all, was not a biography of the man, but a brief sketch of the development of social science teaching in the American universities during the past half-century. The entire historical discipline must be compressed into a few paragraphs, leaving no room for any one individual, no matter how important. His reply to Turner was probably more polite than sincere, saying that the letter was "just what I needed." [27] This obligation fulfilled, he set about writing his article with no reference to the autobiographical letter or anything else.

This did not mean that Turner was neglected, for he was glorified more than any other American historian. After a handful of earlier historians—the greats of the early days of Harvard and Johns Hopkins—had been introduced by name, came his turn in Bernard's account, as the foremost representative of the period of "differentiation and growth": "Frederick Jackson Turner, who received his early training under W. F. Allen, himself an able immigrant from the classics into the social studies, and his graduate training at Johns Hopkins, was added to the Wisconsin staff in 1889. His work in the history of the West amounts to the creation of a new field and a new method which has profoundly affected historiography in this country." [28] That was all. Bernard could have written as he did without any help from Turner, save possibly for the few words about Professor Allen. Turner must have felt, when he read that comment shortly before his death, that his time had been wasted.

If he suffered such doubts, they can be set aside, for in his letter to Luther L. Bernard, no less than in his correspondence with William E. Dodd, Constance L. Skinner, Carl Becker, and Merle Curti, he left behind an invaluable record for a later generation interested anew in his historical concepts. Turner's memory might fail him now and then, or he might not recall the correct initial of a friend or student. He might repeat himself endlessly, telling the same stories of his boyhood, glorifying Professor Allen

27. Luther L. Bernard to Turner, December 1, 1928. HEH TU Box 40.
28. Luther L. Bernard, "The United States," in *Encyclopedia of the Social Sciences*, I, 334. The *Encyclopedia*, XV, 132–33, also contained an article on Turner by his successor at the University of Wisconsin, Frederic L. Paxson. This is a straightforward account of his academic career, stressing his frontier thesis more than his sectional studies, and failing to mention his other contributions. "It can be said with justice," Paxson wrote, "that in the forty years following its enunciation a great part of the writing of American history was reorganized around Turner's frontier hypothesis."

over and over again, over-stressing Droysen's dictum that history was the self-consciousness of humanity, or parading pridefully the names of his students who had made their mark in the academic world. We can, however, forgive Frederick Jackson Turner these sins as we reread his letters. Taken together, and with the repetitions and occasional lapses ignored, they tell us much about the genesis of his frontier hypothesis. They also reveal the depth of his understanding of the past and the extent of his faith in history as a palliative for mankind's woes. As such they form a fitting monument to one of the nation's most original and influential historians.

BIBLIOGRAPHICAL NOTE

The literature on Frederick Jackson Turner and his frontier thesis is voluminous, numbering well into the hundreds of items, but most of it is not directly pertinent to the purpose of this book. Bibliographies are readily available, one of Turner's own writings in Everett E. Edwards, comp., "Bibliography of the Writings of Frederick Jackson Turner," in F. J. Turner, *Early Writings of Frederick Jackson Turner* (Madison, 1938), pp. 233–72; one listing the books and articles about Turner and his thesis in Ray A. Billington, *The American Frontier* (American Historical Association: Service Center for Teachers, Washington, 1971). Hence these works will not be listed here; each secondary book or article cited in the text and footnotes has full bibliographical information provided on its first use in every chapter, and can readily be identified. Mention should be made, however, of one earlier study of immense value: Fulmer Mood, "The Development of Frederick Jackson Turner as a Historical Thinker," *Transactions of the Colonial Society of Massachusetts, 1937–1942*, XXXIV (Boston, 1943), 283–52. This was a pioneer work, written without access to Turner's manuscripts, but it can still be read with profit today.

The manuscript collections that include letters and documents by Turner are less widely known than the secondary literature. They have been, moreover, the principal sources on which this book is based. Hence a description of the most important collections, indicating their nature and the type of Turner materials to be found in each, may be useful. The list that follows describes first specific collections of Frederick Jackson Turner Papers in four libraries, then other collections containing Turner items useful in this study. Other collections, containing letters to and from Turner that do not bear directly on the genesis of his frontier thesis, are not included. Abbreviations used in footnotes are indicated in italics.

A. Frederick Jackson Turner Papers

1. Frederick Jackson Turner Papers, Henry E. Huntington Library and Art Gallery, San Marino, California.[1] Turner was so grateful for his years spent at the

1. A more detailed description of this collection, now out of date, is Ray A. Billington and Wilbur R. Jacobs, "The Frederick Jackson Turner Papers in the Huntington Library," *Arizona and the West*, II (Spring, 1960), 73–77.

Huntington Library that he bequeathed to that institution his library, manuscripts, and correspondence files. Since his death in 1932 the Library has continued to acquire his letters and documents by gift from his former students and friends. Moreover an effort has been made to secure duplicates of Turner's more important letters in other depositories, as well as published works essential to the study of his career, including newspapers and magazines recording his activities. This collection, combined with Turner's own library with its annotations and marginal comments, makes the Huntington Library an essential depository for any serious research on Turner and his ideas. His papers have been open to properly qualified scholars since January, 1960, and have been widely used.

They fall into a number of categories:

a) Correspondence, Manuscripts, and Documents. *HEH TU Box 1.*

(1) General Correspondence. Seventy-two flat boxes of letters and related documents, each in its separate folder, chronologically arranged. Boxes 1 through 52 contain letters to and from Turner, Boxes 53–57 manuscripts of his speeches, diplomas, and similar documents, and Boxes 58–62 ephemera, business papers, pages from pocket diaries, and photographs. Box 63 holds his correspondence with his principal publisher, Henry Holt & Company, much of it microcopied from the Henry Holt & Company archives in the Firestone Library, Princeton University.

(2) Turner-Hooper Correspondence. *HEH TU-H Box 1.* Alice Forbes Perkins Hooper, daughter of Charles Elliott Perkins and husband of William Hooper of Manchester, Massachusetts, began a correspondence with Turner in 1910 that continued until his death in 1932. This is the only sustained body of letters left by Turner. It is housed in ten boxes, the last two containing typed versions of the manuscript letters. The more important letters have been published in Ray A. Billington, ed., *"Dear Lady": The Letters of Frederick Jackson Turner and Alice Forbes Perkins Hooper 1910–1932* (San Marino, 1970).

(3) Family Letters. *HEH TU Box A ff.* Letters between Turner and members of his family, including an important series exchanged with his fiancée between 1887 and 1889, are in eleven boxes numbered A through K.

b) Reading and Research Notes.

(1) Reading Notes and Lectures. *HEH File Drawer 1A ff.* Turner left the Library twenty-two file drawers filled with his notes, clippings, and miscellaneous materials. These have been transferred to cardboard boxes, five boxes to each original drawer, and designated File Drawer 1A, 1B, etc. File Drawers 14 and 15 contain many of his speeches and manuscripts of articles.

(2) Notes on Sectionalism. *HEH File Drawer A1 ff.* Twelve file draw-

ers held the notes for Turner's last book on *The United States, 1830–1850: The Nation and Its Sections*. These also contain most of his notes and earlier speeches on sectionalism. They have been transferred to cardboard boxes, five to each original wooden drawer, and designated File Drawer A1, A2, etc.

(3) Three by Five File Drawers. *HEH 3×5 File Drawer 1 ff*. Nineteen metal 3×5 inch file drawers contain Turner's brief research notes, bibliographical notations, and the like. Drawers 1 and 2 were apparently begun during the 1890s and house notes important to the genesis of his frontier thesis. Drawers 13 through 19 contain the notes used in dictation on his last book.

(4) Manuscript Volumes. *HEH TU Vol. 1 ff*. Twenty volumes of albums, manuscripts, scrapbooks, and the like were compiled by Turner and are housed separately in the collection. These include his Commonplace Books, his early syllabi, and the "Red Book" and "Blue Book," holding letters presented by his students on his leaving Wisconsin in 1910 and Harvard in 1924.

c) Miscellaneous Materials. *HEH TU Black Box 1 ff*.

(1) Newspaper and Magazine Clippings. Nineteen black boxes contain clippings, pamphlets, magazine articles, and other matter that Turner preserved. In them he kept some of the Census Bureau items important in the development of his frontier thesis.

(2) Maps. *HEH TU Maps 1 ff*. Two large boxes hold the many maps Turner drew in connection with his sectionalism studies.

(3) Lantern Slides. *HEH TU Lantern Slides 1 ff*. The lantern slides used by Turner in his classes and lectures fill nine special boxes.

2. Frederick Jackson Turner Papers. Houghton Library. Harvard University. Cambridge, Massachusetts. *Houghton: Turner Papers*. One box contains papers bequeathed to Harvard University by Turner on his retirement from the faculty. In it are three folders: a) Seven letters from Woodrow Wilson to Turner, 1889–1902, and two from W. E. Dodd concerning the origins of the frontier thesis, b) Seven letters from Theodore Roosevelt to Turner, 1894–1898, and c) Letters from Walter Hines Page and other editors of the *Atlantic Monthly* for the period 1896–1899.

3. Frederick Jackson Turner Papers, State Historical Society of Wisconsin Library, Madison, Wisconsin. *SHSW, Turner Papers*. Turner presented the library with three boxes of papers, largely having some local connection. Box 1 contains largely items related to his father, Andrew Jackson Turner, Box 2, a few letters and many manuscripts relating to his teaching at the university, and Box 3 some notes that he took in his classes at the university and some of Professor W. F. Allen's classroom notes.

4. Frederick Jackson Turner Papers, Archives of the University of Wisconsin. The Memorial Library, University of Wisconsin, Madison, Wisconsin. *U. of Wis. Archives, L&S, Turner Corr., 1901–5, Box 1 ff.* Six boxes officially catalogued as College of Letters and Science. Department of History. Turner Correspondence, 1901–1905. Series N. 7/16/2, Boxes 1–6. The first five boxes contain correspondence to and from Turner (most of the latter are carbons) arranged chronologically. The letters deal largely with matters relating to his post as chairman of the school of history, but some have to do with his publishing and scholarly activities. Box 6 has one folder of correspondence, but is filled largely with reports and items having to do with the school of history.

B. Collections of Papers Relating to Frederick Jackson Turner

1. William Francis Allen Papers. State Historical Society of Wisconsin Library. *SHSW: Allen Papers.* One box of papers covering the period from March, 1848 to December, 1889, and consisting largely of Allen's own diplomas, transcripts, and the like. Included, however, are his class records books with notations about Turner and his work.

2. American Historical Association Papers. Manuscripts Division, Library of Congress, Washington, D.C. *L. of C., AHA Papers, Box 1 ff.* The papers fill 211 linear feet of shelf space and contain more than 155,000 items. The boxes for the period 1892–1893 have some material, though disappointingly little, relating to Turner and his paper on the significance of the frontier.

3. Charles McLean Andrews Papers. Historical Manuscrips Division, Yale University Library. *Yale: Andrews Papers.* The only papers important to this study are the letters written in 1888–1889 when Andrews was a fellow student with Turner at the Johns Hopkins University. He wrote weekly to his mother, describing events in detail. Turner is not mentioned, but the letters provide useful background material.

4. Carl L. Becker Papers. Collection of Regional History and University Archives. Albert R. Mann Library, Cornell University, Ithaca, New York. *Cornell: Becker Papers.* The original copies of the letters reproduced in this volume, written from Turner to Becker, are in this collection, together with others over the years. An important collection for any study of Turner.

5. Richard T. Ely Papers. State Historical Society of Wisconsin Library. *SHSW: Ely Papers.* Largely important for Turner's later career, but with some

correspondence during the period just after his year at Johns Hopkins, where Ely taught.

6. Papers of the Harvard Commission on Western History. Harvard University Archives, Widener Library, Harvard University, Cambridge, Massachusetts. *Widener: HC on WH Corr., Box 1 ff*. Twelve boxes of correspondence, in addition to card indexes and other items. Although important in Turner's later life, the Commission correspondence file became a depository for many earlier letters useful in this study.

7. J. Franklin Jameson Papers. Manuscript Division, Library of Congress, Washington, D.C. *L. of C., Jameson Papers, Box 1 ff*. Box 7 of this large collection contains Jameson's letters and notes for the period 1892–1893. Jameson was active in the Chicago meeting of the American Historical Association, where Turner read his paper; but his letters have disappointingly little on the event.

8. Johns Hopkins University Seminar Records, 1886–1890. Johns Hopkins University Archives, Baltimore, Maryland. *Johns Hopkins: Seminar Minutes*. Original handwritten version and typed copies of official minutes of each seminar in history and political science held at Johns Hopkins during this period. Turner served as secretary for one meeting, and at others gave his reports.

9. William F. Poole Papers. The Newberry Library, Chicago, Illinois. *Newberry: Poole Papers*. Twenty-six boxes of letters covering the period 1858–1894, arranged chronologically. Some deal with the 1893 session of the American Historical Association, where Poole served as local program chairman.

10. Joseph Schafer Papers, State Historical Society of Wisconsin Library, Madison, Wisconsin. *SHSW: Shafer Papers*. Most of the Turner correspondence in this file is of a later period, but Schafer wrote much about Turner and often inspired him to reminisce about his formative years.

11. Charles R. Van Hise Papers. State Historical Society of Wisconsin Library, Madison, Wisconsin. *SHSW: Van Hise Papers*. Nine boxes covering the period 1875–1918. Many of Van Hise's papers are in the university's "Presidents File" listed below. Van Hise, as a geologist, influenced Turner's thought and life even before he became president of the university.

12. University of Wisconsin, College of Letters and Science. Administration. Dean's Files. Series 7/1/12–2 and 7/1/2–1. University of Wisconsin Archives,

Madison, Wisconsin. *U. of Wis., C. of L., Dean's Files.* This extensive file contains many letters from and about Turner during his early period at the university.

13. University of Wisconsin, Instructional Reports, Fall, 1886 to Spring, 1910. University of Wisconsin Archives, Madison, Wisconsin. *U. of Wis., Instructional Reports.* Each term members of the faculty filled out reports showing the courses they taught, the number of students, their hours of instruction, and the like. Invaluable in tracing Turner's early teaching career.

14. University of Wisconsin, Presidents of the University, General Correspondence. University of Wisconsin Archives, Madison, Wisconsin. *U. of Wis., Presidents File, Box 1 ff.* Contains 142 boxes of general correspondence, largely directed to the presidents of the university, arranged chronologically, with letters filed alphabetically within each period. Contains many letters from Turner on both his academic and his professional interests. Indexed under individual presidents: Chamberlin Series 4/7/1; Adams Series 4/8/1; Van Hise Series 4/9/1.

15. Woodrow Wilson Papers, Manuscript Division, Library of Congress, Washington, D.C. *L. of C., Wilson Papers, Box 1 ff.* An extensive file, containing many letters to and from Turner in the period 1889–1902, with scattered letters thereafter. These have been summarized in George C. Osburn, "Woodrow Wilson and Frederick Jackson Turner," *Proceedings of the New Jersey State Historical Society,* LXXIV (July, 1956), 208–29, and reproduced in full in the continuing series of volumes being edited by Arthur S. Link, ed., *The Papers of Woodrow Wilson* (Princeton, 1966 ff.).

INDEX

Abreu, Capistrano de: writes on Brazilian frontier, 85.

Adams, Henry: as pioneer in social history, 271.

Adams, Herbert Baxter: as Turner's teacher at Johns Hopkins University, 5–7, 27–29, 39; asks help of William F. Allen, 21; aids extension programs, 45; advice of sought on syllabi, 51–52; comments on Turner's "Significance of the Frontier" paper, 60–61; as leader of Teutonist School of history, 90–91; recommends Walter Bagehot's *Physics and Politics*, 131; arranges 1893 American Historical Association program, 162–65; delays printing of "Significance of the Frontier" paper, 172; urges students not to study American history, 192, 195; as social scientist, 221; teaching of recalled by Turner, 234–35, 291; influence of recalled by Turner, 236.

Adams, Charles F.: on "The New History," 93.

Adams, Charles Kendall: invites Turner to give "Significance of the Frontier" paper, 163; urged to read paper at 1893 meeting, 164–65; fails to appreciate Turner's essay, 171; as pioneer in use of seminar, 258.

Adelphi Literary Society: Turner as member of, 15.

Aegis, The: publishes "Problems in American History" paper, 56–61.

Agrarian Myth: as applied to American frontier, 72–75.

Agricultural history: Turner as pioneer in, 211–12.

Allen, Ethan: Turner on his capture of Ticonderoga, 242.

Allen, William Francis: as teacher of Turner, 5, 7, 15–26; receives Turner's letters, 29, 36; death of, 40–41; Turner's appraisal of, 192, 195; influence of recalled by Turner, 213;

Turner's debt to, 229; teaching of remembered by Turner, 234, 237–39, 258–60, 290–91, 297.

Allport, Floyd H.: use of Turner's techniques by, 268.

Alvord, Clarence W.: Turner's influence on, 212.

American Historical Association: popularity of frontier thesis in, 3–4; invitation to Turner to deliver "Significance of the Frontier" paper before, 60–61; Turner at 1893 meeting of, 159, 161–67; prints "Significance of the Frontier" essay, 172; Turner at 1900 meeting of, 199; meeting of in Ann Arbor, 230; aids in methodological study, 254–55; Turner reads paper before, 259, 267.

American Sociological Society: inaugurates social science encyclopedia, 287.

Andrews, Charles M.: comments on Turner's paper, 60; leads attack on Teutonist school of history, 91; acknowledges Turner's paper on "Significance of the Frontier," 173; student days at Johns Hopkins University recalled, 235.

Angell, James B.: arranges 1893 American Historical Association program, 162, 164; presides at historical congress, 195–96.

Ashton, Mary Jane: boarding house of, 30.

Bagehot, Walter: book by read by Turner, 6; influences of on Turner, 130–32; 155; use of by Turner, 192, 196.

Baily, Francis: 124.

Baird, Robert: 124–26.

Baker, Ray Stannard: mentions Turner in Woodrow Wilson biography, 295.

Bancroft, Frederic: on 1893 American Historical Association program, 163.

Bancroft, George: as romantic historian, 87–88.

Bancroft, Hubert H.: on influence of frontier, 71.

Barnes, Harry Elmer: praises Turner, 210; book by reviewed, 226; consulted by Merle Curti, 255; writes on Turner, 264, 270; reads Curti essay on Turner, 281, 285.

Barrows, Harlan H.: as student of Turner, 272.

Bassett, John S.: praises Turner, 246.

Baxter, James P. III: as student of Turner, 264.

Beard, Charles A.: economic thesis of, 4; writes pragmatic history, 102; praises Turner, 210, criticises Turner, 266–67, 271; employs sectional concept, 267.

Becker, Carl: as pragmatic historian, 102; correspondence with Turner, 219, 223–50; as Turner's student, 221–23; on Turner's skills as teacher, 230–32; as author of essay on Turner, 264, 290, 296, 277–78; reads essay for Merle Curti, 281.

Belaunde, Victor A.: writes on comparative frontiers, 276.

Bellamy, Edward: as critic of society, 76.

Beman, Nathan: as ancestor of Turner, 242.

Bemis, Samuel F.: praises Turner, 228, 246, 274; as student of Turner, 262; consulted on Turner's diplomatic studies, 270.

Benson, Lee: discusses Achille Loria's influence on Turner, 136–38.

Bernard, Luther L.: career of, 288–89; correspondence with Turner, 289–96; prepares encyclopedia article, 287–98; appraisal of Turner by, 297.

Bidgood, Lee: influenced by Turner, 212.

Biological Studies: use of by Turner, 102–08.

Birge, E. A.: explains biological theories, 107.

Blair, Helen: as student of Turner, 212; dedicates book to Turner, 262.

Bonanza Farms: heard of by Turner, 12.

Bourne, George E.: speaks on 1893 American Historical Association program, 163.

Boutmy, Emile: influence on Turner's 1893 essay, 128.

Britt, Barney: killed in Portage, 10.

Brown University: Phi Beta Kappa lecture at, 132.

Bryan, William Jennings: Turner's appraisal of, 189, 194.

Bryce, James: quoted, 77; accepts environmental determinism, 99–100; praises Turner, 226, 235.

Buffalo Bill's Wild West Show: as attraction at Chicago Exposition, 166; as competition for Turner's frontier paper, 172.

Bullock, Charles J.: as friend of Turner, 296.

Burgess, John W.: as social scientist, 221.

Butterfield, Consul W.: book of assigned by W. F. Allen, 19.

Caledonia, Wisconsin: population of, 13–14; Scotch settlers in, 215.

Cambria, Wisconsin: Welsh settlers in, 215.

Carter, Clarence E.: as student of Turner, 274.

Carver, Thomas N.: as friend of Turner, 296.

Census Bureau: use of maps of by Turner, 109–16; effect of announcements of, 156; use of reports of by Turner, 167.

Chamberlin, Thomas C.: favors adoption of extension program, 45; on environmental determinism, 102; influences Turner with concept of multiple causation, 257, 265, 296.

Channing, Edward: leads attack on Teutonist school of history, 91.

Churillon, André: influence of on Turner, 128–29.

Clark, Champ: foreign policy views of appraised by Turner, 189, 194

Clark, John B.: economic views of studied by Turner, 32.

Clay, Henry: cited by Turner, 121–22.

Cole, James A.: recalls Turner's predictions on Woodrow Wilson's presidency, 187, 193.

Collot, Victor: book of read by Turner, 124.

Colonial Society of Massachusetts: Turner as president of, 242.

Colonization: lectures on by Turner, 44–45, 48–56; Turner's lecture on to Madison Literary Club, 53–56.

Columbia County, Wisconsin: as frontier area in Turner's youth, 12–14.

Commercial Revolution: effect of on American agriculture, 76–77.

Commonplace Books: kept by Turner, 22; quotation in, 68.

Commons, John R.: as student at Johns Hopkins University, 235.

Comparative technique: in historical methodology, 89–90.

Contemporary Club: discussion of Henry George by, 129.

Cotton, J. S.: book by used by Turner, 49–50.

Coulter, John L.: as student of Turner, 211, 261.

Cox, Isaac J.: as student of Turner, 274.

Creativity, Psychology of: discussed, 147–52; as applied to Turner, 152–56.

Crissey, Merrill H.: collects Turner letters, 217.

Curti, Merle: career of, 253–54; invited to write on Turner, 254–55; correspondence with Turner, 255–85; prepares essay on Turner, 280–82; essay on Turner cited, 289, 290, 296.

Dana, James D.: accepts environmental determinism, 99.

Darling, Arthur B.: dedicates book to Turner, 228.

Darwin, Charles: impact of on historical studies, 18, 88; accepts environmental determinism, 95–96; effect of on biological theory, 103–08; as creative thinker, 151.

Davis, C. Wood: quoted on closing of frontier, 78–79; demands end to immigration, 81.

Democracy: Turner speculates on influence of frontier on, 22, 125–26, 169; western writers on, 69; E. L. Godkin on, 70; influence of free land on, 141.

Demography: Turner's interest in, 269, 273.

Demoulin, Edmond: as environmental determinist, 96.

Depression of 1873–1896: effect of on western thought, 76–78.

Dewey, Davis R.: as friend of Turner's, 296.

Dewey, John: and pragmatic school, 102.

Diplomatic history: Turner's pride in writings on, 210–11, 228, 246, 262; Turner's contributions to, 274.

Dodd, William E.: career of, 181–83; correspondence of with Turner, 183–201; on nature of historical writing, 198–99; correspondence referred to, 234–35; comment on history by, 277.

Douglas, Stephen A.: quoted on influence of frontier, 73.

Doyle, John A.: books of assigned by W. F. Allen, 20–21; influence of writings on Turner, 49–50.

Draper, Lyman C.: builds State Historical Society of Wisconsin, 95; suggests topic to Turner, 212–13, 237.

Droysen, Johann G.: influence of on Turner, 243–44, 257, 296.

Dunning, William A.: as social scientist, 221.

Dwight, Timothy: book of read by Turner, 124.

Edwards, Everett E.: as student of Turner's, 282.

Edwards, Jason: as writer on West, 74.

Eggleston, Edward: refuses to speak at 1893 American Historical Association meeting, 163.

Ely, Richard T.: as Turner's teacher, 5–6, 27, 31–36; views on stages of social evolution, 53, 113–15, 145; assigns reading in Henry George's works, 129; assigns reading in books of Francis A. Walker, 132; use of Achille Loria's theories by, 136–37; skills as teacher recalled by Turner, 213, 291, 296.

Emerson, Guy: Turner's influence on, 212.

Emerson, Ralph Waldo: quoted on frontier's influence, 68.

Emerton, Ephraim: on 1893 American Historical Association program, 163.

Environmentalism: early acceptance of, 50; Turner on importance of, 54; effect of environment on sections, 58; acceptance of in 1890s, 95–101; Turner's views on, 176, 277–78, 280.

Everest, Kate A.: as student of Turner, 43–44.

Evolutionary Thesis: effect on historical studies, 18; as taught at Johns Hopkins University, 32–36; Turner's speculations on, 24, 44–45; in Wisconsin as observed by Turner, 36; effect on historical writing, 88–90, 95–96; effect of on biological studies, 103–08.

Expansion of Europe: relation to frontier, 18–19.

Extension education: Turner's participation in, 45–53.

Farrand, Max: collects Turner letters, 217, 219; offers Turner position at Huntington Library, 247–48.

Faulkner, Harold U.: writes on statistical techniques, 269; reads Curti essay on Turner, 281, 285.

Fay, Sidney B.: heads methodological study, 255–56; reads Curti essay on Turner, 281, 285.

Findley, William: works read by Turner, 122.

Fish, Carl Russell: writes on comparative frontiers, 276.

Fisher, George P.: reads paper at 1893 American Historical Association meeting, 166.

Fiske, John: praises "Significance of the Frontier" paper, 173, 208.

Ford, Amelia C.: as student of Turner, 211, 262.

Ford, Henry J.: praises Turner's writings in diplomatic history, 211, 246.

Ford, Worthington C.: as friend of Turner, 295.

Fort Winnebago: Turner's boyhood near, 9; Turner's memories of, 243.

Fox, Dixon Ryan: as editor, 218.

Frankfurter, Felix: influenced by Turner's writings, 227.

Franklin, Benjamin: quoted by Turner, 24.

Free Land: economic theory of, 33–36; passing of, 77–79; Henry George on, 130; Achille Loria's views on, 134–41; Turner speaks on to Madison Literary Club, 156–57; Turner's thoughts on effects of, 176.

Freeman, Edward A.: quoted on political history, 91.

Frontier: Portage as example of, 4–5, 9–15; John A. Doyle's comments on, 20–21; interest of Turner in, 23–24; as symbol and myth, 72–75; as remembered by Turner, 216, 276.

Frontier, Closing of: Turner affected by, 55, 75–82, 85–87; Mackinder quoted on, 86–87; census announcement of, 114–15; Turner writes on in 1893 essay, 169–70.

Frontier Thesis: stated by Turner, 3; acceptance of by historians, 3–4; attacks on, 4; development of by Turner, 24; effect of fur trade thesis on, 25–26; expressed in review of *Winning of the West*, 40; in Turner's lectures on colonization, 53–56; developed in paper on "Problems in American History," 56–61; early statements of, 66–72; importance of census publications in developing, 109–16; Turner's reading on, 119–46; Turner's psychological preparation for, 152–56; in essay on "Significance of the Frontier," 167–70; inadequate basis for, 174–76; ascribed to Woodrow Wilson, 182–83; Turner's comments on origins of, 190–92, 214–16, 232–44, 275; Turner's views on, 207–10, 213–14, 228–29, 232–44, 249, 292–94; attacks on, 218.

Fur Trade: Turner's thesis on, 25–26, as stage in settlement process, 36; described by Turner, 44; comments on by Woodrow Wilson, 190–95; thesis on appraised by Turner, 207, 236.

Gannett, Henry: as statistical cartographer, 111–13; influence on Turner recalled, 236.

Garden of the World: image of West as, 72–75.

Garland, Hamlin: writes on West, 74; rebels against eastern domination, 93–94.

Geographical Society of Chicago: Turner lectures to, 272.

Geography: knowledge of by Turner, 26; effect of changing interpretations of on Turner, 95–101; Turner's opposition to geographic determinism, 176; Turner's views on importance of, 210, 224–25, 263.

George, Henry: works of studied by Turner, 32; expresses agrarian discontent, 76; influence on Turner, 129–30, 155, 282–83.

"Germ Theory:" popularity of, 3; as taught by Herbert Baxter Adams, 27–28; Woodrow Wilson on, 30; rise of in Teutonist School, 89–93; Turner's attacks on, 51, 54, 175–76, 244.

German immigrants: in early Portage, 13–14; effect of on free land, 36; study of migration of, 42–44.

Giddings, Franklin H.: quoted, 257, 294; as social scientist, 221; use of statistical maps by, 273; as friend of Turner, 296.

Gildersleeve, Basil L.: quoted on teaching, 229.

Godkin, E. L.: as early writer on frontier influence, 69–70, 123.

Graduate Studies: Turner's interest in, 42–44.

Great Depression: effect on frontier thesis, 3–4.

Green, John R.: as pioneer in social history, 92.

Grignon Tract: Turner prepares essay on, 21–22.

Hale, Edward Everett: on 1893 American Historical Association program, 163; acknowledges paper on "Significance of the Frontier," 173, 208.

Hale, George Ellery: Turner comments on, 250.

Hancock Point, Maine: Turner's summer home at, 230, 248.

Haney, Lewis H.: as student of Turner, 261.

Hanford, Reverend Thomas: as ancestor of Turner, 216, 241.

Hansen, Marcus Lee: as student of Turner, 262.

Harvard University: Turner leaves on retirement, 224–25.

Haskins, Charles Homer: joins history department at University of Wisconsin, 41–42; gives course on geography, 107; helps entertain Woodrow Wilson, 157; on 1893 program of American Historical Association, 163, 165; Carl Becker on, 226–27; student days at Johns Hopkins University recalled, 235, 291.

Hedges, James B.: reads Merle Curti's essay on Turner, 281.

Hegel, William F.: credited with frontier thesis, 123.

Henderson, Archibald: dedicates book to Turner, 228, 262.

Hendrickson, G. L.: at 1893 meeting of American Historical Association, 165.

Henry, William Wirt: on 1893 program of American Historical Association, 163.

Hewes, Fletcher: as statistical cartographer, 112–13.

Hibbard, Benjamin H.: as student of Turner, 211, 261, 262.

Hildreth, Richard: works of read by Turner, 19; as pioneer in social history, 266; quoted, 273.

Hinsdale, B. A.: as pioneer in western history, 94; acknowledges paper on "Significance of the Frontier," 173.

Historical and Political Science Association: hears paper on "Significance of the Frontier," 172.

History: changing concepts of, 87–95; origins of study of western, 93–96; Turner's views on, 45–48, 56–61, 214, 228–30, 234–36, 246–47, 249, 257–75, 278–80, 283–84.

History of the West course: Turner on origins of, 209.

Hockett, Homer C.: dedicates book to Turner, 228.

Holmes, Oliver Wendall: quoted, 249.

Hooper, Mrs. William: letters sent to, 235.

Howard, George E.: comments on paper by Turner, 60.

Howe, E. W.: as writer on West, 74.

Huntington Library: as depository of Turner papers, 7–8, 217–19; Turner joins staff of, 247–48, 250, 289.

Immigration: to Portage and vicinity, 13–14, 215, 239–40; Turner's speculations on, 24; study of at University of Wisconsin, 42–44; Turner on importance of study of, 54–55, 58–59, 80–81; Turner directs students into study of, 262.

Immigration Restriction League: formation of, 81.

Ince, Jonathan: as student of Turner, 242.

Indians: as seen by Turner near Portage, 4–5; wars with reported, 10; removal of from Columbia County, 12–13; in Turner's fur trade thesis, 26; cultural areas concept applied to, 85–86; Turner as pioneer in study of history of, 202; Turner's memories of in boyhood, 215, 243.

Ingram, John K.: economic views of studied by Turner, 32.

Institutional History: Turner's instruction in, 5–6; as taught by William F. Allen, 16–18; as taught by Herbert B. Adams, 27–28; Turner's views on, 214–15, 229, 234–35.

Intellectual History: Turner as pioneer in, 268.

Interdisciplinary Studies: use of by William F. Allen, 17; use of urged by Turner, 47, 58; Turner's views on importance of, 224–25, 233, 246–47, 257–60, 293–94; encyclopedia prepared for, 287–88.

Inventiveness: as frontier trait, 127; Francis A. Walker on, 133.

Ise, John: as student of Turner, 211–12.

James, James Alton: as student of Turner, 283–84.

Jameson, J. Franklin: on 1893 American Historical Association program, 163.

Jefferson, Thomas: on stages of social evolution, 66–67; quoted on frontier, 72–73.

Johns Hopkins University: Turner as student at, 5–6, 26–37; completes doctoral work at, 41; as center for Teutonist School of history, 90; discussion of Henry George at, 129–30; relations between Turner and Woodrow Wilson at, 183, 195–97; Turner's memories of life at, 190, 195–97, 213, 235–36, 259–60, 291.

Johnson, Allen: edits *Chronicles of America* series, 203; as critic of sectionalism studies, 269.

Johnson, Emory R.: as student of Turner, 43, 261; comments on "Significance of the Frontier" essay, 60.

Johnston, Alexander: use of textbook by, 19.

Kipling, Rudyard: recommended by Turner, 229.

Kitchin, Claude: views of appraised by Turner, 189, 194.

Kittredge, George Lyman: seeks Turner as author, 159.

Kriehn, George: reads paper at 1893 American Historical Association meeting, 166.

LaFollette, Robert M.: as friend of Turner, 295.

Lamar, Lucius Q. C.: credited with originating frontier thesis, 123.

Lamarck, Chevalier de: biological theories of, 103–04.

Lamprecht, K. C.: acknowledges "Significance of the Frontier," essay, 173.

Land legislation: study of at Johns Hopkins University, 28.

Land rent: Turner's theories of, 33–36.

Lecuyer, John: in land dispute in Portage, 21–22.

Lewis, George C.: works of used by Turner, 49.

Lewiston, Wisconsin: population of, 14.

Libby, Orin G.: recommended for American Historical Association 1893 program by Turner, 164; as Turner student, 263; mapping techniques of, 273.

List, Friedrich: views of on social evolution, 33, 67.

Lodge, Henry Cabot: refuses place on 1893 American Historical Association program, 163; Turner's appraisal of foreign policy of, 189, 194–95.

Logan, John H.: book of read by Turner, 124.

Lord, Robert H.: asked to comment on Turner, 244.

Loria, Achille: theories of, 50; credited with frontier thesis, 123; influence of on Turner, 134–42, 155–56.

Lowell, Henry Wadsworth: frontier views of, 82.

Lowell, James Russell: quoted on influence of frontier, 68.

Lumbering: as frontier industry in Portage, 11–12; Turner's visits to camps of, 216; Turner's memories of, 243.

Lybyer, Albert H.: writes on use of statistics, 269.

Lynchings: as seen by Turner, 10–11, 243.

Macauley, Thomas B.: on safety valve theory, 67.

McCarthy, Charles: as student of Turner, 274.

Mackinder, Halford J.: closing of frontier, 86–87.

McMaster, John Bach: as pioneer in social history, 92.

Macy, Jesse: reads paper at 1893 American Historical Association meeting, 166–67.

Madison Contemporary Club: Turner speaks before, 44.

Madison Literary Club: Turner reads fur trade paper to, 25, 160; lectures to on colonization, 53–56, 143; talks on free land to, 156–57.

Mahan, Alfred T.: writes on naval history, 92.

Manning, William R.: diplomatic studies of aided by Turner, 274.

Maps: use of by William F. Allen, 17; reveal pattern of westward expansion, 20; use of by graduate students, 44; emergence of science of statistical cartography, 108–14; use of by Turner, 224, 273–74, 281.

Marshall, John: use of books by, 19.

Mason, Otis T.: arranges Indian exhibit for World's Columbian Exposition, 85–86.

Mather, Cotton: quoted, 241–42.

Mead, John: as ancestor of Turner, 242.

Meitzen, August: as pioneer in statistical cartography, 108–09.

Menomonee Indians: removal of from Wisconsin, 12–13.

Merivale, Herman: books of used by Turner, 49–50.

Merk, Frederick: as student of Turner, 262, 264; consulted on Turner's diplomatic studies, 270.

Merriam, C. Hart: develops cultural areas concept, 85–86.

Meyer, Balthasar H.: as student of Turner, 261, 295.

Mill, John Stuart: books of read by Turner, 32; rent theories of, 34–35.

Millikan, Robert A.: Turner comments on, 250.

Milwaukee, Wisconsin: Turner lectures in, 48.

Moran, Thomas F.: as friend of Turner, 197.

Morison, Samuel E.: critical of Turner's views on sectionalism, 263, 269.

Motley, John L.: as romantic historian, 87–88.

Multiple Hypotheses: Turner's use of, 257, 265.

Murat, Achille: works of read by Turner 124.

National Education Association: Woodrow Wilson at Madison meeting of, 157.

Nationalism: study of by Turner, 29–30; Turner's views on, 121–22; effect of frontier on, 125, 133–34; formation of on frontier, 167–68.

Neo-Lamarckians: in biological controversy, 105–06.

New Darwinians: in biological controversy, 105–06.

New England: effect on Turner of visit to, 24; described by Turner, 53.

New England School of History: importance of, 6; Turner's resentment of, 29; attacks on, 40, 93–95; Woodrow Wilson's attack on, 182–96.

New England towns: William F. Allen's study of, 21–22; genesis of as historical controversy, 28; Woodrow Wilson's views on, 30; Turner's views on origins, 51, 54; conflicting theories on origins of, 89–90.

New History: anticipated by Turner, 47–48; emergence of, 91–93; Turner as pioneer of, 270–71, 275.

North American Land Company: Turner's reading on, 121–22.

Odum, Howard W.: edits volume of essays, 221.

Old Pinery Road: followed by Turner, 11–12.

Olsen, Nils A.: as student of Turner, 211, 261.

Osgood, Herbert L.: books of read by Turner, 122–23.

Oshkosh, Wisconsin: Turner lectures in, 51.

Page, Walter Hines: correspondence with Turner, 235; as friend of Turner, 295.

Pan-American Congresses: as symbol of closing of frontier, 55.

Parish, John C.: praises Turner's contributions, 284.

Parkman, Francis: books of assigned by William F. Allen, 19; quoted on frontier influence, 68; as romantic historian, 87–88.

Patten, Simon H.: theories of rent studied by Turner, 32, 35–36; comments on paper by Turner, 60.

Payne, E. J.: his books used by Turner, 49–50.

Peck, John M.: guidebook of read by Turner, 124.

Pelzer, Louis: as student of frontier, 283.

Phillips, Ulrich B.: comments of about Turner, 244; as student of Turner, 274.

Political economy: Turner's study of, 31–36.

Poole, William F.: as chairman of 1893 American Historical Association program committee, 162–65; describes 1893 American Historical Association meeting, 171; delays printing of "Significance of the Frontier" essay, 172.

Populism: ends Garden of the World myth, 74; Turner's views of, 75; expresses western discontent, 76; program of for reform, 78.

Portage, Wisconsin: influence of on Turner, 4–5; Turner's boyhood in, 9–15; Grignon tract in studied by Turner, 21–22; changing social order in, 24; as remembered by Turner, 153, 215–16, 239–40, 243, 291–92.

Powell, John Wesley: on inheritance of acquired characteristics, 106.

Powers, Harry H.: translates Achille Loria, 136–38.

Poynette, Wisconsin: Turner lectures in, 48.

Prescott, William H.: as romantic historian, 87–88.

"Problems in American History" Essay: writing of, 56–61, 144–45; meaning of, 116; dating of writing of, 137; as statement of frontier thesis, 154–55; used by Woodrow Wilson, 158–59, 186, 191, 196–97; discussed with Woodrow Wilson, 160–61; comments on by Turner, 207, 234, 275.

"Problems of the West" Essay: writing of recalled by Turner, 208–09.

Pyre, James F. A.: as historian of University of Wisconsin, 239.

Ranke, Leopold von: as founder of "Scientific School" of history, 88; Turner's views on, 279.

Ratzel, Friedrich: as environmental determinist, 96–98; works of read by Turner, 100–01; influence of on Turner, 267–68, 272; praises "Significance of the Frontier" essay, 173–74.

Redlich, Joseph: praises Turner's article on sectionalism, 226, 246.

Relativism: preached by Turner, 46–47.

Rent: See Land Rent.

Rhodes, James Ford: appraised by Turner, 214; as friend of Turner, 295.

Ricardian Economics: as dominant school, 31.
Ripley, William Z.: as friend of Turner, 296.
Rivers of America Series: origins of, 217.
Robertson, William S.: as student of Turner, 274.
Robinson, Edgar E.: as student of Turner, 284.
Robinson, James Harvey: as social scientist, 221; as pioneer of New History, 270–71, 275; historical views of, 277.
Rogers, James E. T.: as pioneer in economic history, 92.
Romantic School of History: dominance of, 87–88; Turner's disagreement with, 175.
Roosevelt, Theodore: as author of *Winning of the West*, 39–40; compliments Turner on paper, 82; reviewed by Turner, 154–56, 207–08; acknowledges "Significance of the Frontier" essay, 173; correspondence of with Turner, 235; as friend of Turner, 295.
Roscher, Wilhelm: books of used by William F. Allen, 238.
Ross, E. A.: as friend of Turner, 296.
Round, J. Horace: attacks views of Edward A. Freeman, 92.
Royce, Josiah: quoted on sectionalism, 224–25; influence on Turner, 273.

Safety Valve Theory: early expressions of, 67–68; use of by William F. Hegel, 123; use of by Henry George, 130.
Saint Louis: Turner's 1904 speech in 1904, 160, 275.
Salisbury, Rollin D.: invites Turner to lecture, 272; influences Turner's views on sectionalism, 296.
Sanford, Albert H.: Turner seeks place for on 1893 American Historical Association program, 164.
Schafer, Joseph: prints Turner letter, 218; as student of Turner, 262.
Schaper, William S.: as student of Turner, 273–74.
Schlesinger, Arthur M.: as Turner's successor at Harvard University, 254; comments of on Turner, 266.
Schmidt, Louis B.: as student of Turner, 261.
Schouler, James: his history read by Turner, 19, 122; as friend of Turner, 295.
Scientific history: as developed by Herbert B. Adams, 27; rise of school of, 88–90; attacks on by Turner, 48, 90–92, 175–76; Turner's view of, 279.

Scottish settlers: in early Portage, 13–14.
Scribner's Statistical Atlas of the United States: use of by Turner, 112–13.
Sectionalism: study of urged by Turner, 31, 58; revealed in congressional debates, 185; Turner's early study of, 190, 194; discussion of in "Significance of the Frontier" essay, 196; influence of theories on historians, 198–99; Turner's views on nature of, 209, 224–25, 226, 258–59, 263, 293–94; Turner's articles on, 246; Turner's contributions to study of, 267–68; criticism of Turner's ideas of, 269; Turner recalls early interest in, 272–73; Turner's last book on, 289–90.
Seligman, Edwin R. A.: edits encyclopedia of the social sciences, 287–88.
Semple, Ellen C.: as environmental determinist, 97–98.
Shaler, Nathaniel S.: as environmental determinist, 97; read by Turner, 101; lack of influence on Turner, 268, 272.
Shaw, Albert: on closing of the frontier, 81.
Shea, J. G.: books of assigned by William F. Allen, 19.
"Significance of History" essay: preparation of, 45–48.
"Significance of the Frontier" essay: preparation of, 156–65; reading of, 165–70; reception of, 170–76; read to Woodrow Wilson, 186, 197.
Skinner, Constance L.: career of, 203–05; correspondence with Turner, 205–16; publication of Turner letter by, 216–19; comments on autobiographical letter to, 234.
Small, Albion W.: as Turner's teacher at Johns Hopkins University, 5–6, 27, 29–30; comments on Turner's paper, 60; refuses invitation to speak at 1893 American Historical Association meeting, 163; comments on Turner's sectional studies, 210; as social scientist, 221; teaching at Johns Hopkins recalled by Turner, 259–60, 291–92, 296.
Smith, Goldwin: book of read by Turner, 122; work of reviewed by Woodrow Wilson, 182, 197, 234–35.
Smith, Theodore C.: speaks at Turner's retirement banquet, 225; as student of Turner, 264.
Smithsonian Institution: arranges Indian exhibit, 85–86.

Social evolution: Turner's views on, 53; discussed in census publications, 113; Achille Loria's views on, 138; incorporated in "Significance of the Frontier" essay, 168.

Social history: study of advocated by Turner, 46–47; rise of study of, 91–93; Turner as pioneer in, 266; Turner's views on, 271.

Social Science Research Council: sponsors book on methodology, 254–55; sponsors encyclopedia of the social sciences, 287–88.

South: Woodrow Wilson's interest in as section, 6; lack of historical interest in, 29, 235.

Southwestern Wisconsin Teacher's Association: Turner lectures before, 45–46.

Spain, William H.: lynched in Portage, 10.

Spencer, Herbert: on inheritance of acquired characteristics, 106.

State Historical Society of Wisconsin: use of by Turner, 23, 25–26, 94–95, 110, 120–21, 147; "Significance of the Frontier" paper read to, 191, 197; use of recalled by Turner, 212–13; paper before on sectionalism, 224; Turner made fellow of, 230.

Statistics: use of by Turner, 268–69.

Stephenson, George M.: as student of Turner, 211, 262.

Stephenson, Nathaniel W.: praises Turner, 284.

Stine, Oscar C.: as student of Turner, 211, 261.

Stone, William J.: Turner's appraisal of, 189, 194.

Strong, Josiah: on future of United States, 78; favors end to immigration, 80.

Sumner, William Graham: on frontier influences, 70–71.

Taussig, Frank W.: as friend of Turner, 296.

Taylor, Henry C.: as student of Turner, 211, 261; use of theories of by Turner, 284.

Teutonic School of History: dominance of in historical studies, 3; as taught by Herbert B. Adams, 27–28; influence of on Woodrow Wilson, 30; attacked by Turner, 51, 54, 90–93; advocated by Hubert H. Bancroft, 71; popularity of, 88–90.

Thayer, William Roscoe: as friend of Turner, 296.

Thompson, James Westfall: studies of influenced by Turner, 276.

Thoreau, Henry David: quoted on frontier, 68.

Thorpe, Francis N.: comments on Turner's paper, 60.

Thwaites, Reuben Gold: at 1893 American Historical Association meeting, 163, 165, 167; paper of praised, 171; judgment of Turner on, 214; dedicates book to Turner, 262; as friend of Turner, 296.

Tocqueville, Alexis de: describes American colonization, 66–67.

Trimble, William J.: as student of Turner, 211, 261.

Turner, Andrew Jackson: as leading citizen of Portage, 10; ignores "Significance of the Frontier" paper, 171; influence of on Turner, 215–16, 239–40, 264, 291–92.

Turner, Frederick Jackson: frontier thesis of, speculates on its origins, 3–7; papers of at Huntington Library, 7–8; boyhood of, 9–15; as student at University of Wisconsin, 15–23; as graduate student, 23–26; as graduate student at Johns Hopkins University, 26–37; friendship with Woodrow Wilson, 30–31; views on land rent, 32–36; as teacher at University of Wisconsin, 39–61; reviews *Winning of the West*, 39–40; takes over William F. Allen's courses, 40–41; as graduate instructor, 41–44; lecturing and extension courses, 44–53; prepares essay on "The Significance of History," 45–48; lectures on colonization, 53–56; prepares "Problems in American History," essay, 56–61; reads in frontier history, 67–72; belief of in agrarian values, 75–76; effect of closing of frontier on, 76–81; effect of changing historical concepts on, 81–82, 92–93; effect of demands of western historians on, 93–96; effect of changing concepts in geography on, 95–102; exposed to writers on environmental determinism, 100–02; influence of changes in biological studies on, 102–08; benefits from progress in statistical cartography, 108–16; prepares new courses on West, 119–20; prepares for essay on frontier history, 119–46; writing of essay on "Significance of the Frontier," 156–65; reading of essay before American Historical Association, 165–70; reception of frontier essay, 170–76; correspondence of with William E. Dodd, 181–201; his appraisal of Woodrow Wilson, 187–90, 193–95; views of on foreign policy, 188–89, 193–95; correspondence of with Constance L. Skinner, 203–19; comments by on his own writings,

206–07; recollections of undergraduate career and of year at Johns Hopkins, 212–13; recalls ancestors, 216, 240–43; advises on book publishing, 217; correspondence with Carl Becker, 221–50; appraised by Carl Becker, 222–23; books dedicated to, 228; recalls methods and purpose as teacher, 228–31, 260–62, 294; farewell banquet for on retiring from Harvard, 235; moves to California, 247–48; correspondence of with Merle Curti, 255–85; views of on nature of history, 257–66, 271–80, 292–94; reaction of to Curti essay, 282–85; correspondence with Luther L. Bernard, 288–96.

Tyler, Moses Coit: on 1893 American Historical Association program, 163.

Unitarian Review: quoted by Turner, 122.

Van Hise, Charles R.: explains scientific progress to Turner, 107; influences Turner on environmentalism, 101–02; influence of recalled by Turner, 214–15, 296.

Veblen, Thorstein: expresses social unrest, 76; as social scientist, 221.

Vincent, J. M.: publishes Turner bibliography, 206.

von Holst, Hermann: works of read by Turner, 19; refuses invitation to speak at 1893 American Historical Association meeting, 163; appraised by Turner, 214.

Vries, Hugo de: biological theories of, 104–05.

Walker, Francis A.: as pioneer in statistical cartography, 20, 109–11; works of on economy studied by Turner, 32–35; opposes continued immigration, 81; influence of on Turner, 132–34; acknowledges "Significance of the Frontier" essay, 173.

Ward, Lester F.: on inheritance of acquired characteristics, 106; as social scientist, 221.

Washington, University of: Turner's commencement address at, 160.

Webster, Daniel: credited with frontier thesis, 123.

Weeden, William B.: as pioneer in social history, 266.

Weismann, August: biological theories of, 104–05.

Wellington, Raynor G.: as Turner student, 211, 262; dedication of book by, 228, 245.

Welsh: in early Portage, 13–14.

Wesleyan College: Woodrow Wilson at, 30.

Whitaker, Arthur P.: as student of Turner, 262.

Whitman, Walt: quoted on frontier, 74–75.

Wildrick, Pat: lynched in Portage, 10.

Williams, Talcott: praises "Significance of the Frontier" essay, 174.

Wilson, Woodrow: as Turner's Johns Hopkins instructor, 5–6, 27, 30–31; recommends reading of Walter Bagehot, 131; hears "Significance of the Frontier" essay read, 157–60; biography of by William E. Dodd, 181–201; Turner's appraisal of foreign policy of, 187–90, 193–95; Turner's intellectual debt to, 192, 195–96; teaching of recalled by Turner, 213, 291; denies priority in suggesting frontier thesis, 234–35; influence of on Turner, 235–36; praises Turner's historical methodology, 275; as friend of Turner, 295.

Winchester, Caleb T.: seeks Turner as author, 159.

Winnebago Indians: removal of from Wisconsin, 12–13.

Winsor, Justin: advocates theory of environmental determinism, 100; opinion of 1893 American Historical Association program, 163; work of appraised by Turner, 214.

Wisconsin: as example of social evolution, 36; history of studied by Turner, 42–43.

Wisconsin Academy of Sciences, Arts and Letters: Turner reads paper to, 43; acts to broaden Turner's knowledge, 107.

Wisconsin Journal of Education: publishes "Significance of History" essay, 46.

Wisconsin Magazine of History: publishes Turner's autobiographical letter, 218–19.

Wisconsin State Register: published by Andrew Jackson Turner, 10.

Wisconsin, University of: Turner as undergraduate at, 5, 15–23; as graduate student at, 23–26; as member of faculty of, 39–45, 54–61; introduces new courses at, 119–20; recalls teaching at, 209, 213–14, 260–62; recalls student days at, 212–13, 292; Carl Becker as student at, 221–23.

Woodburn, James A.: on 1893 American Historical Association program, 163.

World History: study of advocated by Turner, 47.

World's Columbian Exposition: meeting of American Historical Association at, 161–67.

Wright, Benjamin F.: attacks Turner's frontier theory, 218.

Wright, Chester W.: works of read by Turner, 284–85.

Young, Allyn A.: speaks at Turner's retirement dinner, 225; views on Turner, 244; as friend of Turner, 296.

THE GENESIS OF THE FRONTIER THESIS

A Study in Historical Creativity

by Ray Allen Billington

It is not often that the reader is allowed, as he is in this book, to follow the progress of a major creative venture. The creator, be he inventor, mathematician, or historian, leaves few blaze marks for us along his trail, and seldom indeed do we find the raw material of his research in the form of books consulted, notes taken, or the writing down of his own recollections of the journey.

In the case of Frederick Jackson Turner's remarkable essay, "The Significance of the Frontier in American History," it is the Huntington Library's good fortune to have a wealth of just such material, and to have in Ray Allen Billington a dedicated historian to bring this material to the reader.

For a generation long accustomed to thinking of the frontier as a molding force in our history, it is hard to realize that the thesis seemed so revolutionary when it was first read as a paper at Chicago's Columbian Exposition in 1893. Although it has had a profound effect on historiography since that time, Turner himself never thought of it as the last word. His purpose was not to close, but to open an avenue of historical research. The author's purpose in this book is to retrace the young historian's thinking as the frontier thesis evolved in his mind.

We review Turner's boyhood in Portage, Wisconsin—then itself a part of the frontier. We follow him through his college years, meeting along the way many of the professors whose classes and seminars first sparked in Turner the interest in Western history that was to become one of the ruling passions of his life. We look over his shoulder as he reads and underlines, and we read jottings on three-by-five cards that tell of conclusions drawn or of new ideas as they occur.

The last five chapters are devoted to correspondence between Turner and five of his colleagues, in which he himself tries, at a much later date, to recall the genesis of the frontier thesis. The letters from his colleagues movingly express their admiration and affection. Turner's letters, although sometimes inaccurate as to the small details of his own life, reveal the depth of his understanding of the nation's past, and form a fitting monument for one of America's most original and influential historians.

Ray Allen Billington was William Smith Mason Professor of History at Northwestern University before coming to the Huntington as Senior Research Associate. He has recently edited a book of correspondence entitled "Dear Lady": The Letters of Frederick Jackson Turner and Alice Forbes Perkins Hooper 1910–1932.